The Future of Kurdistan in Iraq

The Future of Kurdistan in Iraq

Edited by Brendan O'Leary, John McGarry, and Khaled Salih

PENN

University of Pennsylvania Press
Philadelphia

10 9 8 7 6 5 4 3 2 1

Published by
University of Pennsylvania Press
Philadelphia, Pennsylvania 19104-4011

Library of Congress Cataloging-in-Publication Data

The future of Kurdistan in Iraq / edited by Brendan O'Leary, John McGarry, and
Khaled Salih.
    p.   cm.
  ISBN: 0-8122-3870-2 (cloth : alk. paper)
  Includes bibliographical references and index.
    1. Kurds—Iraq—Politics and government—21st century   I. O'Leary, Brendan.
II. McGarry, John, 1957–   .   III. Sālih, Khālid.
DS70.8.K8F88   2005
956.7'20443—dc22   2004061229

Frontispiece: Hosney Rasheed in traditional Kurdish dress. Painting by Dlier Rasheed.

This book is dedicated to the memory of Sami Abdulrahman, a man, a husband, a father, a patriot, a liberal nationalist, and a former peshmerga. When he was murdered beside his son in the Erbil bombings of 1 February 2004, he was the deputy prime minister of the Kurdistan Regional Government (Erbil), the secretary of the Kurdistan Democratic Party, and a key figure in the joint inter-party committee preparing for constitutional negotiations. Sami Abdulrahman co-sponsored the conferences that led to this book, initiated its translation into Kurdish, and had planned to write an Afterword. Few politicians truly grace their nations. Sami was one. He will always be missed.

Contents

Note on Transliteration

Our transliteration of Arabic words follows a modified version of the system used by the *International Journal of Middle East Studies*.

The Arabic letter *'ayn* is kept only in Shi'a, Shari'a, and Ba'th.
The Arabic letter *hamza* is not used: Fu'ad is written as Fuad.
The letter H is not used at the end of names: Hillah is written as Hilla, Fallujah as Falluja.

Transliteration of Kurdish words follows a simplified version of Tafiq Wahby and Cecil John Edmonds, *A Kurdish-English Dictionary* (Oxford: Oxford University Press, 1996).

Preface

"Their minds are filled with big ideas, images and distorted facts."
—Bob Dylan, *"Idiot Wind,"* Blood on the Tracks *(1974)*

On 19 March 2003, the United States, the United Kingdom, and a "coalition of the willing" declared war on the Republic of Iraq. The ostensible justification of the war was to terminate the imminent international threat posed by Saddam Hussein's weapons of mass destruction. None of the editors of this collection believed this warrant for the war, and we regretted the war's lack of strict conformity to the standards of international law. But, unlike some critics of the American- and British-led invasion of Iraq, we looked forward to the termination of the political institutions of Ba'thist Iraq and the opportunities that would create for a democratic and just reconstruction. For the Ba'thists had organized *a regime of mass destruction*. It was habitually genocidal by the standards of the 1948 international convention, engaging in "the following acts committed with intent to destroy in whole or in part, a national, ethnic, racial or religious group as such: (a) killing members of the group; (b) causing serious bodily or mental harm to members of the group; (c) deliberately inflicting on the group conditions of life calculated to bring about its physical destruction in whole or in part; (d) imposing measures intended to prevent births within the group; (e) forcibly transferring children of the group to another group" (Article 2 of the Convention on the Prevention and Punishment of the Crime of Genocide, cited in Thornberry 1991).

Ba'thists intermittently exterminated Kurds, Shi'a, Marsh Arabs, Yezidis, and small Christian communities. They deported whole populations of villages and towns, razed villages, systematically practiced torture, and committed every other imaginable gross violation of human rights. The regime was equally politicidal; it sought to kill its political opponents, in whole or in part. Refusal to join the Arab Ba'th Socialist Party was sufficient to be defined as an enemy of the state and liable to torture, deportation, or execution. The regime was also misogynist, indeed gynocidal. Amnesty International and Human

Rights Watch documented organized rapes of women held in custody, the ritualized beheading in front of their families of women defamed as prostitutes, and the relegalization of so-called "honor killings." The minimal estimate of those murdered by Ba'th governments since the early 1980s is 300,000 people. This figure excludes those killed in direct wars with Iran, Kuwait, and the U.S. and its allies, and those killed in wars between Ba'thists and Kurdish insurgents before 1979. Peter Sluglett, a contemporary historian of Iraq, estimates that as many more people, up to 300,000, may have been killed in the spring of 1991 in Saddam's counter-attack against Kurdish and Shi'a rebels (Farouk-Sluglett and Sluglett 2003, 289). Three hundred thousand dead from genocide is the figure publicized in 2003 by the Coalition Provisional Authority (CPA) Director of Human Rights, Sandy Hodgkinson (CBS News 2003). The remains of many of these victims lie in mass graves yet to be scientifically exhumed and properly documented—a task for which the CPA was disgracefully ill-prepared. Three hundred thousand is, however, a low estimate of genocide victims. British Prime Minister Tony Blair said on 20 November 2003 that as many as 400,000 people are buried in the mass graves (USAID 2004). Others, including General Jay Garner, the first American-appointed authority in Iraq, suggest that the victims of Saddam's regime number one million or more (Fineman 2003). The Kurdistan Regional Government estimates that 182,000 people were killed in the 1988 Anfal campaign alone (KRG 2004). Even by Hodgkinson's conservative estimate, the death toll from genocide would constitute a staggering 1.25 percent of Iraq's estimated population.

The regime's genocidal, politicidal, and gynocidal nature should have been the enduring centerpiece of the global political and media attention paid to Iraq from 1968, or at least after 1979 when Saddam became its president-leader (al-Rais al-Qaid). Not so. Oil, weapons of mass destruction, sanctions, and Saddam's self-styled roles as a champion of Palestine and a secularist opponent of Iranian Shi'a ayatollahs received far more extensive consideration. The liberal internationalist interventions against genocide and ethnic expulsion in the Balkans during the 1990s were not widely canvassed as equally appropriate for Iraq. It was felt sufficient to protect Kurds from the air, while Shi'a rebels and the Marsh Arabs were abandoned to Saddam's Republican Guard in 1991 and only benefited from the Allied imposition of a no-fly zone, much too late, in the summer of 1992. Genocide, ethnic expulsion, and coercive assimilation were not seen for what they are: the worst of all governmental crimes, mandating uniform global revulsion and international sanctions.

Regrettably, it is not yet an axiom of democratic governments' foreign policy that mass-destruction regimes be relentlessly and universally opposed and, where prudent and feasible, overthrown. In political judgment, and the public media, the control and termination of mass-destruction regimes should take precedence over the subsidiary, though not entirely unrelated, question of weapons of mass destruction. But, neither President Bush nor Prime Ministers Aznar, Blair, or Howard felt that a war overtly launched against Saddam's mass destruction of the residents of Iraq would win domestic support. They calculated that the alleged existence of externally deployable weapons of mass destruction provided the best public rationale for an invasion. This judgment betrayed their convictions about their own citizens. They believed that only direct, credibly palpable threats to their domestic security would generate support for war, invasion, and regime change in Iraq.

After conducting the invasion successfully on these premises, Coalition leaders found themselves coping with an unanticipated and increasingly embarrassing difficulty: the much-maligned UN inspectors had, almost certainly, successfully terminated Saddam's program to develop or redevelop arsenals of nuclear, chemical, and biological weaponry. The President of the U.S. and the Prime Ministers of the UK, Spain, and Australia and their confidantes then appeared either as awkward liars to their publics, or, almost as embarrassingly, as the dupes of their intelligence agencies, which themselves had probably been duped. The U.S.- and UK-dominated Coalition fought the war without significant advance institutional planning, either for the management of regime collapse, as Karin von Hippel's essay here demonstrates, or for coherent, constructive regime change and transformation, as Peter Galbraith maintains in Chapter 10. In consequence, the Coalition Provisional Authority), nicely satirized as "Can't Provide Anything," initially presided over a chaotic mess, especially in predominantly Arab Iraq. They compounded that mess by creating a climate in which torture has been practiced by U.S. soldiers in Saddam's own dungeons in Abu Ghraib. The sole facts that might be invoked in mitigation of this total betrayal of liberal democratic values were the shame aroused in the Western public and the partial holding to account of the perpetrators. That policy morass and its human repercussions have become the dominant preoccupations of the Coalition members' media.

What was blown away by the winds of policy idiocy in Washington and Westminster, before and after the war, was the prospect of a better justified and far more effective intervention. Coalition leaders got the facts wrong, held distorted images of their own constituents and of Iraqis and Kurdistanis, and missed the important big ideas. The idiot wind reaped its harvest. Poor planning facilitated Ba'thist resistance to occupation. Failure adequately to secure either the external or the internal borders of the occupied territory made Iraq and Kurdistan vulnerable to every suicide-oriented Islamist. The coalition's counterinsurgency policy was not coherently married to constitutional rebuilding and political reconstruction, which are the prime concerns of the writers of this collection. The CPA would eventually waver between rigor in eliminating Ba'thists from public life and rehabilitating them. Policy often seemed designed, at best, to facilitate a hasty exit with minimal losses of Coalition troops. This picture of disarray is, we suggest, far more accurate than the claim in much of the Arab media and some of the Western left that a coherent recolonization of Iraq is under way.

The editors seek to distance this book and its contributors from the thought patterns and agenda of certain neoconservatives in Washington and some New Labourites in Westminster. Bush's and Blair's appraisal of the nature of Saddam's regime, including the view that it would redevelop weapons of mass destruction if it could, was broadly correct, although they radically overestimated its capacities to put up any sustained resistance to American military power. But, like many other observers, we deeply regret the fact that the removal of this genocidal regime was not the centerpiece of the case for war, or the focus of the limited strategic planning for the rebuilding of Iraq and Kurdistan. We accept—indeed, insist—that Saddam's regime would have been both expansionist and committed genocide again had it been allowed to regroup and express its inner dynamics during the 1990s. We regard as naïve the argument of some opponents of invading Iraq that Saddam was "boxed in" and no longer posed a real and imminent threat. It is now known that he was able to manipulate the UN sanctions regime, and the huge corruption in the oil for food program has retrospectively besmirched both the UN and the permanent members of the Security Council (including those who opposed the war on Iraq, notably France and Russia, and those who supported it, the U.S.A. and the UK). The claim that Saddam was boxed in withstands scrutiny only as applied to external or inter-state relations. The regime remained exterminationist domestically, as was evident in the attacks in the marsh regions of the southern governorates in late 1998, a decade after the Anfal campaign against the Kurds. The termination of the Ba'thist regime was therefore a consummation devoutly to be wished. This normative logic has a corollary: the reconstruction of Iraq and Kurdistan needs to be done in such a way that there can be no repetition of genocide, ethnic expulsion, or coercive assimilation. This concern has often been lost sight of, or inadequately considered, since the "liberation" or "invasion" began on 19 March 2003.

Some opponents of the war had entirely rational and well-considered fears about the unilateral use of American power and very reasonable observations about the failure of the U.S.A. and its allies to address other palpable injustices in the Middle East. These critics were right to question whether a preventive war was necessary to destroy a regime believed to have immediately externally usable weapons of mass destruction. But, the case for an interventionist war against a genocidal and expulsionist regime would, we think, have been far more difficult to refute. In apparent naïveté, George W. Bush sought to remind Americans and others that Saddam had "gassed his own people." He may have been unaware that in the late 1980s officials in his father's administration had falsely suggested that Iranian forces had executed those poisonous atrocities. The elder Bush had followed the Reagan administration's tacit determination after 1980 to back Saddam against Iran's ayatollahs as the lesser of two evils. So, some of his officials had been reluctant to accept that Saddam had gassed any people and claimed preposterously that Iranians had gassed their own military allies, very close to their own border, and then brought the destruction of Halabja to the attention of the world's media in a clever and diabolical public relations conspiracy. That Saddam gassed people and committed genocide should not be in question (although reasonable people differ in their estimates of the number of killings). Reading the documentation and data of Human Rights Watch, Amnesty International, Physicians for Human Rights, and the annual reports of Max van der Stoel, the High Commissioner on National Minorities of the Organization for Security and Co-operation in Europe, and the United Nations (UN) Special Rapporteur on Iraq between 1992 and 1999 will quell any doubts among skeptics (see especially Human Rights Watch 1993). These reports are readily confirmed by the burial specialists in nongovernmental agencies (NGOs) who should be engaged in the exhumation of mass graves in Kurdistan and Iraq, for example, Archeologists for Human Rights, or by simple conversations with survivors and eyewitnesses. Those who deny genocidal gassing by Iraq have been eloquently and effectively refuted (Casey 2003). The Baʿthists own record-keeping in any case convicts them. But there was something very misleading in President George W. Bush's claim that the victims of the gassing were Saddam's "people." Tikrit's Sunni Arab Baʿthists were not gassed. Kurds were.

The Baʿthist regime was both ethnically and religiously exterminationist. It embedded a remarkable but horrific series of syntheses. It bellowed a nominally pan-Arab nationalism, invoking all the defeats suffered by Arab peoples in our times, but sat astride a minority Sunni Arab tyranny and made no efforts to achieve Arab unification except through the conquest of Kuwait. It proclaimed itself modern, socialist, and secular, but its party structures were eventually subordinated to a clan of Saddam's cousins. It systematically atomized most of its internal opponents through standard totalitarian routines before its logic drove it toward territorial aggrandizement, declaring war on Iran in 1980 and occupying Kuwait in 1991. From the reservoirs of the treasury of a postcolonial *rentier* oil-producer, it lavishly funded its party, its army, its police, its intelligence services, its domestic repression, and its external military adventures. Its skills in financial and moral corruption enabled it to manipulate the UN sanctions regime. Its attempted conquest of Kuwait proved to be its eventual undoing, although Saddam enjoyed a reprieve of a dozen years.

The Baʿthists came to power in 1968 through a coup. Their success was unusual because it was a comeback; they had been displaced in a prior coup in 1963. The chaos, incompetence, and malevolence they had displayed had produced widespread popular approval for their forcible exclusion from government. But, returned to executive control, they learned how to hold onto power. They took management guidance from the KGB's Yuri Andropov. They sought to make themselves coup-proof in the same manner as the Marxist-Leninist tyrannies of the Soviet bloc, checking and balancing party, army, and state institutions with multiple and rival intelligence services reporting to the dictator, in the manner memorably described in Kanan Makiya's *Republic of Fear*, previously published under the pseudonym of Samir al-Khalil (al-Khalil 1990). The regime was a stunning and stupefying hybrid. At its peak stood one party, one ethnoreligious minority, one region, one clan, one family, and one strongman. Ideologically, it was nationalist, socialist, anti-imperialist, racist, and opportunistically Islamist. Economically, it was a *rentier* oil state, a quasi-Soviet planned system, and welfare statist (or, rather, bribery statist) in its moment of affluence. Its alliances and its military armory before its invasion of Kuwait in 1990 had included tacit or explicit support and the purchase of weapons of mass destruction from the U.S., the USSR, and the major states of the European Union. Avowedly secular, it launched the terminal ambitions of the Anfal campaign against the Kurds by invoking the eighth *sura* from the Qur'an that sanctions the spoliation and looting of nonbelievers. According to *sura* 8: 12, Allah declares: "I shall cast terror into the hearts of the infidels. Strike off their heads, maim them in every limb."

This was not merely bloodthirsty theological poetry; Islam was pressed, when convenient, into the service of the Arabization of Iraq. Even though most Kurds were and are Sunni Muslims, the regime treated them as "infidels" when that was useful. Coup-proof, Soviet-style; affluent when the oil was flowing, unlike Soviet puppet regimes; racist and expansionist, invoking both Arab and pre-Arab civilizational justifications (one division of the Republican Guard was named after Hammurabi, and Saddam erected Assyrian artifacts on the citadel of Erbil), this horrific hybrid would not have fallen through domestic opposition in its Sunni Arab heartlands, ideological doubt, or loss of élan. Like the Nazi dictatorship it resembled, it could lose power only though defeat in war. That is why the editors of this book, like most residents of Iraq, be they Arabs, Turkomen, or Kurds, Muslims, Christians, Yezidis, or Jews, liberals, old communists, or Shiʿa fundamentalists, welcomed the repercussions of the war that President Bush and Premiers Blair, Aznar, and Howard fought for the wrong public reasons. There could be no empathy or nostalgia for Saddam. The sole internal constituency opposed to what became a war of liberation was the much-reduced base of the Baʿthists among Sunni Muslims.

This book, our collective contribution to debates over this most controversial war and its consequences, focuses on the future of Kurdistan in a new Iraq. It does not address, except as necessary, the rest of the former Iraq. After the first, introductory chapter, it also generally ignores the other territories of what some fear and others hope might constitute Greater Kurdistan (except parenthetically, or through historical references). Our book is an appraisal of the immediate past of what is officially called Iraqi Kurdistan by some and "Northern Iraq" by others; it evaluates Kurdistan's likely and desirable futures and its relations with the rest of Iraq. The book offers both analysis and prescription. It is not neutral. It takes the existence of Kurdistan as a political entity as a desirable given, although our contributors have different conceptions of how the relationships between Kurdistan and the rest of Iraq might and should be remade. Some authors envisage variations on autonomy; others foresee variations on a federal unit, a federacy in an otherwise unitary state, or a sovereign Kurdistan. They anticipate many different possibilities in the rest of Iraq. None excludes bleak futures. The history of Iraq does not inspire facile optimism. Although the premises of our contributors are not neutral, we hope readers will agree that none of our contributors betrays scholarly standards in the conduct of argument, or the presentation of evidence.

Our normative arguments are directed toward avoiding any repetition of Iraqi regimes' treatment of their largest national minority, the Kurds; and, equally, toward assisting the equal, fair, and proportional treatment of *all* the peoples of Iraq, whatever their national, ethnic, or linguistic origins, or their religious or nonreligious convictions. Our contributors contest the premise that Iraq has been, is, or should be one nation, or that it has, or should have, just one people. We are not motivated by what some dismiss as fashionable, pious, or politically correct multiculturalism, but rather by enlightened realism. Iraq's sociology and ethnography are incontrovertibly bi-national, arguably pluri-national. They are certainly multiethnic and religiously plural. Our contributors recognize and commend the international and domestic recognition of Iraq's deep diversity. The tone and the arguments herein are at odds with those of certain Arab liberals and integrationist American administrators and academics who, like some authorities under the British mandate, want to invent a single Iraq where all the people are "just Iraqis." We think that they are confusing, either guilefully or naïvely, state-building with nation-building

(Connor 1972). They are at their most naïve when they compare the post-World War II reconstructions of Germany and Japan with the task of reconstructing Iraq. For Germany and especially Japan were essentially homogeneous nations, and their cultural unity facilitated their reconstruction from the ravages of fascism. Iraq has no analogous cultural unity.

An Iraqi state can be rebuilt, although that is by no means guaranteed. It may even be rebuilt as a democracy, as a secular state (or, at least, as a religiously pluralist and tolerant state), as a state that treats women as equals and not as chattels, and one that develops and cherishes all its citizens and children equally. It may be rebuilt as a federation. All of this will be extraordinarily difficult to deliver. But such rebuilding will not work if Iraq is reengineered around the illusion that it has been, is, or can be one nation. Our contributors' conviction is that, although dual and multiple identities play a role in the past and future of Iraq's peoples, it would be irresponsibly utopian to assume that most, let alone all, of the denizens of Iraq can easily be assimilated or merely integrated into a common identity, especially after their differentiated experiences of Ba'thism. If the genocidal destruction of European Jewry helped produce Israel rather than integrationist-minded Jews, no one should be surprised that the Anfal campaign has produced Kurdistan and Kurds rather than integrationist-minded "Iraqi Kurds." If ethnic expulsions and their repercussions produced present-day Bosnia-Hercegovina, Kosovo, and Macedonia, then no one should be surprised that Kurds, Arabs, Turkomen, and Christians dispute the "right of return," settlements, historical claims to indigenous status, and requirements of truth and reconciliation. If pleasant islands can be as ferociously contested as Ireland, Fiji, Cyprus, and Sri Lanka, then why should anyone expect the cramped river beds of Mesopotamia and the freer mountains of Kurdistan to be sites of utopian forgiveness and reconciliation? Given that Beirut, Belfast, and Jerusalem are hotly claimed by rival national or ethnic communities, why should anyone be surprised that Kirkuk might become an epicenter of urban violence if past expulsions, expropriations, forced settlements, and gerrymandering are not properly redressed through demonstrably fair processes? If contemporary peoples have nowhere extensively voluntarily assimilated in their own homelands, why should any reasonable person expect Kurds, Arabs, Turkomen, and Assyrians to set exemplary standards in interethnic and interreligious relations? If in the last two decades your own people—if you belong to one, or just one—had been assaulted, robbed, deported, and forced to speak and write another language, would you now recommend that they turn the other cheek and become "just" citizens of a state "for all" and adherents of "constitutional patriotism," merely because a small minority from among their erstwhile oppressors promise a new era?

These rhetorical questions are intended to convey this book's message that there can, with difficulty, be a new Iraq, but there cannot be "just Iraqis." There must minimally be Kurdistanis, as well as Arab Iraqis, if there is to be a durable, let alone flourishing, political reconstruction. It is our conviction that the recognition of Kurdistan and its just constitutional treatment will be the decisive test of whether there can be a renewed and democratic Iraq. Kurdistan may continue to disprove the thesis that people of predominantly Muslim beliefs cannot become democratic, secular, or tolerant of other nationalities and other ethnic, religious, and linguistic communities. But Kurdistan can pass these tests only on one condition: if it is given sufficient freedom to demonstrate its capacity to do so, by the rest of Iraq, by Iraq's neighbors, and by the great powers.

Only one editor of this book, Khaled Salih, was born in Kurdistan, and he is now a Swedish citizen who was a beneficiary of political asylum. Most of our contributors have had first-hand experience in Kurdistan. Collectively, we refute the proverb that the only friends of the Kurds are the mountains of Kurdistan. The rest of our contributors might be regarded as honorary Kurdistanis, but are neither Kurdish by ethnicity nor Muslim by religion. Readers will assess whether the distance that creates makes their arguments more or less compelling.

This book emerged from two conferences, one held before the war at Odense, Denmark, at the University of Southern Denmark in December 2002, and one held in Washington, D.C., in September 2003, nearly six months after the war had begun. The University of Southern Denmark, the University of Pennsylvania's School of Arts and Sciences and its Solomon Asch Center for the Study of Ethno-Political Conflict, the Kurdistan Regional Government, the Washington Kurdish Institute, and Baban Computers of Erbil jointly funded the conferences. Scholars and practitioners at the first conference addressed the ten years of existence of the Kurdistan Regional Government and Kurdistan National Assembly (www.kurdistan.sdu.dk). This conference was held both to review the longest period of self-government in the history of modern Kurdistan and to assess, warily, the likely future of a post-Saddam Kurdistan if war were to occur. Presentations at this first conference were made by, among others, Brendan O'Leary, Ofra Bengio, Sophia Wanche, Khaled Salih, and Peter Galbraith. The second conference addressed the future of Kurdistan in a reconstructed Iraq. Brendan O'Leary, John McGarry, and Paul Williams made presentations there. Later contributions were sought from Michael Gunter and Molly McNulty, who participated in the Washington conference, and from Gareth Stansfield, who recently published the first comprehensive book on the Kurdistan Regional Government. Subsequently, Galbraith, O'Leary, and Salih were asked to constitute a constitutional advisory team that assists the Kurdistan Regional Governments and the Kurdistan National Assembly. In consequence, this collection has emerged from both pre- and postwar reflections and from the practical experiences of researching and advising in Kurdistan. As we go to press, all the contributions retain their urgency and, we think, have a pressing coherence. But we freely admit we would welcome the eventual redundancy of our arguments.

We owe warm thanks to Peter Agree of the University of Pennsylvania Press for his early support. The final text was edited with the assiduous, skilled assistance of Grey Osterud in Newton, Massachusetts. Salih and O'Leary, working on a mountain in Kurdistan, and McGarry, living in a functioning binational and bilingual federation, finalized this collection via email shortly after the Erbil bombings killed many people whom we had come to know and admire from Kurdistan's principal political parties. We dedicate this book to the memory of one of the most distinguished victims of those bombings. Sami Abdulrahman shared the dream of a free Kurdistan with most of the people with whom he served, but as a realist he would have been content with a free Kurdistan in a free Iraq. The cause for which he lived and died still lives.

References

al-Khalil, Samir (pseudonym for Kanan Makiya). 1990. *Republic of Fear: Saddam's Iraq*. London: Hutchinson Radius.

BBC News. 2001. "Iraqi Kurds' Story of Expulsion." 3 November. <http://news.bbc.co .uk/1/hi/world/middle_east/1614239.stm>.

Casey, Leo. 2003. "Questioning Halabja: Genocide and the Expedient Political Lie." *Dissent* 50(3): 61–65.

CBS News. 2003. "Powell '88 Attack Proves War Case." Halabja, 16 September. <http://www.cbnsnews.com/stories/2003/09/17/iraq/printable573667.shtml> accessed 1 April 2004.

Connor, Walker. 1972. "Nation-Building or Nation-Destroying?" *World Politics* 24: 319–55.

Farouk-Sluglett, Marion and Peter Sluglett. 2003. *Iraq Since 1958: From Revolution to Dictatorship*. London: I.B. Tauris.

Fineman, Mark and John Hendren. 2003. "Garner: 'A Million Iraqi Corpses Possible.'" *Los Angeles Times*, 3 July.

Human Rights Watch. 1993. *Genocide in Iraq: The Anfal Campaign Against the Kurds*. New York: Middle East Watch Report, Human Rights Watch, July, <http://www .hrw.org/reports.1993.iraqanfal/>.

Kurdistan Regional Government (KRG). 2004. "Anfal Campaign." <http://www.krg .org/reference/hrw-anfal/preface.asp>, accessed 1 April 2004.

United States Agency for International Development (USAID). 2004. "Iraq's Legacy of
    Terror: Mass Graves." <http://www.usaid.gov/iraq/pdf.iraq_mass_graves/pdf>
    accessed 1 April 2004.
Thornberry, Patrick. 1991. "The Convention on Genocide and the Protection of
    Minorities." In *International Law and the Rights of Minorities*, ed. Patrick Thorn-
    berry. Oxford: Oxford University Press. 59–85.

PART ONE

Introduction

Chapter 1

The Denial, Resurrection, and Affirmation of Kurdistan

Brendan O'Leary and Khaled Salih

"Nature knows neither an equality of individuals nor an equality of nations; equality is a creation of law and its greatest benefit for those subject to it."
—Karl Renner (1918)

"There is no such place as Kurdistan"

In January 2004, one of us traveled from the city of Erbil, known in Kurdish as Hewlêr, the site of the Kurdistan National Assembly, into the Republic of Turkey to begin a journey to London. The border checkpoint is at Ibrahim Khalil in Kurdish, or Habur in Turkish. By prior agreement, he was not required to go through the usual rigors of inspection by the Turkish military, who are usually more discourteous, inquisitorial, and disobliging than the conventional border police and visa inspectors. No such luck awaited another traveler, a professional consultant who held a U.S. passport and had hitched a ride in the same vehicle. As he later explained in Diyarbakir airport, situated in what is officially southeastern Turkey, a predominantly Kurdish region, he had been detained for two hours. Two military officials had instructed the consultant, in English, to open and switch on his laptop computer, but not, as he initially surmised, as an instance of now routine international security procedures. Instead, they ordered him to use the "find facility" on his computer to search for the word "Kurdistan." To their evident satisfaction and feigned dismay, the term occurred in a number of the consultant's Microsoft Word documents. "There is no such place as Kurdistan," one of the soldiers declaimed. He repeated this assertion throughout the interview—despite the fact that, within two hundred meters of the unofficial hut where such interviews are conducted, there is a public sign, in English, Kurdish, and Arabic, that welcomes visitors to "Iraqi Kurdistan." The soldier ordered the consultant to replace every instance of "Kurdistan" in his laptop computer files with what he insisted was the "correct" expression: "northern Iraq." When this renaming was completed to his satisfaction, the soldier himself hit the "save" key. Thus the existential denial of Kurdistan was locally accomplished through an act of definitional extermination. Listeners to this story, after making the usual acknowledgments of Turkey's human rights record, immediately question the perversity of the officials: "Won't the consultant now be much more sympathetic to Kurdistan than before?" The technically minded insist on the futility of hitting the "save" key: "Once the consultant had his laptop back home, won't he just re-replace 'northern Iraq' with 'Kurdistan'?" These interrogations are entirely sensible, but they miss one of the points of this exercise. Turkish officialdom, especially its military, must keep *itself* in denial of Kurdistan, lest the state's founding ideas be jeopardized. These officials are saying their secular prayers, rooting out the secular heresy of Kurdistan.[1]

Turkish officials are quite distinctive in presently insisting that there *is* no such place as Kurdistan; but they have never been entirely isolated in insisting there *should* be no such entity. The denial of Kurdistan's existence was normal, and normalized, throughout much of the twentieth century. Some Arab politicians on the American-appointed Iraqi Governing Council (IGC), and some American intellectuals who jointly counseled against an "ethnic federation" in 2002–2004, were not the first to seek to deny Kurdistan, great or small. "Greater Kurdistan," which encompasses the lands where Kurds predominated within jurisdictions of the Ottoman and Persian empires, is the dream of the Kurdish nation. This vision had a fleeting moment of partial political realization after World War I (McDowall 2000, 115–50; Edmonds 1957). One of its possible configurations, as presented to Woodrow Wilson by a Kurdish representative at Paris, is shown in Figure 1.1a. Other visions of Greater Kurdistan such as those in Figure 1.1b, c. usually portray a state with a Mediterranean port and a fat crescent-shaped swath of land running from southeastern Anatolia to the Zagros Mountains. Carving out such a nation-state would have had a dramatic impact on its neighbors.

This geopolitical reality explains both the power of "Greater Kurdistan" and the fears the idea generated. It was not to be. In the decisive interval between the Treaty of Versailles (1919) and the Treaty of Sèvres (1920), which reflected the nadir of Turkish fortunes, and the Treaty of Lausanne (1923), which registered Atatürk's successful revival of Turkish power, Greater Kurdistan was politically eliminated. Article 62 of the Treaty of Sèvres had envisaged "a scheme of local autonomy for the predominantly Kurdish areas," and Article 64 specified that within a year "the Kurdish peoples" within this scheme

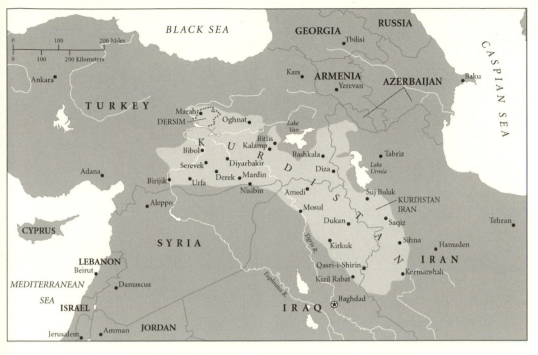

Figure 1.1a. Greater Kurdistan as proposed by Sharif Pasha for the Treaty of Versailles in 1919. Adapted from Natali (2001) by permission of Oxford University Press.

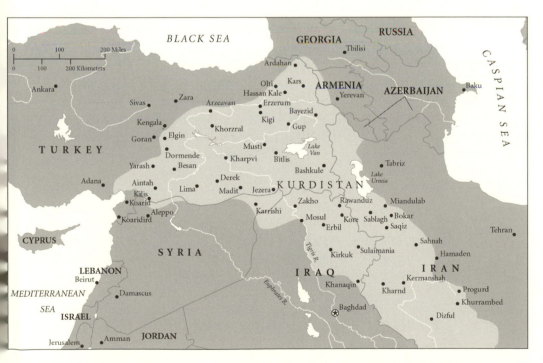

Figure 1.1b. Greater Kurdistan as proposed by the Rizgari Party to the United Nations in 1945. Adapted from Natali (2001) by permission of Oxford University Press.

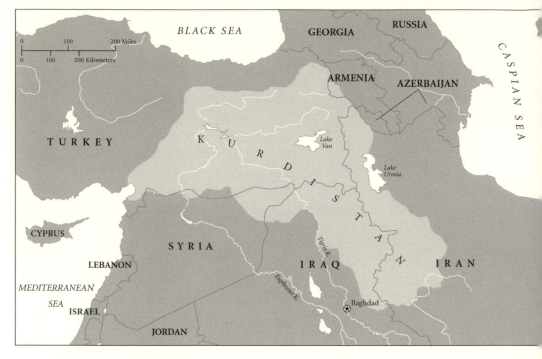

Figure 1.1c. The popular map of Greater Kurdistan found everywhere Kurds feel free. Adapted by the authors.

would have had the right to petition the League of Nations for "independence from Turkey." Instead, Kurdistan was partly digested by two independent rumps of former empires, Iran and Turkey. This was no historic surprise, because Kurdistan and its peoples comprised "march lands," mountains, and frontier tribes that for centuries had passed back and forth between Persian and Turkish overlords. But now, two additional newcomers dined on the body of Kurdistan, territorial constructions of empires new to the region: French-mandated "Syria" and British-mandated "Iraq" (Mufti 1996).

Mustafa Kemal Atatürk's remarkable reconstruction of the rump of the downsized Ottoman Empire was ratified in the Treaty of Lausanne. It codified the defeat of the territorial ambitions of the Greeks, Italians, and Armenians, as well as the plans of the French and the British. It extinguished Greater Kurdistan from the world's official maps. Greater Kurdistan is remembered, however, in the longings and banners of Kurds, especially Kurds of the diaspora, and in the nightmares of its potential neighbors. Greater Kurdistan haunts the states of west Asia in the way the idea of Poland once stalked the powers of eastern Europe: the Habsburgs, Hohenzollerns, and Czars. To stamp out the idea of Greater Kurdistan, the states which incorporated Kurdish populations have adopted the full gruesome repertoire of available strategies: genocide, ethnic expulsion, territorial partition, coercive assimilation, and hierarchical control aimed at disorganizing Kurds and organizing those who feel threatened by them.

Whether Greater Kurdistan will be resurrected just as Poland rematerialized after two world wars is not something anyone, including the authors represented in this book, can presume to know. But the mere idea that it might still matters. It is a "thought-stopper" that inhibits Turkish, Syrian, and Iranian politicians from reconstituting their regimes to make "their Kurds" feel at home. Although the realization of Greater Kurdistan was snuffed out in 1923, the idea often resurfaced in the successive eruptions of "little Kurdistans" in the twentieth century. Various Kurdish movements achieved these liberated territories through military self-help and political struggle. Some Kurds sought an autonomous Kurdistan under the British mandate in Iraq and fought for that objective in the 1920s, only to be defeated by Britain's Royal Air Force and the British-trained armed forces of the Iraqi monarchy. Ismail Agha Simko organized Kurdish resistance to Reza Shah's Iran in the 1920s. After World War II, in December 1945, the "Mahabad Republic," a Kurdish "people's government," was proclaimed in western Iran under the aegis of Qazi Mohammed and the generalship of Mustafa Barzani. It lasted almost a year, until its erstwhile leader, his brother, and his cousin were hanged by the government of the Shah after the Soviet Union decided to leave Iran within Britain's sphere of influence.

"Little Kurdistans" kept appearing despite Iraq's, Iran's, Turkey's and Syria's nation-building programs. In the 1960s, *peshmerga*, "those who face death," sought, fought, and eventually won an autonomy settlement from Iraq's successive republican governments, including the Ba'thists. The Kurdistan Democratic Party (KDP) led by Mustafa Barzani organized the initiative. "Iraqi Kurdistan" had a precarious status between 1970 and 1974, and was crushed when Saddam betrayed the promises he had made. In 1975 Iraq made a deal with the Shah of Iran that was endorsed by U.S. President Gerald Ford and Secretary of State Henry Kissinger. Giving *realpolitik* a bad name, the U.S. and Iran betrayed Barzani and the KDP, which they had been funding. In the late 1970s and early 1980s, the Kurds of Iraq regrouped now under two parties, the KDP, led by Masoud Barzani, and the Patriotic Union of Kurdistan (PUK), led by Jalal Talabani. During the Iran-Iraq war they fought Saddam. In the 1990s, the Kurds of Turkey gave extensive support to Abdullah Ocalan's ferocious PKK (the Kurdistan Workers Party) in an exceptionally bloody war that the state's military won after releasing itself from the limited restraints of Turkey's laws.

The lesser Kurdistan of this book, the Kurdistan in Iraq, is one of many possible Kurdistans that have gone before. This one was established after the first Gulf War, after the American, British, and Turkish governments were prompted, with shame but without foresight, into creating a safe haven for Kurds fleeing the revenge of Saddam. Several of our contributors—Ofra Bengio, Sophia Wanche, and Gareth Stansfield—reflect on its curious formation, and all the chapters address the prospects of this latest lesser Kurdistan. We believe that Kurdistan should have a viable future; but none of us confuse our desires with reality.

Factors Facilitating and Obstructing Kurdish National Aspirations

This capsule history suggests extensive opposition, external and internal, to the formation of both Greater and Lesser Kurdistans. It is not by accident that the Kurds are the largest nation without a state of their own in what the Americans and the British still call the Middle East. Nor is it coincidental that lesser Kurdistans erupt after major wars that shatter prior geopolitical configurations of power. Lesser Kurdistans manifest themselves after shocks to the host regimes allow Kurds to surface as collective political agents. Equally, the record suggests that they are snuffed out after the restabilization of the host regimes. External opposition to Greater and Lesser Kurdistans has been led intermittently by each of the great twentieth-century powers, the British, French, Soviet, and American empires. At particular junctures each great power has decided against sovereign or autonomous Kurdistans because it prefers different allies, or to avoid provoking its current enemies. Neighboring states have been equally ill disposed to the idea of Kurdistan. There has been no organized empathy for Kurds in the discriminatory, exclusionary *wahhabist* royal despotism in the land where Islam originated, Saudi Arabia. Jordan's Palestinians often preferred Saddam and his championing of pan-Arabism to solidarity with a people with whose plight they might have been expected to empathize. Immediately adjacent host states have generally opposed Kurdistans emerging within their neighbors' territories. In 1983 Turkey signed an agreement with Saddam allowing Turkish forces officially to enter Iraq in hot pursuit of the PKK. It also put both the KDP and the PUK under pressure. From 1991, despite assisting the formation of the safe haven by not filling the vacuum created by Saddam's withdrawal of his government from "his" Kurdistan, Turkish governments insisted on the right to pursue the PKK and often sealed their borders as a pressure tactic. For tactical reasons, Syrian, Iraqi, and Iranian regimes have been more likely than Turkey to support Kurdish political movements within their neighbors' borders. The PUK was initially supported from Damascus, and governments in Tehran have supported both the KDP and the PUK. Nevertheless, the neighboring host states shared a common perceived interest in repressing Kurdish nationalism and generally acted on that interest.

The host states have, predictably, been most adamantly opposed to the emergence of a meaningful Kurdistan on their own soil. Only outright apologists suggest that these states have been genuinely hospitable toward Kurds within their borders, or accommodating toward Kurdish identity. Throughout this book, we have deliberately used expressions such as the "Kurds of Iraq" to represent statements about residence. We have avoided common expressions such as "Iraqi Kurds," "Turkish Kurds," or "Iranian Kurds," which suggest identities and affinities that cannot be taken for granted. We do not deny that some Kurds partially identify themselves as Iraqi, Turkish, Iranian, or Syrian. Nor does our usage imply that no Kurds have been assimilated. Our terminological caution registers the fact that we do not share the assumption of the respective host states that they own "their" Kurds, or the belief that the respective Kurds feel that they belong to their hosts.

The conduct of these host states throughout the twentieth century is partly explained, although not excused, by their respective demographic profiles. The demographic facts are, of course, disputed, and precise details are a matter of controversial conjecture. The last relatively undisputed census in Iraq was conducted in 1957 or, some would say, 1947; both the 1957 and 1977 census data were subsequently rewritten by Ba'thist demographic police, notably in the oil-rich and heavily Kurdish governorate and city of Kirkuk. Bear in mind that since Turkey officially comprises only Turkish citizens, its official statisticians do not collect data on ethnic and national minorities. And it should never be forgotten that Syria is effectively an ethnic and religious minority tyranny of Alawis, a fact that Damascus prefers not to advertise (Haklai 2000). These considerations highlight shared demographic insecurity within the dominant regimes of the host states. It was no accident that in 1937 these opponents of Greater Kurdistan signed a treaty in the Persian palace of Saadabad to recognize one another's borders and to avoid manipulating the other states' Kurdish populations.

The demography of the dominant community in these host states is remarkably varied. In Turkey and Iran, Kurds have faced tyrannies of the majority ethnos and the sustained imposition of that majority's Turkish or Persian ethos and language. In Iran the majority is Shi'a, the bulk of the Kurdish minority Sunni. The Turkish and Turkified majority in Turkey is proportionally larger than Iran's Persian *Staatsvolk*. In Iraq and Syria, by contrast, Kurds have shared a common subordination to ideologically mobilized ethnoreligious minorities (Sunni Arabs and Alawis respectively), though both states have Arab demographic majorities. Despite data manipulation, scrupulous scholars do not dispute the general demographic profile of these four states and the Kurdish proportion in each. Table 1.1 shows one estimate of the Kurdish populations of Iraq, Turkey, Iran, and Syria (adapted from McDowall 1992, 12).

These data are highly suggestive. Kurds comprise nearly one in four of Iraq's population and almost one in five of Turkey's. Their demographic weight is much less in Iran and Syria, where they comprise approximately one in ten of each state's population. A Greater Kurdistan encompassing most of this Kurdish population might form a nation-state of over twenty-five million persons. Its numbers would match an Iraq without Kurds. Combining elementary demographic calculations with elementary geographic analysis makes it obvious that two of the potential sites of lesser Kurdistans, those in "southeastern Turkey" and "northeastern Iraq," have contiguous and dense concentrations of Kurds near mountainous and forested environs favorable to the sustained conduct of guerrilla warfare, at least until recent changes in military technologies. These regions are the nuclei of what pan-Kurdish champions term Northern and Southern Kurdistan and the epicenters of the most sustained Kurdish resistance to assimilation. Politics is never reducible to demography and geography, however. Kurds have been differentially treated by their host states, and eighty years of attempted incorporation in these varied states has left its imprint, differentiating the Kurds, undermining the cohesiveness assumed in the dream of Greater Kurdistan, and altering the Kurdish diaspora. The varied comparative treatment of Kurds is essential to understanding their contemporary politics.

Denials of Kurdistan, Kurdish, and Kurds have been most thoroughly routinized in "Kemalism," the codified beliefs of Kemal Atatürk, the founder of modern Turkey, who appreciated the salience of recognizing and not recognizing national identities. Before his moments of decisive victory in 1923–1924, he successfully mobilized some Kurds under a pan-Islamic and neo-Ottoman platform against Western foreign powers, Christian Armenians, and Assyrians. At certain junctures he contemplated both cultural rights and territorial autonomy for Kurds. But these proved no more than tactical conveniences, which he dispensed with when he consolidated his regime. Kemalism was built around the defense of the new Turkish rectangle, the abandonment of the Arab components of the Ottoman empire, the replacement of Islam by secular

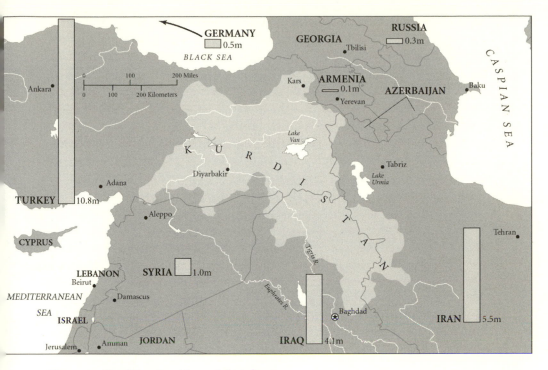

Figure 1.2. Kurdish minorities and their hosts.

TABLE 1.1. NUMBER AND PROPORTIONS OF KURDISH POPULATIONS IN THEIR "HOST" STATES

Kurdish population	Absolute population size (000)	Estimated population share (%)
Iraq	4,100	23
Turkey	10,800	19
Iran	5,500	10
Syria	1,000	8
Other states	1,200	n/a
Total	22,600	

Source: McDowall (1992), adapted: his estimations assume Kurdish demographic growth rates at the average of the states within which they reside.

Turkish nationalism as the official ideology of the new regime, and, not least, the coercive assimilation of all within Turkey, through educational and linguistic standardization into one Turkish ethnos (Kazancigil 1981; Gellner 1994b; Cizre 2001). Atatürk's disciples declared that Kurds, notwithstanding their protestations, were not what they said themselves to be, but rather "mountain Turks." Inspired by the full vigor of French Jacobin assimilationist logic, Kemalism affirmed that there were no minorities in Turkey. All its citizens were Turks, period. The positive side of Turkey's nation-building program—its republicanism, its anti-aristocratic spirit, and its effort to de-Islamicize the Turkish state—has been celebrated by intellectuals in France, at Princeton University, and some unlikely observers (Gellner 1994b). But it hid a darker underbelly: the attempted eradication of (formerly) territorially compact national, ethnic, and religious minorities.

The state of Turkey is still "nation-building"—that is, nationalizing a state on the foundations of a single ethos, ethnos, and language. It has had no patience for dual or multiple identities among its citizens. Turkish nation-building has mandated not just the definitional but also the cultural and even physical destruction of other nations within its borders. Late Ottoman, Young Turk, and Turkish regimes successively assaulted, expelled, exterminated, or coercively assimilated Armenians, Greeks, and Kurds: 1,883,000 were murdered in genocidal purges by twentieth-century Turkish regimes (Rummel 1997, 209ff). The Armenians and the Greeks of Turkey now have their nation-states and have settled some scores with their former masters, although the survivors of Turkish hospitality live outside their ancient homelands of Asia Minor and Eastern Anatolia. The Kurds of Turkey have not been so lucky. The revolts led by Sheikh Said in 1925, the Koybun insurrection of 1929–1930, and the Dersim rebellion of 1937–1938 were all crushed. The Turkish army "found control of Kurdistan to be its prime function and *raison d'être*. Only one out of 18 Turkish military engagements during the years 1924–1938 occurred outside Kurdistan. After 1945, apart from the Korean War and the invasion of Cyprus, 1974, the only Turkish army operations continued to be against the Kurds" (McDowall 2000, 198).

Under the pressures of "implacable Kemalism," some Kurds assimilated and have tried to forget their Kurdish roots. The Kurdish language has not been a public language in Turkey. Educated Kurds speak and write Turkish in public; for them, Kurdish has become a language of the home (Hassenpour 1992). In his trial, the PKK leader Ocalan defended himself—if that is what he did—in Turkish, not Kurdish. Sustained, concerted pressures on the Kurdish identity in schools, workplaces, and public media, the eradication of Kurdish villages, and the deliberate dilution of areas of Kurdish concentration have been pulverizing. The Kurds of Turkey are less Kurdish than they once were. They are now much more dispersed; Kurds are said to comprise three million of Istanbul's residents. They migrate within Turkey to the west and from Turkey to Europe, where they sometimes blend, especially in Germany, with *echte* (authentic) Turks. The PKK has dissolved, renamed, or reconstituted itself, abandoning claims both to independence and to federal status for the

Kurdish-majority zones of Turkey. Kurdish voters and potential politicians in Turkey shift among permutations of seeking cultural rights, working with "soft" pan-Islamists who recognize them as fellow Muslims and as Kurds so long as the first identity takes precedence, and hoping that Turkey's possible entry into the European Union will bring relief. In sum, at the turn of the twenty-first century, the Kurds of Turkey are disorganized, repressed, partially assimilated, and partially depoliticized. They live with a legacy of decades of repression, their most recent defeats having left their traditional rural habitat scorched beyond immediate repair.

The Turkish state inherited and reengineered Ottoman state capacities and put them to work making Kurds into Turks, with some brutal success. The Iranian state, under novel shahs or novel ayatollahs, also inherited absolutist state capacities and deployed them against the Kurds. Having experienced an independent Kurdish Republic in 1945, Pahlavi kings and their Shi'a theocratic successors determined that there should be no recurrence. Less demographically and geographically threatened by Kurds than either Turkey or Iraq, Iran has managed the Kurds within its borders with less overall bloodshed. The words "Kurds" and "Kurdistan" were not prohibited. In fact, Iran has an administrative region called "Kurdistan," although it includes only part of historic Kurdistan in Iran, and it has never been an authorized site of Kurdish self-government. Iran has often hosted Kurdish refugees from Iraq and occasionally offered tactical support to Kurdish movements in Iraq, notably during the latter stages of the Iraq-Iran war of 1980–1988 (Koohi-Kemali 2003). Iran's ayatollahs have been somewhat less opposed to Kurds qua Kurds than the secular zealots of Kemalism and the Ba'thist pan-Arab nationalists of Syria and Iraq. They have, however, been equally fixated on preventing a self-governing territorial Kurdistan within their Islamic Republic, and they have been better disposed toward Shi'a than Sunni Kurds.

Immediately after the overthrow of the Shah, before the consolidation of Khomeini's Islamic republic, liberal politicians negotiated with the Kurdish parties of Iran. The Kurdish parties sought wide-ranging territorial autonomy (encompassing areas without a Kurdish majority) and a single Kurdistan within a federated Iran. Tehran offered linguistic and cultural rights, minority rights in the constitution, and the appointment of Kurdish officials in Kurdish areas. The prospects of a compromise were destroyed by conflicts within the regime and by divisions among Kurds—between Sunni and Shi'a, between conservatives, leftists in the Kurdistan Democratic Party of Iran, and ultra-leftists in the Komola organization. Shi'a clerics eventually overturned the draft constitution's commitment to equal rights for "Persians, Turks, Kurds, Arabs, Baluchis, Turkomen, and others," insisting that none were minorities, but all were brothers in Islam (Menashri 1988). The theocrats and their supreme leader came down in favor of "Muslim patriotism," much as fashionable European liberals today proclaim their piety by endorsing "constitutional patriotism." In both cases a cosmopolitan universalism is invoked to reject ethnic particularisms, but conveniently leaves the ethos of the dominant community uncompromised. The *pasdaran*, the Islamic Revolutionary Guard, as well as Tehran's army, enforced the Shi'a brand of philosophical universalism. Kurds boycotted the constitutional referendum. During the next two decades, indigenous Kurdish movements were comprehensively defeated. Their leaders were assassinated, their fighters were beaten on the battlefield, and their organizations became generally disordered. Much as the Kurds of Turkey live in hope that the European Union will bring relief, so the Kurds of Iran anticipate that liberal and reformist challenges to theocracy in Iran will alleviate their political plight. But for now the slogan of "democracy for Iran, autonomy for Kurdistan" is a dream.

Ba'thists in Syria, like their counterparts in Iraq, oscillated between treating Kurds as potential Arabs and as an enemy nation. Amid its ferocious internal power struggles, post-colonial Syria has been as coercively assimilationist as Turkey: outlawing Kurdish in the workplace in 1986, banning ethnic (Kurdish) political parties, and not permitting education in the Kurdish language (van Dam 1979, 1996). Its leaders have moved Kurds from within the rims of their borders, where they posed perceived security risks, to the interior; they have diluted areas of Kurdish settlement. Arab nationalists realized that traditional Kurdish notables had been Ottomanist; they resented France's reliance on minorities, including Kurds, to maintain control over Syria under the mandate. They came to think of Kurds as potential fifth-columnists, potential allies of the former colonial power, Israel, and Turkey. And they treated them accordingly. In the Jazira region, local Kurds, who included both refugees who had come from Turkey in the 1920s and long-standing communities, were condemned as illegal immigrants in the early 1960s, stripped of their Syrian citizenship, and eventually encapsulated by an Arab *cordon sanitaire*, built along the Turkish and Iraqi borders, an engineered belt of Arab settlement (*al-hàzam al'arabi*) on lands where Kurds had been dispossessed. Kurds in "sensitive" regions are often denied identity cards because they are regarded as "guests." Marginalized, disorganized, and dependent, the Kurds of Syria seemed until very recently to pose no significant threat to the status quo. Indeed, the regime had been so confident of its control that many Kurds are enrolled in the Syrian army at lower ranks. The fragmented, unrecognized, and frightened Kurdish political parties of Syria had confined their aspirations to cultural rights. Most have dropped "Kurdistan" from their names, desperately signaling their renunciation of territorial ambitions (McDowall 2000, 478). Yet in March 2004, after the signing of the Transitional Administrative Law of Iraq, which recognized the Kurdistan of Iraq, the Kurds of Syria showed surprising cohesion and coordination in Qamishli after a regime-sponsored pogrom provoked riots (Agence France Presse 2004).

The neighboring host-states are the persistent veto powers that obstruct a Greater Kurdistan. There is no immediately feasible prospect of little Kurdistans in Turkey, Iran, or Syria; and a fortiori no present-day prospect of Greater Kurdistan. Kurdish cultural rights may get footholds in a liberalized Turkey within the European Union, a post-theocratic Iran, and a post-Baʿthist Syria, but these prognoses are multiply uncertain. In all three host states, Kurdish advocates of autonomy, though themselves defeated, achieved comprehensive ascendancy over their co-nationals who advocated independence or pan-Kurdish struggle. The political organizations of each of these Kurdish communities presently have autonomy, not independence, as their maximum feasible objective. This is more than a pragmatic accommodation with the ways things are; it is increasingly a set of entrenched dispositions. This inclination suggests that, whether dream or nightmare, Greater Kurdistan is not imminent. No one can credibly use that idea to argue against a fair and just constitutional settlement for the Kurds of Iraq. The expression of that fear, especially by the Turkish, Iranian, or Syrian governments, should be rejected as paranoia, or as rationalization that inhibits the constructive and just treatment of their minorities.

The Emergence of Kurdistan in Iraq

The little Kurdistan of this book, the Kurdistan in Iraq, is no dream and no nightmare. It has existed despite formidable external and internal difficulties since 1991. Under prudent political leadership and with considerable luck, it may be able to consolidate, especially since the regime of its Iraqi host-state has been dismantled. Why has this Kurdistan become more viable and enduring than the others that have gone the way of all flesh? One answer lies in the sheer demographic weight and territorial concentration of Kurds within Iraq (see Figure 1.3), at least by comparison with their presence in Syria and Iran. It was impossible for Baʿthist Iraq wholly to eradicate, expel, or assimilate them, even though versions of all these strategies were attempted. In a democratized Iraq, the combined vote-share of Kurds will be between one fifth and one third of those who vote, depending upon the yet-to-be established facts of Iraq's current ethnic demography and comparative rates of voter turnout, but

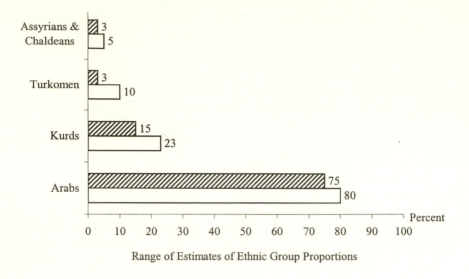

Range of Estimates of Ethnic Group Proportions

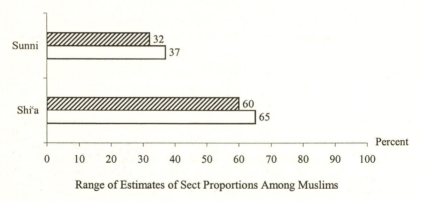

Range of Estimates of Sect Proportions Among Muslims

Figure 1.3. Estimates of minimum and maximum proportions of Iraq's nationalities and sects. Lewis (2003); CIA (2004); NZZ (2002); McDowall (1992).

few doubt that probably between one fifth and one third of Iraq's electorate would vote for parties that insist on the distinctiveness of Kurdistan.

The second explanation of the relative strength of this Kurdistan is that Iraq was a weak state before the Ba'thists consolidated their power, an evaluation shared by its English-language academic specialists (Batatu 1978; Dann 1969; Dodge 2003; Farouk-Sluglett and Sluglett 2003; Longrigg 1968; Marr 1985; Mufti 1996; Tripp 2002). Its military and bureaucratic capacities were far less than those of post-imperial Turkey or monarchical Iran. It was therefore less able to control, or coercively assimilate Kurds. "Iraq" was a British invention, in the full meaning of that noun. Its territory was a novel juxtaposition of three separately administered Ottoman *wilayets* (see Figure 1.4); its monarchy was an import from Arabia to fulfill a promise made to other Arabs; its dragooned peoples were involuntary citizens of an entity none had sought; and its public management developed under the influence of British India's colonial administration. The arranged marriage of Mesopotamia and southern Kurdistan had a poor start. Its political birth was rocked by a large-scale tax rebellion, primarily among Shiʿa tribes. This unrest was followed by Kurdish revolts, insurrections with both a traditional tribal character and the full flavor of modern nationalism: Sheikh Mahmud had a Quran strapped to his arm "like a talisman," on the flyleaves of which was written in Kurdish Woodrow Wilson's twelfth point and Anglo-French promises to liberate the peoples of the Ottoman Empire (Wilson 1930, 129, cited in McDowall 2000, 158). To economize on the costs of control, the British refused to permit the development of a conscript army and deployed the RAF as their preferred high technology instrument of order, policing, and tax enforcement (Edgerton 1991). Although the British reneged on early promises to both the League of Nations and Kurdish notables to grant official autonomy to Kurdistan, they did not completely stamp on the idea and usually talked about it in the future perfect conditional. Later, in their formal submissions to the League of Nations they lied about the implementation of these promises, equivocating because they wanted to appease the Arab nationalists around King Faisal and to exit from governing Iraq (Dodge 2003). Reducing imperial overload was then their dominant priority. Some British officials at least encouraged bilingualism in Kurdistan and education in Kurdish, though that did not ensure the bureaucratic entrenchment of these cultural rights. While Kurds did not administer Kurdistan, at least in the higher ranks of the civil service, Kurdish tribal notables remained essential for the minimal maintenance of state functions, and proved useful parliamentary ballast against Arab nationalists in the early 1920s.

Neither the British nor their tutelary Arab Iraqi successors achieved full statal penetration of tribal Kurdistan in the 1920s and 1930s. Upon formal decolonization in 1932, the Kurdish-dominated former *wilayet* of Mosul had not been politically, administratively, or culturally integrated with the rest of Iraq. At the handover, Britain "wittingly abandoned the Kurds to an Arab government intent upon evading" the reduced pledges of cultural rights for Kurds that had been made to the League of Nations (McDowall 2000, 171). But the British did not leave the Kurds of Iraq cowed. The peculiarities of British social policy in mandatory Iraq—minimal administrative development, buttressing rural as opposed to urban entities, and creating or reinforcing *sheikhs* (depending upon which historical anthropology one believes) and sometimes

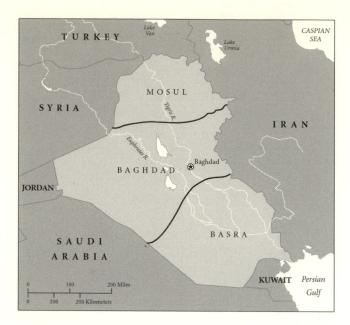

Figure 1.4a. Mandatory Iraq invented from the three Ottoman *wilayets* of Basra, Baghdad, and Mosul. Adapted from BBC map. The precise boundaries of the Mosul *wilayet* were not agreed on until 1926; see McDowall (2000, 146).

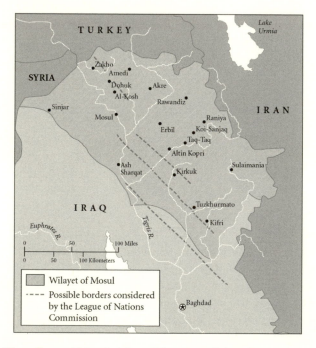

Figure 1.4b. The *wilayet* of Mosul. Adapted from Bomli (1929).

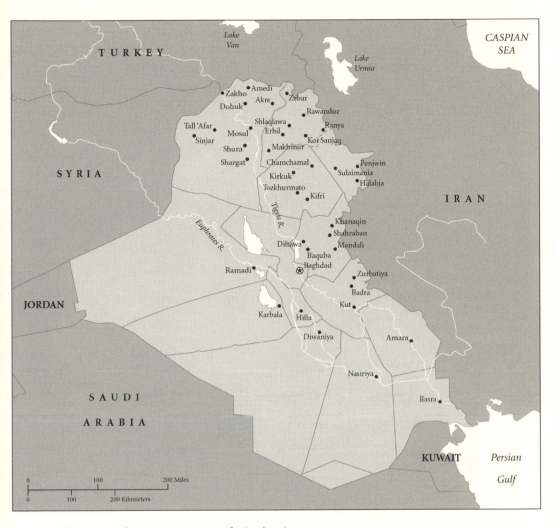

Figure 1.4c. The 14 governorates of Mandate Iraq.

aghas (landlords)—may have assisted in preserving the combination of traditional Kurdish culture and modernizing elements that animated Kurdish nationalism. Under the mandate, and indeed under the monarchy, the Kurds of Iraq were less repressed, or less successfully repressed, than the Kurds of the neighboring states (Farouk-Sluglett and Sluglett 2003, 26)—with the emphases on the word *less* in both of those clauses.

Independent monarchical Iraq (1932–1958) was not a strong state, though its leaders had the ambition to make it one. This landlords' regime was more rigorous in repressing class-based discontent than ethnic differences. King Faisal, though not well disposed to Kurds *qua* Kurds or to Kurdish speakers, wanted them as "confessional ballast"; he believed that as Sunnis they might check the demographic preponderance of Shi'a in his novel kingdom. Faisal's Arab nationalist advisors saw Kurds as troublesome, but as potential Arabs. West Asia's first post-colonial kingdom displayed bewildering instability, with an extraordinary number of attempted coups originating within the monarchy. Executive instability was accompanied by bursts of horrific violence and ethnic outrages against Assyrians in the 1930s and Jews in the 1940s (Kedourie 1984 (1952); Salih 1996a). A parade of politicians succeeded one another as premiers and ministers, bereft of significant support from political parties or organized social bases. They varied between pro- and anti-British, or pro- and anti-imperial orientations. These divisions among Arabs developed into controversies over pan-Arabism versus Iraqi patriotism, republicanism versus monarchism, and land reform versus landlordism (Salih 1996b).

The emergence of intra-Arab conflicts gave Kurdish leaders regular opportunities to advance demands for cultural, administrative, and territorial rights, especially when Baghdad politicians felt they needed to widen support for their governments. Kurds sought recognition of their language and administrative control of Kurdistan. Several different general theories of the emergence of nationalism apply to the Kurds of Iraq (and to other Kurds). In strongly "modernist" explanations, nationalism arises during the breakdown of caste-based agrarian empires and their displacement by industrializing societies that insist on cultural, especially linguistic, homogenization. Nationalism takes a strongly conflictual form among those excluded from high-status positions because they are deemed to lack a "high culture" (Gellner 1983; see O'Leary 1998). On a related account, nationalism emerges, especially within colonial entities, in response to literacy and print media that facilitate the imagining of a new horizontal community of co-nationals. This type of nationalism is expected to be especially strong among educated persons whose social mobility in public administration is blocked (Anderson 1991). In a less modernist theory, by contrast, nationalism is considered as a form of collective action especially likely to arise in response to any alien "direct rule" of a region previously governed through its own modes of autonomy (be they tribal, patrimonial, feudal, or modern) (Hechter 2000; for a non-instrumentalist account, see Connor 1994).

During the period from the decline of the Ottoman Empire to the end of the Hashemite monarchy in Iraq, the Kurdish case fits all three of these frameworks. Urbanization and modernization, especially in the Mesopotamian plains, and underdevelopment in the mountains of Kurdistan highlighted the emergent contrast—and significant disparity in life-chances—between Arab "high culture" and traditional Kurdish "low culture." Educated and urbanized Kurds experienced both discrimination and pressures to assimilate. The emergence of written Kurdish, albeit in different alphabets (Latin in Turkey and an adaptation of Arabic in Iran and Iraq), facilitated a cultural Kurdish imagination in which the excluded could take pride and organize. The efforts of the British and the Hashemites to penetrate Kurdistan with modern direct rule and to replace tribal governance and patronage with more "impersonal," bureaucratic but Arabized administration provoked the traditional notables of Kurdistan to defend their privileges and eventually led some to make common cause with the new urbanized and professionalized Kurds who had different grievances and agendas. Workers and peasants were the last to be mobilized behind Kurdish nationalism. Nationalists had to compete with the Iraqi Communist Party (ICP) for the support of workers, a task made easier by the strength of pan-Arabism, Nasserism, and Ba'thism among Arab workers. The peasantry was the least educated sector of the population and the last to acquire a modern Kurdish political identity, and their interests, at least when they ceased to be clan members, were at odds with those of the traditional notables, especially those who had become landlords.

The historical sociology of Kurdish nationalism may therefore be briefly summarized as taking the following stages. First, tribal notables, aggrieved at their displacement from their traditional local forms of rule, sought the restoration of customary modes of autonomy. They were defeated. Some accepted integration into the new order as landlords, but others made common if competitive cause with new intellectual and urban nationalists and eventually brought significant numbers of workers and peasants into their ranks. This model applies to the emergence of the Kurdistan Democratic Party of Iraq, under the leadership of a traditional notable, Mustafa Barzani, possessed of first-class military skills, and a range of able urban intellectuals, notably Ibrahim Ahmed and Jalal Talabani.

The Hashemite monarchy was destroyed in the July 1958 revolution. In the republican decade before the Ba'th coup, serious divisions and rivalries among Arab politicians and military gave the KDP leverage in Iraqi politics, as communists, Iraqi patriots, Nasserites, and even Ba'thists successively wooed its leaders. Between 1958 and 1961, between 1965 and 1966, and in the early years of the second Ba'th regime, Kurds briefly won formal concessions on language rights, recognition as a constituent co-nationality in the provisional constitution, and promises of decentralization or territorial autonomy. Implementation was another matter. The very weakness of the Arab leaders willing to make deals with the Kurds led them to backtrack when concessions led to dissent or anger within their Arabist constituencies. But even after the Ba'thists returned to power in 1968 they tried to accommodate the Kurds, both in central government ministries and through far-reaching offers of autonomy in 1970. These efforts were, of course, undermined by their determination not to allow oil-rich Kirkuk become part of autonomous Kurdistan and by their deliberate efforts to take advantage of rivalries among Kurds.

The sustained weakness of the Iraqi state from 1920 until the high tide of Ba'thist ascendancy (1975–1990) created multiple opportunities for the emergence of Kurdish agendas and for a Kurdistan in "South Kurdistan." Iraqi leaders, interested in consolidating their power, found the idea of Kurdistan thinkable, negotiable, and even sensible. The political and administrative implications of an *Iraqi* Kurdistan, while unwelcome to Arabists, were not beyond the pale. Some would even contend that intra-Kurdish divisions contributed as much as Arab hostility to blocking the emergence of a functioning Kurdistan before the mid-1970s (that is how we read McDowall 2000). The emergence of Kurdistan after Saddam Hussein's defeat in the Kuwait war in 1991 was thus not an accident. It had its roots in the prior development of the state of Iraq. In 1992, Kurdistan's voters were able to elect a National Assembly to sit in an Erbil parliament building. It had been commissioned by none another than Saddam Hussein, who had staffed it with collaborators.

The third answer to the question of why this Kurdistan emerged and has proved more durable than its historical precursors lies in the sustained organizational continuity of Kurdish nationalist groups within Iraq. Again, this is a comparative evaluation. No nation, manifest or latent, is a homogeneous monolith. Kurdistanis, like people of other nations, vary by dialect, region, and religion (Shi'a, Sunni, Feyli, Yezidi, Christian, and Jew). Kurdish society has urban-rural cleavages; in the recent past deep-rooted conflicts between landlords and peasants arose from monarchical Iraq's encouragement of an exploitative Kurdish *agha* class. Moreover, tribalism, factionalism, and splits correctly constitute the standard historical narratives of organized Kurdish nationalism.[2] The traits these stories manifest have been the major internal obstacles to the creation of both Greater and Lesser Kurdistans. Emphasis on the fissiparous nature of Kurdish organization is as common among observers of the Kurds today (Randall 1997; van Bruinessen 1992, 2003; McDowall 2000; Stansfield 2003) as it was during the early twentieth century (Edmonds 1957; Wilson 1930, 1931). This factionalism may be seen as rooted in the paradoxical but nonetheless intimate connection between particularistic "tribal" loyalties and universalistic "modern" nationalist ideologies. Anthropologically speaking, nomadism in a mountainous topography is conducive toward segmentary lineage systems, which in turn may facilitate both the generation of egalitarian warriors and the salience of kin and clan loyalties over statal dispositions

(Gellner 1969, 1981, 1991, 1994a). The "tyranny of cousins" has certainly been part of Kurdish culture, along with fratricide, feuding, and fatuous divisions. The bewildering alphabet soup of historic Kurdish party organizations bears some semblance to the parody of left-wing national liberation movements in Monty Python's *Life of Brian*. Even today some Kurdish militants, on minimal evidence, are very quick to categorize outsiders as supporters of the KDP or the PUK, displaying a party sectarianism worthy of Mao's last disciples in Europe. Kurds of all classes, both sexes, and various age-cohorts tell outsiders that the disunity of Kurdish organizations, whether in the diaspora or within each of the host-states, makes the Kurds their own worst enemies. Being divided renders a people vulnerable to being ruled and further divided. Turkish, Iranian, Syrian, and Iraqi leaders have been adept at taking advantage of these divisions, through intrigue, funding, bribery, and assassination. Kurdish nationalist movements might be said to have two natural equilibrium conditions: no leaders, and too many leaders.

But it is precisely by these standards of disunity that the Kurds of Iraq have differed from Kurds elsewhere. They have been better organized both to conduct armed and political struggle and to nurture and maintain their constituency. Even their infighting has, in the end, been less crippling than have the conflicts among their counterparts. Mustafa Barzani, the first powerful leader of the Kurdistan Democratic Party (KDP), whether under house arrest or in exile in the Soviet Union, dominated the politics of the Kurds of Iraq from the 1930s until his death in Washington, D.C., in 1979. Even though his roots lay in tribal power configurations, which often adversely affected his conduct in the eyes of his critics, he nevertheless institutionalized his charismatic authority and achieved discipline, especially military discipline, among contentious Kurds. Many other Kurdish parties emerged among the Kurds of Iraq, most notably Jalal Talabani's Patriotic Union of Kurdistan (PUK), but Barzani and his peers had pioneered an enduring organizational capability, especially party cadres and *peshmerga,* that all its potential rivals were obliged to emulate. In uneasy cooperation (and sometimes open conflict) with Ibrahim Ahmed and Jalal Talabani, Barzani led Kurds toward a post-tribal and modern nationalist politics.

From 1961 until 1975 Barzani and his *peshmerga* were occasionally bloodied, but they avoided devastating defeats though astute marshalling of resources; and in 1966 they routed the Iraqi army in a full-scale engagement at Mount Handrin. Even though the Ba'thists eventually defeated the KDP in 1975, after the Shah of Iran and the U.S. withdrew their support, the KDP reappeared in the 1980s, after Mustafa Barzani's death, as a sustained opposition force, along with the PUK. The KDP, led by Masoud Barzani, and the PUK, led by Talabani, have often put their respective parties first in intra-Kurdish struggles, but sufficiently often enough they have put the interests of the Kurds of Iraq first—as when they ruthlessly dropped leftist Iranian Kurdish organizations in the 1980s in return for a free hand against the Ba'thists, or when they cooperated with Ankara against the PKK. These two party organizations, with established social bases, ideologists, mythologies, and military capabilities, with all their limitations, and their past histories of schism, were ready to be parties-of-government in 1991–1992. The voters of free Kurdistan, with obvious enthusiasm and in an almost even allocation, gave the two of them 89 percent of their votes.

Free Kurdistan, 1991–2003

The creation of a safe haven by the U.S. and the UK in April 1991, a military exclusion zone and a no-fly zone north of the 36th line of latitude, allowed this free Kurdistan to emerge from Ba'thist Iraq. The safe haven was an ad hoc response by the UK, U.S., and Turkey to the presence in Turkey and Iran of over two million refugees who had fled from Saddam's revenge on Kurdish and Shi'a rebels. Saddam subsequently withdrew his forces and his administration from Kurdistan, hoping that a sustained economic boycott would bring the land-locked Kurds to their knees and encourage infighting between the Kurdish parties. Uncertain of continuing American and British support and fearfully determined to avoid a repetition of genocide, Barzani and Talabani sought to negotiate recognition of the new entity directly with Baghdad. They also sought the inclusion in Kurdistan of Kirkuk, Khaniqin, and Mandali, as had been previously anticipated in negotiations with Mustafa Barzani in March 1970. Even though Saddam was deeply weakened, no deal was done. Armed conflict soon resumed, only to reach a rapid stalemate. A line of control was consolidated, separating free Kurdistan from the rest of Iraq with a de facto border that ran from near Zakho on the Turkish border to the Iranian border and encompassed the three major Kurdish cities of Dohuk, Erbil, and Sulaimania (see Figure 1.5). Freed from Saddam's direct rule, the Kurds of Iraq elected a Kurdistan National Assembly in May 1992, in the first free and fair parliamentary elections in the history of Iraq, and arguably in any part of historic Kurdistan. The election was closely contested. It was won by a whisker by the KDP in what proved to be a two-horse race; third parties and independents garnered just over 10 percent of the vote between them (there were separate Christian minority lists). The distribution of the vote showed that the KDP was totally dominant in Dohuk, the PUK enjoyed a three-to-one advantage in

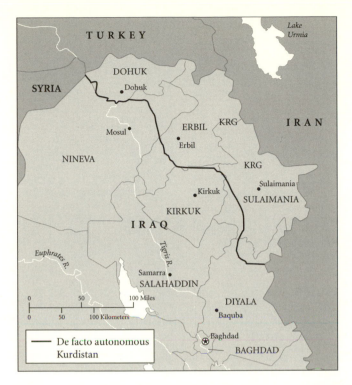

Figure 1.5. De facto Autonomous Kurdistan, 1991–2003. Adapted from KRG map.

Sulaimania, and Erbil was evenly divided between the parties.[3] Agreement was reached to establish a power-sharing Kurdistan Regional Government (KRG), although both party leaders avoided taking executive positions.

The story of free Kurdistan in the dozen years between the war over Kuwait and the war to remove Saddam may be told in two ways, the malign and the benign (for one extensive field report, see Stansfield 2003). Taking the malign perspective, one can contend that the division and near balance between the parties and their failure to create unified security forces facilitated disastrous episodes of civil war in the mid-1990s. It seems unfair to blame power-sharing itself for the breakdown into conflict, as some observers do. Both parties had expected to win, and the marginal loser, the PUK, found losing or not winning very difficult—as in Ireland's 1922–1923 civil war, voices were heard to say that the people had no right to be wrong at the ballot box. Past schisms between the parties produced widespread distrust between the parties' respective cadres that their leaders were unable or unwilling to control. Fighting that began in the lower ranks over trivial disputes was insufficiently controlled by the senior party leaderships. Each eventually stooped to bring in

Tehran and Baghdad to aid their respective causes, before sanity prevailed under the pressure of local civil society. The inter-party conflict had to be mediated by the United States—in conferences held in Drogheda, Ireland, Rambouillet, France, and Ankara, among other efforts. The repercussions of these conflicts were approximately three thousand dead and a territorial division of free Kurdistan into two executive jurisdictions, KRG (Erbil) and KRG (Sulaimania), dominated by the KDP and the PUK respectively. The two executives co-exist with a single legislature, the Kurdistan National Assembly. Each unit now provides its part of free Kurdistan with a government and a prime minister, cabinet, and ministries. Currently, Nechirvan Barzani in Erbil and Barham Salih in Sulaimania are respectively the KDP and PUK prime ministers.

There has been no serious internal fighting since 1997, and Kurdistan has had none of the major crime or terrorism problems associated with failed states or other unrecognized entities, such as Somaliland or Abkhazia. Indeed, it seemed in late 2003 that conflict had finally been resolved with an agreement to re-create a unified government of all Kurdistan, but to date that has not happened. One of the diasporan Kurdish web sites runs two competing countdown diaries: on one side it displays the number of days since the KDP and the PUK agreed to form a unified government, and on the other it displays the number of days until the U.S. restores sovereignty to Iraq (see <www .kurdistanobserver.com>). This conjunction is meant and received as a telling criticism. The division between political parties and the territorial division of the two executives make it easier for opponents of Kurdistan to deny that it is one entity, and to reject the idea that it should be treated as one entity in discussions of the constitutional future of Iraq. The descent into civil war meant that the renewal of the Kurdistan National Assembly through fresh elections was postponed, and postponed again after the onset of the Gulf War in 2003. The mandate of a parliament elected in 1992 is less and less credible, domestically and internationally. All this constitutes the malign downside of this experiment in self-government.

The benign perspective on free Kurdistan peeks through, however, even in the darker picture painted above. Since 1991 it has been much better for all, minorities included, to live within Kurdistan than in the rest of Iraq. All the cabinets of Kurdistan have included members of religious and linguistic minorities and members who do not belong to either of the two dominant parties. Even the Arab opposition party leaders spent time in Kurdistan in the 1990s. UN data suggest that Kurdistan has performed better across a range of key human development indicators, as emphasized by Molly McNulty in her chapter on children. The deleterious impact of UN sanctions on the rest of

Iraq is not the sole cause of this disparity; it has also been due to better governmental performance in Kurdistan. There have been no government-organized or government-sanctioned human rights abuses of minorities or women in Kurdistan. There are two ministries of human rights, led by able men and staffed by many women. There are female ministers. The Kurdistan National Assembly recently criminalized "honor killings," a rare move among the Muslim countries of the Middle East.

Although frequently satirized as embryonic "Barzanistan" and "Talabanistan," both the KDP- and the PUK-led governments have, we argue, proved to be more than the "eighteenth-century tribal confederations" suggested in a moment of exasperation by one of their most astute long-time observers (McDowall 2000, 462; see also Stansfield 2003). In the executives they control, the two parties temper patronage with merit and, contrary to stereotypes, they draw upon highly educated personnel to fill both ministerial and administrative positions, independent of lineage, region, or prior commitment to the existing leaders. Both have partially differentiated party from government, a feat often not successfully executed by many European parties. Both have allowed and nurtured judicial independence. There are female judges and lawyers. The rule of law and economic freedom have encouraged small and medium-sized enterprises. Kurdistan is networked, both with mobile phones and by the internet. Its electricity supplies are far more stable than those in many allegedly more developed countries. The Kurdistan National Assembly has remained in being as the common parliament of both executives: a symbol of the desire for unity and a plausible center of unity once fresh elections take place.

It may reasonably be claimed, despite the civil conflict between them, that both parties and their executives rose to the challenge presented by Saddam's blockade. They have developed Kurdistan. We might even argue that the division into two governments gave each KRG executive incentives to perform at least as well as the other. There are no significant allegations or evidence of corruption, and none is so far suggested at the senior level, among the prime ministers, ministers, senior civil servants, and top party leaders. The two regimes have been fairly frugal and honest. The land they inherited was charred, scorched by Saddam's deforestation, environmentally damaged, bombed out, ravaged by decades of war, deportation, refugee movements, and displacements. A large proportion of the population of Kurdistan had lost their economically active heads of household to war, genocide, disappearance, or exile. The Kurdistan Regional Governments succeeded in bringing back some of the prosperous residents of the diaspora to invest in the rebuilding of their country. They negotiated successful development programs with the

United Nations, through their share of the "Oil-for-Food" Program. They did the same with NGOs and international nongovernmental organizations (INGOS). They have developed their own administrative capacities. For the first time in its existence, Kurdistan has generally smooth, functioning roads that link and integrate its major cities and villages. Customs on commerce— and smuggling—funded government revenues, but a low tax and reduced oil-welfare environment have encouraged self-help in place of the dependency encouraged during Saddam's ascendancy. The landscape is being restored and reforested. There is plentiful evidence of private entrepreneurial activity. Local agriculture benefited from boycotts by the government of Iraq and has progressed to meet local urban needs, though it remains underdeveloped. Refugees and internally displaced persons are looked after and being resettled. Schooling is organized, free, and compulsory, although implementation varies. An educated generation has emerged with English rather than Arabic as its world language. Universities are developing technical and engineering capabilities. Hospitals and medical services work. The two governments are secular and have not allowed Muslim zealots to have their way on the sale of alcohol, the dress of women, or so-called honor killings. The police are uniformed, disciplined, and trained to be civil; foreigners usually complain that the traffic police are too relaxed! The *peshmerga* are being partially demobilized and reconstructed as police officers and border guards, and may be converted into a trained national guard or mountain rangers. Free media criticize the governments and parties; although the two main television stations are still too close to the two main parties, their partisan tilt results from their own deference rather than the instructions of the respective party leaders. There is no widespread or palpable evidence of destitution or begging in the major cities, though the housing stock leaves a great deal to be desired. Until the twin Erbil bombings of February 2004, Kurdistan was a haven of tranquility by comparison with the rest of Iraq.

Actually existing free Kurdistan is no paradise. It has a long way to go to develop the full capabilities of its men, women, and children. Its economic development cannot continue on its previous path. Kurdistan's governing institutions can no longer expect funding through special UN programs or irregular customs. They must develop their own fiscal capacity, and sought to do just that in the negotiation of the Transitional Administrative Law. The region needs to be able to develop its own natural resources—water, minerals, oil—and its hydroelectric power industry in a secure legal environment that will encourage inward investment in and diversification of the regional economy. It will benefit from free trade with the rest of Iraq, although some of its enterprises will suffer. Understandably, its talented and well-educated professionals too often seek to emigrate along the diasporic family chains built during several decades of political persecution, exile, and economic exigency. The political turmoil of the mid-1990s casts a shadow of apprehension, though it also serves as dire warning that the consequences of division include the possible loss of Kurdistan. Some suggest that the territorial division of Kurdistan between the two party-dominated executives is a resolution of conflict. It has created two legitimate governments with tolerated opposition (an argument along these lines is developed in Stansfield 2003). If so, it is an ad hoc resolution, not one for the long term: fresh regional elections will oblige the parties to produce a durable institutional settlement.

Prospects for the Future: Reextinction or Flourishing Autonomy?

On 6 March 2003, shortly before launching the invasion of Iraq and the forcible overthrow of Saddam Hussein, President George W. Bush made a rare statement in a press conference about the regime change he wished to see: "I'm convinced that a liberated Iraq . . . will provide a place where people can see that the Shiʿa and the Sunni and the Kurds can get along in a *federation*. Iraq will serve as a catalyst for change, positive change . . . replacing this cancer inside Iraq will be a government that represents the rights of all the people, a government which represents the voices of the Shiʿa and Sunni and the Kurds" (Bush 2003, 7–8 of 13-page transcript, emphasis added). Although Bush did not elaborate on what kind of federation he had in mind, many took him to have been endorsing a tripartite federation built on Arab Sunni, Arab Shiʿa, and Kurds as the major constituencies of territorial units (Gelb 2003). This interpretation, however, was soon resisted within his administration. His advisors started to gloss over his statement and to declare that a recognizably American version of a federal arrangement was what the President had in mind, especially after the creation of the Coalition Provisional Authority (CPA).

Expatriate Iraqi intellectual activists and some American-educated academics spelled out this American model publicly (Makiya 2003; Dawisha and Dawisha 2003). They sought a nonnational, or nonethnic, federation in which all citizens would just be "Iraqis"—a model of "territorial" or "administrative" federalism which allegedly would resemble that of the U.S. Brendan O'Leary and John McGarry critically evaluate these arguments in their essays that follow. The resonance of these arguments among other reasons flowed from America's commitments to its alliance with Turkey. Turkey's fear of the secession of Kurdistan matched America's fear of a pan-Shiʿa state built through the expansion of Iran into southern Iraq. On the part of some Arab liberals, by contrast, the motivation for territorial federation presents itself as a difference-blind constitutional patriotism. But, however they are put, the arguments of the Arab liberals, such as the honorable Makiya and the naïve Dawishas, as well as those of the anti-Kurdish and anti-federalist Turks with whom they are in de facto alliance, are propositions for the reextinction of Kurdistan.

Consistent with the theses of the Dawishas and Makiya, L. Paul Bremer III, "The Administrator" of the CPA, in "papers" and "non-papers" circulated in December 2003 and January 2004, advocated a federation based on the idea of Iraq's 18 governorates that date back to Saddam Hussein (see Figure 1.6). These papers were circulated shortly before the making of the Transitional Administrative Law of March 2004 (for further discussion, see the chapters by O'Leary and Peter Galbraith). The relevant governorates, including jurisdictions that Saddam had expressly reengineered for purposes of ethnic manipulation, especially in Kirkuk, were, remarkably, presented as "non-ethnic" or as ethnically neutral. The implication, which also remained undeclared, was that "actually existing Kurdistan" should accept its dissolution into the preexisting governorates and bits of governorates that its current territory encompassed. Some Arab liberals and some within the CPA may even have naively hoped that the divisions between the KDP and the PUK executives could be resolved through a formula based on the old governorates, creating two or three mini-Kurdistans. Bremer himself expressed difficulties in understanding why the Kurds were not happily embracing a federal model based on Iraq's governorates. Some Arab politicians, who had previously supported Kurdish demands for their own federal unit in Iraq, returned from exile and started to air their opposition to the existence of Kurdistan from new positions in Baghdad.

The coalition-appointed Iraqi Governing Council (IGC) collectively had started to proceed in the same direction, with encouragement and steering from Bremer. On 15 November 2003, in a quickly arranged agreement with the CPA, Jalal Talabani, leader of the Patriotic Union of Kurdistan and a Kurdish rotating president of the Governing Council, was persuaded to sign an Agreement in which it was declared that an element of the fundamental law would include "federal arrangements for Iraq, to include governorates and the separation and specification of powers to be exercised by central and local entities" (CG-CPA 2003). Talabani subsequently repudiated the relevant clause, by publishing a qualification; he had recognized that the Arabic version of the text might be read as an endorsement of Saddam's governorates and therefore of the dismemberment of Kurdistan's existing integrity. The CPA's web site summary on a "timeline to a sovereign, democratic and secure Iraq" excluded any

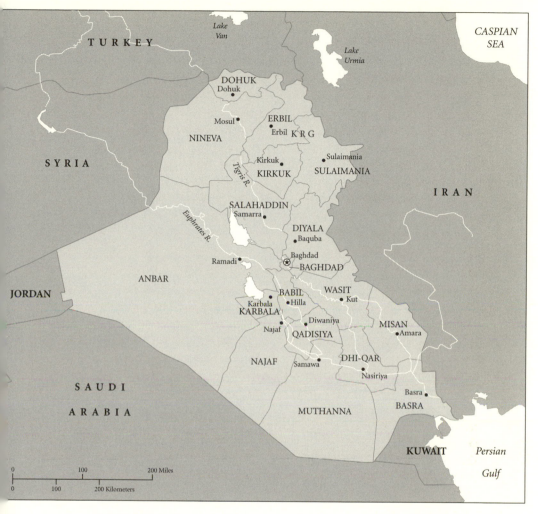

Figure 1.6. The 18 governorates of Saddam Hussein. Adapted from UN map.

reference to this controversial clause (CPA Agreement 2003). Thereafter, the joint Kurdish leaderships made it plain that while the rest of Iraq was entitled to have governorates, Kurdistan qua Kurdistan would, by contrast be *a* unit in the future federation, or there would be no agreed transitional law, let alone any prospect of an agreed permanent constitution.

Despite the existence of free Kurdistan between 1991 and 2003, and despite the fact that the *peshmerga* were the sole internal forces to assist the U.S.-led coalition in the liberation of Iraq, it had become thinkable, within six months of declaring victory, for the American occupation authorities to contemplate, by oversight or design, the re-extinction of Kurdistan. This thinking, or indifference, had several sources. First, Arabists and Turkists were often preeminent in the U.S. State Department and UK Foreign Office and present in the Coalition Provisional Authority. The Arabists wanted to appease Iraqi and pan-Arab opinion as part of weakening the Ba'thist and Islamist resistance. (On 14 March 2004, a search of the CPA web site turned up zero— repeat, zero—references to "Arabization," whether in Kirkuk or elsewhere). The Turkists wanted to calm Ankara, even though Turkey had voted against joining the overthrow of Saddam, not even by permitting U.S. forces to traverse its territory and air space. (Interestingly, when the CPA web site's own search engine is run, very little that is positive comes up on Kurds or Kurdistan, and nothing commensurate with Kurdish suffering; most of the results are about Turkish "sensitivities" toward Kurdish demands; and, tellingly, the CPA web site is published in English and Arabic, but not Kurdish; see <www.cpa-iraq.org>.) Second, the CPA was fixated on its public international commitment to the territorial integrity of Iraq, which pushed it toward favoring a recentralized Iraq despite whatever knowledge its officials had of the history of Iraq's past treatment of Kurds, or of their recent alliance with Kurdistan. The displacement of General Garner by Ambassador Bremer was part of this commitment. Third, the CPA was influenced by some conventional wisdom in the American political science community that opposes ethnic or multinational federations, which John McGarry and Brendan O'Leary address in their chapters. Fourth, until matters reached this pass, the Kurdish leadership had presumed too much on its status as allies of the Americans. It then fought a successful rearguard action for recognition of the distinctiveness of Kurdistan.

The lesson of this episode remains pertinent. The denial or reextinction of Kurdistan remains thinkable, among both Arabs and Americans, and is still demanded by many Turkish politicians, as Sophia Wanche and Michael Gunter explain in their overviews of Ankara's perspectives. This constellation of interests would have preferred central and local entities, rather than federal and regional entities. They sought as many federal units as possible to dissolve Kurdistan and to avoid creating any potential "Shi'astan" and "Sunnistan," as O'Leary argues in his chapter. This strategy had been foreshadowed in a report written by the Democratic Principles Working Group (DPWG), Iraqis chosen and supported by the U.S. State Department to envision the transition to democracy in Iraq (DPWG 2002). They opposed both bi-national and multinational federation and concluded that "it is extremely unlikely that a federation of many national and ethnic groups would be any kind of an improvement on a federation made of only two [Arab and Kurdish] large groups"

(DPWG 2002). Reasoning that such a division "will turn nationality and/or ethnicity into the basis for making territorial claims and counterclaims, especially with regards to high profit resources located in one region and not another," they proposed "territorial/administrative" federalism, arguing that the alternative to nationality is "territoriality," offering each separate region its share of "national resources" (oil revenues included), according to the relative size of its population. In this view, "territorial" or "administrative" criteria have "greater credibility" among Iraqis and the international community because national and ethnic divisions have acquired a bad name since the wars in Lebanon and former Yugoslavia, and because of the tendency among some Iraqi "nationalities to cloak nationalist arrangements in territorial garb" (DPWG 2002, 94). The convergence between these liberals and classical Marxists is interesting: both reduce ethnic, national, and religious identity claims to codifications of material interests. The DPWG did not say whether material interests played any role in arguments against a resource-rich Kurdistan or for a Kirkuk freed from the repercussions of ethnic expulsions and induced Arab settlements.

If trying to relaunch the governorates as meaningful public authorities was the practical Trojan horse to destroy Kurdistan from within, the ideological attempt to re-deny the existence of Kurdistan was rather different. The standard discursive strategy among Arab liberals and some CPA officials has been to insist that there is but one *people* in Iraq, to refer only to the "Iraqi people," to Iraqi citizens and individuals, to "just Iraqis," as well as to make synonyms of state and nation in the word Iraq. The DPWG argued against the domination of Iraq by the (Sunni) Arabs and proposed instead that the future democracy must elevate "the Iraqi character of the state above all considerations of race, ethnicity and religion" (DPWG 2002, 95). As the author of those lines later explained, a democratic Iraq "will be one that by definition exists for all its citizens equally, regardless of race, ethnicity, or religion. And that means an Iraq that will not imagine itself as an *Arab* nation" (Makiya 2003, 9–10). Kanan Makiya believes that the new Iraqi constitution should "elevate the Iraqi-ness of Iraq over all other factors to express what we have in common" and should therefore "avoid formulations that prioritize one group over another." Makiya desires Iraq to be neither "an Arab nation with a Kurdish minority" nor "an Arab and Kurdish nation with other nationalities" (International Crisis Group 2003, 11). This argument is at once a reversion to old-style Iraq-first patriotism (*wataniyya*), as opposed to ethnic pan-Arab nationalism (*qawmiyya*), and an effort to advertise the commitment of Arab liberals to "civic nationalism," "constitutional patriotism," and "republican citizenship"—all the current buzzwords of Western liberalism deemed acceptable in polite company. Exponents of this argument obviously include those keen to prevent both Shiʿa and Kurds from reconstituting Iraq in their national or religious interests. They also include those genuinely hostile to the recognition of ethnic and sect-based politics. Remarkably, however, those Iraqis so persuaded appear to speak Arabic (or Turkomen) as their first language and are usually secular or Sunni Arabs.

This liberal ideological argument, even when well motivated as in Makiya's case, is thin and corresponds to no ethnographic realities in Iraq. It may be possible to reconstruct a shared Iraqi citizenship and identity, but only on the basis of the explicit recognition and expression of dual or multiple identities, be they national, religious, or linguistic. Eventually this was the route taken in the Transitional Administrative Law, as O'Leary argues in Chapter 2. The liberal ideological argument is also doubly false in simple factual terms. There is not just one Iraqi *people*. Even the Baʿthists recognized this fact in their 11 March 1970 accord with the KDP in which they promised to amend the interim constitution to read "The Iraqi people is made up of two nationalities, the Arab nationality and the Kurdish nationality." Kurds and Arabs are members of different nations, each with a different language, history, and ethos. Second, it is false because it implicitly denounces Kurdistan as an ethnic entity. It is true that Kurdistan certainly contains "Kurd" within its name, just as England contains "Anglo," France contains "Frank," and Denmark contains "Dane." But Kurdistan and its parties are at least as civic nationalist in disposition as the English, French, Danes, and Arab liberals, and unlike the latter they have proved themselves to be such in government. Within Kurdistan, minority rights in language, schooling, and religion have been protected. All citizens under both of Kurdistan's functioning executives are equals and treated as such. Kurdistani is not synonymous with Kurd, any more than Iraqi should be synonymous with Arab.

For many Kurdistanis, the 15 November 2003 document and the arguments of the Arab liberals created anxiety, which dampened the joy they felt at the overthrow of Saddam and his subsequent arrest. They feared that another betrayal of promises awaited them. In several public meetings, Masoud Barzani, president of the KDP, repeatedly insisted on two principles for the future of a renewed Iraq: power-sharing between the Arabs and the Kurds, and treating Kurdistan as one geographic and political entity in the proposed federal system. Both were essential to achieve national rights for the Kurds. Barzani explicitly rejected the idea that a federal Iraq should be based on the old governorates, because in such an arrangement the Kurdish identity, distinctiveness, and existing rights would be lost (*Khebat*, 13, 15 November, 18 December 2003). Kurdistan's parties were not about to accept reintegration into Iraq on the terms proposed by the Arab liberals and their American sponsors. The Kurdistan National Assembly (KNA) had already in 1992 proposed, through a parliamentary bill, a draft constitution for a two-unit federation in a future Iraq, one to encompass Kurdistan and another to encompass the rest of Iraq. It had been drafted by the KDP but approved by the PUK (Kurdistan Democratic Party 1992a, b). The KNA renewed this declaration in October 2002.

Kurdish politicians and media reminded Arab politicians that the majority of the Iraqi opposition forces, with U.S. sponsorship, had adopted Kurdistan's proposal of a federal Iraq in 1992 and had reiterated this commitment in 1999 and 2002 (*Khebat*, 18 December 2003). Federation had been accepted in principle by a clear majority of the organized opposition groups, and as late as December 2002 the Iraqi opposition conference in London agreed that the permanent constitution of post-Saddam Iraq should be drafted in such a way that "the national composition of Iraq" was enshrined (Political Statement 2002). The Kurdish leadership insisted on these commitments to win concessions in the making of the Transitional Administrative Law (TAL) that was negotiated in February 2004 and ratified in March. Among other things, the TAL recognized multiple nationalities, made Kurdish an official language of the federation, recognized the existing territory of Kurdistan, the Kurdistan National Assembly, and the Kurdistan Regional Government, and granted the region its own internal security. As important, de facto, Kurdistan negotiated a veto on the ratification of the permanent constitution (for details see the three chapters by O'Leary; Eklund, O'Leary, and Williams; and Galbraith).

Kurdistan is, in short, legally secure for now. Its existence is official. Its status can be both secured and extended. Kurdistan can live within a new Iraq, and live well, but Kurdistanis will not be "just Iraqis." And the rest of Iraq will have to accommodate those changes if stability is to be achieved and maintained. The partners in the new federation might do well to start by designing a new flag and new currency notes. The current flag of Iraq has three colors: red for courage, white to symbolize generosity, and black to reflect the success of Islam in Iraq. In different ways all three colors are symbols of pan-Arabism. They are not inclusive toward Kurds, Turkomen, Christians, or Jews. The three stars on the current flag, contrary to a misleading anecdote that is given widespread credence, do not stand for Shi'a, Sunni, and Kurds; nor do they signify the three Ottoman *wilayets* of Mosul, Baghdad, and Basra. Rather, they are a legacy of a very different and wholly failed federalist project: one to unify Egypt, Syria, and Iraq under pan-Arabism. A new, pluralist federal flag will have to accommodate Kurds and Kurdistanis, as well as Iraq's smaller nationalities and non-Muslims. The new currency notes sustain the difficulty in treating Iraq as comprising just an Arab nation. The "Bremer dinars," as they are known, have symbols under which phrases including "Arab" and "Islam" are printed in Arabic, but when a famous waterfall in Kurdistan is displayed the Kurdish language is not used, nor is its location specified. Kurds as well as other minority peoples of the federation will no doubt argue for a pluralist as well as a stable currency.

We hope we will not be misunderstood. We editors, like most of our contributors, are liberals, but we are not difference-blind liberals. We think it is political fantasy for Kanan Makiya and others to ask Kurds—or Shi'a, for that matter—to forget the history of modern Iraq. Survivors do not forget genocide or deportation. It is utopian to expect the Kurds to abandon their long struggle to be recognized as a nationality in exchange for merely having their individual human rights protected by an Arab majority, or a Shi'a Arab majority. In contrast to the view that the new Iraq should be based just on individual human rights or on allegedly non-ethnic governorates, and to arguments that deny the national and religious character of political conflicts in Iraq, the contributions to this book propose different concepts, arrangements, mechanisms, and rights to create a durable, democratic, and pluralist peace. These proposals are often based on the experiences of federations and power-sharing arrangements that have proved effective elsewhere, whether in transitional arrangements, or as durable elements of their political institutions. Essentially these proposals rest on a shared commitment to protecting and developing the autonomy of Kurdistan and the hope that Kurdistan may flourish within a renewed Iraq. If these contributions assist that process, the editors and authors will be satisfied.

The Structure and Contents of the Book

The rest of this book, like Gaul and Iraq, is divided into three parts. We begin with debates over the future. Part Two, "Federative Possibilities," contains three essays. Chapter 2, "Power-Sharing, Federation, and Federacy," by Brendan O'Leary, reconsiders and revises arguments made before and shortly after the war that overthrew the Ba'thists. The author argues that Kurdistan *and* the rest of Iraq would best be reconstituted in a bi-national, multi-ethnic, and multi-religious federation. He maintains that pluri-national federal arrangements are desirable, and that "consociational arrangements" in the federal government are needed to stabilize Iraq's fledgling experiment in democracy. The exponents of "non-ethnic" federation, he counters, advance shallow arguments, which are overreliant on the distinctive U.S. experience and evaporate when exposed to any quantum of light. But, just because their claims are shallow, they cannot be politically dismissed. Bad arguments often win in politics.

O'Leary analyzes the Transitional Administrative Law, evaluates likely difficulties ahead if Kurdistan and the rest of Iraq are to function separately and
jointly, and makes recommendations on future electoral and party law
arrangements and how Kurdistan might organize its internal governance.
Chapter 3, John McGarry's "Canadian Lessons for Iraq" complements
O'Leary's essay. McGarry shows that at least one bi-national federation, Canada, has functioned and flourished for a century and a half. He suggests persuasively that Canada, Belgium, and Switzerland provide better role models
and road maps for Iraq than the centralized federation that American academics and administrators are overly prone to idealize. If the conventional wisdom
of American political science on so-called "ethnic federations" were correct,
then Canada would and could not exist. McGarry spells out the erroneous
assumption made by the political scientists dispensing such advice. Envisaging
Kurdistan as a future Quebec, McGarry draws on this comparison to offer
informed advice on what may best stabilize Iraq as a functioning federation.
In Chapter 4, "Negotiating an Iraqi Federation," Karna Eklund, Brendan
O'Leary, and Paul Williams consider both the negotiation environment and
the crunch issues that will make or break the drafting and ratification of the
permanent constitution. They also place the prospective negotiation of the
permanent constitution within theories of the origins and maintenance of federal bargains. The authors offer some hope—although readers are advised to
follow carefully the numerous assumptions they specify, and the conditions
they insist must be present, for a successful federal resolution. Skeptics are
equally free to read this chapter as specifying the impossible conditions that
Iraq will have to satisfy to make a viable federal bargain, although that is not
the authors' intent. Molly McNulty, a specialist in international law, human
rights, and public health, who has recently consulted in Iran, concludes our
discussion of federative possibilities. She focuses on a typically neglected subject in post-conflict sites, the rights and needs of children in constitutional
design and the affirmative duties of government in these respects. Extracting
lessons from four federations—India, Canada, Switzerland and Belgium—she
suggests the merits of incorporating the International Covenant on the Rights
of the Child into the constitution and law of Iraq and Kurdistan, and makes
recommendations on how the federal and federal units' affirmative duties
might best facilitate children's development.

Part Three, "Legacies of the Past," contains four essays. Chapter 6, by
Ofra Bengio, composed on the cusp of the 19 March 2003 war, provides a historian's perspective on Kurdish autonomy in Iraq. The author of a detailed
analysis of Saddam's discourses (Bengio 1998), she considers the past, reviews
likely scenarios for the development of Kurdistan, and concludes with fasci-

nating reflections on a passage from one of "Saddam"'s novels. The idea that the relations between Kurdistan and Arab Iraq resemble those of marriage was one of Saddam's less unpleasant fantasies. It was curiously apposite, because Kurdistanis regarded the marriage as arranged by the British and saw themselves as a battered wife held in thrall by a succession of violent husbands, passed to each brother in line after the violent death of his older predecessor. The metaphor of an arranged and coerced marriage is doubly appropriate because international law has no formal divorce procedures for regions. In Chapter 7 Sophia Wanche, a consultant to the International Crisis Group, reflects on interviews she conducted among Kurdistan's peoples before the March 2003 war. Wanche captures their mixed emotions of fear and anticipation: enthusiasm for deposing Saddam, and fear of being betrothed again to a Baghdad government. It is rare to have such timely research before a war; in the regrettable absence of resources for a proper survey, Wanche's work will remain the benchmark from which to assess the subsequent development of public opinion in Kurdistan. One remarkable development in public opinion was prefigured in her analysis. Nearly two million Kurdistanis petitioned their leaders to demand a referendum giving them the option of voting for independence. That figure suggests that there are limits beyond which representative Kurdish politicians cannot go and keep their jobs or their lives, in making compromises with potential Arab political partners in the constitutional renewal of Iraq. Chapter 8, by Gareth Stansfield, draws on his extensive field research in free Kurdistan. "Governing Kurdistan" is an insightful and astringent review of divisions between the KDP and the PUK which adversely affected the politics of free Kurdistan between 1991 and 2003. Stansfield then argues for the codification of the outcome of the conflict between the two parties: the organization of Kurdistan into two separate administrations. His prescription may prove an accurate prediction, although many friends of Kurdistan and many in the Kurdish diaspora will regret an enduring division. In Chapter 9, Michael Gunter provides analysis of how the most powerful neighboring state has perceived the emergence of Kurdistan and an Iraqi federation that recognizes Kurdistan. Hostility and suspicion are paramount, as he shows, but interpreting the past and reading the runes does not lead him to believe that Turkey's elites relish a formal and extensive intervention in Kurdistan. To the contrary: he suggests that Turkey's candidacy to join the European Union may fetter its traditional animosity to Kurdistan and oblige it to follow a more imaginative post-Kemalist politics.

Part Four, "Immediate Issues," encompasses four current appraisals both inside and outside Kurdistan. In Chapter 10, "What Went Wrong," Peter W. Galbraith, former U.S. ambassador to Croatia, addresses one of the burning issues in contemporary U.S. and international politics. Irrespective of the merits of the case for going to war against Saddam, what went wrong in the planning and implementation of the U.S. occupation? Exactly how did the U.S. and the CPA so rapidly exhaust the goodwill they had earned among Sh'ia Arabs and Kurds in particular? Why has a policy mess and fierce resistance in Arab Iraq emerged? Originally the first of the John Kenneth Galbraith lectures, and previously published in the *New York Review of Books*, Galbraith's lecture has already stirred the waters within the U.S. foreign policy community. It has provoked thinking on a three-state future, which Galbraith carefully presents as the only realistic alternative to the loose federation that Kurdistan has sought and continues to seek. The editors believe Galbraith's essay will remain a key guide on the prospects now opening before the organizers of the US intervention. His appraisal nicely matches the independent evaluation by Karin von Hippel in Chapter 11. Von Hippel is a specialist both on U.S. efforts to export democracy in the 1990s (von Hippel 1999) and in the regulation of political violence. Her arguments will be of interest to all international relations scholars and students of interventions. Von Hippel's essay should be mandatory reading in the U.S. Congress when full oversight of the administration's intervention and occupation takes place. She nevertheless concludes by suggesting that for all its flawed nature this American intervention should "stay the course."

Most of the chapters here make analyses of—or recommendations toward—the constitutional design of any future federation in Iraq, and particular on Kurdistan's status in such a federation. In Chapter 12, "Kurdistan in a Federal Iraq," Peter Galbraith sums up the constitutional prospects facing Kurdistan. With Brendan O'Leary and Khaled Salih he was part of an international constitutional advisory team employed on-site by the Kurdistan National Assembly and the Kurdistan Regional Governments before and after the making of the Transitional Administrative Law. A long-time advocate of the Kurdish cause, Galbraith has professional skills in negotiation. He maintains that Kurdistan has greater leverage over the making of any final constitution in Iraq than some might suggest or fear. The leaders of Kurdistan respect his voice, so he is likely to be listened to as well as heard. Galbraith's essay is followed by a Postscript, "Vistas of Exits from Baghdad" written by Brendan O'Leary. It attempts to bring readers up to date with the fast pace of developments since these essays were finalized in the spring of 2004. It reprises the origins of the war to overthrow Saddam, the failures of the CPA, especially in constitutional reconstruction, and the strange death of the Transitional Administrative Law, and sketches likely futures and tough choices for Kurdistan.

Notes

Epigraph: Karl Renner, *Das Selbstbestimmingsrecht der Nationen in Besondere Anwendenung auf Öesterreich* (1918), quoted in Stourzh (1991, 68).

1. This story is not unusual. In March 2004 the same editor, Brendan O'Leary, accompanied Michael Ignatieff, director of Harvard's Carr Human Rights Center, across the same checkpoint in the other direction. All of Ignatieff's printed materials in his possession (mostly articles from the web) containing the terms "Kurd" and "Kurdistan" were confiscated. On 11 May O'Leary returned to the same checkpoint. This time he had his text of Iraq's Transitional Administrative Law, Appendix II of this book, confiscated because, the military official explained, it contained the word "Kurdistan," which "we don't like." His printed materials discussing the ethnic demography of Kirkuk were also confiscated. Such behavior is incompatible with Turkey's international treaty commitments and its application for membership of the European Union.

2. Martin van Bruinessen, the leading contemporary anthropologist specializing in the study of the Kurds, often observes that the model of segmentary lineage systems (and its portrait of alignments and feuds) corresponds well with the map of social reality that many Kurdish tribesmen have in their heads.

3. Data from the May 1992 elections suggest that, contrary to many interpretations, it is incorrect to assume that either tribal affiliation or dialect (Kurmanji-speaking in the north and west or Sorani-speaking in the south and east) neatly explains the party identifications of Kurdish voters in Kurdistan. That the vote was divided 50:50 in Erbil and 75:25 in Sulaimania stops such facile readings. Only Dohuk's voting fits the stereotype. The authors suggest, on the basis of their own interviews, that party identification among many voters may owe much to which party mobilized male family members to join the *peshmerga*, although a survey would be required to test whether this factor is as important as we suspect.

References

Agence France Presse. 2004. "Kurdish Unrest in Syria Echoes Iraq Conflict." 18 March.

Anderson, Benedict. 1991. *Imagined Communities: Reflections on the Origins and Spread of Nationalism*: London; Verso.

Batatu, Hanna. 1978. *The Old Social Classes and the Revolutionary Movements of Iraq: A Study of Iraq's Old Landed and Commercial Classes and of Its Communists, Ba'thists, and Free Officers.* Princeton, N.J.: Princeton University Press.

Bengio, Ofra. 1998. *Saddam's Word: Political Discourse in Iraq.* New York: Oxford University Press.

Bomli, Pieter Elias Johannes. 1929. *L'Affaire de Mossoul.* Amsterdam: H.J. Paris.

Bush, George W. 2003. "President George Bush Discusses Iraq in National Press Conference." White House (East Room), 6 March. <http://www.whitehouse.gov/news/releases/2003/03/print/20030306–8.html>.

Central Intelligence Agency (CIA). 2004. <http://www.cia.gov/cia.publications/factbook/geos/iz.html>. Accessed 30 April 2004.

Cizre, Ümit. 2001. "Turkey's Kurdish Problem: Borders, Identity and Hegemony." In *Right-Sizing the State: The Politics of Moving Borders*, ed. Brendan O'Leary, Ian S. Lustick, and Thomas Callaghy. Oxford: Oxford University Press. 222–52.

Connor, Walker. 1994. *Ethnonationalism: The Quest for Understanding*. Princeton, N.J.: Princeton University Press.

CPA-Agreement. 2003. The November 15 Agreement: Time Line to a Sovereign, Democratic and Secure Iraq. November. <http://www.coalition.org/government/AgreementNov15.pdf>.

Dann, Uriel. 1969. *Iraq Under Qassam*. Jerusalem: Israel Universities Press.

Dawisha, Adeed and Karen Dawisha. 2003. "How to Build a Democratic Iraq." *Foreign Affairs* 82 (3): 36–50.

Dodge, Toby. 2003. *Inventing Iraq: The Failure of Nation Building and a History Denied*. New York: Columbia University Press.

Democratic Principles Working Group (DPWG). 2002. *Final Report on the Transition to Democracy in Iraq*. Washington, D.C.: DPWG.

Edgerton, David. 1991. *England and the Aeroplane*. London: Macmillan.

Edmonds, Cecil J. 1957. *Kurds, Turks and Arabs: Politics, Travel and Research in North-Eastern Iraq, 1919–1925*. London: Oxford University Press.

Farouk-Sluglett, Marion, and Peter Sluglett. 2003. *Iraq Since 1958: From Revolution to Dictatorship*. London: I.B. Tauris.

Gelb, Leslie H. 2003. "The Three-State Solution." *New York Times*, 25 November.

Gellner, Ernest. 1969. *Saints of the Atlas*. London: Weidenfeld and Nicolson; Chicago: University of Chicago Press.

———. 1981. *Muslim Society*. Cambridge: Cambridge University Press.

———. 1983. *Nations and Nationalism*. Oxford: Blackwell.

———. 1991. "Tribalism and the State in the Middle East." In *Tribes and State Formation in the Middle East*, ed. Philip S. Khoury and Joseph Kostiner. London: I.B. Jannis; Berkeley: University of California Press. 109–26.

———. 1994a. "Tribal and International Law: Between Might and Right." In *Subduing Sovereignty: Sovereignty and the Right to Intervene*, ed. Marianne Heiberg. London, Pinter. 116–25.

———, ed. 1994b. "Kemalism." In Gellner *Encounters with Nationalism*. Oxford, Blackwell. 81–91.

Governing Council-Coalition Provisional Authority (GC-CPA). 2003. Agreement on Political Process. Baghdad, 15 November. <http://www.cpa-iraq.org/audio/20031115_15_Nov_GC-CPA_Agreement _final.html>

Haklai, Oded. 2000. "A Minority Rule over a Hostile Majority: The Case of Syria." *Nationalism and Ethnic Politics* 6 (3): 19–50.

Hassenpour, Amir. 1992. *Nationalism and Language in Kurdistan*. San Francisco: Mellon Research University Press.

Hechter, Michael. 2000. *Containing Nationalism*. Oxford: Oxford University Press.

International Crisis Group (2003). *Iraq's Constitutional Challenge*. Baghdad and Brussels: ICG Middle East Reports 19, 13 November.

Kazancigil, Ali. 1981. "The Ottoman-Turkish State and Kemalism." In *Atatürk—The Founder of a Modern State*, ed. Ergun Özbudun and Ali Kazancigil. London: Hurst.

Kedourie, Elie. 1984 (1952). "Minorities." In Kedourie, *The Chatham House Version and*

Other Middle Eastern Studies. Hanover, N.H.: University Press of New England. 286–317.

Koohi-Kemali, Farideh. 2003. *The Political Development of the Kurds in Iran: Pastoral Nationalism.* New York: Palgrave Macmillan.

Kurdistan Democratic Party. 1992a. Draft Constitution of the Federal Republic of Iraq. Erbil: Kurdistan National Assembly, <http://www.krg.org/docs/Federal_Const.asp>.

———. 1992b. Draft Constitution of the Iraqi Kurdistan Region. Erbil: Kurdistan National Assembly, <http://www.krg.org/docs/K_Const.asp>.

Lewis, Jonathan Eric. 2003. "Iraqi Assyrians: Barometers of Pluralism." *Middle East Quarterly* (Summer) 10 (3). <http://www.meforum.org/article/558>. Accessed 30 April 2004.

Longrigg, Stephen H. 1968. *Iraq, 1900 to 1950.* Beirut: Libraire du Liban.

Makiya, Kanan. 2003. "A Model for Post-Saddam Iraq." *Journal of Democracy* 14 (3): 5–12.

Marr, Phebe. 1985. *The Modern History of Iraq.* Boulder, Colo.: Westview Press.

McDowall, David. 1992. *The Kurds: A Nation Denied.* London: Minority Rights Publications.

———. 2000. *A Modern History of the Kurds.* London: I.B. Tauris.

Menashri, David. 1988. "Khomeni's Policy Toward Ethnic and Religious Minorities." In *Ethnicity, Pluralism, and the State in the Middle East,* ed. Milton Esman and Ithamar Rabinovich. Ithaca, N.Y.: Cornell University Press.

Mufti, Malik. 1996. *Sovereign Creations: Pan-Arabism and Political Order in Syria and Iraq.* Ithaca, N.Y.: Cornell University Press.

Natali, Denise. 2001. "Manufacturing Identity and Managing Kurds in Iraq." In *Right-Sizing the State: The Politics of Moving Borders,* ed. Brendan O'Leary, Ian S. Lustick, and Thomas Callaghy. Oxford: Oxford University Press.

Neue Zürcher Zeitung (NZZ). 2002. <http://www.nzz.ch/english/background/2002/08/06_kurds.html>. Accessed 20 April 2004.

O'Leary, Brendan. 1998. "Gellner's Diagnoses of Nationalism: A Critical Overview *or* What Is Living and What Is Dead in Gellner's Philosophy of Nationalism?" In *The State of the Nation: Ernest Gellner and the Theory of Nationalism,* ed. John A. Hall. Cambridge: Cambridge University Press. 40–90.

Political Statement. 2002. "Political Statement of the Iraqi Opposition Conference." The Iraqi Opposition Conference, London, 14–17 December. <www.krg.org/docs/Opposition-Political-statement.pdf>.

Randal, Jonathan. 1997. *After Such Knowledge, What Forgiveness? My Encounters with Kurdistan.* New York: Farrar, Straus and Giroux.

Rummel, Rudolph J. 1997. *Death by Government.* Foreword Irving Louis Horowitz. London and New York: Transaction Publishers.

Salih, Khaled. 1996a. "Demonizing a Minority: The Case of the Kurds in Iraq." In *Nationalism, Minorities and Diasporas: Identity and Rights in the Middle East,* ed. Kirsten Schulze, Martin Stokes, and Colm Campbell. London: I.B. Tauris. 81–94.

———. 1996b. *State-Making, Nation-Building and the Military: Iraq, 1932–1958.* Göteborg: Göteborg University.

Stansfield, Gareth R. V. 2003. *Iraqi Kurdistan: Political Development and Emergent Democracy.* London: Routledge.

Stourzh, Gerald. "Problems of Conflict-Resolution in a Multi-Ethnic State: Lessons from the Austrian Historical Experience." In *State and Nation in Multi-Ethnic Societies: The Breakup of Multinational States*, ed. Uri Ra'anan, Maria Mesner, Keith Armes, and Kate Martin. Manchester: Manchester University Press, 1991.

Tripp, Charles. 2002. *A History of Iraq*. Cambridge: Cambridge University Press.

Uriel, Dann. 1969. *Iraq Under Qassem: A Political History, 1958–1963*. Tel Aviv: Praeger.

U.S. Department of State. 2002. <http://www.state.gov/r/pa/ei/bgn/6804.htm>. Accessed 30 April 2004.

van Bruinessen, Martin. 1992. *Agha, Shaikh and State: The Social and Political Structure of Kurdistan*. London: Zed Books.

———. 2003. "Kurds, States and Tribes." In *Tribes and Power: Nationalism and Ethnicity in the Middle East*, ed. Faleh Abdul-Jabara and Hosham Dawod. London: Saqi. 165–84.

van Dam, Nikolaos. 1979. *The Struggle for Power in Syria: Sectarianism, Regionalism and Tribalism in Politics, 1961–78*. London: Croom Helm.

———. 1996. *The Struggle for Power in Syria: Politics and Society Under the Asad and the Ba'ath Party*. London: I B. Tauris.

Von Hippel, Karin. 1999. *Democracy by Force: U.S. Military Intervention in the Post-Cold World*. Cambridge: Cambridge University Press.

Wilson, Arnold. 1930. *Loyalties: Mesopotamia, 1914–1917*. London: Oxford University Press.

———. 1931. *Mesopotamia, 1917–1920: A Clash of Loyalties*. London: Oxford University Press.

PART TWO

Federative Possibilities

Chapter 2

Power-Sharing, Pluralist Federation, and Federacy

Brendan O'Leary

"I did not draw my principles from my prejudices but from the nature of things."
—*Montesquieu, Preface to "The Spirit of the Laws," 1748*

On 8 March 2004 Iraq appeared to have an interim constitution, the "Law of Administration for the State of Iraq for the Transitional Period," known generally as the Transitional Administrative Law (TAL), reprinted in this book as Appendix 2. It was negotiated by the members of the Governing Council, under U.S. supervision, and ratified by the Coalition Provisional Authority (CPA) Administrator, Paul Bremer (Governing Council of Iraq 2004). The UN Secretary-General's special advisor, Lakhdar Brahimi, subsequently claimed that "No one said it is a constitution" (CPA 2004), but I am not alone in so classifying the text negotiated under the auspices of the body that the UN recognizes as the lawful occupation authority. The TAL specifies the procedures under which the permanent constitution will be made and ratified, organizes the laws that regulate the executive, legislative, and judicial branches of the state and its territorial governance, establishes a bill of rights, and places both absolute and supermajoritarian constraints on how the text itself can be changed. It therefore matches the requirements of one authoritative definition of a constitution as "the rules which establish and regulate or govern the government" (Wheare 1966, 1). Whatever Brahimi thinks, the TAL is formally an interim constitution, but whether it will be an operative transitional constitution remains to be seen. As this book went to press, it seemed possible that the Bush administration, intent on a hasty exit, might restore sovereignty to an Iraqi transitional government either with the TAL abandoned, or with its validity dependent upon the affirmation of the transitional government. This chapter examines the provisions of the TAL in depth, uncertain whether it is appropriately treated in the present continuous or in historic tenses.

The TAL envisaged the restoration of sovereignty to Iraq on 1 July 2004, and stipulates that an Iraq-wide assembly, elected no later than 31 January 2005, will draft a permanent constitution by 15 August 2005, which will be "ratified if a majority of the voters in Iraq approve and if two-thirds of the voters in three or more governorates do not reject it" (Art. 61). This clause grants a veto to the people of "actually existing Kurdistan" (and others in functioning governorates) on the nature of the future federation. Under the TAL Kurdistan therefore has bargaining leverage to shape the final "system of government" that Article 4 declares "shall be republican, federal, democratic, and pluralistic." The first of these four adjectives is not controversial: Iraq will be a republic. The archaic romanticism of restoring the Hashemite monarchy has been rejected. It had notably been proposed in *Foreign Affairs*, the flagship journal of the U.S. foreign policy community (Dawisha and Dawisha 2003, 42). Advocating a Hashemite restoration as reassurance for the Sunni Arabs was naïve. It would not have reassured the Sunnis, because the proposal ignored the secular republican and republican Islamist dispositions of most of them, and the idea certainly would have been resisted by both Shi'a Arabs and the Kurds. Although republics in the Arab-dominated world have, thus far, been undemocratic, so have its monarchies; kingly authority in Jordan, Saudi Arabia, Morocco, Oman, Kuwait, and the Gulf emirates is neither limited nor properly parliamentarized (Halliday 2000). It is the last three adjectives in Article 4 of the TAL that evoke more controversial concepts: federation, democracy, and pluralism. What sort of federation will most effectively make Iraq both democratic and pluralistic? What model of federation best suits Kurdistan? The answer proposed here is power-sharing within a "pluralist federation" for Iraq and "federacy" arrangements for Kurdistan—elements of which are already embedded in the potential interim constitution.

The Number of Peoples: "Monism" or "Pluralism"?

Arguments about "peoplehood" are critical in politics (Smith 2003: 4). The premise here is that Iraq does not comprise just one people, although the peoples of Iraq may agree in the permanent constitution to share a federal citizenship. The TAL articulates a viable compromise on this deeply controversial matter. The preamble, which is integral to the law (Art. 1(c)), refers to "the people of Iraq" in the singular, as does Article 10. By contrast, Article 7(b) declares that Iraq is "a country of many nationalities, and the Arab people in

Iraq are an inseparable part of the Arab nation." This phrasing repudiates the Ba'thist treatment of Iraq as an Arab nation and recognizes non-Arab people(s). The Arabs of Iraq are no longer an official *Staatsvolk*, but rather one of many nationalities. The phrasing of this provision is, however, unjust because the Arabs of Iraq are not alone in being part of a wider nation; the Kurds of Iraq are not recognized as "an inseparable part of the Kurdish nation," and the Turkomen, Assyrians, and Armenians might make analogous complaints. But historic injustice is recognized. The legally operative preamble declares that mechanisms will be established to ensure the erasure "of the effects of racist . . . policies and practices"; thus, the interim constitution repudiates past "Arabization" programs, though not expressly by name. Iraq's deep diversity of nationalities—Arabs, Kurds, Turkomen, Assyrians, and Armenians—is constitutionally acknowledged. These named nationalities have linguistic rights in Article 9, although only Arabic and Kurdish are official languages of the federation. This norm reflects the demographic weight of the Arab and Kurdish nationalities. Elsewhere the TAL guarantees "the administrative, cultural, and political rights of the Turcomans, ChaldoAssyrians, and all other citizens" (Art. 53 (d)), which, appropriately interpreted, permits these national minorities self-government in their own languages, schools, and religious affairs, and access to public administration in their own languages, where their numbers mandate it. In summary, the interim constitution preserves a formal monism through a common federal citizenship (one), but qualifies it through a pluralist recognition of multiple nationalities (many) and the practical treatment of (two) Kurds and Arabs as the most linguistically significant communities. Iraq is in actuality *pluri-national* and bilingual, and this official constitutional recognition in the TAL provides the necessary basis for a flourishing federation.

Why "pluri-national"? For most purposes, the terms "pluri-national" and "multi-national" may be treated as synonyms, but there is a formal case for the former expression. A "pluri-national federation" describes a state in which there are multiple recognized nations, whose respective nationals may be both concentrated and dispersed, and in which individuals may identify with one, more than one, or none of these nations. The prefix "pluri" helpfully describes cases of "not one"; that is, it covers both "two" and "more" and suggests that national identity or identities may be variable in intensity, and that the federation may comprise both conflicting and compatible identities. "Multi-national federation," by contrast, is often interpreted as indicating spatially discrete and homogeneously adjacent nations, as requiring three or more nations, as suggesting that each national identity is held exclusively, and that each national has only one national identity possessed with the same intensity. The TAL foreshadows a pluri-national federation.

Iraq is also religiously pluralist and it has atheists among it citizens. Does the interim constitution reflect this pluralism? Article 7(a) recognizes "Islam . . . [as] the official religion of the State" and states "the Law respects the Islamic identity of the majority of the Iraqi people and guarantees the full religious rights of all individuals to freedom of religious belief and practice."[1] This article may appear to recognize only a single religion, but minority religions are implicitly recognized, and "freedom of religious belief" includes the freedom to have no religious belief. Islam's preeminence is undercut in three additional ways. First, Islam is said to be "a" rather than "the" source of legislation. Second, "No law that contradicts the universally agreed tenets of Islam, the principles of democracy, *or* the rights cited in Chapter 2 of this Law may be enacted during the transitional period" (emphasis added; Chapter 2 is the Bill of Rights). Theocracy is rejected by recognizing pluralism or schism within Islam: the "universally agreed" and distinctive "tenets of Islam" are few. The essential core is defined by monotheism, Muhammad's status as Allah's messenger, Allah's status as the author of the Quran, and the duties of the faithful (Rodinson 2002; Gellner 1981). Beyond that core, multiple legal and theological traditions flourish, creating much finer distinctions than the divisions between Sunni and Shiʿa. Third, the meaning of Article 7a depends on the interpretation of the "*or*" italicized above. On the most reasonable reading, any law that violates "the principles of democracy" or the bill of rights would be invalid, even *if* it did not contradict the "universally agreed tenets of Islam." On commercial grounds I would not recommend that a Kurdish publisher issue a translation of Salman Rushdie's *Satanic Verses*, but such a decision would be constitutionally protected, both by the "right of free expression" (Art. 13(b)) and by the pluralist reading just given to Article 7(a); it should be illegal to ban the book, or to pass a law banning it. *Fatwas* have no universally binding legal force, so Iraq is, at least according to the TAL, constitutionally pluralist in religious affairs. The state has one official, majority religion (with plural if not pluralist traditions), but requires respect for minority religions and offers tacit protections for nonbelievers. The TAL provides the minimum guarantees of pluralism necessary for a flourishing federation. Whether the TAL will function, and whether Iraq's judges will interpret the law in this manner are another matter, yet to be confirmed or falsified.

Federation for Iraq: Integrationist or Pluralist?

The TAL makes Iraq both pluri-national and religiously pluralist. Kurdistan sought these provisions, will want to ensure they are not lost in the permanent constitution, and will seek to have the federation established as a voluntary union of its constitutive peoples. The TAL also sought to establish a federal democracy. Under its provisions free and fair competitive elections to public office will take place, with a free media; freedom of political and religious expression and association are protected (Art. 15(c)); individual human rights are entrenched, including "the rights stipulated in international treaties and agreements" (Art. 23); and the democracy is governed by the rule of law. But, what does the TAL imply in its "federal" promise? Answers require agreement on the concept of federalism, the institutions of federation, and types of federation.

Federalism as a political philosophy commends "shared-" and "self"-government (Elazar 1987; King 2001), which is reflected in the TAL: "The system . . . shall be . . . federal . . . and powers shall be shared between the federal government and the regional governments, governorates, municipalities, and local administrations" (Art. 4). As a philosophy, however, federalism is compatible with a whole range of federal political systems, including confederations, federations, federacies, associated states, leagues, and cross-border functional authorities (Watts 1998). The TAL envisages a federation, as seen in the distinction between the "federal government" and the other federative entities, such as "governorates" and "regional governments." Federations are distinct federal political systems, first invented in 1787 in Philadelphia. In federations at least two governmental units, the federal and the regional, enjoy constitutionally separate competencies, although they may have concurrent or shared powers. The federal and regional governments are co-sovereign (whereas in a confederation the member states retain sovereignty), and both are empowered directly to deal with their citizens. In a democratic federation, citizens directly elect some legislative components of both the federal and the regional governments. Federations are "covenantal"—that is, the authority of each federal entity, be it federal or regional, is derived from the constitution, not from another government (Elazar 1987). The federal government usually cannot unilaterally alter the horizontal division of powers: constitutional change affecting the division of competencies and the boundaries of units requires consent from both tiers of government. Federations require a codified constitution; they normally have a federal supreme court charged with upholding the constitution and umpiring differences between the governmental tiers;[2] and they require a bicameral legislature, one chamber of the citizens as a whole and one that represents the regions or federative units. These are the core features of a federation. The TAL for Iraq envisages a federation in nearly all these respects and bans the federal government from reorganizing the regions and the governorates during the transition. There is one excep-

TABLE 2.1. POLAR CONTRASTS IN THE DESIGN AND OPERATION OF FEDERATIONS

	Integrative	*Pluralist*
Decision-making within the federal government	Majoritarian	Consensual
Powers of the federation versus the regions	Centralized	Decentralized
Recognition of identities	National	Pluri-national
Example	U.S.A.	Switzerland

tional silence. The interim constitution makes no reference to a second chamber, or senate. That remains to be negotiated in the drafting of the permanent constitution, and will be a matter on which Kurdistan will have much to say.

Federations vary in three key but interlinked ways: in their degree of "consensual" or "majoritarian" decision-making in the federal government, which is affected by the organization of executive, legislative, and judicial powers; by the distribution of powers and competencies between the federal and regional governments; and, lastly, by whether they are "national" or "pluri-national." Although permutations of these three major axes of variation are possible, federations cluster into two polar types. "Integrative" federations are majoritarian, centralized, and national; "pluralist" federations are consensual, decentralized, and pluri-national (see Table 2.1). In what follows, I elaborate on the variations, clarify the relevant evaluations of the TAL, and suggest what needs to be done to ensure the consolidation of a pluralist federation in Iraq.

Majoritarian or Consensual?

Federations vary in the extent to which they are "majoritarian"—the extent to which they constrain a federation-wide majority from imposing its political will on federal or regional minorities. All federations place some constraints on the powers of federation-wide majorities, but do so to strikingly different degrees (Stepan 1999). The TAL constrains a normal majority in the federal government from amending the TAL itself. That requires a "three-fourths majority" of the future federal assembly and "the unanimous approval of the presidency council" (Art. 3). The same article absolutely prohibits the transitional federal government from abridging the bill of rights, extending the TAL, delaying the holding of the first required elections, affecting religions or religious communities, or reducing "the powers of the regions or governorates" (including Kurdistan). A federal majority is constrained in these respects, at least for now; and a federal super-majority is required to weaken the pluri-national and bilingual character of the federation. But, a simple federal majority in the future assembly may write the draft of the permanent constitution, since Articles 60 and 61 place no super-majoritarian constraints on its drafting. That is why, from Kurdistan's perspective, the constraint built into Article 61(c) is so important. It stops the permanent constitution from being ratified if three governorates (Dohuk, Erbil, and Sulaimania) within the Kurdistan region that are overwhelmingly Kurdish vote against the draft constitution by a two-thirds majority.

A majoritarian federation concentrates political power at the federal level and facilitates executive and legislative dominance either through a popularly endorsed executive president or through a single-party prime minister and cabinet which has the confidence of the federal house of representatives. A consensual federation, by contrast, has inclusive executive power-sharing and representative arrangements in the federal government, institutionalizes proportional principles of representation and allocation of public posts and resources; and has mechanisms, such as the separation of powers, bills of rights, monetary institutions and courts, which are insulated from the immediate power of a federal governing majority. On this design choice, Iraq as a whole, Kurdistan, Kurds, and the small nationalities in particular, should seek a consensual federation. Kurds and the smaller nationalities would be long-run losers from the creation of a strongly majoritarian federation, in which either an Arab or a Shi'a Arab majority might threaten their national, linguistic, and cultural identities, as well as their regional and economic interests. Sunni Arabs, too, have an interest in constraining the power of a potential federal majority that might be inimical to their religious and other interests. Shi'a, or Shi'a Arabs, are the most tempted by a majoritarian federation, but they may be less homogeneous than some of them hope and others fear, given differences among them in class, religiosity, and dispositions toward Iran and other neighboring states (Gardner 2003; Jabar 2003).[3] The perspectives of Muhammed Baqir al-Sadr, executed by Saddam in 1980, exist among Shi'a and diverge from the political Islam of Khomeini and his successors. His grandson, Moqtada al-Sadr, the paramilitary leader, espouses a brand of Shi'a Islam that is unashamedly theocratic, whereas Grand Ayatollah al-Sistani's orthodox and more learned Shi'a theology does not insist on a clerical executive. Historically communism was strong among the Shi'a of Iraq, so some of their voters may support secular left-wing parties. There are secular Shi'a, and significant numbers of religious Shia do not agree that political leadership should be monopolized by clerics. Two analysts rightly remark on a "dangerous tendency in the West to equate secular with Sunni and Islamist with Shi'ite" (Fuller and Francke 1999, 108). In fact, Shi'a intellectuals, especially in Iran, have argued strongly against the political imposition of Islam in ways that have no counterpart among Sunni Muslim scholars (Soroush 2002). All this suggests we should expect political heterogeneity among Shiʿa in open politics, including among Shiʿa Arabs. In any case, the more homogeneously Shiʿa Arabs mobilize, then the greater the likelihood is that they will generate a countervailing coalition of minorities.

The minorities, including Kurds, want to ensure power-sharing within the federal government, at least for an extended transitional period. This logic explains why Kurdistan advocated the following in the negotiation of the TAL:

(1) an indirectly elected and inclusive collective presidency with veto powers over national, religious, and linguistic legislation;
(2) a federal cabinet, broadly or proportionally representative of Iraq's pluralism, including its linguistic and party pluralism;
(3) proportional representation in the federal electoral systems (both for the federal assembly and the senate), and the proportional allocation of public posts in executive, bureaucratic, and judicial posts to the recognized nationalities and religious minorities.

The TAL partially met some of these requirements, but not others. It foresaw an indirectly elected collective presidency. Three persons are to be elected to a presidential council on a single list by a two-thirds majority of the federal assembly's votes (Art. 36 (a)). But this provision does not guarantee that at least one of the members will be from a non-Arab minority group. Although the presidential council shall act by consensus (Art. 36(c)), no single member possesses a veto to wield in defense of national, linguistic, or religious minorities. The TAL requires that the prime minister be chosen unanimously by the presidential council, or by a two-thirds majority of the federal assembly if the presidential council does not agree on a candidate (Art. 38(a)). These provisions are super-majoritarian and consensual, at least so long as no party or community comprises a two-thirds bloc in the assembly. But, the presidency may only dismiss the prime minister or cabinet ministers, after due process, for corruption (Art. 41). When the prime minister takes office, he or she and the cabinet may operate in a standard majoritarian way, requiring the support of a majority of the assembly and taking votes within the cabinet by simple majority (Arts. 41, 42). The prime minister does not have to propose a cabinet representative of Iraq's diversity. He or she is, in effect, in charge of the armed forces (Art. 39(b)). The TAL is silent on electoral law and on proportional representation, affirmative action, or quotas in public positions. A sub-clause of Article 4, "the federal system shall [not] be based upon . . . origin, race, ethnicity, nationality or confession," might be read to outlaw affirmative action or quotas. Knowing the negotiating history of this clause, I suggest that it should be read strictly as seeking solely to prevent regional governments or governorates from having their boundaries decided by these criteria. The same clause mandates the design of the federal system on the basis of "geographic and historic" realities, which might support the proportional inclusion of historic nationalities in federal bureaus. In short, the TAL has consensual features in its federal design, although others remain to be established. In negotiating the permanent constitution, Kurdistan will seek to have these features developed.

Federations vary in how they organize executive, legislative, and judicial powers. In general, majoritarian federations fuse executive and legislative powers; create strong first chambers and weak second chambers; and have strong federal judiciaries appointed by federal majorities in the executive or first chamber. By contrast, consensual federations separate legislative and executive powers, create strong second chambers representing the constituent regions, and have strong regional judiciaries and a regional role in the selection of federal judges. Federations are only fully consensual if they do not create strong single-person presidents, or senates that are mirror images of the house of representatives.

The negotiators of the TAL agreed to divide the transitional executive (Article 35), although they did not agree its personnel—at the time of composition of this essay the members of the transitional executive are still not known, further evidence of the poor U.S. administration of its occupation authority. The presidential council is to be a collective head of state, but not the head of government: that is the prime minister, who presides over the cabinet (the Council of Ministers). The presidential council, if it is not unanimous, *may* have the ability to block the ratification of treaties and agreements because it "shall recommend passage of a law [by the Assembly] to ratify such treaties and agreements" (Art. 39(a)). It is moot here whether "shall" in Article 39(a) overrules the unanimity provisions governing the conduct of the presidential council (Art. 36(c)). (This ambiguity might reflect confusion during the negotiations.) Apart from appointing the premier and overseeing the undefined "higher affairs of the country," the collective presidency is to have one major power. It "may veto any legislation passed" by the assembly, within fifteen days, though that veto may be overridden by a two-thirds majority of the assembly (Art. 37). This power gives a unanimous presidential council a veto over the likely proposals of the premier and cabinet, so a prudent premier and cabinet will clear legislative proposals with at least one member of the presidential council.

In the making of the permanent constitution, the design of the executive might be productively reconsidered. First, a collective and fully executive presidency, indirectly elected by the senate and the house of representatives, on the model of Switzerland, might be advocated, removing the need for a prime minister. This feature would create some of the merits of a parliamentary system—an executive chosen by the legislature—and some of the benefits of a presidential system—an executive that cannot, except by impeachment, be destroyed by the legislature. At the same time, it would avoid some of the key defects of a single-person presidency or an overly powerful premier in an ethnically and religiously divided state. Second, the presidential council might be expanded beyond three members. The Swiss federal council has seven members. A proportional representation and allocation rule, such as d'Hondt, could be used to fill the council (for details, see O'Leary, Grofman, and Elklit 2005). The collective presidency could then nominally appoint ministers from parties in proportion to their strengths in the federal lower chamber, again using the d'Hondt rule for the proportional allocation of portfolios: the largest party would have an entitlement to the first choice of ministerial portfolio, the next largest the second choice, and so on. All this would allow for further diversity within the presidential council and the ministers working under them and ensure parties access to office according to their strength in votes or seats won. This proportional policy would not involve reserve posts or set asides for national, ethnic, or religious minorities. But third, and reinforcing the previous proposal, there should be a constitutional requirement to ensure that senior civil servants are representative of Iraq's national, linguistic, and religious diversity.

The TAL is silent on the design of the second legislative chamber that a meaningful federation must have. Kurdistan will not be alone in wanting a strong second chamber, or senate, to protect the interests of the regions and the minority nationalities and religious communities. It will be especially keen to do so if the first federal assembly election generates either a two-thirds Arab majority or a two-thirds Shi'a majority. Some federations create very powerful second chambers. The U.S. Senate is more powerful than the House of Representatives because of its special powers over treaty-making and nominations to public office, including federal judges and ambassadors. Other second chambers, such as those in Canada, India, and Belgium, are weak (Watts 1998, 2001), but Canada and Belgium protect their regions through cabinets that are representative of the major regional identities and interests. Federations also vary in how they represent their regions in their senates. Australia, Brazil, and the U.S.A., for example, allow equal representation of each of their regions in the senate, generating massive over-representation for small units such as Tasmania or Rhode Island. Others, such as India, adopt more proportional representation of the regions in the second chamber. Senators may be directly elected by citizens within their regions, as in the U.S., or indirectly elected by their respective regional assemblies (or regional executives), as in Germany.

On these design choices, the Kurds of Iraq, as the late Sami Abdulrahman made clear, will favor a senate that has strong powers over constitutional matters, the approval of federal judges, and the federal budget, provided that the senate is appropriately structured. They will want the senate to have a defined role and a super-majority requirement in making constitutional changes. They might want to have elections to the senate staggered, as in the U.S. or Germany. Kurdistan, like Baghdad, will prefer a senate proportional to population. Equality of all the federated units and normal voting rules would mean that the federative entities outside Kurdistan could outvote Kurdistan by a ratio of 15 to 1 (or 13 to 1, depending on how one counts the governorates, a controversial subject addressed below), even though the respective population ratios are no more than 4 to 1. By contrast, a proportionally elected or indirectly elected senate would give Kurdistan approximately a 25 percent share of the representation if its boundaries are expanded to encompass Kirkuk. Given some of its past preferences, Kurdistan might seek to negotiate a senate constructed on bi-national principles (Kurdistan Democratic Party 1992)—that is, it might argue for full parity of representation with the rest of Iraq in a senate that has veto powers over constitutional change—perhaps in return for accepting a more majoritarian house of representatives, or federal executive. Parity may not be necessary to achieve the same objective. The senate could be required to operate with a concurrent majority of senators from Kurdistan as well as from the rest of Iraq in approving federal judges, treaties, and constitutional changes. Such proposals will need to ensure that historic national and religious minorities within Kurdistan and the rest of Iraq are represented in the Senate. Allowing the regional and governorate assemblies to elect representatives to the senate using the single transferable vote would facilitate that. The single transferable vote is a sophisticated preferential and proportional voting system which legislators would easily master, and would ensure the senate reflected the internal diversity of Iraq's regions and governorates. Nevertheless, reserved seats for the smaller nationalities may still be required in the senate if they are to be represented.

The TAL provides a strong federal bill of rights (Arts. 10–23), which will protect individual human rights against federation-wide majorities, and which, after the restoration of sovereignty to Iraq, should also protect Iraqis from abuses by coalition troops. The new federal judiciary will be non-majoritarian because human rights are not "majoritarian" per se. But if the federative entities do not play a direct role in the selection of judges, through the senate or other mechanisms, there is a danger that the federal judiciary will not be representative of Iraq's national, religious, and linguistic diversity, which could affect judicial interpretation of the clauses that make Iraq plurinational, religiously pluralist and officially bilingual. If the TAL is implemented there will be a nine-member federal supreme court (Art. 44), with the right to strike down unconstitutional laws, regulations, and directives (Art. 44(c)). A pool of regionally representative candidates for the Supreme Court is envisaged (Art. 44(e). A tenured, self-governing, and self-appointing judiciary is mandated (Art. 45). Those provisions will certainly achieve the separation of powers, but they do not guarantee democratic oversight, except in cases of moral turpitude, corruption, or infirmity. They also do not ensure regional representativeness, though that could develop informally. Federal judicial supremacy is established in the TAL, and Kurdistan and the other federative entities are aware that activist judiciaries may take federations in directions not envisaged by the makers of original constitutions (Zines 1991). Consequently, Kurdistan will seek assurances in the permanent constitution that the federal judiciary will be representative of Iraq as a whole and that Kurdistan's legal distinctiveness is assured.

Centralized or Decentralized?

Federations differ, second, in the distribution of powers and competencies between the federal and regional governments. In some federations, the powers of the federal government are constitutionally circumscribed and delimited; in others, it is the regional governments that have their capacities specified and delimited. In "German" federations, the federal government makes broad policy and law while administration and implementation are in the hands of *Länder* (regional) governments, empowering both tiers with distinct enabling and blocking powers. In all federations, the constitutional division of competencies (even as interpreted by the courts) may not be an accurate guide to the policy-making autonomy held by the separate tiers. The superior financial and political resources of one tier (usually the federal) may allow it to weaken the other tier's capacities, as has happened in the U.S., where the federal government's preeminence is established. Indeed, the proportion of public expenditure allocated (or taxes raised) by regions as opposed to federal governments may be a better guide to their autonomy and power than the text of the constitution (for discussions of such measurements see Lijphart 1979, 505; Watts 2001 29).

In the making of the TAL, the initial negotiating positions over the distribution of competencies were highly polarized. Given the persistent history of repressive, indeed genocidal dictatorial government from Baghdad, Kurdistan did not want to endorse a strong federal government, at least in its region, and Kurdistan's National Assembly put forward detailed proposals to that effect (Kurdistan National Assembly 2004, and see Appendix 1 of this book). These included ensuring the continuity of Kurdistan's government, territory, and laws, and proposals to have:

(1) legal supremacy within Kurdistan (Art. 1);
(2) Kurdistan's National Guard established from the retrained *peshmerga*, and to exclude the Iraqi armed forces from Kurdistan save when granted permission (Art. 2);
(3) exclusive ownership of natural resources within Kurdistan, confining federal control to petroleum reservoirs currently in commercial production (Art. 3);
(4) fiscal autonomy, including the right to raise taxes and discretion in expending federal block grants (Art. 4); and
(5) Kurdistan's assent to the ratification of the permanent constitution (Art. 5).

Kurdistan, in short, sought to attain maximum feasible domestic public policy autonomy and to delimit the federal government's writ in Kurdistan. By contrast, the Arab parties and the American occupation authorities proposed a very strongly majoritarian, centralized and mono-national federation. Given their persistent partial possession of central governmental power, Sunni Arabs retain, for now, a centralist political culture. Shi'a Arabs are also tempted to create a strong federal government, although they also want to ensure the direction of resources and powers to poorer southern governorates. Arab views, which the U.S. strongly supported, were consolidated in what became known as the "Pachachi draft," after Adnan Pachachi, a Sunni Arab member of the Governing Council.[4] This plan envisaged a "national" or a "central" (not a "federal") government with uninhibited supremacy to make law throughout the federation on any matter, in control of integrated armed and intelligence forces, and having exclusive competence in foreign policy, monetary policy, fiscal policy and borrowing, and ownership of natural resources— all with no recognition of Iraq's diversity. The Pachachi draft declared the Kurdistan Regional Government to be "a subordinate level of the government of Iraq" (a wholly antifederal mode of thought), eliminated the Kurdistan judiciary, and envisaged an entirely centralized non-federal judiciary. It proposed that the constitution be ratified by a simple majority of Iraq's citizens.

The TAL was a compromise between these strongly divergent positions. A federal majority in the future assembly is to be constrained. Article 57 reserves to the regions and governorates powers that are "not exclusively reserved to the Iraqi Transitional Government." Article 56(c) arguably places a duty on both the federal government and the federative entities to devolve and decentralize government and administration "where practicable." If the TAL operates there will be a strong federal government in Arab-dominated Iraq, where there will be unified armed and security forces and where the governorates will be heavily dependent on the federal government. But, if the TAL operates, the federation will be bi-national in practice, because Kurdistan, which is *not* a mere aggregation of previous governorates, is distinctive. For now, it is the sole region. Its borders, which as of 19 March 2003 cut across prior governorates, are recognized (see Figure 2.2 below). It will have its own police and "internal security" arrangements, although the federation will apparently secure the border. Its judiciary is not abolished. The Kurdistan National Assembly has the right to "amend the application" of any federal law within Kurdistan (Art. 54(b)), although not matters within the exclusive competence of the federal government. These federal matters are spelled out in Article 25: foreign policy, federal defense and security policy, formulating fiscal policy, the management of natural resources (which has to occur with consultation with the federated entities), Iraqi citizenship, immigration and asylum, and the regulation of telecommunications policy. For now, the TAL points both ways: toward a centralized federation in predominantly Arab Iraq, and toward a more decentralized federation as regards Kurdistan; toward a strongly centralized federation in the management of natural resources and fiscal policy, but toward a decentralized federation if the benefits of natural resources are equitably distributed, if the federative entities are genuinely consulted over their use, and if fiscal policy is confined to general steering. Kurdistan may be expected to renegotiate the clauses on natural resources in the drafting of any proposed final constitution (see Chapters 4 and 12).

The variations between majoritarian or consensual and centralized or decentralized federations are *not* variations on the same theme. A federation might be decentralized but strongly empower a federation-wide majority; and a federation might be centralized but consensual in organizing regions' share in power in the federal government. These distinctions matter in deciding whether a federation will have an integrative or pluralist character. Integrative federations are both majoritarian and centralized; pluralist federations are both consensual and decentralized.

National or Pluri-National?

The third important distinction among federations deeply animated the negotiators of the TAL. A federation may be conceived, on the one hand, as
national (mono-national), or, on the other hand, as pluri-national (multi-
national). National federations aspire to national homogeneity—that is, to
prevent internal national and ethnic differences from having lasting political
salience. Their goal is "nation-building": one nation, one federation, *ein Volk,
ein Bund.* Proponents of national federations sometimes reject this labeling of
their position. They say that they advocate "territorial federations" (Wimmer
2003–4). But this naming is deceptive and misleading, because all federations
are necessarily territorial—that is, comprised of multiple federative entities
with distinct territories. Exponents of national federation in fact oppose, or
rather denigrate, what they call "ethnic federations," federations designed to
grant territorial powers to more than one nationally, ethnically, culturally, or
linguistically differentiated group, and which specifically enable such groups
to be territorially concentrated majorities—that is, to have regions within
which they are the dominant group. The appropriate name for what they
oppose is pluri-national federations.

The U.S. is the paradigm of a national federation. It is now integrative,
indeed assimilationist, as well as centralizing; and it facilitates majoritarianism
when any political party captures the presidency and both legislative houses.
The U.S. federation inspired many of the Arab liberals who negotiated the TAL
and many of the American lawyers working for the Coalition Provisional
Authority. It was they who named the federal assembly "the National Assembly." Many American-educated intellectuals, political scientists, and constitutional lawyers propose national federations to manage post-colonial and
post-communist societies. The U.S. model has had its emulators. The Latin
American federations of Mexico, Argentina, Brazil, and Venezuela adopted it
at various junctures in their histories. Germany, Austria, Australia, Malaysia,
and the United Arab Emirates are also national federations, though the emirates are scarcely democratic. The earliest advocates of national federalism in
what became the Netherlands, the German-speaking Swiss lands, the U.S., and
the Second German Reich were "stepping-stone" nationalists. Federation was
"to unite people living in different political units, who nevertheless shared a
common language and culture" (Forsyth 1989, 4). Federation provided a
united external security regime, a task that confederations were less well-
equipped to perform (Riker 1957, 1964, 1975).

Proponents of national federations often have a distinct animus against pluri-national or ethnic federations, which they regard as divisive and likely to collapse through secession. But selective amnesia about American political development is usually evident in the arguments of those who extol the U.S. experience. As it expanded southwestward from its original largely homogeneous citizenry of the thirteen founding colonies—a citizenry which, of course, excluded enslaved Africans and Native Americans—no new territory received statehood in the U.S. federation unless minorities were outnumbered by White Anglo-Saxon Protestants (Glazer 1983). So the U.S. federation, far from being "non-ethnic," was built around a *Staatsvolk*. Sometimes the technique deployed was to gerrymander state boundaries to ensure that Hispanics or Indians were outnumbered, as in Florida. At other times statehood was delayed until new settlers could swamp the region's long-standing residents. America's nation-builders were even cautious about immigrant groups concentrating too much in given territorial locales, lest this give rise to ethnically based demands for self-government. Public land was denied to ethnic groups per se to promote their dispersal: Welsh immigrants were dissuaded from setting up their own self-governing barony in Pennsylvania (Gordon 1964, 133). This is why the U.S. federation shows "little coincidence between ethnic groups and state boundaries" (Glazer 1983, 276). It would be more precise, however, to say that the sole coincidence is between white majorities and state boundaries, and that that is no coincidence. Celebration of the homogeneity of the founding people was evident in the now sacrosanct *Federalist Papers*. In the words of John Jay: "Providence has been pleased to give this one connected country to one united people—a people descended from the same ancestors, speaking the same language, professing the same religion, attached to the same principles of government, very similar in their manners and their customs, and who, by their joint counsels, arms and efforts, fighting side by side throughout a long and bloody war, have nobly established liberty and independence" (Madison, Hamilton, and Jay 1987 (1788), Paper II, 91).

Jay's propagandist claims ignored the Indians, Africans, Catholics, and non-English-speakers in the newly independent thirteen states. But it takes little historical knowledge to argue that no one could plausibly advance Jay's arguments during the making of Iraq's interim constitution. Its founding people were the same as the founding people of the U.S., namely the British! Iraq may be contiguously connected on maps, but it has not had a united people, descended from the same ancestors, who speak the same language, or profess the same religion. Islam divides them at least into Shi'a and Sunni. The peoples of Iraq neither flow from a common stock nor are united by a common immigrant or assimilationist experience. They have not "by their joint counsels, arms and efforts" fought a combined war of national liberation. Only

Kurdistan's *peshmerga* fought with the Coalition; the Shiʿa Arabs were reluctant to rise, given their previous abandonment to Saddam's mercies by the 1991 coalition; and some Sunni Baʿthists, *wahhabist* Islamists, and al-Sadr's Shiʿa paramilitaries continue to fight the Coalition occupation. Some Arab liberals argued that Iraq should be treated as if it comprised one united people, but the if is a giveaway (Makiya 2003). That the peoples of Iraq "should" be "just Iraqis" is a just a point of view; it confirms no fact.

Elementary comparisons of "historical starting points" may convince impartial readers of the inappropriateness of American national federation as a model for Iraq's future. There is no equivalent to a sufficiently homogeneous founding people, blessed by Providence or Allah. There are Arabs, Kurds, Turkomen, Assyrians, and Armenians. There are different kinds of Muslims, as well as Christians, Yezidis, and Jews (see Figure 2.1 and Table 2.2). The Shiʿa of Iraq are mostly Arab, not Persian, though there are a small number of Shiʿa Kurds, Turkomen, and Arabized Persians (Fuller and Francke 1999, 87). The Shiʿa Arabs, especially if they return disproportionately from exile, will see their demographic and electoral weight confirmed in the first elections and new census. They have the potential to be a *Staatsvolk*, a dominant people in control of the state, but are unlikely to constitute much more than 60 percent of the electorate. Between them, Sunni Arabs, Kurds, and others will resist any strongly religiously assimilationist project that (some) Shiʿa Arabs might attempt.

The Arab liberals and centralizers and the American occupiers sought a national federation essentially by trying to stop the formation of "Kurdistan," "Shiʿastan," and "Sunnistan." They feared that a "three-state solution," corresponding roughly to the demographic concentrations of Kurds, Sunni Arabs, and Shiʿa Arabs, would be a prelude to a secessionist free-for-all. They wanted to deny the possibility that Kurds, Shiʿa Arabs, and Sunni Arabs would aggregate to create their own national (Kurd versus Arab) or religious (Sunni Arab versus Shiʿa Arab) regions. In this respect, Saddam's refusal to let Kirkuk be part of an autonomous Kurdistan in the 1970s served their purposes. While not denying Saddam's injustices, the Coalition Provisional Authority was adamant that Kirkuk could not join Kurdistan before the making of the permanent constitution—a perspective that was also motivated by the wish to appease Ankara. In the making of the TAL, the problem for the Arab liberals and centralizers (and the American occupiers) was that free Kurdistan already existed, and that Shiʿa Arab leaders wanted to aggregate at least some governorates to create more viable regions. In the interim constitution they were obliged to recognize actually existing Kurdistan (Art. 53) and to allow any of

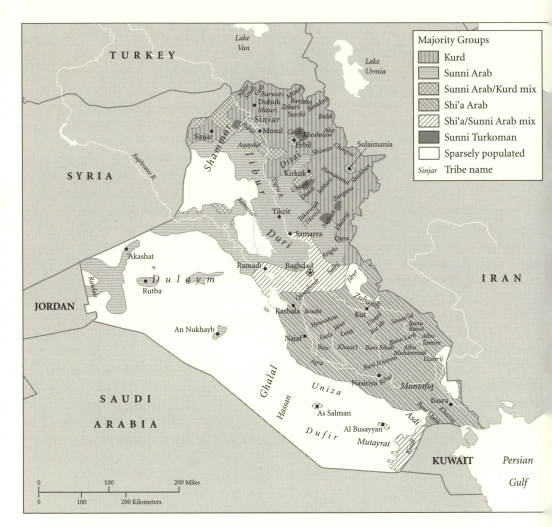

Figure 2.1. The concentration and distribution of nations, religious communities, and tribes. CIA Iraq Country Profile, January 2003. <http://www.lib.utexas.edu/maps/middle_east_and_asia/iraq_ethno_2003.pdf, 18 April 2004>. The CIA spellings are transliterated versions of Arabic: we have altered their spellings.

TABLE 2.2. ESTIMATIONS OF THE PROPORTIONS OF NATIONALITIES AND
CONFESSIONS IN IRAQ

	Estimates (%)	
Group	*High*	*Low*
Ethnicity/nationality		
Arabs	80	75
Kurds	23	15
Turkomen[a]	10	3
Assyrians and Chaldeans[b]	5	3
Others	1	0[c]
Confession		
Muslims	98	94
Shi'a[d]	65	60
Sunni[e]	37	32
Christians	5	3
Others[f]	1	0[c]

Sources: CIA, U.S. State Department, KRG(s), McDowall (1992), Iraqi Turkomen Front (websites), or interviews by authors.

Iraq's demography is a minefield, because no reliable census has been conducted since 1957 (some say 1947). The true proportions (and freely chosen identifications) of nationalities and confessions may lie outside the range of each of the estimates reported here. None of the estimates in either the high or low columns sum to 100 percent for obvious reasons, and of the Shi'a and Sunni estimates do not add to either 98 or 94 for the same reasons (see also Figure 1.2).

There is a standard joke in today's Iraq: "The peoples of Iraq are at a reconciliation conference. Turkomen, Kurdish, and Chaldo-Assyrian speakers precede an Arab speaker. Each of them gives preposterously high estimates of their nationalities' population-share. Then the Arab speaker starts his presentation, with heavy irony, 'Speaking on behalf of the Arab minority in Iraq . . .'"

a. The high estimate is from the Iraqi Turkomen Front, <http://www.ecoi.net/doc/en/iq/content/7/7657–7858>. No one else credits it.

b. These estimates combine Assyrians and Chaldeans: some refer to Chaldo-Assyrians and insist that they are one group; others regard each group as distinct; others say that there are Assyrians, Chaldeans, and Chaldo-Assyrians.

c. Rounded to nearest whole number percent.

d. Almost all Shi'a Muslims in Iraq are Arabs. The Feyli Kurds comprise the Shi'a Kurds, of whom approximately 200,000 are said by Kurdish sources to have been expelled from Baghdad and Iraq by Saddam.

e. Sunni Muslims are fairly evenly divided between Kurds and Arabs.

f. "Others" include Zoroastrians, Yezidis (who are Kurds), and Jews.

up to three former governorates (except Baghdad and Kirkuk) to aggregate into regions (Art. 53(c)).

What the Arab centralists and their American supporters were, and still are, trying to do is to make the federative entities "non-ethnic" and "non-religious." This thinking is linked to a mode of thought articulated by Donald L. Horowitz (1985) and applied to Iraq by Andreas Wimmer (2003). Wimmer's article is revealingly titled "Democracy and Ethno-Religious Conflict in Iraq," which seems to imply no conflict of nationalities exists and that the ethnic and religious conflicts are fused. In fact, it is more accurate to say that there has been an ethnonational conflict between Kurds and Arabs and a sectarian conflict among Arabs, between Sunni and Shi'a Arabs. The underlying argument of Wimmer, following Horowitz, is that a federation should be built on balance-of-power principles, encouraging intraethnic or intrareligious competition and creating incentives for intergroup cooperation, by designing regions without ascriptive majorities (Horowitz 1985, ch. 14, 15).

There are, however, only two possible routes to implement this strategy in Iraq: to ensure that no federative entities have any ethnic or religious group as a majority or to divide up the homeland concentrations of the three major groups. The first is not feasible for reasons subsequently elaborated. The second route is technically feasible, and it is the one the Arab centralizers and American occupation authorities have sought to promote. Arab national federalists argue that the new Iraqi federation should be built around the eighteen governorates (provinces) of Ba'thist Iraq. The Dawishas, for example, advocated maintaining "Iraq's present administrative structure, under which the country is divided into 18 units" (Dawisha and Dawisha 2003, 39; for similar advocacy of the 18 provinces see Bronson et al. 2003; Yavuz 2004). On the same page, however, the Dawishas insisted that the Kurds should have their own territorial "unit in the federal structure." This proviso is, on the face of it, contradictory, since it means that at least three governorates and several fractions of former governorates that comprise actually existing Kurdistan do not have federative status. Whatever it means, the argument is challenged by the de facto boundaries of Kurdistan, which cut across prior governorate jurisdictions (see also Salih 2004, 124).

The key problem with the "18 governorates model" (see Figure 2.2) from the perspective of national federalists is that it will not do the job they want. The boundaries of Saddam's governorates would not in fact prevent either ethnic or religious groups from having local territorial majorities. Kurds are a demographic majority in at least three, Dohuk, Erbil, and Sulaimania, and probably "Tamim" (Saddam's name for his restructured Kirkuk governorate). Shi'a Arabs are a demographic majority in at least nine: Basra, Muthanna, Misan, Dhi-qar, Qadisiyah, Wasit, Babil, Karbala, and Najaf, and probably in Baghdad. Sunni Arabs are almost certainly a demographic majority in the remaining four: Anbar, Diyala, Salahaddin, and Nineva. To achieve their goal, the Arab liberalizers and centralizers would have had to ban or place a strict limit on the voluntary aggregation of governorates. In the TAL they succeeded in banning aggregation as regards Kirkuk, the boundaries and status of which

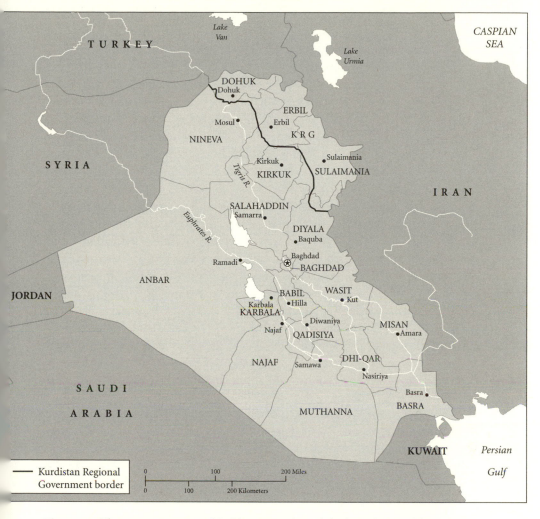

Figure 2.2. The 18 governorates of Saddam Hussein and the boundaries of the Kurdistan Regional Government in the TAL.

are left for later resolution, and Baghdad, but not otherwise. They have achieved a partial victory at the price of apparent absurdity. Kurdistan *and* all 18 governorates are recognized as federative entities, which means that Kurdistan has three governorates recognized within it: and that it contains fragments of two others, Diyala and Ninevah (see Figure 2.2). These governorates are divided, both in fact and in administration, so their constitutional recognition is either a face-saver, or foreshadows attempts to use the governorates as "Trojan horses" to undermine the integrity of Kurdistan. Banning immediate aggregation has stopped the formation of "Shiʿastan" and "Sunnistan" for now, but Kurdistan has survived, and its higher status may well encourage many Shiʿa and Sunni Arabs to aggregate their governorates and move toward a "three-region" settlement.[5]

The administrative division of the Kurdish, Sunni, and Shiʿa heartlands is technically possible, but Kurdistan has resisted the project, and Sunni and Shiʿa Arabs might eventually join them in resisting the division of their zones. For non-Kurds to divide up Kurdistan would require the armed intervention of the Coalition occupiers or future UN forces; ergo, it is not going to happen. The sole non-Kurdish army that could do the job is Turkey's, but that might terminate Turkey's prospects of entry into the European Union (a key issue for Ankara's elites, as Michael Gunter's subsequent chapter makes plain). However, more than the demographic, ethnic, and religious differentiation of Iraq's population constrains those who advocate a national federation based on Saddam's 18 governorates. The physical distribution of the communities, if data on this matter can be trusted, prevents the creation of federative entities in which none of the three communities enjoy a majority. Figure 2.1, based on U.S. Central Intelligence Agency analyses, shows the Herculean labor the requisite engineering would require. It is probably not technically feasible to design any contiguous regional boundaries that would not leave the Shiʿa Arabs dominant in several, and noncontiguous regions are always bitterly resisted. It would be impossible to draw boundaries in which Arabs and Shiʿa would be minorities in every region.

Designing credibly sized federative entities to prevent regional ascriptive majorities would require parallel crescent-shaped boundaries running from the south to the north. Such a map might have some strange aesthetic appeal, but it would be extraordinarily politically difficult, foolish, and divisive. In the case of the Kurds, such a strategy would partition Kurdistan and add significant non-Kurdish population and territories into each new unit. These design principles would return the Kurds to armed conflict with the rest of Iraq. No nationally mobilized people in recent history has voluntarily accepted or peacefully acquiesced in the externally imposed partition of its homeland, and the Kurds have just fought to regain control over (part of) their homeland. In short, no better plan for provocative conflict exists than to redesign the territorial boundaries of the new federation to prevent Kurds, Sunnis, or Shiʿa from having regions or governorates in which they are the demographically and electorally dominant group. Sensible American political scientists, otherwise attracted by integrationist federations, do not make the mistake of arguing against letting Kurds have their own region, including Kirkuk (Brancati 2004).

The TAL, in my view, marked an overall defeat for the integrationists—

the national, centralist, and majoritarian federalists of Iraq. A defeat, but not a rout, and they will fight for their position again in the making of the final constitution, or by seeking to prevent the TAL from operating. What of the opposing position, that of the pluralists who sought a consensual, decentralized and pluri-national federation? They had the advantage of starting from better historical and sociological appraisals. Article 4 of the TAL appears to give victory to both sides: "The federal system shall be based upon geographic and historic realities and the separation of powers, and not upon origin, race, ethnicity, nationality, or confession." Since the geographic and historic realities include the current and past existence of Kurdistan and the racial, ethnic, national, and confessional territorial concentrations of Iraq's major peoples, these stand opposed to the last part of the clause. It is rare in a constitutional text to see such an exquisite conjunction of rival political visions. But the pluri-nationalists won the practical victories and can consolidate this success in the final constitution. It is imperative that they do so; otherwise Iraq will not function and an implosion and civil war may follow.

Advocates of pluri-national federations seek "to unite people who seek the advantages of a common political unit, but differ markedly in descent, language and culture" (Forsyth 1989, 4). They wish to recognize, express, and institutionalize at least two national cultures on a durable and often a permanent basis. They reject the integrationist and assimilationist dispositions of national federalists, which they see as the programs of the dominant ethnonational, religious, or linguistic community. They believe it is possible, though not guaranteed, for the citizens of federations to have dual or plural loyalties—a patriotic attachment to the federation and a nationalist attachment to their homeland. They believe it is wrong to assume a priori either that plurinational federations will lead to the abuse of the rights, interests, and identities of regional minorities, or that they will necessarily facilitate secessionists. Pluri-national federation has been advocated within both liberal and Marxist traditions and has a significant following within the Anglophone academy (Hechter 2000; Keating 2001; Stepan 1998, 1999). Pluri-national federations are defended as devices to hold peoples together, as well by those who emphasize the merits of territorial autonomy for historic national minorities. Plurinational federations are workable. Switzerland and Canada are among the world's oldest continuous constitutional regimes; they have lasted in recognizably similar forms since 1848 and 1867 respectively. India, another plurinational federation, is post-colonial Asia's sole enduring democracy.[6]

Exponents of pluri-national federations, in Iraq and elsewhere, face one recurrent and apparently powerful criticism. In the twentieth century, plurinational federations or "multi-national federations" had "a terrible track record" (Snyder 2000, 327). They have broken apart or failed to remain democratic throughout the communist and post-communist world (Yugoslavia, Czechoslovakia, and the USSR; Ethiopia "lost" Eritrea). Such federations also collapsed in much of the post-colonial world, in sub-Saharan Africa, South Asia, and the Caribbean (Watts 1996; for discussions of the breakdown of federations see O'Leary 2001; Franck 1968; Hicks 1978; Watts 1971). But, the picture is emphatically not unremittingly bleak, and some American political scientists in particular overgeneralize from the post-communist and post-colonial experiences. There are major enduring pluri-national federal democracies, notably Canada, Switzerland, and India. There *may* be new ones: Belgium, Spain, Indonesia, Nigeria, South Africa, and perhaps the European Union. Therefore, consideration of the factors that promote the breakdown *and* the success of pluri-national federations are instructive in considering the future of Iraq (see Table 2.3).

The comparative evidence strongly suggests that pluri-national federations are more likely to break down if they were put together coercively (as were the Soviet Union and Yugoslavia). A successful federation in Iraq must be a voluntary union, not regarded as an American or UN imposition. Its respective and prospective units must ratify it. That is why Kurdistan, de jure or de facto, must be able to vote to endorse any freely negotiated final constitution. A foundational act of cooperation is more likely to promote sustained accommodation.

Pluri-national federations are vulnerable to breakdown at the moment of liberalization of totalitarian or authoritarian regimes. The secessions from the USSR, of Slovenia and Croatia from Yugoslavia, and of Bangladesh from Pakistan conform to this pattern. The American intervention in Iraq opened the possibility of subsequent break-up—or, if one prefers, of ratifying its break-up. The U.S. decision to hold Iraq together, but to encourage its supervised democratization *may* work. To succeed, the federation will have to have the full repertoire of liberal democratic institutions, universal adult suffrage, competitive elections, freedom for political parties and interest groups, the rule of law, human rights protections, and a free media. Iraq is a test case for those who think Arab culture, especially Arab Islamic culture, is inimical to democracy.

Pluri-national federations that maltreat at least one of their constituent nations are vulnerable to dissolution. The first Malaysian federation failed to resolve tensions between the Malays and Chinese; Pakistan's federation was oppressive toward Bengalis; and India has been oppressive toward Kashmir, where it is still engaged in counterinsurgency (Bose 2003). In Iraq, constructive relations based on mutual recognition will have to be built between the three

TABLE 2.3. FACTORS PROMOTING THE FAILURE AND SUCCESS OF PLURI-NATIONAL
FEDERATIONS

Pluri-national federations are likely to fail if:	*Pluri-national federations are likely to succeed if:*
1a. They are established and maintained through coercion	1b. They are voluntary unions of constituent peoples
2a. They are run by either totalitarian or mono-national authoritarian governments before they democratize	2b. They are established as democracies and maintained as democracies
3a. They maltreat nations, especially those situated on the territorial perimeter of the federation	3b. They recognize nations and grant them territorial self-government and/or cultural rights
4a. They experience severe distributive conflicts over natural resources or fiscal policy	4b. They manage distributive conflicts equitably
5a. They experience centralizing coups, putsches, or maneuvers that threaten the federation's founding pact	5b. They centralize only with the consent of the nations, and they decentralize to solve potential conflicts
6a. They have a *Staatsvolk* that behaves as in 1a, 2a, 3a, or 5a	6b. They have a *Staatsvolk* that is sufficiently confident to accommodate minority nations
7a. They are strongly majoritarian in the federal government, leading to 1a, 2a, 3a, and 5a	7b. They share power in consociational ways, especially important when there is no *Staatsvolk*
8a. They have interventionist and irredentist neighbors	8b. They do not have interventionist and irredentist neighbors
9a. "Exit" seems a better choice than "voice"	9b. "Voice" appears a better choice than "exit"
10a. They are economically stagnant or block the development of particular regions	10b. They promote economic development

Source: Synthesis and adaptation of arguments in McGarry and O'Leary (2003) and O'Leary (2001).

largest national and religious communities—Kurds, Sunni Arabs, and Shiʿa Arabs—as well as the smaller minorities of Turkomen, Christians, and others. This process will require substantive redress for historic injustices against Kurds, Shiʿa Arabs, and others, as well as just treatment in the future. It is a tall order.

Pluri-national federations that fail to develop or maintain economic distributive and redistributive formulae regarding natural resources, economic policy, taxation, revenue-sharing, and public expenditures that are widely regarded as fair are vulnerable to disintegration. Czechoslovakia's break-up was partly centered on the divergent economic interests of its two major units; Nigeria and Canada have experienced severe conflicts over related issues. In Iraq, robust, adequate, and fair agreements have to be built over the ownership and sharing of Iraq's natural resources. Some have sensibly suggested that Kurdistan (including Kirkuk) should own its natural resources, but that politically sensitive formulae operate to distribute revenues and royalties across the federation (Brancati 2004).

The breakdown of pluri-national federations has often been the immediate result of centralizing coups, putsches, or maneuvers, rather than the work of secessionist movements. The conduct of many Serbian politicians in Yugoslavia before 1991 and the failed coup of hard-line communists in the USSR immediately preceded the collapse of these federations and prevented their possible democratic reconstruction. A coup preceded Nigeria's descent into civil war in 1966. These vistas should serve as a warning to Arab Iraqi centralizers tempted to pressure all of Iraq into an integrated federation. Kurds and others will seek multiple constitutional checks, including international arbitration mechanisms, to inhibit future efforts to centralize the federation. Kurds are understandably concerned that an Arab-dominated governing coalition in Baghdad might seek to undermine Kurdistan's newly won constitutional status, and that some Shi'a Arabs want to dictate a majoritarian formula.

Pluri-national federations may fail if they have a dominant people, a *Staatsvolk*, that approves or is complicit in the coercion and maltreatment of other nations. According to its critics, the Bharatiya Janata Party in India, if it had become preeminent among Hindi-speakers, might have so maltreated India's minority nations that multiple secessions would become inevitable. However, a pluri-national federation may well benefit from having a *Staatsvolk*, provided it conducts itself appropriately—as it may be more likely to do in a democratic environment. All other things being equal, a *Staatsvolk* can be assured it is secure and live with what it will regard as the costs of bi- or multi-nationalism, bi- or multi-lingualism, and bi- or multi-religiosity. It may have the practical power to resist secession, but, more constructively, the capacity to be generous to discourage secession. Majoritarian federations, by their very nature, are likely to be perceived by minority nations as coercive, authoritarian, oppressive, exploitative, and centralizing, or as prone to display these traits. Therefore, majority nations, such as the Arabs of Iraq, may find consensual institutions are worthwhile investments to maintain the loyalty of the minority nationalities to the federation.

Pluri-national federations that lack a *Staatsvolk*, if they are to survive as democratic and durable entities, must have cross-community power-sharing practices in the federal government. These practices must encompass the interests of all the national, ethnic, and ethnoreligious communities with the capacity to break away or promote instability. Neither the presence of a generous or powerful *Staatsvolk* nor cross-community power-sharing practices in the federal government ensure the survival of a democratic pluri-national federation; but, judging by the twentieth-century record, the presence of one of these features is a necessary condition of enduring federations (O'Leary 2001). Iraq has a potential *Staatsvolk*, Shi'a Arabs, although several factors tell against their possible dominance. They have not been the historically dominant people; and it is unlikely that they will be politically homogeneous provided they get a fair stake in the new order. It is Kurdistan's view that power-sharing in the federal government as well as autonomy within the regions is necessary to stabilize the federation. Federalism, after all, mandates "shared rule" as well as "self-rule." The exclusion of national, ethnic, or religious communities from representation and power from the federal government is a sure recipe to promote conflict and secession. Durably democratic multi-national federations, such as Canada, Switzerland, and Belgium, have had what political scientists call "consociational practices" in their federal governments: cross-community executive power-sharing, proportional representation of groups throughout the state sector including the judiciary, and formal or informal minority veto rights (Lijphart 1977; O'Leary 2003a). It has also been argued that India has been at its most stable when its executive was descriptively inclusive of that federation's diverse religions and linguistic communities (Adeney 2002; Lijphart 1996). This comparative evidence strongly suggests that Iraq needs a federal executive that is cross-community and cross-regional in character. That is why, unlike some (Yavuz 2004), Kurdistan's leaders took the collective presidency of the Governing Council as a portent of sensible compromises, and it is why I share Kurdistan's reservations about the possible scope of prime ministerial power in the TAL.

Pluri-national federations are more likely to be stabilized if they have non-interventionist neighbors, especially if they have non-irredentist neighbors that do not seek to play major roles in the lives of their cross-border co-ethnics or co-religionists. These external conditions for the success of pluri-national federation in Iraq are not difficult to spell out. Turkey, Syria, Iran, and Saudi Arabia will have to keep out of Iraq's territory and avoid sponsoring paramilitary organizations of any kind. Turkey will have to reduce its current dispositions to manipulate the Turkomen and forget its ambitions over Mosul, which Kemal Atatürk abandoned nearly eighty years ago. The willingness of the Bush administration's national security advisor, Condoleezza Rice, to encourage the deployment of Turkish troops in Iraq in 2003 suggested amazing insensitivity on these matters. It immediately opened tensions between

Iraq's new foreign minister, Hoshyar Zebari, and Ahmad Chalabi, one of the rotating presidents of the new Governing Council (Knowlton 2003). The subsequent veto of the deployment of Turkish troops by the Governing Council and its acceptance by the Turkish government suggested incoherence in the upper echelons of the Bush administration, where it seems to have been believed that the "Muslim" identity of Turkish troops would be better than the "Christian" identity of the Coalition occupiers. That Arabs had revolted against the Ottomans and that Kurds might fear the major historically genocidal state in the region were facts that were somehow discounted. Not only will the neighboring powers have to keep out of Iraq, but the Coalition occupation forces will eventually have to withdraw in a manner that will avoid an immediate implosion—no easy step. Again these are tall orders, though thay are not as impossible as some suggest. Syria, Iran and Saudi Arabia have strong incentives not to provoke the U.S.; Turkey wants to join the EU.

Nations in federations, like citizens and consumers confronted with decline in the quality of states or private organizations, may be conceived of as having three choices: exit, voice, or loyalty (Hirschman 1970). If "exit" seems a better choice than "voice," both politically and economically, for nations trapped within a federation, then the federation is likely to be doomed. A pluri-national federation that is democratic leads minority nations at least to consider "voice" before "exit." Democratic arrangements allow the representatives of national, ethnic, and religious communities to engage in dialogue and open bargaining, which facilitate the development of political cooperation. They protect individual rights and collective organization in civil society that may check systematic transgressions against these communities. Federations that protect collective identities create collective security and may facilitate the emergence of interethnic and interreligious cooperation and even enable secularization to proceed in less fraught confrontations.

Pluri-national federations that are economically stagnant or block the development of particular regions create strong incentives for "exit," especially if the best alternative to federation seems to promise more prosperity. Conversely, prosperous and developing federations are more likely to endure than those which are not. One should not exaggerate the power of materialism in politics. It would be wrong to insist that prosperity is a necessary starting condition for the success of multi-national federation. Switzerland and Canada did not start rich, and India is far from being rich. But, other things being equal, federations that over time facilitate increasing per capita prosperity, have better prospects of success. Democratization and economic prosperity cannot be assured in advance, but nothing in Iraq's cultures or communities' talents need necessarily prevent them.

This review of the factors that make pluri-national federations fail and work has suggested the sheer magnitude of what is required if Iraq is to be a democratic and functioning federation. Two considerations need to be kept in mind by skeptics. First, the TAL has plainly stepped toward the pluri-national and pluralist model: constructive analysis should therefore focus on how to make this negotiated outcome flourish. Second, those who quite reasonably think the prospects for a pluri-national federation in Iraq are grim need to explain why either a unitary state or an integrated, majoritarian, centralized and mono-national federation would be more likely to win the loyalty of Iraq's minority nations and confessions. There is strength in the view that Iraq can only be a democratic state if it is also a pluri-national federation, a decentralized federation, and a consensual federation—in short, a pluralist federation. More precisely still, *bi-national, multiethnic,* tolerantly *religiously plural,* and *multiregional.* Bi-national, because there are two major nationally mobilized and linguistically distinctive collective communities, Kurds and Arabs. Multiethnic, because there is a range of other ethnic communities, notably Turkomen, Assyrians, and Armenians, who will need to have institutional recognition and protections, both at the federal and regional levels. Religiously plural, both to manage the divide between Shiʿa and Sunni, their internal divisions, *and* the non-Muslim religions, as well as those who have no religion. It is certainly difficult; it is not impossible. The real choice is between such a pluralist federation and the break-up of Iraq.

Pluralist Federation and Consociation

The preceding arguments combine federal and consociational principles (Lijphart 2004). Consociational principles include cross-community executive power-sharing, proportionality, autonomy rights, and veto rights (O'Leary 2003a). Recommendations have already been made on how to enhance power-sharing in the federal executive. The other three principles require further development.

Pluralist federations can function without proportional representation electoral systems (cf. India and Canada), but are better secured through such systems (cf. Spain and Belgium). Proportional representation electoral systems do what they say: they match the proportions of seats won in legislatures to the votes cast for parties (or candidates, in the case of the single transferable vote). They are fair, and they are also properly "majoritarian": they generally ensure that the government is in fact supported by a real rather than an artificial majority of voters (Nagel 2000). Before the making of the TAL it was my view, consistent with the pluralist and consociational logic articulated here, that the lower chamber of the federal parliament should be elected by proportional representation. The TAL, though silent on the electoral system to be adopted as the electoral law, may terminate the necessity of defending this position at length because it mandates that one in four members of the future federal assembly must be women and that there must be "fair representation for all communities," including small nationalities (Art. 30).

Article 30 must therefore exclude winner-take-all or double-ballot electoral systems in single-member districts, which are not "fair" and can not achieve the goal of one in four female parliamentarians except through forcing all-female contests in one quarter of the districts, which would fall foul of the bill of rights article that prohibits discrimination on grounds of sex (Art. 12). In consequence, the drafters of the electoral law, at least if they wish to be consistent with the TAL, must choose one of three standard systems:

(a) a party-list system (in either multi-member regional districts, with compensation at the federal level for any disproportionality introduced at the regional level, or in a federation-wide single district);
(b) an additional-member system with proportional compensation at the federal level (in which half the seats might be allocated in districts, and half through a federal list, where female candidates might be over-represented); or
(c) the single transferable vote in multi-member districts (which might also have compensation at the federal level for any disproportionality at the district level, or for low female representation).

The party-list system would be the simplest, and could be implemented either in an Iraq-wide electoral district, or organized on regions, including respect for Kurdistan's boundaries, with compensation at the federal level for any disproportionality at district levels. From the perspective of the small national minorities, there are two easy ways to secure their fair representation: through reservation, which would allocate them quotas of seats after a fair census; or through having very large districts and no threshold so that their candidates have a fair chance of being elected. From the perspective of Kurdistan, the electoral districts must respect its territorial integrity; that is, there must be no electoral districts that cut across its boundaries. No federations have electoral districts which cut across the territorial boundaries of the constituent units. Provisions to make the governorates the electoral district boundaries would reprise the controversy over the status of the governorates and would reflect an attempt to create a non-federal voting system. Equally, Kurdistan will oppose attempts to introduce cross-regional or distributive requirements on parties in elections to the federal parliament. Such requirements aim to reward parties with support throughout the federation. This would not be fair, because it would be biased toward Arab parties and be overtly discriminatory. Again, such proposals would constitute an effort to create an integrated federation, ideas that have been aired in the American academy (Wimmer 2003; Brancati 2004) and that need to be rejected as recipes for conflict. The negotiation of the electoral rules for the second chamber will not be decided until the permanent constitution, but again proportionality (perhaps using the single transferable vote among regional assembly electors to choose federal senators) would be consistent with a pluralist federation.

Autonomy is necessarily embedded in federal territorial governance, but two matters require special consideration. The federal parliament and other institutions will have to operate in two and possibly three languages (Arabic, Kurdish, and perhaps English as a neutral post-colonial language), and a decision will have to be made on which language is authoritative for constitutional adjudication by the supreme court. Younger Kurds may advocate English rather than accepting the primacy of Arabic. Regional parliaments will have to decide whether their regions will be bilingual in schooling, or monolingual with support for second or third languages, and will have to make similar decisions about their other public institutions. All federal and regional bureaucracies should be mandated to have at least bilingual capacities (which will not require every employee to be bilingual). The linguistic rights of ethnic and religious minorities who will nowhere be regional majorities, such as the Turkomen, Chaldeans, Assyrians, and Jews, may need further clarification under both federal and regional bills of rights. They should be entitled to proportional public funding for their schools and special support to protect their linguistic heritage.

Executive power-sharing, proportionality, and autonomy have to date been shown to be potentially amenable to constructive negotiations, but the agreement of veto rights will be much more controversial. Some Shiʿa Arabs have already taken umbrage at Kurdistan's de facto veto over the ratification of the permanent constitution—and the U.S. may yet defer to Shiʿa sentiment on this matter. The proposed ratification process is not a matter which solely benefits Kurdistan: it also gives veto power to three Sunni-dominated governorates. Bills of rights, if properly judicially protected, create certain veto rights, but the TAL largely protects only individual rights. Given Iraq's deep diversity it would be best if each region had its own constitution and its own bill of rights, to be interpreted or applied to regional parliamentary legislation solely by its own regional supreme court. It should also be made difficult to change those features of the constitution that would protect Iraq's bi-national, multilingual and religiously pluralist character. One rule would require that any constitutional change have two-thirds support in the lower federal chamber, a concurrent majority of Kurdistan and the rest of Iraq's senators, and the consent of a majority of regional parliaments, with one of those parliaments necessarily including the Kurdistan parliament on any matter affecting the national interests of Kurdistan. However it is designed, a Kurdistan veto on constitutional change is necessary—and may need protection in an international treaty. Veto power might be supplemented by a Kurdistan opt-out right (which other regions could adopt if they chose). For example, Kurdistan might negotiate to have the right to opt out of any law or policy adopted by the federal parliament (after passage of a resolution to that effect by two-thirds of its assembly members and senators and two-thirds of the members of its regional parliament).

Combining federal and consociational principles is crucial to creating a democratic Iraq. There is no workable alternative if Iraq is to be democratized and if the reconstructed state's relationships with Kurds and Kurdistan are to be based on recognition, partnership, and equality. No one imagines this will be easy. But, to test the realism of these arguments, consider how they might apply to two controversial sites and questions.

First, let us shift from the "F" word to the "K" words. The Kirkuk governorate outside the city (even after Saddam's boundary changes) is predominantly Kurdish, whereas the city (even after coercive "Arabization" under the Ba'thists) has a mix of Arabs, Kurds, Turkomen, and Christians (see Appendix to this chapter, and Figure 2.3a, b). The obvious solution to this disputed area, proposed by the leadership of Kurdistan, is to create a local power-sharing arrangement within Kirkuk governorate and city underneath the Kurdistan regional government which would be protected within Kurdistan's constitution and possibly within the federal constitution. In reciprocity, Mosul should have power-sharing arrangements for the Kurdish minority within a likely Sunni-dominated region. The TAL, however, has delayed the final status of Kirkuk. Instead, a fair process has been designed (Arts. 58) that should reverse the consequence of Saddam's demographic manipulations, through expulsions, expropriations, and "Arabization programs." The UN may be required to appoint an arbitrator (Art. 58 (b)) to make final recommendations. A fair settlement would guarantee local consociational arrangements in Kirkuk city, irrespective of the final status of the governorate. The issue remains a live one.

A second issue is military. On the logic of federal principles, there should be regional guards as well as a federal military, and both should cooperate on the borders of Iraq, with the rights of mobilization and deployment of the federal army subject to the unanimous consent of the collective presidency. These matters remains to be definitively settled (see Chapter 4) but as this chapter went to press it seemed likely that Kurdistan would keep its *peshmerga*, albeit as mountain guards, and that the federal army would not be deployed in Kurdistan.

Federation for Iraq and Federacy for Kurdistan

The arguments so far have focused on the design of the federation of Iraq; the final negotiation of such a federation is addressed in Chapter 4. While heavily focused on Kurdistan's interests, I have not so far addressed Kurdistan's internal governance and how that will affect its relations with the federation. Kurdistan can argue that Article 52 of the TAL mandates a consensual rather than majoritarian federation, because it states that the federal design should "prevent the concentration of power . . . that allowed the continuation of decades of tyranny and oppression." That principle enables it to stake its claim for the redesign of the federal executive, to ensure proportionality in the federal legislatures and courts, and to maintain control over its domestic security. Indeed Kurdistan's strikingly asymmetrical status in the TAL makes it likely that it can evolve into a "federacy" (O'Leary 2003b; Rezvani 2003). A federacy is a unit of government which is asymmetrical in relation to others. In a unitary state, a federacy is a distinctive governmental unit with an entrenched federal relationship with the central government, normally embedded in a constitutionally entrenched statute of autonomy. In a federation, a federacy is a distinctive semisovereign entity, culturally different from the other units in the federation, which may enjoy different powers to those units, or choose to exercise the same powers differently. A federacy is not a part, or, better, not an identical part of the systemwide federation; it creates a semi-sovereign territory different in its institutions and constitutional competencies from the rest of the state. The division of powers between the federacy and the federal government is constitutionally entrenched, cannot be unilaterally altered by either side, and has established arbitration mechanisms, domestic or international, to deal with difficulties that might arise between the federacy and the federal government. These are objectives Kurdistan will seek in the negotiation of the permanent constitution. Federacy is not devolution: it is not a revocable gift from the federal government. Rather; it is a right that is domestically constitutionally entrenched, so that the federacy can veto any changes in its status or powers, and, ideally, its status and powers are internationally protected in a treaty. In making the TAL, Kurdistan's negotiators did not seek to stop Arab Iraq from adopting a centralized U.S.-style national federation if that was what Arabs wanted, provided it was not imposed on Kurdistan. They knew that they had no right, or capacity, to impose their preferred federation on all of the rest of Iraq, but they insisted they had every right to insist on their preferred federal arrangements for Kurdistan as one means through which they could exercise national self-determination. In effect, then, they sought a federacy for Kurdistan.

Kurdistan's asymmetry and propensity to become a federacy is evident in several ways. Under the TAL it is the sole region; all the other federative entities are governorates. It has been recognized as it was before 2003, as free Kurdistan, as have its laws not in conflict with the TAL. Its prior status has not been declared illegal; to the contrary, it has been regularized. Its National Assembly has been recognized by that name. Of the federative entities, it alone may amend federal legislation. It is the largest federative entity in territory and (except for the capital region of Baghdad) in population. It is the sole federative entity dominated by another, non-Arab, nationality, the Kurds. It is the only federative entity whose citizens predominantly speak the other official language of the federation, Kurdish. It is the one entity likely to convert its army into its own national guard, and it is unquestionably the sole entity granted exclusive jurisdiction in policing and internal security. Kurdistan *is* different. It will, of course, seek to see these differences affirmed in the final constitution and will want default mechanisms in the event of breaches of the constitution by the federal government.

Kurdistan has to address several questions that bear on its status as a federacy and on the stability of the federation. The first is its own internal governance. The Kurdistan Democratic Party (KDP) and the Patriotic Union of Kurdistan (PUK), having resolved their civil war, are committed to a unified region, national assembly, and government. One issue is whether they can or should fulfill this objective. In a subsequent chapter, Gareth Stansfield argues eloquently that the KDP and the PUK are incapable of organizing unification and should regularize the existing division of Kurdistan instead. That is certainly one possibility that time will test. But several features of the TAL, if it becomes operational, will force the two dominant governing parties in Kurdistan to make decisions: governorates, elections, and the prospective party law. The TAL recognizes the governorates within and across Kurdistan, and indeed grants three of them, not Kurdistan per se, a potential veto on the constitution. Although Kurdistan could aggregate its governorates, it would be prudent to do so only after the ratification of the permanent constitution. What its parties must do is to stop Baghdad parties and bureaucrats making these governorates into meaningful entities for governance that undercut Kurdistan's integrity.

The way to do this is through pact-making among elites and using the discipline of their party members in the governorates. They can then spend time considering their own preferred modes of decentralization for Kurdistan and insist in the final federal constitution, as is standard in federations, that the Kurdistan region should have the right to organize its own internal local government arrangements. One reason they will need to do this is because they will need to think through how Kurdistan will be governed if Kirkuk does indeed join Kurdistan, as all Kurdish parties want. If that merger happens, there will then be four major urban locations in Kurdistan: Dohuk, Kirkuk, Sulaimania, and Erbil. Kirkuk will require special arrangements because of its large Turkomen and Arab populations. It would make sense to share some of the functional and symbolic parts of the governance across these cities. Erbil should remain the site of the National Assembly, but Kurdistan's regional supreme court could be in Kirkuk, and the regional cabinet could rotate between Erbil and Sulaimania. Dohuk and Sulaimania could be the centers of internal security: the police and the Kurdistan Mountain Rangers or the Kurdistan National Guard. The ministries and their officials should be spread fairly across the four cities, giving all the major cities a stake in Kurdistan's governance.

It would make a great deal of sense, before the simultaneous regional and federal elections that have to be held before 31 January 2005, for the two major parties, the KDP and the PUK, to make a double pact. One part of this pact would be to create a temporary government of national unity in Kurdistan before the elections, but intended to endure for the first legislative term of the regional assembly. This would guarantee that neither party would completely lose power within Kurdistan and that each would be less vulnerable to "divide and rule" tactics from Baghdad. They should agree in advance to give all parties, large and small, shares in the cabinet of national unity, according to their respective shares of seats in the Kurdistan National Assembly, reserving some ministries for minorities. Such a government of national unity would enable the parties to agree the drafting and implementation of Kurdistan's own constitution, as the TAL now radically affects the provisions of its previous draft (Kurdistan Democratic Party 1992a, b). It would assist in ensuring that Kurdistan speaks with a unified regional voice during the making of the permanent constitution.

It would also make sense for a second pact before the first elections to the federal assembly. For Iraq as a whole, a Kurdistan National Alliance should be formed to maximize votes and seats for what will, after all, be a constitutional convention as well as a federal assembly. It would galvanize Kurds outside the existing Kurdistan region, including those in Kirkuk and Baghdad. An alliance would not require the KDP and the PUK to merge, but it would require them to form a common electoral alliance. They should argue for *apparentement* (permitting parties to present a joint party list) in the electoral law, and share a common whip in the first federal assembly. The purpose here would be to develop a common national mandate of principles for the making of the permanent constitution. This double-pact proposal is not intended to stifle democratic life—other parties will and should challenge the big two parties in Kurdistan—but rather to consolidate the democratization of Kurdistan and to create a united front in the federal assembly.

Conclusion

Neither pluri-national federations nor consociations are guaranteed to work: there have been many, many failures. Objectively there are several reasons to be pessimistic about the prospect of a pluralist federation in Iraq; indeed reasons for pessimism exceed those that might inspire hope. There are therefore no constitutional elixirs or panaceas. Lest it be forgotten, it may well be the case that the leadership of the two major parties in Kurdistan are more moderate than their public, which has, in the main, happily enjoyed its dozen years of de facto independence and does not welcome reincorporation into a state which has practiced genocide, ethnic expulsion, and coercive assimilation at their expense. Arab leaders may only have a brief opportunity to make a feasible federal bargain with Kurdistan that can hold.

The alternatives to pluralist federation and power-sharing, such as a wholly unitary Iraq, or pretending that Iraqi Arabizing nationalism was successful throughout Iraq, do not pass muster. The arguments from within the Bush administration, the CPA, and the Arab liberals, who commend variations on the U.S. national, centralized, and often majoritarian federation, evaporate when exposed to light. With luck they will leave little residue. The real alternatives to a genuine pluralist federation for Iraq and federacy for Kurdistan are either a continuing occupation or an implosion, with secessions accompanied by interventions from neighboring states. Reasonable people differ on the motives behind and the justice of the U.S.-led war to overthrow Saddam's regime. Fair-minded people all agree that the U.S. has not presided over a well-managed occupation, even before the scale of human rights abuses in former Ba'thist prisons became apparent. But, it would be helpful if political thinking inside and outside Iraq and within the United Nations, which may return to Iraq in the summer of 2004, supported the pluralist ideas advanced here while they have some prospect of being voluntarily institutionalized. The principal danger is that the United Nations, saturated with a new anti-Americanism, and inclined to appease pan-Arab opinion, will unwind the constructive possibilities created by the TAL. Tacitus remarked in his *Annals* that in one of their wars of conquest the Romans created a desert and called it peace. Let us hope when all the Americans, British, Australians, and Polish soldiers leave the deserts of Mesopotamia and the mountains of Kurdistan that a fledgling federation will remain to create a flourishing peace. The alternatives are deeply unpleasant.

Appendix: The K Words: Kirkuk Governorate and Kirkuk City

Kirkuk City and Governorate are the most hotly contested of the "disputed areas" whose final status is not resolved in the TAL, and will have to be settled in the negotiation of the permanent constitution. The last relatively reliable census in Iraq was held in 1957, but the Ba'thists subsequently tampered with its records. In that partially disputed census, of the three largest communities in the whole governorate, namely Arabs, Turkomen, and Kurds, the Kurds constituted the plurality, approximately 48 percent of the governorate as a whole, and 49 percent if the unknown and foreign citizens are excluded. Outside Kirkuk city Kurds were indisputably the majority community. By contrast in the city, in the middle of the governorate, and then home to less than a third of the governorate's population, Turkomen (37.6 percent) were the largest group, just outnumbering Kurds (33.3 percent), who in turn outnumbered Arabs (22.5 percent). There was a significant category of "unknowns" (4.2 percent) who were probably mostly illiterate Kurds. Figures 2.3a and 2.3b represent the data. The most objective summation of the 1957 demography is that Kirkuk was a multi-ethnic city surrounded by a larger and heavily Kurdish population in the governorate.

What the situation is in 2004 no one knows for certain. All the populations have probably grown in size, but Kurds and Arabs have likely had higher birth rates than Turkomen and Assyrians, although it is a fool's game to project demographic data from fifty years ago. The author has heard and received absurd estimates from all communities. The most preposterous figures have consistently been from correspondents from the Turkomen and the Assyrian communities, which I interpret to reflect the fears, and fantasies, that accompany ethnic tension, especially among small groups who fear extinction. We can be certain of one fact: that Saddam continued to induce Arabs into Kirkuk and to "denationalize" its Kurds, Turkomen, and Assyrians in the 1990s confirms that his Arabization project was far from complete. And we can be cer-

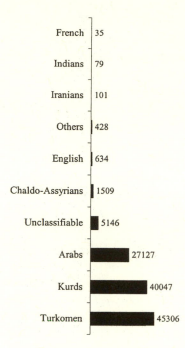

French | 35
Indians | 79
Iranians | 101
Others | 428
English | 634
Chaldo-Assyrians | 1509
Unclassifiable | 5146
Arabs | 27127
Kurds | 40047
Turkomen | 45306

Figure 2.3a. Population of Kirkuk City, 1957.

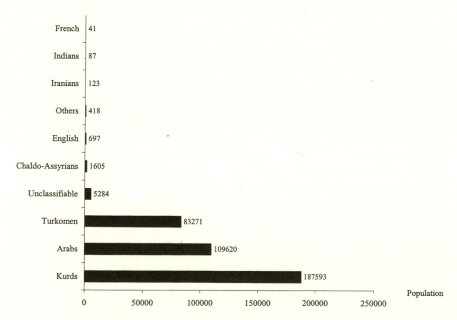

French | 41
Indians | 87
Iranians | 123
Others | 418
English | 697
Chaldo-Assyrians | 1605
Unclassifiable | 5284
Turkomen | 83271
Arabs | 109620
Kurds | 187593

Population

0   50000   100000   150000   200000   250000

Figure 2.3b. Population of Kirkuk Governorate, 1957.

tain of one more fact. The return of some Kurdish expellees in 2003, and the flight of some Arab settlers, has led to a de facto reversal of some of Saddam's work. It is uncertain what the demographic and electoral picture will be even if all expelled Kurds return, but possible that Kurds would prove to be at least the plurality group in the city, and the majority group in the governorate.

Incorporating Kirkuk governorate and city in an autonomous (or an independent) Kurdistan has been a consistent objective of Kurdish nationalists. They have four sets of arguments. The first set is geographic. Any traveler by road from Hewlêr (Erbil) to Kirkuk city, even today, observes no visible geographic demarcation between Kirkuk and actually existing Kurdistan. In spring exactly the same green flat fields surround each side of the road as far as the horizon that is ringed by the same mountain range. The oil field near the city is the first sign of any material difference in the landscape, and that is a recent and man-made difference. The second set of arguments is historic and national. The region, although not always the city, has been part of Kurdish-speaking civilization for at least two centuries, and Kurds maintain that even though it has numerous significant minorities that should not affect its Kurdish national status. Many nations have regions in which there are large minorities; and the Kurds maintain that they have treated and would treat their minorities much better than Arab or Ba'thist governments have treated Kurds. The third medley of arguments is demographic. Kurds argue that were it not for deliberate demographic manipulation they would constitute the majority group in both the region and the city. The manipulation has taken multiple forms. Under the Hashemite monarchy Arab settlers were encouraged to develop the region's agriculture. Under the republic non-Kurds were deliberately preferred over time in employment in the oil field and related industries. Ba'thists expelled Kurds (and Turkomen) from the city and the region. Citizenship records were falsified, properties confiscated, and Arab settlers, largely Shi'a Arabs from the South, were induced by special bonuses and privileges to settle in the city. The boundaries of the governorate were redrawn by Saddam, and the governorate was renamed "Tamim" ("nationalization"). The redrawing excluded strongly Kurdish-majority rural zones from the governorate, and incorporated strongly non-Kurdish (mostly Sunni Arab) rural zones.

The fourth stream of Kurdish argument is moral. They argue that recent ethnic expulsion and coercive "Arabization" should not be rewarded and treated as irreversible "facts on the ground," and that efforts to reverse these injustices should not be treated as equivalent to the original crimes. Had the consequences of Kurds' higher birth rates prevailed, had they merely had equal opportunities for employment in the oil industry, and had there been no expulsion and induced settlements, no one would now question that the region is Kurdish by geography, history, and by demographic head-count. Sometimes, of course, Kurds offer less convincing arguments, for example, that Kirkuk is sacred to their civilization, or is their historic capital. But bad arguments need not impair good ones. There is no doubt that the Kurds' geographic, historic, national, demographic and moral arguments are also motivated by Kirkuk's natural resources, which would dramatically boost Kurdistan's development prospects.

Non-Kurds in Kirkuk city and governorate are differentiated. They are, however, not Kurdish politically; and they do not favor an independent Kurdistan. But, on the other hand, they are not uniformly hostile to Kurds, or toward an officially recognized Kurdistan region; and most, when pressed, recognize that the Kurds have suffered injustices. In the highly segregated city, Arab and Turkomen districts are materially much better off to the naked eye. The professional Assyrians of the city appear intent on keeping their heads down, and would live with any settlement that minimized the threat of communal violence. Some Arab politicians in the city have told me that they are now the majority in the city, that Kirkuk is, and has been, an Iraqi city, that it is the right of citizens everywhere to settle where they will within a state, and that the sole reason for the Kurdish claim to Kirkuk is oil: the Kurdish claim was raised by Mustafa Barzani in search of black gold, rather than because of geography, history, nationality, demography, or morality. Some gravely warn that the Kurdish claim and efforts to reverse what some Arabs call "alleged expulsions" will create a crisis. They also accuse Kurdish *peshmerga* of organizing the expulsion of Arabs. There is, however, a noticeable difference in disposition between the Sunni and Shi'a Arab politicians. The former, "old city" Arabs, seem keener on constructive cross-community relations, and are recognized to have this orientation by local Kurds (both those residing in the city and those who have been expelled). The Shi'a Arabs, perhaps reflecting their more recent and settler status, appear both more antagonistic and fearful toward Kurds, and more concerned to narrate Shi'a grievances in the South, than the ones experienced by Kurds "in the North." Poor Kurdish returnees with whom I spoke, especially the younger ones, distinguished the Arabs in the city by religion, Shi'a and Sunni, and favored the latter—but, on questioning, assured me the distinction was based on the fact that the former are mostly recently settlers, and not upon their own sectarian preferences. Turkomen politicians are not homogeneous in their readings of the city's recent history, although they privately concede they have probably lost their plurality status. The Turkomen politicians who are sponsored by Ankara find it difficult to explain why Turkey did nothing for them during the high-tide of Saddam's Arabization; and they have no good answers when told that their estimates of the Turkomen population require preposterously sized Turkomen families who are nowhere to be found. The Turkomen Shi'a politicians, by contrast, have no truck with secularist Turkey. They are contemptuous of the Turkomen Front sponsored by Ankara, and look likely to create alliances with Sh'ia Arab politicians. Saddam's manipulations have definitely had one significant impact on the political controversy that surrounds the city and the governorate. In the 1960s and 1970s Kirkuk's status was an issue in which northern communities in Iraq, that is, Kurds, Sunni Arabs, Turkomen, and Assyrians, had an emotional and material stake. But now, thanks to Saddam's efforts, all communities in Iraq, and all their responsible and ambitious politicians, have emotional and material stakes in its status.

Notes

This chapter updates and radically revises addresses given to the conferences on "Multi-Nationalism, Power-Sharing and the Kurds in a New Iraq, held in Washington, D.C., on 12 September 2003 (O'Leary 2003), and on "Autonomy Arrangements" held by the Norwegian Foreign Ministry in Oslo, 14–15 November 2003. It benefits from being part of the on-site advisory team that advised Kurdistan during the making of the transition law, but reveals no confidences from that process. Thanks are especially owed to John McGarry, research funds provided by the United States Institute of Peace, the Lauder chair, and the Dean of the School of Arts & Sciences at the University of Pennsylvania. Many thanks to Sahar Ghazanfar, Arend Lijphart, Ian S. Lustick, Tom Lyne, John McGarry, Iain McLean, Molly McNulty, Tanni Mukhopadhyay, Jack H. Nagel, Khaled Salih, Rogers M. Smith, and many, many people in Kurdistan, especially Kamilia Boya, who explained the situation of Christian minorities, and Falah Mustafa Bakir, whose translation skills helped me tremendously. Presenting the analysis on 17 March 2004 at the Aweza Club in Hêwler, to two hundred citizens of Kurdistan who had read the text at least as carefully as I had kept me on my toes.

The identities and data in the Appendix from the 1957 census were translated by Sahar Ghazanfar. The impressions conveyed above are the result of the author's visits and interviews in the region in the spring of 2004.

1. Expert comparative constitution-watchers will note the resemblance to a subsection of Article 44 of Ireland's 1937 Constitution (now repealed), which recognized the Catholic Church as the religion of majority of the people, while protecting the religious rights of others. What was progress in Ireland in 1937 may be progress in Iraq in 2004.

2. Switzerland is exceptional in not having a federal supreme court; the referendum device functions to leave the citizenry of Switzerland and the cantons free to determine the constitutionality of any federal law.

3. Confusion on the demographic weights of Shi'a and Sunni remained heavily evident among influential Americans. Henry Kissinger, America's foremost "realist," as late as January 2002 managed to write in the *Washington Post* of "the Sunni majority

that now dominates Iraq" ("Phase II and Iraq," 13 January, B7), a mistake that has been satirized as an example of "magical realism" (Smyth 2003, 565–67).

4. This text is not published, or directly available on the internet. But a prior version of it appeared in *Asharq-al Awsat*, 14 February 2004, under the heading "Draft Law of Administering the Iraqi State for the Transitional Period Proposed to the Governing Council." I wrote a short critical op-ed on "the Pachachi draft" (O'Leary 2004a).

5. Shortly after the U.S. occupation, I suggested a five-region model (O'Leary 2003c). The idea was that it might offer an emergent resolution of the differences between the two-unit federation preferred by Kurdistan; the three-unit model favored by others (e.g., Gelb 2003); and the 18-unit model of the Arab liberals. Baghdad and Kurdistan (with disputed territories restored to it) have comparable populations and have distinct reasons for being treated as two regions. Voluntary aggregation of governorates would generate a Sunni Arab-dominated region in their "triangle" and one or two Shi'a regions in the South. A five-region model would create roughly balanced populations, grant self-determination to three communities, and create a pluralist capital region. The five-unit model would also make the design of a collective presidency easier: if one president came from each region there would normally be three Shi'a, one Sunni Arab, and one Kurd without requiring quotas. This idea is not yet precluded by what happened in the making of the TAL, because aggregation of governorates can be agreed in the making of the permanent constitution. Two- and three-unit federations have a poor track record, which provides another argument in favor of a five-unit federation. Canada and Australia, with populations in the same range as Iraq, have ten- and six-unit federations respectively, and both have some very small units, such as Tasmania and Prince Edward Island.

6. India's federation is partially pluri-national, but in our typology of polar contrasts in federations (Table 2.1) it is much more of an "integrative" than a "pluralist federation." It is highly centralized (granting the federal government the right to impose emergency presidential rule on India's provinces, and the right to create new provinces); and it is potentially majoritarian (or "pluralitarian") because under the electoral system of plurality rule in single member districts the Lok Sabha and the executive can be—and have been—dominated by single-party governments with significantly less than 40 percent of the popular vote.

References

Adeney, Katharine. 2002. "Constitutional Centring: Nation Formation and Consociational Federalism in India and Pakistan." *Journal of Commonwealth & Comparative Politics* 40 (3): 8–33.

Bose, Sumantra. 2003. *Kashmir: Roots of Conflict, Paths to Peace*. Cambridge, Mass.: Harvard University Press.

Brancati, Dawn. 2004. "Is Federalism a Panacea for Post-Saddam Iraq?" *Washington Quarterly* 27 (2): 7–21.

Bronson, Rachel, ed. 2003. *Guiding Principles for U.S. Post-Conflict Policy in Iraq*. New York: Council on Foreign Relations.

Dawisha, Adeed and Karen Dawisha. 2003. "How to Build a Democratic Iraq." *Foreign Affairs* 82 (3): 36–50.

CPA. 2004. Coalition Provisional Authority briefing with UN Special Representative Lakhdar Brahimi and Massoud Barsani, president, /Iraqi Governing council, Baghdad, Wednesday, 14 April. <http://www.cpa-iraq.org/transcripts/20040414 _brahimini_barzani.html.>

Elazar, Daniel. 1987. *Exploring Federalism.* Tuscaloosa: University of Alabama Press.

Forsyth, Murray, ed. 1989. *Federalism and Nationalism.* Leicester: Leicester University Press.

Franck, Thomas M. 1968. *Why Federations Fail: An Inquiry into the Requisites for Successful Federation.* New York: New York University Press.

Fuller, Graham E. and Rend Rahim Francke. 1999. *The Arab Shiʿa: The Forgotten Muslims.* New York: St. Martin's Press.

Gardner, David. 2003. "Time of the Shia." *Financial Times,* August 30/31, W1-W2.

Gelb, Leslie, H. "The Three-State Solution." *New York Times,* 25 November 2003.

Gellner, Ernest. 1981. *Muslim Society.* Cambridge: Cambridge University Press.

Glazer, Nathan. 1983. "Federalism and Ethnicity: The American Solution." In *Ethnic Dilemmas, 1964–82,* ed. Nathan Glazer. Cambridge, Mass.: Harvard University Press. 274–92.

Gordon, Milton. 1964. *Assimilation in American Life: The Role of Race, Religion and National Origins.* New York: Oxford University Press.

Governing Council of Iraq. 2004. Law of Administration for the State of Iraq for the Transitional Period (Transitional Administrative Law; TAL). Baghdad Governing Council of Iraq and Coalition Provisional Authority. <http://www.cpa-iraq.org/ government/TAL.html>

Halliday, Fred. 2000. "The Fates of Monarchy in the Middle East." In *Nation and Religion in the Middle East.* Boulder, Colo.: Lynne Reinner. 91–108.

Hechter, Michael. 2000. *Containing Nationalism.* Oxford: Oxford University Press.

Hicks, Ursula K. 1978. *Federalism, Failure and Success: A Comparative Study.* London: Macmillan.

Hirschman, Albert O. 1970. *Exit, Voice, and Loyalty: Responses to Decline in Firms, Organizations, and States.* Cambridge, Mass.: Harvard University Press.

Horowitz, Donald L. 1985. *Ethnic Groups in Conflict.* Berkeley: University of California Press.

Jabar, Faleh A. 2003. *The Shi'ite Movement in Iraq.* London: Al Saqi Books.

Keating, Michael. 2001. "Managing the Multinational State: Constitutional Settlement in the United Kingdom." In *The Dynamics of Decentralization: Canadian Federalism and British Devolution,* ed. Michael Keating and Trevor C. Salmon. Montreal: McGill-Queen's University Press.

King, Preston. 2001. *Federalism and Federation.* 2nd ed. London: Frank Cass.

Knowlton, Brian. 2003. "U.S. Aid Offer Prods Turkey on Troops for Iraq."*International Herald Tribune,* 10 September, 3.

Kurdistan Democratic Party. 1992. Draft Constitution of the Federal Republic of Iraq. Draft Constitution of the Federal Republic of Iraq Erbil Kurdistan National Assembly. <http://www.krg.org/docs/Federal_Const.asp>

Kurdistan National Assembly. Kurdistan Region's Constitutional Proposal (Special Provisions for the Kurdistan Region of Iraq) Patriotic Union of Kurdistan website, 2004 (cited February 19 2004). <http://www.puk.org/web/htm/news/nws/krg040220.html.>

Lijphart, Arend. 1977. *Democracy in Plural Societies: A Comparative Exploration*. New Haven, Conn.: Yale University Press.

———. 1979. "Consociation and Federation: Conceptual and Empirical Links." *Canadian Journal of Political Science* 12 (3): 495–515.

———. 1996. "The Puzzle of Indian Democracy: A Consociational Interpretation." *American Political Science Review* 90 (2): 258–68.

———. 2004. "Constitutional Design for Divided Societies." Journal of Democracy 15 (2) (April): 96–109.

Madison, James, Alexander Hamilton, and John Jay. 1987 (1788). *The Federalist Papers*, ed. Isaac Kramnick. Penguin Classics. Harmondsworth: Penguin.

Makiya, Kanan. 2003. "A Model for Post-Saddam Iraq." *Journal of Democracy* 14 (3): 5–12.

McGarry, John and Brendan O'Leary. 2003. "Federation, Conflict-Regulation, and National and Ethnic Power-Sharing." Paper presented at the Annual Conference of the American Political Science Association, Philadelphia, 29 September.

Nagel, Jack H. 2000. "Expanding the Spectrum of *Democracies:* Reflections on Proportional Representation in New Zealand." In *Democracy and Institutions: The Life Work of Arend Lijphart*, ed. Markus M. L. Crepaz, Thomas A. Koelble, and David Wilsford. Ann Arbor: University of Michigan Press. 113–27.

O'Leary, Brendan. 2001. "An Iron Law of Federations? A (neo-Diceyian) theory of the Necessity of a Federal Staatsvolk, and of Consociational Rescue." Fifth Ernest Gellner Memorial Lecture. *Nations and Nationalism* 7 (3): 273–96.

———. 2003a. "Consociation: Refining the Theory and a Defence." *International Journal of Diversity in Organisations, Communities and Nations* 3: 693–755. <http://www.DiversityConference.Publisher-Site.com>

———. 2003b. "The Kurds Must Not Be Betrayed Again." *Financial Times*, 24 March, 23.

———. 2003c. "Multi-National Federalism, Power-Sharing, Federacy, and the Kurds of Iraq." Paper presented at Conference on Multi-Nationalism, Power-Sharing, and the Kurds in a New Iraq, Cafritz Foundation Conference Center, George Washington University Washington, D.C., 12 September. <http://www.krg.org/docs/federalism/federalism-iraqi-kurds-paper-sep03.pdf>

———. 2004a. "The U.S. Is Brewing Up a Disaster for the Kurds." *Los Angeles Times*, February.

———. 2004b. "A Transitional Law Worth Fighting For." *Financial Times*, 11 April.

O'Leary, Brendan, Bernard Grofman, and Jorgen Elklit. 2005. "Divisor Methods for Sequential Portfolio Allocation in Multi-Party Executive Bodies: Evidence from Northern Ireland and Denmark." *American Journal of Political Science* 49 (1) (January): 184–97.

Rezvani, David R. 2003. "Federacy: The Dynamics of Semi-Sovereign Territories." Unpublished manuscript.

Riker, William H. 1957. "Dutch and American Federalism." *Journal of the History of Ideas* 18: 495–521. Reprinted in *The Development of American Federalism*. Dordrecht: Kluwer, 1987. 43–67.

———. 1964. *Federalism: Origin, Operation, Significance*. Boston: Little, Brown.

————. 1975. "Federalism." In *Handbook of Political Science*, ed. Fred I. Greenstein and Nelson W. Polsby. Reading, Mass.: Addison-Wesley. 93–172.

Rodinson, Maxime. 2002. *Muhammed: Prophet of Islam*. New York: Tauris Parke.

Salih, Khaled. 2004. "Kurdish Reality in an Emerging Iraq." *Middle East Policy* 11 (1) (Spring): 122–26.

Smith, Rogers M. 2003. *Stories of Peoplehood: The Politics and Morals of Political Membership*. Cambridge: Cambridge University Press.

Smyth, Frank. 2003. "Saddam's Real Opponents." In *The Iraq War Reader: History, Documents, Opinions*, ed. Micah L. Sifry and Christopher Cerf. New York: Simon and Schuster. 565–67.

Snyder, Jack. 2000. *From Voting to Violence: Democratization and Nationalist Conflict*. New York: W.W. Norton.

Soroush, Abdolkarim. 2002. *Reason, Freedom and Democracy in Islam*. Oxford: Oxford University Press.

Stepan, Alfred. 1998. "Modern Multinational Democracies: Transcending a Gellnerian Oxymoron." In *The State of the Nation: Ernest Gellner and the Theory of Nationalism*, ed. John A. Hall. New York: Cambridge University Press. 219–42.

————. 1999. "Federalism and Democracy: Beyond the U.S. Model." *Journal of Democracy* 10 (4): 19–34.

Watts, Ronald L. 1971. "The Survival or Disintegration of Federations." In *Options for a New Canada*, ed. Ronald L. Watts and Douglas M. Brown. Toronto: University of Toronto Press. 15–30.

————. 1996. *Comparing Federal Systems in the 1990s*. Kingston, Ont.: Institute of Intergovernmental Relations/Queen's University.

————. 1998. "Federalism, Federal Political Systems, and Federations." *Annual Review of Political Science* 1: 117–37.

————. 2001. "Models of Federal Power-Sharing." *International Social Science Journal* (March): 23–32.

Wheare, Kenneth. 1966. *Modern Constitutions*. New York: Oxford University Press.

Wimmer, Andreas. 2003–4. "Democracy and Ethno-Religious Conflict in Iraq." *Survival* 45 (4): 111–34.

Yavuz, M. Hakan. 2004. "*Provincial* not *Ethnic* Federalism in Iraq." *Middle East Policy* 11 (1) (Spring): 126–31.

Zines, Leslie. 1991. *Constitutional Change in the Commonwealth: The Commonwealth lectures Delivered at the University of Cambridge on 8, 15, and 22 November 1988*. Cambridge: Cambridge University Press.

Chapter 3
Canadian Lessons for Iraq

John McGarry

The view that Iraq should be structured as a federation, which enjoys the status of a norm among the American and British occupation authorities, and has significant support within Iraq, should be welcomed. It indicates a desire to move beyond the authoritarian, centralized Ba'thist regime that oppressed all Iraqis, and particularly the Kurdish and Shi'a communities. The consensus, however, masks a deep dissensus over the form that a federation should take. Iraq's future stability hinges on the outcome of this debate.

A common view among American (and American-educated or U.S.-based) academics is that Iraq and countries like it should have federations based on the U.S. model, which is seen as promoting nation-building, stability, and unity. The U.S. federation has a very strong federal government and an electoral college which requires successful candidates for the presidency to have broad-based regional support. Crucially, its internal state boundaries were purposely drawn to deny self-government to national or ethnic minorities. In contemporary jargon, they were "territorial" or "administrative" in nature (McGarry and O'Leary 2003). Americans support this model because of its success in their own country, which has survived intact for more than two centuries despite a bloody civil war and which has welded unity out of diversity—*e pluribus unum*. This endorsement has been reinforced by the failure of federations that have deviated from the U.S. model. Several prominent American academics point to the disintegration of the Soviet Union, Yugoslavia, and Czechoslovakia as flowing primarily from the fact that all three were pluri-national federations; their constituent units were dominated by national communities that took advantage of democratization in the early 1990s to break up the federations (Brubaker 1996; Bunce 1999; Leff 1998; Roeder 1991; Snyder 2000).[1] Even Daniel Elazar, the late doyen of federal studies, who argued that federalism could be used to promote peace between different communities, was skeptical that a pluri-national *federation* would work. In his view, confederation was a more feasible option for power-sharing among national communities (Elazar 1994, 167–69).

American-style federalism is sold not only for its allegedly centripetal effects but also because of its liberty-protecting qualities. The separation of powers among the executive, legislative, and judicial branches of the federal government is viewed as a barrier against the abuse of power. So is the division of powers between the federal and state levels, as long as the states are not controlled by ethnic or national factions. Pluri-national federalism, by contrast, is seen as harmful to liberty, because it entrusts power to ethnic groups and their ethnocentric elites. Seymour Martin Lipset argued that minority nationalists were involved in a "revolt against modernity," while Elazar thought that they tended "to subordinate all free government to [their] uncompromising position" (Lipset 1985; Elazar 1994, 128–29, 163–64). Eric Nordlinger, while supportive of the accommodation of minorities through power-sharing, rejected territorial autonomy on the grounds that it would allow the region's "dominant segment to ignore or negate the demands of the minority segment" (Nordlinger 1972, 21–32). In a recent article on Iraq, Andreas Wimmer worried that "federalisation may heighten, rather than reduce the risks of gross human rights violations, especially for members of ethnic minorities living under the rule of the majority government in a federal unit" (Wimmer 2003, 123). The popularity of such arguments in the United States may be related not just to the success of the American model but also to its historic pathologies. The American civil war, which cost half a million lives, followed a prolonged and profound political polarization between one section founded on slavery and another based on "free soil, free labor, and free men." The then federal structure did not resolve, but rather exacerbated, this conflict. And, although the civil war destroyed slavery and brought the South back into the Union, the federal structure of the U.S. government allowed the South to reimpose and enforce white supremacy for a century after Emancipation.

The problem with proposing a U.S.-style federation for Iraq is that the two countries are very different in vital respects. The United States, while ethnically diverse, is nationally homogeneous. Neither its immigrant-based ethnic minorities nor its sizable African American minority have a significant sense of themselves as separate peoples or nations who are entitled to political self-government. Iraq, by contrast, is nationally heterogeneous. It has a large minority, the Kurds, which is territorially concentrated in its ancestral homeland, possesses a distinct culture, including a distinct language, and sees itself as a nation entitled to self-determination. A more appropriate analogue for Iraq is Canada, the United States northern neighbor.

In Canada, the Québécois, like the Kurds of Iraq, around one fifth of the state's population, consider themselves a distinct nation with their own culture.[2] With a different demographic profile from the United States, Canada has a different type of federation: it is more decentralized than the United States; one of its provinces is dominated by the Québécois; and by convention, Québec's politicians are proportionately represented within the federal government. In spite of these arrangements, Canada is, like the United States, one of the longest surviving states in the world. It has been in existence since the United States fought its disastrous civil war, and has had no similar experience. Québec has not been a site for the promotion of ethnic chauvinism. Its respect for human rights and civic inclusiveness is comparable to that of the leading liberal democracies.

Surprisingly, given the proximity of Canada and the United States, the Canadian experience of federation is virtually invisible to the American academy, including those who make recommendations for Iraq. If it is mentioned at all, it is considered as something to avoid because of the erroneous presumption that Canada is on the verge of dissolution. This chapter proceeds by discussing three broad lessons from Canada that should be considered in Iraq: (1) lessons for self-government; (2) lessons for shared government; and (3) lessons for human rights protection.

Lessons for Self-Government

There are two questions here: who is the self that should enjoy self-government, and what should be the scope of self-government? The answer to the first question from those who take their cue from the United States is that the self should be territorial or administrative communities, and not ethnic or ethnoreligious groups. Brancati suggests that internal borders in Iraq should be "drawn *across* ethnic and religious lines" (Brancati 2004). Wimmer argues that "the current situation in Iraq provides an opportunity to introduce a non-ethnic federalism" (Wimmer 2003, 124). A spokesman for the American-backed Iraqi National Congress stresses that "the important point is that it must be administrative federalism rather than ethnic federalism" (*International Herald Tribune* 2003; see also Makiya 2002). In practice, it would be virtually impossible to create federal units in Iraq that were not dominated by one ethnic community or another, particularly Arabs, or by one ethnoreligious community or another, particularly Shi'a. So, what opponents of ethnic federalism appear to be against is a federation that is centered on ethnicity or religiosity—that is, a federation that is based on three units, representing the Kurds,

Shi'a Arabs, and Sunni Arabs, respectively; a federation of two units, Kurds and Arabs; or a federation that gives any of these communities its own single constituent unit. For opponents of ethnic federalism, the most frequently proposed form of federation is based on the 18 governorates, or administrative provinces, of Saddam's Iraq (*International Herald Tribune* 2003; Dawisha and Dawisha 2002; Brancati 2004; Walen 2003). This would have the effect of dividing Kurds, as well as Shi'a and Sunnis, into a number of different administrative units.[3] In the minds of its supporters, this division would make it more difficult for Kurds to secede. It would also, supposedly, bring advantages familiar to readers of James Madison's *Federalist 10*: it would open up intra-Kurdish (as well as intra-Shi'a and intra-Sunni) divisions; facilitate the construction of interethnic and cross-cutting alliances; increase the prospects for shifting coalitions; and strengthen Iraqi nation-building at the expense of Kurdish nation-building (Madison et al. 1788).[4]

The Kurds, on the other hand, would prefer independence, which is hardly surprising, given the way they were treated by the Ba'thist regime and the relative security and prosperity they have enjoyed since 1991. Since this is not feasible, they have proposed instead that Iraq be organized as a loose bi-national federation, with one Kurdish and one Arab unit (Kurdistan Democratic Party 1992). The Kurds have rejected the partition of Kurdistan, notwithstanding well known intra-Kurdish divisions, which critics of ethnic federalism point to as evidence for the feasibility of an 18-province federation (Wimmer 2003, 124). The Kurdish position is that such divisions, consistent with self-determination principles, should be managed within Kurdistan, by decentralization or power-sharing.

Canada's federation is an outcome more of history and democracy than of purposive constitutional design. Nevertheless, one of its ten provinces, Québec, has a dominant francophone majority, which comprises the bulk of Canada's francophones. If applied to Iraq, the Canadian model would suggest a single federal unit including most Kurds and in which Kurds form a strong majority. Québec has been a separate administrative unit since 1791, just four years after the convention at Philadelphia that gave rise to the American federation, although it was temporarily united with Ontario between 1841 and 1867. Self-government for Québec has not led to the break-up of Canada, as supporters of the U.S. model of federation might expect, although there has been a strong separatist movement in the province, currently in retreat.[5] No serious Canadian academic or politician believes that Canada's stability or unity would be strengthened if Québec were partitioned into a number of provinces. If such an approach was broached, most would regard it as destabilizing and utterly counterproductive. Québec's partition has occasionally been mooted in

Figure 3.1. Canada's provinces and territories. The territories are the Yukon Territory, Northwest Territories, and Nunavut. They enjoy powers of self-government, but do not have the same constitutional status as provinces.

the context of the province's secession from Canada, the idea being that areas of the province inhabited by natives or anglophones should be allowed to stay part of Canada (Reid 1992). When this has been suggested, it has produced a visceral reaction from Québec's leaders, both federalist and separatist, who consider all of Québec as their national homeland, including areas in which the francophone presence is weak (*Toronto Star* 1997).

The fact that Québec is largely francophone has not led the predominantly English-speaking remainder of Canada to constitute itself as a single federal unit. Instead, "English Canada" comprises nine provinces, which reflect distinct regional and historical communities. Since English-speaking Canadians (like Americans) see the federal government as their national government and defender of their culture, they have not needed an alternative site for collective self-government.[6] As the overwhelming majority of Canada's population, English-speaking Canadians have tended to reject the idea of parity that is implicit in the concept of a two-unit federation, or confederation, when ideas of this sort have been suggested by Québec nationalists. One advantage of Canada's combination of ethnonational federalism (for Québec) and territorial federalism (for the rest of Canada) is that it has helped Canada to avoid the problems associated with dyadic (two-unit) federations, such as pre-1971 Pakistan, Czechoslovakia, or Serbia and Montenegro. As there is little opportunity for shifting alliances in such federations, issues are more likely to be zero-sum in nature, and politics more difficult (Watts 1999, 112–14). Two of these three have broken up, and the other appears likely to do so. In Canada, issues have often pitted Québec against the rest of the country, particularly when the instrument of a state-wide referendum has been used to settle a divisive issue. However, the fact that English-speaking Canada comprises a number of provinces has mitigated this difficulty by providing opportunities for cross-cutting and unifying alliances, particularly between Ontario and Québec, Canada's first and second most populous provinces respectively.[7] From the Western Canadian perspective, in fact, Canada is divided at least as much along an axis between Western Canada and Québec-Ontario as it is along an ethnic or linguistic axis.[8]

What evidence is available from Iraq suggests that a federation structured like Canada's would be more likely to secure agreement, and more in keeping with self-determination principles, than one that divides the Kurdish homeland into several units, or the Kurds' preferred model of a two-unit federation of Kurdistan and "Arabistan." The Canadian model would allow Kurdistan to continue to be governed as a single national unit, as its leaders and people want. Any partition of this region by non-Kurds would have to be imposed by the U.S.-led Coalition. This appears unlikely, since the Kurds were key military allies of the U.S. in the overthrow of Saddam. The U.S. also announced in January 2004 that Kurdistan would be allowed to continue as an autonomous region after power in Iraq is transferred to a sovereign transitional government in July of that year (*New York Times* 2004a). As Brendan O'Leary has shown in chapter two, Kurdistan is now recognized in the Transitional Administrative Law, or interim constitution.

If Kurdistan is allowed to keep its region intact after the transitional period, it does not follow that Arab Iraq should also comprise a single province. How Arab Iraq constitutes itself should be a matter for Arabs in Iraq to decide. It is less clear what their preferences are than those of Kurds, but there is unlikely to be a sizable Arab constituency in support of the Kurdish proposal for a two-unit federation. First, Arab Iraq is regionally and, even more saliently, religiously divided. Second, there are Arab Iraqi nationalists who, like Canadian nationalists, identify with the whole county (Iraq), and not just with part of it (Arab Iraq). These Iraqi nationalists, who include the supporters of a territorial federation in Iraq, are likely to think that their need for self-determination can be satisfied by Iraq's central government, rather than by a government in Arab Iraq. Third, Arab Iraqis will almost certainly balk at the notion of parity implicit in the Kurdish proposal for a two-unit federation—that is, the suggestion that a unit containing eighty percent of Iraq's population is equal to one containing twenty percent (to use one set of plausible demographic estimates). All of these factors favor the division of Arab Iraq into multiple provinces. Ironically, this proposal, by providing for the possibility of cross-cutting alliances between Kurds and distinct elements of the Arab majority, may be more in the interest of Arabs, and more conducive to Iraq's stability, than a two-unit federation of Kurdistan and "Arabistan."

Boundary issues aside, the preference of some American academics is for a relatively centralized federation. Byman criticizes federalism for Iraq because he thinks it would produce a weak central government that would have difficulty maintaining order or state unity (Byman 2003, 56–57, 65–66). Others are more supportive of federalism but, sharing Byman's concerns, insist that the federal government should be paramount. Walen writes that the "national" [sic] government should remain "strong" (Walen 2003). Adeed Dawisha and Karen Dawisha argue that Iraq's federal government "must" have control over all strategic assets, including petroleum (Dawisha and Dawisha 2003, 38). The comparative evidence indicates, however, that pluri-national federations like Canada are less centralized than nationally homogeneous federations like the United States. If federal government revenues as a share of total governmental revenues are used as a measurement of relative centralization, Canada and Switzerland (48 percent and 45 percent, respectively) emerge as the world's most decentralized federations, while the United States, Australia, Austria, and Germany (66, 69, 73, and 64 percent respectively), all mono-national federations, are much more centralized (Watts 1999, 46).[9] The reasons are straightforward. In mono-national federations, there is trust in the federal government to act impartially on behalf of all citizens. There is also no contradiction between a relatively strong central government and the principle of national self-determination. The federal government, because it can claim to speak and act on behalf of the whole nation, may have greater legitimacy than regional governments. In pluri-national federations, minority nations are less likely to trust the federal government, as they will have at best a minority presence in it. They are also likely to seek a substantial degree of power for their own units, in keeping with the principle of self-determination.

Given the low levels of trust that exist within Iraq, particularly between Kurds and Arabs, and the Kurdish desire for self-rule, the prospects for agreement on a centralized federation must be considered low. What might a functioning decentralized federation look like? To begin with, it will allocate powers that are traditionally seen as provincial, such as education, health care, culture, and local government, to Iraq's provinces. However, provinces within some pluri-national federations have been pushing beyond these traditional jurisdictions, into areas that, in mono-national federations, lie securely under federal control. It would be surprising if the Kurds did not push in this direction also. The Canadian provinces of Québec and New Brunswick (which has a sizable francophone minority) both have seats in La Francophonie, the French-speaking equivalent of the Commonwealth, while Québec and other Canadian provinces engage in "para-diplomacy," operating trade missions and consulates in New York, Paris, and London. Belgium allows its constituent units a role in formulating Belgium's European Union policy when this affects the jurisdiction of its units, and the recent UN plan for Cyprus envisaged a similar role for its constituent parts. Bosnia-Hercegovina's two entities, the Federation of Bosnia and Hercegovina and Republika Srpska, have powers under the Dayton Accords to make external agreements. They have used these to conclude treaties with Croatia and Serbia respectively. A role for a federation's constituent units in defense is less common, but not unprecedented. Bosnia-Hercegovina's two entities control their own armies, and other self-governing units control their own militias and paramilitary police forces. This practice is likely to appeal to the Kurds of Iraq, at least as a transitional measure until mutual confidence across communities has been built up. Iraqi Arabs should note that eight years after the Dayton Accords, Bosnia's two federal units have begun to integrate their armies' command structures, so a generous stance at the outset need not have centrifugal effects (*Economist* 2003, 74).

Contrary to the Dawishas' claim that "as in other federal states, . . . Iraq's petroleum must remain in the hands of the central government" (Dawisha and Dawisha 2003, 38), in some cases oil is under the jurisdictional control of a federation's constituent units. In Canada, it is the provinces that own natural resources including, in Alberta's case, oil. In practice, the management and control of oil is a shared matter, as the Canadian federal government is responsible for regulating interprovincial and international commerce. Alberta's ownership of oil has not meant that only it benefits from the resource. Canada has an equalization program, agreed between the federal and provincial governments and entrenched in the constitution, which provides for the sharing of wealth across the federation. In the case of Iraq, giving the Kurds control of oil resources in their territory could be married to a similar redistributive program.

Ensuring that Iraq's regions have adequate jurisdictional powers will not be enough to guarantee regional autonomy. For this to occur, the regions will also have to secure an adequate revenue base. Without this, they will have the impression of power but not the substance. Even in Canada, where many of the provinces do have substantial fiscal resources at their disposal, the Canadian federal government has been able to influence priorities within provincial areas of jurisdiction, such as health care, by offering funds to the provinces in exchange for the adoption of federal policies. Canada's provinces, particularly Québec, have responded by demanding that federal funds be provided unconditionally, or that the provinces be able to opt out of federal programs in provincial areas of jurisdiction while receiving monetary compensation. For those regions in Iraq which have sufficiently robust economic bases, it will be enough to ensure that the regions have adequate taxing powers. Alternatively, all of Iraq's regions could insist on unconditional block grants from Iraq's federal government, fixed on a per capita basis.

An issue that Iraq's constitution-makers will have to confront when considering the division of powers is the degree of symmetry or asymmetry in the federation. The American model is one of a symmetrical federation in which all fifty states of the Union enjoy the same jurisdiction. In pluri-national federations, however, units that are controlled by minority nations usually seek asymmetrical arrangements, and most pluri-national federations have allowed some degree of asymmetry (Watts forthcoming, 12). The demand for asymmetry is often a question of status as much as functionality: minority nations tend to resist the idea that their nation's unit is the equivalent of *one* of the majority nation's provincial units, and seek to promote the notion of the state as a pluri-national partnership rather than a multi-provincial partnership. This vision is implicit in the Kurds' preference for a dyadic federation, with one Kurdish and one Arab unit. The difficulty is that such demands are likely to be resisted by the majority in the rest of the federation, which may fear that a special status for the minority's unit, which highlights its position as the homeland of a separate people, will facilitate secessionism (see McGarry 2002, 434–35). One technique for dealing with a minority's desire for asymmetry, without compromising the principle of provincial equality, is to offer more power to all provinces, with the expectation that only the minority's will take this up. In Canada, this approach has resulted in Québec being the only province to have its own pension plan and collect its own income taxes (Watts 1999, 67). Provisions in the failed Meech Lake and Charlottetown constitutional proposals (1987–1992) would have allowed provinces to opt out of statewide social programs (for which federal and provincial governments shared the costs), while retaining federal funds, as long as they established their own programs that met certain federation-wide objectives.

This pragmatic approach, whereby a formal constitutional symmetry is maintained, has not resolved the issue in public debate. The unwillingness of English Canada to accept Québec federalists' wish that Québec be recognized as a "distinct society" in the Constitution, and that Canada be seen as a partnership between two peoples has often undermined these federalists and strengthened Québec's secessionists. The failure of the Meech Lake Accord in 1990, which would have offered such recognition, resulted in unprecedented levels of support for secession and, five years later, in a referendum that almost led to the dissolution of the country. Canada's experience suggests that plurinational federations should not seek to emulate nationally homogeneous federations by treating symmetry as a cardinal value.[10]

Lessons for Shared Government

When pluri-national federalism is defended as a method of conflict regulation, the emphasis is usually on how it can provide minorities with guaranteed powers of territorial self-government. Sometimes it is also argued that a virtue of federalism is that it avoids the "winner takes all" outcome associated with Westminster-type regimes: a group that is excluded at the center may be able to console itself with regional power. Thus, Hanf argues that "federalism reduces conflict by allowing those political forces excluded from power at the top the opportunity to exercise regional power" (Hanf 1991, 43). However, this emphasis on *self*-rule downplays the fact that federalism is also about *shared* rule and that even decentralized federations normally entrust some important powers to the federal level. A federation that fails to provide for a minority role in the federal government is likely to be unstable, or to fall apart. There is evidence that the absence of such a role contributed to the failure of several pluri-national federations, including the former communist federations of the Soviet Union and Yugoslavia, the federation of the West Indies, the first Nigerian republic, and the federation of Nyasaland, Southern Rhodesia, and Northern Rhodesia (see McGarry and O'Leary 2003). This evidence is not considered by critics of pluri-national federations, who prefer to see them as unstable and centrifugal because they give *too much* power to minority representatives.

Some American academics have stressed the need for inclusive government at the federal level, but argue this can be provided through the U.S. model, or mild variations of it. The institution of the presidency is regularly touted as one that can and should stand above faction, providing a unifying effect. It is said to promote state-wide parties over regional parties, as only candidates from the former have a realistic prospect of winning office (Brancati 2004, 18). Donald L. Horowitz, an American political scientist and lawyer who has studied divided societies in depth, does not assume that a president will automatically rise above faction to represent the whole nation. Rather, he argues that this is only likely to happen if it is a requirement for winning office. To achieve this, he generally proposes a variation on the U.S. electoral college, which requires winning candidates to achieve broad support across several states, rather than piling up huge majorities in a small number. In his view, electoral systems in divided societies should require winning candidates to win votes throughout the country's *ethnic* regions, and not just a plurality or majority overall (Horowitz 1991, 177–83). Horowitz's ideas have recently been recommended for Iraq by Wimmer (Wimmer 2003, 122; see also Brancati 2004, 17; Byman and Pollack 2003, 128–29). Alternatively, Philip Roeder focuses on the American separation-of-powers doctrine as the key to inclusivity and power-sharing (Roeder forthcoming). The facts that federal power is separated into three distinct (executive, legislative, and judicial) branches, that elections and appointments for the three branches are staggered, and that elections for the presidency and each chamber of Congress are based on different constituencies erect safeguards, in his view, against a monopolization of power by a particular constellation of interests (also see PILPG 2003, 40).

There are limits to all of these purported benefits of the U.S. model. The chief danger with a conventional presidential executive in a divided society is that the winning candidate may represent only his or her own group, and not the whole "nation." This problem occurred in Sri Lanka, Sudan, and in Rwanda before the 1994 genocide. Horowitz's proposal attempts to deal with this, but even if a president were to be elected in Iraq according to the distribution requirements he suggests, with some support from all groups, the president is nonetheless more likely to come from the larger groups, Arabs or Shi'a. Such politicians are more likely to satisfy the plurality or majority and distribution criteria than politicians from minority communities. It is also not clear why the current leaders of Iraq's different communities would consent to an arrangement that would exclude them from executive power, or that would give them the prospect of power only if they reconstructed themselves as politicians with inter-ethnic appeal. Horowitz's model runs the risk that if no candidate meets the distribution requirement—that is, if voters are not prepared to vote across ethnic lines in sufficient numbers—the country would end up with no executive. This almost happened in Nigeria, where a version of this model was adopted in 1979. A president was elected only because Nigeria's

Supreme Court intervened to declare that the leading candidate had satisfied the distributional criterion, when he plainly had not. These problems help explain why Horowitz's ideas have hardly ever been tried, and why they are unlikely to be tried in Iraq.

The purported advantages of the separation of powers doctrine depend on no single group being able to comprise a majority of the electorate, particularly a permanent one. Where such a majority exists, the separation of powers model may not look that different in practice from the fusion of powers associated with the Westminster model: it may deliver majority rule in all three branches of government. Even when no single group is in a majority position, the benefits of the separation of powers model require *shifting* coalitions, with no single community excluded over the long term. If this is to work, group boundaries must be permeable, or the distance and proximity among all groups must be more or less equal. The problem is that neither of these conditions is likely to exist in Iraq for the foreseeable future. The Shiʻa may come to constitute a political majority in their own right, and even if they do not, the divisions among Shiʻa, or among Arabs, are likely to be less prominent than those between Arabs and Kurds. Even if matters do not transpire this way, the possibility that they might should be enough to frighten Kurds, and possibly Sunnis, away from the separation of powers model.[11]

An alternative to these variations on the American model is the Canadian practice of power-sharing among the leaders of different ethnic and national communities. This practice goes back to the union of the two provinces of Upper and Lower Canada (Ontario and Québec) between 1841 and 1867, when it was, arguably, at its most extensive. Conceived of by the British imperial authorities, and by some anglophones, as an arrangement that would provide for the suppression of francophones, the United Canadas developed an elaborate, albeit informal, "consociational" politics (Noel 1990). Each government was a bi-ethnic coalition headed by dual premiers, one from each language community. The executive as a whole required the confidence of both the English and French sections of the legislature. The passage of legislation also required concurrent majorities. When it became increasingly difficult for the government to secure such majorities, the union was dissolved into Ontario and Québec in 1867. The two then joined with the provinces of Nova Scotia and New Brunswick to form the new federation of Canada.

The Ontario anglophones who had first conceived of federation saw it as a mechanism for dominating francophones at the federal level of government. This thinking was based on the Westminster model, according to which the party or parties that commanded a majority in the legislature comprised all of the executive. In spite of this, the Canadian federal government quickly developed many of the characteristics of consociational power-sharing that had marked the union of 1841–1867. Even though single-party governments have been the norm, the executive has continued to be broadly representative of both language communities. By the latter part of the twentieth century, it had become customary for the prime minister to be bilingual. Indeed, for thirty-four of the past thirty-six years, the prime minister has come from Québec, a response, in part, to the threat of Québec separatism.[12] It is likely that this has played an important role in maintaining Canadian unity. As a leading Québec journalist wrote recently, sovereigntists "openly pray" for the day when federal parties are no longer led by a Québec leader and when the prime minister has to defend Canada in Québec through a translator (Hebert 2003). A rough proportionality within the executive is mirrored by proportionality in the federal bureaucracy and formal proportionality within the Supreme Court. Under the Supreme Court Act of 1949, three of the court's nine justices must be from Québec.

These measures, which help to ensure that the federal institutions are representative of francophones, are complemented by formal requirements that the federal legislature, courts, and bureaucracy operate in both English and French. Indeed, as part of Canada's Charter of Rights and Freedoms, Canadian citizens are entitled to federal government services in either English or French, irrespective of where they live, where numbers warrant. This includes the right of members of both linguistic communities to be educated in their mother tongue. Beyond this, the federal government provides public broadcasting (television and radio) throughout the country in both official languages, offers financial support to artists and academics in both communities, and mandates that all goods sold in Canada carry bilingual labels.

Canada's power-sharing practices have clear attractions for Iraq's Kurdish and Sunni Arab leaders in particular. Critics of consociationalism in Iraq argue that it would threaten Iraq's unity because it would hand power to ethnocentric elites (Wimmer 2003, 122), but it seems more plausible to argue that it would have centripetal effects, as it would give minority leaders a stake in the center and protect their interests. Some details of the Canadian model are likely to raise legitimate concerns among Iraq's minorities, however. As in its Swiss and Indian counterparts, important aspects of Canadian power-sharing are informal. There are no legal or constitutional requirements that Québec or francophone politicians be included in the federal government. Indeed, Canada's main opposition party, the Conservatives, currently has no seats in Quebec and it would be possible for it to become the government of Canada without winning any. Second, the federal government has not always represented majority or plurality opinion in Québec (or among Québec's francophones). Since 1993, the biggest party in Québec at the federal level has been the separatist Bloc Québécois, but Québec's representatives in the federal government have been from the governing Liberal Party of Canada. Third, Québec's politicians, whether at the federal or provincial levels, have no formal role in shaping or vetoing federal legislation. Canada's upper legislative chamber, the Senate, which might be expected to represent the federation's units in the legislative process, is appointed by the federal government. Lacking democratic legitimacy or an alternative political base in the provinces, it has not been willing to challenge the House of Commons legislative agenda.

Because Iraq lacks Canada's culture of cooperation and associated levels of trust, the Kurds, and possibly the Sunni Arabs, are likely to want something different from Canada's informal and limited consociational practices. They will probably insist on a form of power-sharing that is formally guaranteed, represents a broad swath of minority opinion, and gives minority leaders a key role in the legislature as well as the executive. For such arrangements, they will have to look beyond Canada, to Belgium, Bosnia-Hercegovina, and Northern Ireland, or to the recent UN plan for Cyprus. Each of these cases formally provides for power-sharing in the executive. The Belgian federal cabinet must be composed of an equal number of French- and Flemish-speakers. Under the Dayton Accords, Bosnia-Hercegovina's government is presided over by a rotating presidency, based on one Bosniac and one Croat from the Federation of Bosnia-Hercegovina, and one Serb from Republika Srpska. In Northern Ireland, under the Good Friday Agreement, there is a First and Deputy First Minister, who are elected as a team by a concurrent majority of nationalist and unionist Assembly members, and a ten-member cabinet that is allocated sequentially among the parties in proportion to their share of seats in the legislature. The UN plan for Cyprus provided for a Presidential Council of six members, with at least two from each of its Turkish and Greek constituent units. The presidency and vice-presidency would rotate among its members. The likelihood that Iraqis will agree on formal consociational institutions is reasonably high. The interim twenty-five-member governing council provides a template. It is comprised of thirteen Shi'a Arabs, five Sunni Arabs, five Sunni Kurds, one Turkomen, and one Christian. The presidency rotates monthly among nine of the members.[13]

As these examples suggest, there is seldom a consensus in favor of an American-style single person presidency in divided societies. When presidential models have been chosen in these cases, they have been collective in nature. Switzerland, historically a divided society, has married a formal seven-person Federal Council to informal consociational practices. Lebanon has a single-person presidency, but this is part of a hybrid presidential-parliamentary system in which most executive power since 1989 has been held by the prime minister. In April 2004 it seemed that the UN mediator, Brahimi, would propose a hybrid executive for the transition foreshadowed in the TAL: a prime minister and a three-person presidential council (a president and two vice-presidents).

There are also several cases where a minority has been given a formal veto over legislation. In Bosnia-Hercegovina, laws can be vetoed in either chamber by two thirds of the representatives from either constituent unit. If a law is declared to be destructive of a vital interest of the Bosniac, Croat, or Serb communities by a majority of that community's representatives in the upper chamber, a concurrent majority of the three groups' representatives is needed to pass it. In Northern Ireland, stipulated key measures require the support of 60 percent of the Assembly, including at least 40 percent of nationalist and unionists respectively. Belgium's constitution describes a range of laws for which a special majority is needed: two thirds of the total votes, including a majority of the Flemish- and French-speaking members, in each of the two legislative chambers.[14] The UN plan for Cyprus proposed that decisions of its legislature should require the approval of both chambers by simple majority, including one quarter of voting senators from each of its two Greek and Turkish constituent units. Special matters should require the support of two fifths of senators from each unit. Northern Ireland's Agreement and the UN plan for Cyprus provide additional formal, albeit indirect, ways in which minorities can be protected from legislation offensive to their interests. They both envisage bills of rights that would impose limits on the legislature. This form of indirect protection requires an impartial and activist judiciary.

Not all of these power-sharing alternatives are equally desirable. Some of them predetermine the beneficiaries of the protections: they name the identity groups that are to be protected in advance of elections. This privileges some groups over others, or over those who do not identify with groups, and it arguably helps to entrench group identities. Thus, Bosnia's rules for executive composition discriminate against ethnic communities other than Bosniacs and Croats in the Federation of Bosnia and Hercegovina, and other than Serbs in Republika Srspka, as well as against those who prefer nonethnic identities. They create an incentive for people to vote for Bosniac, Croat, or Serb politicians, as these politicians have more institutional clout than other ethnic or non-ethnic politicians. Such rules are offensive to liberal critics of consociational power-sharing arrangements, who cite them as reasons to avoid group-based power sharing in favor of the difference-blind protections offered by the American system. The rules also do not provide the flexibility that may be needed to address demographic change. If the French-speaking (Walloon) share of the Belgian population declined precipitously, it would give rise to problems because French-speakers have constitutionally guaranteed parity in cabinet. The difficulties that can occur can be seen from the case of Lebanon, where Maronite Christians were entitled under the 1943 National Pact to the presidency, the most important executive office, while Christians were guaranteed a majority of seats in the legislature. The steady growth of the Muslim population destabilized this arrangement and helped to foment a civil war in 1975. The issue was dealt with by the Ta'if Accords in 1989, which transferred most executive power to the Sunni prime minister and established parity in the legislature between Muslims and Christians.[15] This solution is far from perfect, however, as the guarantee of parity continues to provide disproportional representation to Christians, and this will become more obvious if Christian numbers continue to decline.

It is possible, however, to entrench the practice of power-sharing without predetermining the beneficiaries, or significantly overrepresenting minorities. While Northern Ireland's First and Deputy First Ministerships are effectively guaranteed to nationalists and unionists, its other ten cabinet positions are allocated according to the difference-blind d'Hondt system. Any party that wins the requisite share of seats in Northern Ireland's Assembly is entitled to a corresponding share of cabinet positions regardless of whether it is a nationalist, unionist, or nonethnic party. In a federal Iraq, the Kurdish minority could be guaranteed a share of power in the federal government by a rule similar to that used for Northern Ireland's cabinet, or by stipulating that each of Iraq's constituent federal units should have representation on a collective presidency. A minority veto over legislation in specific areas could be provided by requiring a sufficiently weighted legislative majority in the lower level of the senate. The possibility of legislation unacceptable to minorities could be minimized through a well-constructed bill of rights and a representative judiciary.

One American writer on Iraq has argued that protections at the federal level should be sufficient to allow minorities to accept a strong central government (Walen 2003). The argument seems intuitively plausible: the better the minority's position at the federal level, the more likely it is to consent to a strong federal role. The logic, however, fails to grasp what is involved in claims for national self-determination: a desire for *self*-government. Even on pragmatic grounds alone, the most that a minority can be guaranteed at the federal level is a blocking role. This option is unlikely to be as attractive as the positive power to enact and implement policies within one's federal unit. Just as self-government without shared government will be insufficient to protect minority interests, the reverse is also true.

Lessons for Human Rights Protection

A major objection to pluri-national federalism is that it allegedly leads to human rights infringements. The problem is said to arise for two reasons. First, ethnic populations are usually interspersed, and it is impossible to create homogeneous federal units. The result is that federal units invariably have ethnic minorities. Second, as pluri-national federalism gives power to ethnocentric elites and nationalist movements, it facilitates the abuse of such minorities. Critics of pluri-national federalism in Iraq warn that Kurdistan will have Sunni Arabs, Turkomen, and other minorities in its midst. Kurdish autonomy, it is claimed, will result in revenge attacks against them (Wimmer 2003, 125; see Brancati 2004, 10–11). Some warn that a Kurdish autonomous region will be bad even for some Kurds: those who live outside the Kurdish region will suffer discrimination (*New York Times* 2004b).

One response to these arguments is that *denying* autonomy to ethnic minorities infringes their individual rights. Kymlicka has argued persuasively that a precondition for the meaningful exercise of individual rights is that it occurs within one's own secure cultural context, and that the maintenance of such a context requires political autonomy for one's community (Kymlicka 1995). Another response is that whatever way the state is structured, as a unitary state, a pluri-national federation, or a federation in which internal boundaries intersect minority groups, there will be majorities and minorities. An Iraq federation constructed on the American model would have Shiʿa or Arab majorities in most of its provinces, and a unitary Iraq would have a Shiʿa and Arab majority. It is not clear that these majorities would be any more benign than a Kurdish majority within Kurdistan. There will clearly be a need to ensure rights protection, however Iraq is structured.

Canada's example provides two grounds for thinking that pluri-national federalism need not lead to human rights abuses within federal units. First, Québec shows that minority nationalism and minority control of a federal unit need not involve a "revolt against modernity." Its leaders have generally eschewed ethnic nationalism in favor of an inclusive civic nationalism based on Québec.[16] The attitude of Québecois nationalists to minorities is little different from that of American nationalists: every citizen is entitled to equal treatment, and newcomers have a responsibility to learn the dominant language. Québec has adopted a wide-ranging Charter of Human Rights and Freedoms, which, although it is a product of the Québec legislature and capable of being overridden by it, has been used to defend minorities against provincial legislation.

There are reasonable grounds for expecting that a Kurdistan regional government would treat its minorities well. As early as 1953, the Kurdish Democracy Party changed its name to the Kurdistan Democratic Party to be more inclusive of non-Kurds (McDowall 2000, 297), and the current PUK premier, Barham Salih, has been actively trying to promote a Kurdistani identity. Minorities have been treated well since Kurdistan gained autonomy in 1991 and are represented within both the KDP and PUK governments.[17] Kurdistan is currently in the process of adopting a bill of rights. This civic virtue has strong pragmatic underpinnings. The Kurds are surrounded by powerful enemies, inside and outside Iraq. They do not want to invite intervention, or to alienate international support by trampling on the rights of Turkomen or Arab minorities. With fellow Kurds living as oppressed minorities in neighboring states, the Kurds of Iraq have reason to set a good example: the abuse of Turkomen would give Turkey an excuse to continue repressing its Kurds, while a liberal policy in Kurdistan will strengthen Turkish liberals.

Second, the Canadian example underlines that federal units are not immune from federal intervention: they can be made subject to a state-wide bill of rights. Canada's Supreme Court, using the Canadian Charter of Rights and Freedoms, has intervened to protect the rights of native minorities throughout Canada, francophone minorities outside Québec, and the anglophone minority inside Québec. In this respect it has acted like its American counterpart, which has upheld the rights of minorities in the Deep South and elsewhere. As Iraq is likely to adopt a state-wide bill of rights, this will provide an additional safeguard against the abuse of minorities within federal units, including Arab minorities in Kurdistan, Kurdish minorities in Arab provinces, and those who are neither Kurds nor Arabs throughout Iraq.

Canada's experience also shows, however, that the protection of rights is not as straightforward as it may appear. A state-wide charter, depending on which rights are protected and which are not, can be an integrationist device that is used to thwart the autonomy enjoyed by minorities. Canada's Charter of Rights and Freedoms was the creature of Pierre Trudeau, the anti-Québec nationalist prime minister, who saw it as an instrument to promote a strong Canadian identity at the expense of a Québec identity. The charter protects the standard individual rights of freedom of religion and freedom from discrimination and so on, and it also protects the linguistic rights of francophone and anglophone *minorities* throughout Canada's provinces. For Québec nationalists, however, it does not do enough to promote the right of the francophone *majority* in Québec to enjoy self-government and to protect its culture. The result is that Québec's government has not ratified the charter. In the minds of Québec's leaders, the Canadian Supreme Court has not always been able to balance the linguistic rights of the province's anglophones with the need for Québec, as the only francophone unit in North America, to protect its culture against anglicisation. One of Québec's post-charter constitutional demands has been that it should be recognized as a "distinct society" and that its government should be given the task of protecting and promoting its distinct culture. If judges were required to interpret Canada's Charter of Rights and Freedoms in this light, it is thought, they would be better able to balance the conflicting rights of Québec's two linguistic communities than at present. Québec negotiated for such a clause during constitutional negotiations that took place between 1987 and 1992, but these failed, providing the backdrop for the referendum on sovereignty in 1995.

These difficulties suggest that, while Iraq should adopt a federation-wide bill of rights that protects both individual rights and the rights of minorities within provinces, this should be done consistently with the rights of Kurds, as a distinct national community, to exercise self-government and protect Kurdish culture within the Kurdish region. An Iraq bill of rights might also usefully entrench a right to power-sharing at the federal level. The inclusion of these features would provide an additional safeguard against their being overturned in the future.

Conclusion

This chapter should not be read as suggesting that Canada has resolved its Quebec question. From the perspective of Quebec nationalists, including those who are open to remaining part of Canada, the Canadian federation has several shortcomings, which need to be addressed. The chapter should also not be read as suggesting that Iraq can become like Canada or any other relatively stable pluri-national federation simply by adopting the institutional arrangements described here. The success of these arrangements in other settings has depended on a willingness among political elites to compromise that may not be forthcoming in Iraq. The Canadian practice of decentralized federalism and power-sharing, it should be recalled, has been based at least as much on a spirit of elite accommodation as on facilitative institutional rules. In some ways, in fact, accommodation has worked in Canada in spite of institutional obstacles, including a parliamentary system that is based on the Westminster (majoritarian) model of government. Other cases where constitutions have prescribed power-sharing but there has been little cooperation, such as Bosnia-Hercegovina, should also caution us against expecting too much of institutions.

If power-sharing and pluri-national federalism fail in Iraq, it is likely to be because its communities and their leaders are so polarized that they cannot work together. This suggests that prospects for the American model of federation, which does not allow collective self-government to the Kurds, or ensure them a share in power at the federal level of government, are much worse than prospects for the arrangements suggested here. The choice that Iraq faces is likely to be the same choice faced by other societies that are deeply divided along national lines: not between a nation-state model and a pluri-national state model, but between a pluri-national federation and division into two or more states.

Notes

I would like to thank the Social Sciences and Humanities Research Council of Canada for funding my research.

1. A pluri-national federation is one in which two or more national communities enjoy self-government. Critics of pluri-national federalism generally refer to it as "ethno-federalism" or "ethnic federalism," which suggests regional governments that are ethnocentric rather than inclusive in their policies. I use the term "pluri-national" rather than the more conventional "multi-national," as the latter is too closely associated with "trans-national" business corporations, that is, corporations that are located in two or more states.

2. There are obvious differences between the Kurds and Québécois. The latter consider themselves not a "minority" but one of Canada's "two founding peoples" a formulation that rankles Canada's indigenous peoples as much as its nonindigenous English-speakers. The Québécois are also contained within Canada. Indeed, as the term Québécois suggests, they are contained within the province of Quebec, having largely cut ties with the French-speaking population outside that province. The Kurds in Iraq have little difficulty with being described as a minority, and do not see themselves as one of Iraq's founding peoples, although they seek to be a partner in Iraq's "refounding." Most Kurds in Iraq also see themselves as part of a larger Kurdish nation which stretches into Turkey, Syria, and Iran (see Chapter 1). A sizable proportion of Kurds in Iraq, perhaps as many as one-fifth, live outside the territory governed by the Kurdistan Regional Government. It is possible that autonomy for Iraqi Kurdistan will affect ties between Kurds inside and outside this region, as Québec's autonomy has affected relations among "les Canadiennes" (French-speaking Canadians).

3. The Kurds would likely have control of three provinces (Dohuk, Erbil, and Sulaimania) and a significant presence in Kirkuk.

4. Adeed Dawisha and Karen Dawisha argue that an 18-province federation would increase "healthy political competition for resources—even within various ethnic or religious communities" (Dawisha and Dawisha 2003, 39). Walen writes that "it would be hard to achieve the virtues of federalism—the many different factions operating in shifting coalitions . . . if there were only three large, ethnically based provinces" (Walen 2003; see also Makiya 2002; Byman 2003). More generally, Horowitz argues that splitting ethnic groups into different regions "heightens intraethnic divisions, for

fractions of groups may have greater incentives to cooperate across group lines than do entirely cohesive groups" (Horowitz 2000, 259).

5. Québec is currently governed by the federalist Liberal party, and its premier, Jean Charest, is a committed Canadian. He was a key leader of the "No" side during the 1995 Québec referendum on sovereignty.

6. Similar reasoning explains why England does not seek self-government. As the English constitute an overwhelming majority of the United Kingdom population, they identify with the UK government as their national government.

7. English-speaking Canada is an amalgam of seven distinct colonies that decided to join together between 1867 and 1949, and two provinces that were created from federal crown territories in 1930. It is one thing to recognize that this largely organic development has allowed for the possibility of cross-cutting cleavages, and quite another to advocate the forced partition of a nation's territory into several units in order to promote such cleavages.

8. From the late nineteenth century until today, the two largest and most central provinces have been close allies. Partnerships have been routinely established between the premiers of the two provinces, including Mercier and Mowat, Hepburn and Duplessis, Johnson and Robarts, Bourassa and Peterson, and even between the separatist premier Bouchard and his counterpart Harris in Ontario.

9. The same pattern emerges from Lijphart's research. He measured the degree of centralization in ten unitary states and five federations (Austria, West Germany, the U.S., Australia, and Canada), using as his indicator central government spending as a proportion of GNP. The ten unitary states were more centralized than the federations, with average centralization indices of 85 and 71 respectively. Canada was the least centralized of the fifteen states, with a centralization index of 57 compared to 75 for the U.S. (1979, 504).

10. A defining feature of federation is that it constitutionally guarantees self-government. This feature, which distinguishes federation from devolution or decentralization in unitary states, makes it more attractive to minority nations. In a unitary state, the center can devolve substantial power to regional governments, but is free unilaterally to alter these powers, or to abolish the regional governments, as the United Kingdom did with respect to Northern Ireland in 1972. In a federation, the constitution, including changes affecting the division of powers, can be altered only by constitutional amendment, and in all federations except India this requires the support of both levels of government. While this broad formula generally suffices in mononational federations, minority nations in pluri-national federations may insist on a veto for their own unit. This provision would preclude the possibility of constitutional change acceptable to a sufficient proportion of the majority nation's units, but unacceptable to the minority. It would also be more consistent with the minority's view of the state as a pluri-national partnership. In Canada, prior to 1982, there was no formal amendment formula. There was an understanding, at least in Québec, that constitutional change required the consent of the federal government and all provinces, and that Québec therefore had a veto. However, the Constitution Act of 1982 was passed without Québec's consent and contained a formalized amendment formula that made it possible to introduce future changes in the same way. The issue helped give rise to a constitutional crisis, and eventually, to a referendum on sovereignty in 1995, which separatists came within one percentage point of winning. The federal government

responded after 1995 by passing federal legislation indicating that it would not approve constitutional change without Québec's consent. As this indirect veto for Québec is part of a federal statute and revocable by the federal parliament, it has only partly addressed Québec's concerns. Given this experience, it may be prudent to ensure that, whatever constitutional amendment formula is adopted in Iraq, it provides a veto for Kurdistan, at least on those issues it considers fundamental, such as language, culture, and the division of powers.

11. Adeed Dawisha and Karen Dawisha offer a variation on American "separation of powers" thinking (Dawisha and Dawisha 2003, 43–44). They propose "splitting the executive between a weak president and a prime minister," who would have "different power bases and may come from different parties." There are two problems with this line of thinking. First, as the president they envisage would be weak, with "limited, largely symbolic powers," it is difficult to see how this proposal would constitute a separation of "powers." Second, without formal constitutional provisions that prohibit it, it is quite possible that the president and prime minister could come from the same party, with the same support base.

12. The convention that the prime minister be bilingual gives a tremendous advantage to Québec francophones; they are less than 20 percent of Canada's total population but more than 40 percent of Canada's bilingual population. These figures are based on calculations from Statistics Canada at <http://www.statcan.ca/english/Pgbd/demo19a.htm.> See also *Globe and Mail* 2004. Bilingualism is effectively required not just for the prime ministership but also for the leadership of all the major federal political parties.

13. On 1 September 2003, the Governing Council appointed a cabinet that was also representative of Iraq's ethnic make-up.

14. The special majority mechanism is described in Art. 4 (3) of Belgium's constitution. The constitution can be accessed online at <http://www.oefre.unibe.ch/law/icl/be00000_.html>

15. The Ta'if Accord can be found at <http://www.jinsa.org/articles/articles.html/function/ view/categoryid/136/documentid/314/history/3,651,136,314>, accessed 4 January 2004.

16. The exception is Jacques Parizeau, premier of Québec at the time of the referendum in 1995. After the result was announced on the night of the referendum, he famously, and accurately, blamed his narrow defeat on "money and the ethnic vote." "Money" apparently meant the wealthy anglophones of Montreal. The "ethnic vote" clearly referred to those recently arrived immigrants who are from neither English-speaking nor French-speaking backgrounds, and who are overwhelmingly federalist.

17. Two critics of a pluri-national federation in Iraq nonetheless note that "basic civil liberties are secure" in Kurdistan (Byman and Pollack 2003, 124).

References

Brancati, Dawn. 2004. "Is Federalism a Panacea for Post-Saddam Iraq?" *Washington Quarterly* 25 (Spring).

Brubaker, Rogers. 1996. *Nationalism Reframed: Nationhood and the National Question in the New Europe*. Cambridge: Cambridge University Press.

Bunce, Valerie. 1999. *Subversive Institutions: The Design and the Destruction of Socialism and the State*. Cambridge: Cambridge University Press.

Byman, Daniel. 2003. "Constructing a Democratic Iraq: Challenges and Opportunities." *International Security* 28 (1): 47–78.

Byman, Daniel and Kenneth M. Pollack. 2003. "Democracy in Iraq." *Washington Quarterly* 26 (3): 119–36.

Dawisha, Adeed and Karen Dawisha. 2003. "How to Build a Democratic Iraq." *Foreign Affairs* 82 (3): 36–50.

Elazar, Daniel J. 1994. *Federalism and the Way to Peace*. Kingston, Ont.: Queen's Institute of Intergovernmental Relations.

Globe and Mail (Toronto). 2004. "Canadian Bilingualism Is Still Just a Good Intention." 28 February.

Hanf, Theodor. 1991. "Reducing Conflict Through Cultural Autonomy: Karl Renner's Contribution." In *State and Nation in Multi-Ethnic Societies: The Breakup of Pluri-National States*, ed. Uri Raʿanan, Maria Mesner, Keith Armes, and Kate Martin. Manchester: Manchester University Press. 33–52.

Hebert, Chantal. 2003. "Harris Won't Fly in Quebec." *Toronto Star*, 22 October.

Horowitz, Donald L. 1991. *A Democratic South Africa: Constitutional Engineering in a Divided Society*. Berkeley, University of California Press.

———. 2000. "Constitutional Design: An Oxymoron." In *Designing Democratic Institutions*, ed. Ian Shapiro and Stephen Macedo. New York: New York University Press.

International Herald Tribune. 2003. "Choosing a Template for Iraq." 3 October.

Kurdistan Democratic Party. 1992. Draft Constitution of the Federal Republic of Iraq.

Kymlicka, Will. 1995. *Multicultural Citizenship: A Liberal Theory of Minority Rights*. Oxford: Oxford University Press.

Leff, Carol Skalnik. 1998. *The Czech and Slovak Republics: Nation Versus State*. Boulder, Colo.: Westview Press.

Lijphart, Arend. 1979. "Consociation and Federation: Conceptual and Empirical Links." *Canadian Journal of Political Science* 12 (3): 499–515.

Lipset, Seymour Martin. 1985. "The Revolt Against Modernity." In Lipset, *Consensus and Conflict: Essays in Political Sociology*. New Brunswick, N.J.: Transaction Books. 253–93.

Madison, James, Alexander Hamilton, and John Jay. 1788. *The Federalist Papers*. Ed. Isaac Kramnick. Reprint Harmondsworth: Penguin, 1987.

Makiya, Kanan. 2002. "A Model for Post-Saddam Iraq." 3 October. Available online at <http://www.benadorassociates.com/article/140>

McDowall, David. 2000. *A Modern History of the Kurds*. London: I.B. Tauris.

McGarry, John. 2002. "Federal Political Systems and the Accommodation of National Minorities." In *The Handbook of Federal Countries, 2002*, ed. Ann L. Griffiths. Montreal: McGill-Queen's University Press. 416–47.

McGarry, John and Brendan O'Leary. 2003. "Federation, Conflict-Regulation and National and Ethnic Power-Sharing." Paper presented to the American Political Science Association, Philadelphia, 29 August.

New York Times. 2004a. "U.S. to Let Kurds Keep Autonomy." 5 January.

New York Times 2004b. "Self-Rule Timetable Cited to Decision; Federal State at Stake." 5 January.

Noel, S. J. R. 1990. *Patrons, Clients, Brokers: Ontario Society and Politics, 1791–1896.* Toronto: University of Toronto Press.

Nordlinger, Eric A. 1972. *Conflict Regulation in Divided Societies.* Cambridge, Mass.: Center for International Affairs, Harvard University.

PILPG (Public International Law and Policy Group). 2003. "Establishing a Stable Democratic Constitutional Structure in Iraq: Some Basic Considerations (May)." Available online at <www.pilpg.org>

Reid, Scott. 1992. *Canada Remapped: How the Partition of Quebec Will Reshape the Nation.* Vancouver: Canada Pulp Press.

Roeder, Philip G. 1991. "Soviet Federalism and Ethnic Mobilization." *World Politics* 43 (January): 196–232.

———. Forthcoming. "Power-Dividing as an Alternative to Ethnic Power-Sharing." In *Sustainable Peace: Democracy and Power-Sharing After Civil War*, ed. Philip G. Roeder and Donald Rothchild. Ithaca, N.Y.: Cornell University Press.

Snyder, Jack. 2000. *From Voting to Violence: Democratization and Nationalist Conflict.* New York: W.W. Norton.

Toronto Globe and Mail. 2004. "Canadian Bilingualism Is Still Just a Good Intention." 28 February.

Toronto Star. 1997. "Bouchard Vows to Call Snap Vote if Top Court Rules Against Québec." 1 December, A1, 11.

Walen, Alex. 2003. "Federalism for Postwar Iraq." *FindLaw's Writ*, 10 April. Available online at http://writ.news.findlaw.com/commentary/20030410_walen.html.

Watts, Ronald L. 1999. *Comparing Federal Systems.* Montreal: McGill-Queen's University Press.

———. Forthcoming. "Multinational Federations in Comparative Perspective." In *Multinational Federations.* ed. M. Burgess and J. Pinter.

Wimmer, Andreas. 2003. "Democracy and Ethno-Religious Conflict in Iraq." *Survival* 45 (4): 111–34.

Chapter 4
Negotiating a Federation in Iraq

Karna Eklund, Brendan O'Leary, and Paul R. Williams

"A tremendous amount of propagandizing and even political organizing has been based on the mistaken premise that somehow, if people just work hard enough for it, federation will occur. It is perhaps unkind to disturb such naïve faith, but the hope of scientific enterprise is that the more people know, the more effectively they can act."
—William Riker, "Federalism" (1975, 131)

This chapter considers the negotiation of the prospective "permanent constitution" of Iraq. If by February 2005 Iraq has a functioning elected assembly, that body will sit simultaneously as its constitutional convention. Under the provisions of the Transitional Administrative Law (TAL), the formal negotiations may therefore last no more than six and a half months because the draft constitution has to be ready by 15 August 2005, before a campaign for ratification can begin. The referendum must be held not later than 15 October 2005. The TAL, Iraq's interim constitution analyzed by Brendan O'Leary in Chapter 2, provides a benchmark against which to assess unresolved and likely future controversies over the making of a permanent constitution. We make several assumptions here, none of which may withstand political change, violent turmoil, or a precipitous U.S. withdrawal; and we make them knowing they may transpire to be incorrect. The first is that Iraq will shortly have a formally sovereign transitional government. The second is that the Transitional Administrative Law (TAL) will remain substantially in force, rather than being put to one side when the United Nations returns to Iraq. Thus, the terms of the TAL will regulate political behavior during the rest of 2004 and most of 2005. Third, we assume that by early 2005 elected politicians will be engaged in meaningful negotiations, and that Iraq's neighbors will not decide its constitutional future. Fourth, we assume (and hope) that Iraq will not be so wracked by national, religious, or merely criminal violence that negotiations are pointless. Lastly, we assume a non-zero probability that the permanent constitution will move from the status of a document to a fundamental norm that substantively regulates Iraq's institutions.

These assumptions may all turn out to be false; but, as we write, they are not certainly false. This chapter considers the environment in which the TAL was negotiated, by comparison with the one in which the permanent constitution will be negotiated; the likely crunch questions that will make or break constitutional reconstruction; and, lastly, explanations of why federal bargains are made.

The Negotiating Environment

Drafting a permanent constitution is a contentious process for any emergent democracy. The challenges are substantially magnified in Iraq because of its lack of democratic experience and its complex mosaic of national, ethnic, religious, tribal, and geographic identities and interests. Saddam Hussein's genocidal regime and the history of conflictual relations between Iraq's national communities (primarily Arabs vs. Kurds) and religious sects (primarily Sunni vs. Shi'a Muslims) lead many to predict a politics of antagonism rather than accommodation. During 2004–2005 Iraq will be in a quandary. The continued presence of multinational forces after the departure of the Coalition Provisional Authority, coupled with the relatively new and untested internal security forces in Arab Iraq, will attract the wrath and strategic malice of some violent Arab nationalists and *wahhabist* Islamists from both within and outside of Iraq. The April 2004 insurrection of Moqtada al-Sadr's "Mahdi Army" indicates that there will also be Shi'a Arab organized violence. Everyone inside and outside Iraq expects organized violence before and after the formal restoration of its sovereignty as of July 2004.

The permanent constitution will be drafted in a threatening atmosphere. It will also be drafted in a bad neighborhood: Iraq is surrounded by suspicious and potentially hostile states. These neighbors' records as parliamentary democracies range from highly dubious (Jordan, Kuwait) to deeply flawed (Turkey, Iran[1]), or nonexistent (Syria, Saudi Arabia), and their records as liberal democracies are no better. Perhaps as significant, the permanent constitution will be negotiated under the accusation that its outcome is compelled by the transitional administrative law, which was heavily steered, if not dictated, by the the CPA Administrator, Ambassador L. Paul Bremer III of the U.S. Arab political leaders, especially Shi'a Arab political leaders, have declared that the TAL, particularly its rules for making the permanent constitution, illegitimately usurps the will of "the people of Iraq." The supporters of Grand Aya-tollah Ali al-Sistani have already argued this case, even though their five members on the Governing Council were part of the unanimous agreement of the TAL.

The interim constitution was negotiated and agreed without any pretense of transparency, serious public education, or extensive democratic deliberation (Governing Council of Iraq 2004). Its manufacture displayed, almost in text-book fashion, many of the carefully crafted habits developed by American negotiators, notably in the Balkans (Holbrooke 1998). The Americans used their standard repertoire of negotiating techniques,[2] with some success, to:

1. *Control the text*, either directly or by proxy (using advisors to Arab members of the Governing Council).
2. *Agree the text in English* (although there was simultaneous translation into Arabic, no texts were provided in Kurdish or other minority languages).
3. *Accept only cosmetic (and obfuscatory) changes on controversial matters of fundamental importance* (see, for example, the clause on natural resources).[3]
4. *Prematurely close discussion on deeply conflictual matters* (for instance, the final status of Kirkuk).
5. *Impose an artificial deadline of 28 February 2004 to create a sense of urgency,* and offer the restoration of sovereignty on June 30 as a reward for a settlement.
6. *Isolate leaders* (for example, separating Kurdistan's key leaders, Barzani and Talabani, from their key aides, peers, and specialist advisors in their parties and the Kurdistan National Assembly).
7. *Flatter leaders* (American advisors visited al-Sistani's followers and encouraged Governing Council members to visit him).
8. *Politely intimidate key leaders* of national and religious communities by warning of chaos if a settlement were not made.
9. *Reduce all parties' expectations.*
10. *Insist on secrecy and on the letter of past "agreements" reached through "non-papers"* (when secrecy was not necessary, and there had been no formal agreements).
11. *Clear away "irrelevant" moral arguments in the interest of "practicalities."*
12. *Induce leaders, rather than their immediate subordinates, to be the negotiators* (the one leader who resisted and remained outside the Governing Council, the Shi'a cleric al-Sistani, proved to be one of the hardest bargainers, obliging the Americans to seek the help of the United Nations on the feasibility of holding elections).

While the American negotiators did not succeed in having all their preferences satisfied (and not all their preferences were coherent),[4] they significantly constrained and shaped others' preferences, especially their sense of which of their preferences were feasible. This pressure was exerted effectively enough to provoke a predictable backlash against the TAL, which may harm the making of the permanent constitution.

The negotiation of the permanent constitution will, paradoxically, be both assisted and rendered difficult by the absence of the Americans and the British as formal third parties. Their absence will make its negotiation an intra-Iraqi affair. But, for all their defects, the Americans and the CPA provided the "mediation with muscle" that allowed the TAL to be made, despite deep disagreements. As Senator Joseph Biden, the senior ranking Democrat on the U.S. Senate Foreign Relations Committee, put it in April 2004: "We are about to give over authority to an entity that we haven't identified yet, knowing that whatever that entity is, there's going to be overwhelming turmoil between June 30 and January, when there is supposed to be an election. Who is the referee? Who is the graybeard?" (Barringer 2004). Variations on this perspective are held by the negotiators on the Governing Council, whatever their views on the TAL that they all signed. The Americans, under either a Bush or a Kerry administration, will be able to do little more than offer their "good offices" in the making of the permanent constitution. They will want to be seen to take a back seat during that process.

If the TAL is upheld, the future negotiations will be a much more public, transparent, and democratic process than the one through which the TAL was drafted. Since the assembly is tasked with drafting the constitution, its detailed content is likely to be written by a broadly inclusive parliamentary committee, probably assisted by experts, that will report to the presidential council, the prime minister and cabinet, and plenary sessions of the assembly. It would be sensible for such a committee to hold hearings, receive written and oral submissions, and travel throughout Iraq. The committee would also benefit from holding conferences on federations and organizing visits for parliamentarians and public officials to functioning democratic federations. It will also have to organize a public education program to persuade citizens of Iraq to ratify the draft constitution.

In the absence of the American-dominated Coalition Provisional Authority, only three formal rules will structure the negotiations if the TAL operates: the majoritarian, the federal, and the default rules. The first is straightforward: the draft constitution can be passed by a mere majority of the new Iraqi assembly. The second is not straightforward, but it is principled. In accordance with a federalizing logic, the constitution must be ratified with the support of a majority in an Iraq-wide referendum and must not be opposed by two-thirds of the voters in any three of the eighteen former governorates (Governing Council of Iraq 2004, Art. 61c). This federal rule creates a "qualified majority" for popular ratification. These two rules, the majoritarian drafting rule and the federal ratification rule, will, if they are kept, bias outcomes in the negotiations, but in productive ways. The rules require political leaders to win popular support both for their negotiating positions *and* for any settlement they reach. The federal ratification rule requires that at least one third of the voters in each of sixteen of Iraq's former eighteen governorates endorse the final constitution, ensuring that its ratification has a high threshold of popular support and widespread territorial endorsement. Though widely interpreted as "Kurdistan's clause," Article 61 (c) formally empowers all locally concentrated majorities in Iraq (Shi'a Arabs, Sunni Arabs, and Kurds) with a de facto veto over ratification of the constitution. These rules oblige Iraq's newly elected leaders to engage in extensive public education, because otherwise they would not win a popular or qualified majority for whatever they agree. Numerous reconciliation conferences and intercommunity public dialogues resembling those initiated by Masoud Barzani, president of the Kurdistan Democratic Party, in Kurdistan in March 2004 will be required. The leaderships will have to build a sufficient consensus. The manufacture and ratification of the permanent constitution will require sustained broadcasting programs, brochures in multiple languages, and simplified "question and answer" booklets on the meaning of the draft constitution. Films, videos, organized radio discussions, and extensive popularization of the constitution will be essential, particularly for illiterate voters. This campaign will have to be conducted in a milieu in which only Kurdistan has extensively institutionalized parties; in Arab Iraq, one cannot assume that party leaders who broker a draft constitution will secure the voters' support in the ratification referendum.

The third rule is more tacit in its logic and will operate in the background. It is the default rule. What happens if the ratification referendum fails? The answer, according to Article 61(e) of the TAL, is that the TAL remains in being and a new federal assembly would have to be elected under the same electoral law. Although the Coalition's response to such an impasse is unpredictable, we assume that Coalition troops will not be completely withdrawn until the permanent constitution is ratified. A federal assembly that acts in a solely majoritarian way and proposes an insufficiently acceptable constitution will end up with the status quo ante.

The implications of the default rule cut at least two ways. The default option may produce a cycle in which a Shi'a Arab majority in the assembly proposes an unacceptable constitution to the rest of Iraq, which then rejects it, creating an automatic dissolution of the assembly, fresh elections, and a possible repetition of this scenario. The constructive alternative suggests that the threat of instability that nonratification would create will induce a Shiʿa Arab majority, or any other majority coalition in the assembly, to negotiate a widely acceptable constitution. The stark procedural consequence of the federal and default rules in the TAL is that a Shiʿa Arab majority that insists on majority rule over federalism (and liberalism) will not be able to make a constitution with the assent of enough of the rest of Iraq. That is why, in the spring of 2004, many Shiʿa Arab leaders, prompted by al-Sistani, proclaimed their desire to overturn Article 61 in its entirety; they may shift to argue that the UN, rather than the U.S. should provide the appropriate roof for making the rules for making the constitution; or simply argue for the sovereignty of the new Iraqi national assembly. Provided the TAL is validated during the restoration of Iraq's sovereignty it specifies the rules, but that does not mean it cannot be amended. But to abolish Article 61 legally, Shiʿa Arabs will need three-quarters of the future assembly to agree that it is worth provoking Kurds and other minorities in this way, and the three members of the presidential council (who have to be elected by a two-thirds majority in the assembly) would have to agree that adding fuel to the fire is a good idea. That seems to us both an undesirable and an unlikely prospect. If the TAL is undone illegally, Iraq will be plunged into chaos. In that event, the rest of this chapter will likely be consigned to the trash can of speculative writing. We shall assume, although we cannot be certain, that enough elected and responsible Shiʿa Arab leaders will prefer negotiating an agreed draft permanent constitution to dictating a unitary state under their auspices, especially because they cannot confidently expect the American military to enforce, or acquiesce in, any straightforward bid to seize power.

The leaders of Kurdistan have an important bargaining advantage, especially if they act as a bloc. They know that in at least three governorates, Dohuk, Erbil, and Sulaimania, they can mobilize over two thirds of the voters to vote down an unacceptable draft permanent constitution. If the status quo created by the TAL is acceptable to them, as it has been so far, it may constitute what negotiation theorists call their "batna" ("best alternative to a negotiated agreement") although in this case their batna is a previously negotiated agreement (Fisher and Ury, 1981, 1987; Brams, Dougherty, and Weidner 1994; Hall 1993; Raiffa 1982; Zartman 1996; Zartman and Rubin 2000). To put the situation bluntly, in order to ensure the complete restoration of Iraq's sovereignty through the withdrawal of American troops and the ratification of the permanent constitution, Arab party leaders may have to offer Kurdistan a better deal than it obtained in the TAL. More subtly, as long as Kurdistanis believe that the U.S. will not acquiesce if a Shi'a Arab or Arab-dominated coalition attempts to break the TAL illegally, then Kurdistan maintains this strategic bargaining advantage. But it will only have this advantage as long as this belief is widely shared and as long as Kurdistan presents a united front in the negotiations. If any Arab-dominated coalition succeeds in attracting one of Kurdistan's major parties into a side deal, then "Kurdistan's veto" may not operate. How likely is this scenario? Arab party leaders controlling a majority of the federal assembly may calculate that the Kurdistan Democratic Party (KDP) could deliver a two-thirds "no" vote in Dohuk, that the Patriotic Union of Kurdistan (PUK) could deliver a two-thirds "no" vote in Sulaimania, and that jointly the two parties could deliver the same result in Erbil. But, they may also calculate that if they could peel away one of these parties from a united Kurdistan front, they would be able to ratify the permanent constitution by getting over one third of the vote in two of these governorates. Yet, even conceding that they could split Kurdistan's two major parties, they still could not know whether that could deliver the relevant party's previous supporters in sufficient numbers. After all, Kurdish voters might regard such a side deal as an act of "national treachery," especially if the rival Kurdistani party makes that accusation. Indeed it is possible that the batna of Kurdish voters differs from that of Kurdistan's leaders; that is, they may want even more from the permanent constitution than their leaders think is feasible, which places a further constraint on Arab politicians.

We now make some assumptions that may prove unwarranted, although they are currently widely shared in Iraq. First, in the elections for the transitional Iraqi national assembly, predominantly Shi'a Arab political parties will collectively have more support than Kurdistan's political parties; Kurdistan's two major parties will jointly have more support than parties dominated by Sunni Arabs; and the pan-Iraq, pan-Arab, and pan-Islamist parties will be represented in smaller numbers. These electoral results will be more likely if the assembly is elected on a system of proportional representation. Second, we assume that an agreement endorsed by all three major communities' representative leaders will easily pass the referendum thresholds. Third, it follows, on most variations of the first two assumptions, that there is only one possible "winning coalition" by which just two of three major national or religious groups could ratify the constitution over the opposition of the third group. A coalition of Shi'a Arabs and Kurdistanis would easily carry 50 percent in an Iraq-wide referendum, and it would have a good chance of carrying at least one-third of the vote in sixteen governorates. At least two Sunni-dominated governorates are vulnerable to such a coalition, because Kurdish and Shi'a Arab voters may add up to close to one third of probable electors within them, and no community anywhere ever votes completely as a bloc. By contrast, an Arab coalition of Shi'a and Sunnis could never win a third of the vote in a referendum in Kurdistan's encapsulated governorates against the will of both Kurdistan's principal parties, while a largely pan-Sunni alliance of Kurdistan's parties and Sunni Arabs might not even get 50 percent of the assembly to approve a draft constitution. This analysis does not predict that Kurdistan will seek to create a "minimum winning coalition" with Shi'a Arabs; in fact, we think that Kurdistan will prudently seek widespread consensus for the new constitution. What we are emphasizing is Kurdistan's pivotal position. What Kurdistanis and Shi'a Arabs agree is likely to go into the permanent constitution.

The logic bears summary. A well balanced and flourishing pluri-national and religiously pluralist federation in Iraq will work best if it is endorsed widely throughout Iraq. Kurdistan may have "pivotality" in the making of the permanent constitution, especially if the TAL applies. Its batna is the TAL—provided that Coalition troops do not leave or threaten to leave precipitously.[5] If they remain united, Kurdistan's parties are essential for any coalition that wishes to see a draft constitution passed by the federal assembly *and* ratified by the qualified majority procedure. Moreover, for different reasons both Shi'a and Sunni Arab leaders should want to make a political deal with Kurdistan's political leaders to restore Iraq's full sovereignty and to have a functioning political order. Kurdistan, the part of Iraq with the greatest historic interest in the right to self-determination, including secession, is now paradoxically essential to Iraq's immediate future constitutional order—at least if that order is to be constitutional and democratic, and ratified according to the TAL.

The Crucial Negotiating Questions

What then are the crunch issues that will decide whether a durable federal bargain can be made between Kurdistan's parties and the parties of predominantly Arab Iraq?[6] One of the authors of this chapter, Paul Williams, foresaw at the Washington conference which preceded this book that the primary issues for the Kurds of Iraq would be territorial autonomy, resources, security, and power-sharing. These issues are woven through the multiple questions that any constitutional committee must address during the drafting of the permanent constitution. We examine the first three of these issues, focusing on possible bargains. Then we examine power-sharing as part of a general consideration of federal bargains. We do not discuss at length the issues that Kurdistan regards as "non-negotiable": recognition of its existence, the federal recognition of the Kurdish language, the reversal of Saddam's injustices in Kirkuk, the work of the "property claims commission,"[7] the operations of a fair process to permit the incorporation of Kurdish majority areas in Kirkuk and other disputed territories into the Kurdistan region, or Kurdistan's management of its policing and internal security arrangements. These likely "break" issues for Kurdistan are addressed by other authors in this book, so we refer to them only as they affect the making of feasible bargains.

Territorial Autonomy

Arab political leaders (and some small minorities) are likely to continue to prefer a unitary state or a centralized federation. If Shiʻa Arab parties mobilize the Shiʻa vote successfully, we might see a shift to a federalist disposition among strategic Sunni Arab politicians and their supporters. It is our experience that many Sunni Arabs still do not think they are a minority. The main advantage of a unitary Iraq or a centralized federation, according to its exponents, is that it would substantially further efforts to maintain an Iraqi political identity (Makiya 2003). But, Kurdistan and all of the expatriate opposition groups expressly rejected a unitary state before the U.S. liberation of Iraq, and Kurdistan insisted on and won a commitment to a federal system in the TAL. A unitary Iraq therefore cannot meet the threshold requirements of the permanent constitution.

In practice, Kurdistan has sought "asymmetrical federalism," while being accused of seeking a confederation or secession. It wants jurisdiction over cultural, social, and economic matters, education, and natural resources. It has been willing to cede to the federal government jurisdiction over traditional federal government competencies, including foreign affairs. Retaining portions of the Kurdistan army,[8] the *peshmerga*, has been its preference (the U.S. has a state-organized National Guard). Despite their well-recognized difficulties (Stansfield 2003), Kurdistan's institutions have functioned fairly successfully for the past twelve years, especially its ministries of finance, education, human rights, agriculture and irrigation, and reconstruction and development. Its voters are content with the autonomy they have had, and particularly the freedom from Baghdad governments that they have enjoyed. The practical implementation of asymmetrical federation would be straightforward. In the draft permanent constitution, it would require Kurdistan's competencies to be enumerated and reserved and the federal government's competencies expressly delimited. An unambiguous designation of responsibilities and shared powers might reduce power struggles. This bargain was foreshadowed in the making of the TAL. Kurdistan was willing to let the rest of Iraq be highly centralized, as long as such arrangements did not automatically apply to Kurdistan: it sought an "opt-out." In short, "constitutionally entrenched asymmetrical territorial autonomy" (ceata), would be better than Kurdistan's batna.

The most likely negotiating response of centralists when others demand asymmetrical arrangements is a reduction in the special region's role in the federal government. Arab negotiators may have to pay heavy costs, however, if any draft constitution reduces Kurdistan's share of power in the federal government: they may have to accept an expansion in Kurdistan's territorial extent (the resolution of Kirkuk's final status is foreseen in the TAL), and they may have to concede Kurdistan and other regions ownership of their unexploited natural resources. In the eyes of some Arab politicians, such a deal would threaten to create the de facto confederation that they claim to want to avoid. We think that, with side payments,[9] Kurdistani and Arab negotiators might agree an asymmetrical arrangement, but to assure its passage in the referendum both Sunni and Shi'a Arab leaders would have to endorse it. Yet, some Arab Iraqi nationalists (and any pliant Turkomen whom Ankara can direct) would be unhappy, and might claim that such a settlement foreshadows secession and campaign against its endorsement in the constitutional referendum.

Kurdistan's leaders have to market their federal design preferences to the rest of Iraq, especially if Kurdistan's territory is to be expanded. Philosophical federalism will not help them much. Four pitches might. First, the rest of Iraq will achieve the restoration of full sovereignty in return for accepting federation and will secure Kurdistan as its defense ally against possibly hostile neighbors. The second would be for Kurdistan to embrace some doctrine of symmetry and for the Arab parties to concur. This plan would not, however, be symmetry based on the "18 governorates" model. An alternative symmetrical federation would involve encouraging other parts of Iraq to amalgamate to create regions modeled on Kurdistan's own territorial range and functions. After the exit of the CPA, which ruled out such ideas, a significant constituency for a three-region (Gelb 2003) or a five-region federation (O'Leary 2003) may develop (see Figures 4.1. and 4.2).[10] Were that to happen, many conflicts attached to parity of esteem between regions and governorates would be avoided. The third pitch, which would be difficult to make, would be for Kurdistan to agree to relinquish some of its preferences over the design of the federal government (e.g., in the collective presidency and the senate) in return for Arab embrace of asymmetrical federalism and granting Kurdistan veto rights over constitutional change. That arrangement is, after all, one way to describe the bargain made in the TAL (see Chapter 2). The last pitch would

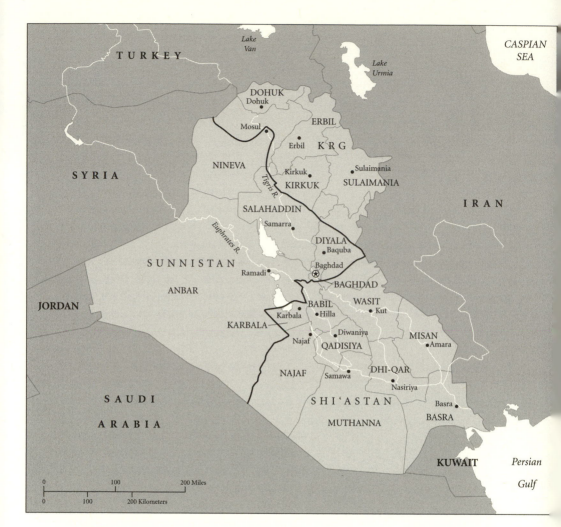

Figure 4.1. A "three regions" model (Khaled Salih). This is just one possible three regions model in which an expanded Kurdistan would be recognized, along with Sunnistan and Shiʿastan, names that are meant to be illustrative (they have no present legal or formal significance). It bears emphasis that any borders between these putative regions would be disputed.

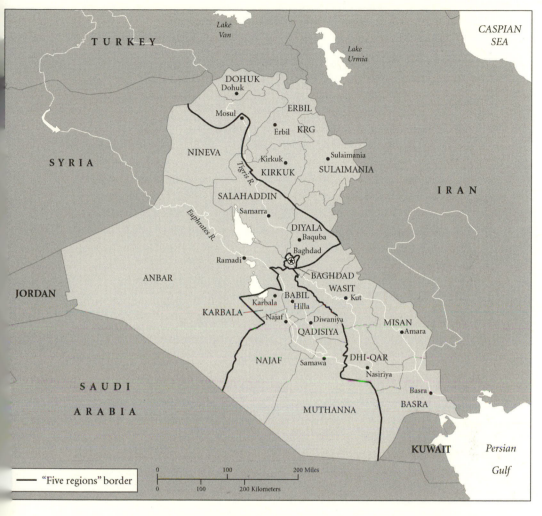

Figure 4.2. A "five regions" model (Khaled Salih). This is just one possible five regions model in which an expanded Kurdistan would be recognized. It operates from the internal divisions the CPA used to organize itself. It bears emphasis that any borders between these putative regions would be disputed.

involve constructive proposals on the questions of resource-sharing that would win support in Arab Iraq.

Resources

Generally, in a federation the minimal powers allocated to the federal government include defense, foreign affairs, monetary policy, financial equalization, and management of the federal economy's macro-economy. Interregional transportation and debt management are often, but not always, federal functions. By contrast, in most federations the minimal powers allocated to the constituent regional units relate to language, culture, education, health, natural resources, and social policy. The TAL meets most of these minimal desiderata, but not on the ownership of natural resources or the management of debt. Might there be any movement on these competency questions from the provisional bargain reached in the TAL? The TAL delimits exclusive federal competencies (Art. 25; see Appendix 2 and Chapter 2 in this volume). No one can expect Kurdistan to agree to expand the range of exclusive federal competencies without very extensive payoffs, such as guaranteed territorial expansion, greater participation in the operation of the federal government, or ownership of its natural resources.

The ownership of natural resources and control of the revenues they produce is one of the most hotly contested questions awaiting resolution. Kurdistan sought regional ownership of currently unexploited natural resources in negotiating the TAL. It will revisit this position in the making of the permanent constitution. It may gain support from some Shiʿa politicians in the south, where oil resources are also located. Central Iraq, the predominantly Sunni Arab belt outside Baghdad, is largely without oil. The allocation of the benefits to be derived from Iraq's natural resources, especially its oil resources, is predictably controversial. Any visitor to Kirkuk city is struck by the contrast between the dilapidated housing in the Kurdish locations (whose inhabitants were forbidden to repair their homes) and the superior accommodations in the "Arabization zone." The most resource-rich city in the world is the historic home of mistreated, expropriated, and expelled Kurds and Turkomen. Debate is underway over the control of oil production, the royalties and revenues generated by its sale, and the methods by which the extraction infrastructure could be maintained and upgraded.

The permanent constitution must define whether individual citizens, private corporations, regional governments, or the federal government own the oil reserves, or whether they are shared. It must provide a formula for deciding how local, regional, and federal governments benefit from the money derived from the sale of oil on the open market—as well as who must pay the bill to rehabilitate the decaying infrastructure. Any morally decent framework for sharing natural resources must take into account four considerations: population; territory; the location of underground resources, which may straddle jurisdictions; and past practices. Past practices did not function for the benefit of the people of the Iraq, especially those in the regions where known natural resources are concentrated. Kurdistan may argue that the best framework would be a system of royalty and oil revenue allocation that gives regional governments exclusive control over resources within their boundaries and requires them to pay a certain percentage of the revenue generated by oil resources to the federal government. This model has been successfully implemented in other federations; John McGarry discusses the Canadian example in chapter 3. The regional distribution of Iraq's national and sectarian groups means that the redistribution of resources to traditionally disenfranchised and persecuted communities (primarily Shi'a Arabs in the south and Kurds in the north, but also all non-Arabs in Kirkuk) would be achieved under a settlement that allows regional ownership of resources. Such a bargain would put control of oil development and revenue in the hands of regional and local officials, who would be more directly accountable to the citizens of their regions. This arrangement seems fair, but would it be acceptable? What room is there for bargaining between Kurdistan and the rest of Iraq on these issues?

A coalition between southern Shi'a Arabs and Kurdistanis in favor of regional natural resource ownership may develop, but there will also be a strong pan-Arab and likely Arab plus Turkomen coalition (likely supported by the U.S. and the UK, judging by the behavior of CPA officials in 2003–2004) against Kirkuk becoming part of Kurdistan *and* against the oil revenues of Kirkuk accruing to Kurdistan. It might be prudent for Kurdistan to agree that Kirkuk's oil fields belong to the federation in return for most of Kirkuk's territorial incorporation into Kurdistan's jurisdiction (a bargain that would trade oil for national territory). To achieve its other goals and maintain flexibility, Kurdistan might differentiate oil from other natural resources such as water, natural gas, and minerals, accepting that oil reserves would be federal property as long as its own population derived proportional benefits from oil revenues. Regional ownership of non-oil natural resources would help insure that no future federal government could suffocate Kurdistan's development.

Hard and unpredictable bargaining will definitely occur in this domain. Other resource questions will also be controversial. Kurdistan has the right to tax under the TAL, but the federal government created by the TAL is, in principle, fiscally powerful: it formulates fiscal policy, issues currency, and regulates customs, commercial policy across the federative entities, and a general policy on wages (Governing Council of Iraq 2004, Art. 25). Kurdistan has little experience of sophisticated tax collection, but neither has the rest of Iraq. If Kurdistan cannot win full fiscal autonomy, it will seek to ensure constitutional entrenchment of a per capita block grant; and, like regions in other federations, it will want the right to borrow and to issue its own bonds.[11] Trade-offs may be made between natural resources and fiscal powers. The Arab parties are more likely to want tax administration and collection to be a federal matter; Kurdistan is more likely to be insistent on receiving its authorized tax revenues than administering their collection. Politicians excel at making bargains on such matters if they do not directly affect national or ethnic symbols.

Military and Other Armed Forces

The third bundle of issues for Kurdistan and the rest of Iraq concerns the retention of the existing Kurdistani armed forces and the reorganization of the Iraqi military. Some confederations offer precedents for the existence of a protective force under the command of a regional government. Bosnia-Hercegovina's entities have their own armies. Lessons drawn from the experiences of other federations suggest that the retention of some regional armed force may be crucial to the success of the initial bargain: Canada's army has ethno-linguistic regiments, and like many federations Canada has regionalized policing. These are formally viable options for Kurdistan that need not threaten the overall national defense of Iraq.

Kurdistan won control over local policing and its own intelligence services in the TAL. Kurdistan already has its own police forces, and there are impressive police academies in Erbil and Sulaimania.[12] Police in Kurdistan and elsewhere in Iraq must be as representative as possible of their regions, and a constitutional directive to this effect would be helpful. We do not, however, expect the formal organization of policing to be as controversial as in some other post-conflict sites, precisely because the police organizations that were most abusive of human rights have been disbanded, and because regionalization of the function will regulate conflict.

Military security is another matter. The Arab parties and influential sections of American public opinion have called for Kurdistan's *peshmerga* to be disbanded (Editorial 2004; but see Naab 2004). Kurdistan will probably insist on maintaining its control over the *peshmerga* during the transitional period, especially if Iraq's security deteriorates further after the departure of the CPA. It insists that the *peshmerga*[13] are not "militia" or "paramilitaries," not the equivalents of the Shi'a Revolutionary Council's Badr Brigades, or indeed al-Sadr's "Mahdi Army." According to the former CPA coordinator in Kurdistan, the *peshmerga* are "a well-trained infantry fighting force that operates professional training academies for its officer force in Zakho and Qala Chiwalan" (Naab 2004). *Peshmerga* veterans have been receiving pension payments alongside Saddam's dissolved forces.

The KRG executives have downsized the *peshmerga* from the previous war footing, converted many soldiers into police officers, civil defense units, and de-deforestation patrol corps, and allowed some to be recruited into an

Iraqi border patrol. Kurdistan's preference is to have a Kurdistan National Guard, which it sought in the negotiation of the TAL. The U.S. National Guard might offer a model for a regional guard that would operate within a federal system of government. Such a force is routinely under regional control, but is subject to federal control under certain conditions. In the U.S., state governors command the National Guard, but they become a federal force under the federal chain of command when ordered to active duty by the president. Kurdistan will likely seek to retain this type of protection force even if some members of the *peshmerga* decide to participate in the federal armed forces. The Arab parties prefer wholly integrated military structures, as do the Americans who have sought to encourage Kurdish confidence in an integrated force by appointing the former head of the KDP's *peshmerga*, Bruska Shaways, as secretary general of the defense ministry, that is, as the senior civil servant (Chan 2004).[14] What remains controversial is whether Kurdistan retains a separate military capability; its leaders in certain circumstances may be willing to concede a federal command structure, but that would be the outer limits of their flexibility: achieving security is after all more important than formal sovereignty. The federal government could recognize the *peshmerga* and subject them to the authority of the federal presidential council, the prime minister and the defense ministry, but permit their separate organization. In contrast to the former Iraqi army, Kurdish *peshmerga* were not subject to Ba'thification and not involved in genocidal or expulsion operations against minority nationalities.

Kurdistan may be partially persuadable here, but no one should overestimate its flexibility. Kurdish troops, especially Kurdish regiments, would prevent the federal army from becoming an Arab army, so there may be a prudential case for partial integration. Trained *peshmerga* soldiers could be placed at high levels, and other Kurds could be included in civilian oversight committees, thus securing the army's place as a defender of all the citizens of Iraq, not just the Arabs who might otherwise be preeminent.

In light of Iraq's military history and its military's mistreatment of the Kurds, it will be essential to separate the external from the internal defense of the federation and its regions. Creating civilian control over the military, limiting the mission of the federal army to external defense, and confining internal security to internal police forces were all agreed in the TAL. Negotiating some of these matters to a conclusion in the final federal bargain will be a litmus test of the success of the overall federal bargain. But policing, in principle, is settled, as is the structure of federal civilian control over federal armed forces. Whether Kurdistan will have its own guard, or accept that separate predominantly Kurdish regiments will be integrated into the Iraqi armed services, remains subject to bargaining. The military basis of federal bargains conveniently brings us to a famous argument in political science.

Explaining Federal Power-Sharing Bargains

In the best-known explanatory theory of federalism, the late Bill Riker treated federations as "bargains" reached between rational prospective federal political leaders and leaders of the constituent federative entities (Riker 1964, 1975). He dismissed economic, cultural, and philosophical explanations of federations as vague, worthless, or empirically falsified. Inspecting the historical record and applying rational choice thinking he claimed that at the core of a successful federal bargain lay the achievement of a larger territory, better tax capacities, and raising a more effective military (Riker 1964, 11). He hypothesized that two conditions must necessarily be present for a federal bargain:

(1) The politicians who offer the bargain desire to expand their territorial control, usually either to meet an internal military or diplomatic threat or to prepare for military and diplomatic aggression and aggrandizement. But, though they desire to expand, they are not able to do so by conquest. . . . Hence, if they are to satisfy the desire to expand, they must offer concessions to the rulers of the constituent units. . . .
(2) The politicians who accept the bargain, giving up some independence for the sake of union, are willing to do so because of some external military-diplomatic threat . . . or they desire to participate in the potential aggression of the federation. (Riker 1964, 12)

He called these necessary suppositions the "expansion" and "military" conditions.

Riker's conditions seem to be present in today's Iraq. Arab politicians would like to reintegrate Kurdistan into Iraq. They cannot, presently, reconquer Kurdistan—although, to be frank, we must acknowledge that some want to do so. They all seek a strong Iraq to withstand possible aggression from Turkey, Iran, and Syria. They differ in their perceptions of external threats: some Shi'a are well-disposed toward Iran, and some Sunni Arabs toward Syria, but in late 2003 all members of the Governing Council unanimously opposed a Turkish military intervention to support the Coalition troops. Some, but not all, Arabs see an external threat from *wahhabist* terrorists and other religiously motivated Islamists, many of whom are regarded as Saudi and Yemeni exports. Not many Arab politicians share Saddam's aggrandizing fantasies, though some still talk of Kuwait as Iraq's "nineteenth governorate." Not all Shi'a Arab leaders have been positively disposed to Iran, even if they spent time in exile there. Several Shi'a religious leaders wish to reestablish Najaf's and Karbala's previous religious prestige—positions they lost after the Ba'th Party came to power and after the Iranian revolution of 1979. The presence of Riker's expansion condition, in our view, is met by Arab Iraq's desire to reintegrate Kurdistan, rather than by any ambition among Arab politicians to expand Iraq beyond its internationally recognized borders. Since they cannot (now) conquer Kurdistan, they must offer its leaders a federal bargain.

Riker's military condition may also seem satisfied in the possible federal bargain we are considering. The Kurdistan of Iraq, which pan-Kurdish nationalists call "Southern Kurdistan," emphatically does not want to participate in potential aggression by an Iraqi federation. It wants no part in any repetition of Saddam's adventurism. But, Kurdistan definitely faces an "external military-diplomatic threat." Its autonomous existence after 1992 owed much to the support of three great powers, the U.S., France until 1996, and the UK. These powers have expressly declared their hostility toward any formal secession by Kurdistan from Iraq and have stopped Kurdistan from incorporating the Kurdish-majority territories that its *peshmerga* liberated during the war in the spring of 2003. Turkey, Syria, and Iran openly regard a formally independent Kurdistan as a standing incitement to "their" Kurds, and these neighboring states often behave as if they regard an "ethnic federation" in Iraq in the same way. Kurdistan has unquestionably benefited from its alliance with the U.S. in 2003, but, unlike Israel, it has no significant American constituency, and it is vulnerable to any withdrawal of U.S. military and diplomatic support. It experienced a catastrophic "sell-out" by the U.S. in 1975 and another in 1991 before the creation of the "safe havens." Twice bitten, thrice shy. The complaint that "the United States has worshipped at the altar of a unified yet unnatural Iraqi state . . . a false state" (Gelb 2003) is understandable; but, even though Kurdistan's leaders share the sentiment, they cannot rely on sentiment. They must deal with a U.S. administration that inherits a long-standing diplomatic tradition of alliance with Turkey and with a State Department that does not wish to antagonize pan-Arab public opinion further by assisting the break-up of Iraq. In the absence of any American appetite or capacity to organize regime change in Iran, Kurdistan's leaders know that they have little immediate prospect of achieving diplomatic recognition, or membership of the United Nations, as an independent state. Their land-locked position makes them keenly aware of the costs of nonrecognition and the potential costs of externally unsupported independence. They express this view by saying that they have no friends but the mountains. The external military and diplomatic threats that Kurdistan faces make it entertain a federal bargain.

But, that said, Riker's theory of federal bargains rests on the tacit premise that the prospective federative entities share sufficient common interests to make a federation in response to shared military and diplomatic threats or opportunities. Any knowledge of the history of Kurdistan and the rest of Iraq punctures that tacit premise (see Chapter 1). In an elegant transformation of Riker's argument, Anthony Birch, reflecting on the formation of the Nigerian federation, suggested the following as "a substitute":

A necessary condition for the establishment of a federation is that the political leaders of all the territories involved should believe that union would either (a) help to protect one or more of the territories from an external or internal threat, whether actual or potential, to the security of the established regime or (b) enable them to benefit from the improved diplomatic or military position that the larger unit could be expected to enjoy; though it is not necessary that the considerations influencing the leaders of the various territories should be identical. (Birch 1966, 32)[15]

The Riker-Birch model of the foundational federal bargain matches the current circumstances in Kurdistan and the rest of Iraq. The considerations facing the different leaders and their interests are not identical. Kurdistan seeks a federal bargain to achieve security, to expand its officially recognized national territory within Iraq, and to achieve institutional recognition (which *may* help it acquire independence in emergency conditions). It seeks a federal bargain out of prudence, while Arab Iraq is weak, in the knowledge that when Arab Iraq is stronger it will recover its unitary and centralist inclinations. Arab Iraq, by contrast, contains leaders willing to entertain a bargain to recover lost territory and resources, to recover full sovereignty, and to make Iraq stronger in the face of its neighborhood. Both Kurdistan and the rest of Iraq see one another both as existential security threats *and* as potential partners in a marriage of convenience. A federal bargain may establish a political equilibrium.

Still, the Riker-Birch theory only specifies the necessary conditions for a foundational federal bargain. We think that the necessary conditions exist for such a bargain to be reached in the negotiation of the permanent constitution. But these conditions cannot be presumed sufficient, and were these conditions to disappear any foundational bargain that is made might not be sustained. What would best sustain a settlement are power-sharing arrangements in which the benefits exceed the costs for the foundational partners, here seen as Kurdistan and Arab Iraq. The cost for Kurdistan is to refrain from claiming independence, along with whatever other institutional and resource costs it incurs in making this bargain. The cost for Arab Iraq is to abandon the project of making Iraq an Arab nation-state, along with whatever other institutional and resource costs it incurs from the bargain. Arabs are more likely to see as costs the power-sharing institutions that Kurdistan will insist on as benefits.

So, if the foundational bargain is to succeed, the negotiations must ensure that at least some Arab Iraqis regard the power-sharing institutions as in their interests.

The design of five key formal institutions will be at stake in the final federal bargain. We outline the main considerations here.

The federal executive. Kurdistan and Sunni Arab Iraq are likely to prefer a collective executive; Shi'a Arab politicians, by contrast, are likely to want a majoritarian and single-person executive. The TAL compromised these positions. It created a three person collective presidency *and* a potentially (once elected) strong premier and cabinet (that need not be representative of Iraq's diversity).

The senate. Kurdistan will want a senate controlled by regional interests, formed by elections, nominations, and mandatory instructions from the regional and federative entities. It will want the senate to be strong on constitutional matters, especially oversight of judicial appointments. If Shi'a and Sunni Arab politicians embrace a three- or five-region federation, cutting a deal on the design of a senate will not be difficult. But, if most of them persist in preferring the 18-governorates model, the design of the senate will be conflictual.

The supreme court. Kurdistan will want to ensure a regionally representative supreme court and to have a convention of co-decision or unanimity on any matter affecting the distribution of competencies between the federal government and the regions or federative entities. It may win some support for this position from Sunni and Shi'a Arab politicians, but it is not presently evident.

Electoral institutions. Kurdistan, and at least some other federative entities and the smaller nationalities, will want authentic federal and pluralist electoral practices: electoral jurisdictions drawn to conform to federative units; staggered elections or nominations to the senate; and a proportional representation system to elect the federal assembly and the collective executive. These institutions express and protect diversity and inhibit populist majoritarianism. Shi'a Arab politicians may be expected to prefer the converse.

Constitutional renewal. Kurdistan will want to have any permanent constitution to be very difficult to change without its consent. For constitutional amendments it may seek a qualified majority of citizens, that is, a popular majority in a referendum, including in Kurdistan; and a qualified majority in the federal assembly and the senate. It may seek to have certain provisions in the constitution made absolutely irreversible. Arab politicians will be divided in response to these demands, but whether there will be a sufficient "winning coalition" no one knows.

It should be a truism that formal institutions matter. It may seem abstract to reflect on them while the cities of Fallujah and Baghdad boil, the cities of Mosul and Kirkuk simmer, and U.S. troops are guilty of torturing prisoners, but the successful negotiation and widespread popular endorsement of formal institutions are necessary to prevent much worse and more prolonged violence and abuses. These institutions will have to be made by political parties which will include parties from Arab Iraq that have never had governmental responsibility. Political parties, according to many, including Riker, are the key to functioning federations. Although readers may come across claims to the contrary, political scientists do not agree about how they matter, let alone on how they can be designed to govern federations effectively. In any case, we lack practical knowledge (as does every one else at present) about parties in Arab Iraq. We cannot know what support the parties mushrooming in the rest of Iraq will be able to mobilize, or whether their leaders will have sufficient political responsibility to make a sustainable federal bargain. Apart from the two major parties from Kurdistan whose leaderships are tested, who have governed, and whose preferences we know, we are all in the dark. That is just one reason we have written this analysis of the making of the permanent constitution from the perspective of Kurdistan.

Conclusion

It was very improbable that a federation would be made in Philadelphia in 1787 and subsequently ratified by a qualified majority of American states by 1789. It will be even more improbable to negotiate a federation in and between Baghdad, Erbil, Sulaimania, Fallujah, Mosul, Najaf, Karbala, and Basra during the remainder of 2004 and 2005. But sometimes the improbable happens. It requires little thought to foresee or predict disaster, but we hope that this realistic assessment of the negotiation difficulties ahead forearms those arranging or rearranging the marriage of convenience between Kurdistan and the rest of Iraq.

We conclude, first, by emphasizing what we have not said. We have not claimed that Iraq is universally populated by rational agents who know their utility functions and will therefore, subject to our assumptions, negotiate and ratify a federal equilibrium bargain of the kind that we recommend, and that Brendan O'Leary has outlined in Chapter 2. We recognize that Iraq is a deeply disturbed political environment, and that Arab Iraq, in particular, is wartorn, recovering from totalitarian repression, and filled with armed, unemployed, deprivileged and dispossessed men. It is also punctuated with local conflicts that may not be nationally, religiously, or ethnically motivated. We recognize that Iraq is seen by both American neoconservatives and Islamic *jihadists* as a battlefield where civilizations clash, and that most of Iraq's neighbors have in the past, and are now, engaged in spoiling covert interventions of one kind or another (especially Turkey, Iran, and Syria). We recognize that in negotiations between Arab Iraq and Kurdistan, and between Shi'a Arabs and Sunni Arabs, symbolic politics, estimations of group honor, and comparative evaluations of group prestige and worth may end up playing greater roles than rational calculations of net group benefits and costs. We have not "essentialized" Kurds, Shi'a Arabs, and Sunni Arabs. We recognize that these names signify political categories which do not mobilize all encapsulated by them; but we have analyzed the threats and opportunities facing likely politicians who will have reasonable claims to representing these groups. We insist, however, that intra-group divisions may be as important as divisions between groups in determining whether a durable bargain will be made. Each major group minimally has three dispositions and factions: hard-liners, moderates, and the uncommitted. The resolution of their competition will determine the drafting and ratification of the permanent constitution.

We have not, we think, committed any of the multiple fallacies of which Donald Horowitz complains of academic specialists in conflict-resolution (1990a, b, 2001). We have assumed neither that whatever is acceptable will be negotiated, nor that whatever the negotiators agree will be acceptable to their publics. And we have assumed neither that the permanent constitution will be the product of one coherent plan nor that a coherent plan would necessarily work. What we have suggested is that the TAL, itself the product of bargaining, if it is allowed to function, will bias the outcomes of the negotiation of the permanent constitution in ways that are acceptable to Kurdistan, and may be acceptable to enough politicians and voters in Arab Iraq. We have not assumed automatic success in ratifying the permanent constitution. To the contrary: we have emphasized the difficulties facing any draft permanent constitution. We do not, however, think that constitutional design is an oxymoron just because a constitution may be the product of multiple interests and, like success, may have many parents. Design need not presume a single designer, and negotiations may give a constitution a coherence (and a design) that no one fully intended.

We have labored to ensure we are not misunderstood, but for a purpose other than intellectual defensiveness. The analysis here suggests that as a result of the TAL a permanent constitution might be made that meets high normative standards, and which able politicians might have incentives to make, support, and operate. But we will not be surprised if that does not happen. A young minister from Kurdistan might have made the right prediction in conversation with one of us: "The Transitional Law is the first, very best, and very likely the last, constitution Iraq will ever have."[16] It should be of interest that that minister does not want to be right.

Notes

This chapter has benefited from the critical comments of Peter Galbraith.

1. On being asked by one of the ambassadors of the holders of the European Presidency whether Turkey was ready for entry into the European Union, one of us replied that he could confidently say that Turkey was ready for entry into the Soviet Union.

2. We have benefited from Ambassador Peter Galbraith's experience in these matters.

3. "The Iraqi Transitional Government shall have exclusive competence in the following matters: . . . (E) Managing the natural resources of Iraq, which belongs [sic] to all the people of all the regions and governorates of Iraq, in consultation with the governments of the regions and the administrations of the governorates, and distributing the revenues resulting from their sale through the national budget in an equitable manner proportional to the distribution of population throughout the country, and with due regard for areas that were unjustly deprived of these revenues by the previous regime, for dealing with their situations in a positive way, for their needs, and for the degree of development of the different areas of the country" (Governing Council of Iraq 2004, Art. 25).

4. The TAL, because of the preferences of the CPA, requires federal, Kurdistan regional assembly, and governorate elections to be held on the same day (Art. 57(b)), an administrative nightmare for the UN electoral assistance division, and creates the problem that Kurdistan's recognized boundaries cut across the recognized governorates' boundaries.

5. What matters here is not that Kurdistan would be vulnerable to the troops of Arab Iraq, although that would be a risk over the long run. The key vulnerability would be either a Turkish invasion (see Michael Gunter's discussion in this collection), or an Iranian invasion.

6. The analysis here ignores the smaller minority nationalities and sects, because their numbers do not make them "pivotal." We do not think that their interests *should* be neglected. To the contrary. Description and prediction are not the same as prescription. The interests and rights of the smaller nationalities and sects will be decided by the generosity or meanness of the larger parties and by any external leverage the smaller nationalities and sects can exert. The analysis here does suggest a strategy: sensible leaders of the smaller nationalities should promote a viable pan-Iraq federal deal that is acceptable to Shi'a Arabs and Kurds. It would be morally appropriate for them to assist Sunni Arabs as well, but it would only be strategically essential if joining with Sunni Arabs would make them collectively an essential coalition partner for the ratification of the constitution.

7. Estimates of the numbers of internally displaced people before the 19 March

2003 U.S.-led war were summarized in a Brookings Report as ranging from "600,000 to 800,000 in the North of the country [i.e., primarily Kurdish-majority zones] and up to 300,000 in the Center/South i.e., in Arab Iraq]" (Fawcett and Tanner 2004, 1). Individuals, parties, religious figures, and businesses are now asserting claims against the government and Ba'th party from all across the country. The Governing Council has initiated a property claims resolution scheme that addresses adjudication, remedies and compensation, and implementation. The commission must organize a widespread public call for property claims, establish clear procedural standards, dates of eligibility and fair filing deadlines, define the eligibility and classification of claimants, and define evidentiary burdens. Equitable redress and compensation must be provided to those forcibly removed by Arabization, as well as to the secondary occupants of property in which tenancy or ownership rights are in dispute. Each affected person, including those forcibly displaced and the secondary occupants of property in which tenancy or ownership rights are in dispute, must have the right to effective legal remedies, including a hearing by an independent and impartial tribunal. A formal right of return or compensation for all forced removals and nationalized properties needs to be declared and organized. The TAL contains welcome safeguards for private property rights and a just compensation clause. Legislative analysis, repeal, and reform will need to accompany the property claims adjudication process. Property claims in Kirkuk must be addressed immediately. The Governing Council should establish an official body with a representative national and religious makeup and international oversight. Property restitution is vital for the promotion of reconciliation, reconstruction, and economic development within Iraqi society.

8. The *peshmerga* are not, as American commentators often mistakenly suggest, a militia, that is, "a group of people trained to be soldiers who are not part of the permanent army" (Longman Advanced American Dictionary). They are a permanent army, lawfully constituted and subordinated to the Kurdistan National Assembly and its two current executives, the Kurdistan Regional Governments, and under the executive direction of the respective Ministries of Peshmerga. They are regulated according to the Law Regarding the Ministry of Peshmerga, Law Number 5, 1992, October 1 (Kurdistan National Assembly: Laws and Regulations Issued by the Kurdistan National Assembly for the period June 4 1992 to December 31 1992, vol. 1, published in Kurdish and Arabic, Erbil 1997, Ministry of Culture), amended in Amendment Number 1 1996 Regarding Kurdistan Army.

9. "Side payments" is a term of art in bargaining theory; they are not secret bribes to negotiators, but deals made on issues that are incidental to the main issue in the controversy that make the overall deal go down well.

10. Carole O'Leary cites two sources who suggested a five-region model before the war (O'Leary, C. 2002, 20, and n. 9): DPWG (2002) and Karkouti (2002). The DPWG's discussion is very brief and refers to group members who had proposals for 2, 5, 7, 14, and 18 regions (or governorates) (DPWG 2002, 97). The Karkouti reference is a press report on the DPWG, but does not mention the five-region model. The five-region model proposed by one of the authors of this chapter (O'Leary 2003) is conceived as a way of achieving an indirectly and regionally elected collective presidency (with 3 Shi'a Arabs, 1 Kurdistani, and 1 Sunni Arab) that might reflect likely demographic and democratic distributions in Iraq without requiring quotas. These two authors O'Leary are not related (except by likely ancestral tries of which they are

unaware), although they share a common interest in Kurdistan and in a five regions model of a feasible federation.

11. Article 25a defines formulating "sovereign debt policies" as in the exclusive jurisdiction of the federal government: it does not appear to prohibit Kurdistan from fund-raising through borrowing or issuing bonds.

12. One of the authors has visited and heard lectures at both, and witnessed significant numbers of Arabic and Turkomen speakers being educated as cadets alongside Kurdish speakers (March 2004).

13. *Pesh* means "to stand in front of" and *merga* means "death," so the idiomatic translation is "those who face death." This word, whose components are of Persian origin, may have originated in the Mahabad Republic (see Chapter 1).

14. The same article reports that Ambassador Bremer has drafted executive orders for the Iraqi troops to act under the command of U.S. forces (presumably until the withdrawal of Coalition troops) (Chan 2004). Remodeling of Iraq's defense institutions has taken place in consultation with the Governing Council, but under the terms of the TAL may be altered by Iraq's transitional assembly.

15. There are other criticisms of Riker's theory that we shall not consider here. First, it most effectively addresses "voluntary unions," but is less helpful with "imposed federations": India's federation was imposed by the British, and its post-independence and post-partition structure was decided by the center, not in negotiation with the states—but that also explains why some say its constitutional structure is not federal. Some say the post-war German and Austrian federations were impositions, not Rikerian bargains, but they have nevertheless held together, and the German federation has expanded. Second, some critics say that Riker's focus on the military and diplomatic sources of federal bargains is overdone (Dikshit 1971, 1975; King 1982, 2001). They counter that Australia's federal bargain was not fundamentally driven by military considerations. Others claim that the European Union is now a federation (McKay 1996), and that, in consequence, Riker's theory is either falsified, or needs to be modified to describe federations as bargains made under perceived "threats," whether the threats be military, economic, or cultural. Riker's own views on these matters was provisional (Riker 1996).

16. Off-the-record conversation on 6 April 2004, Erbil, Kurdistan.

References

Barringer, Felicity. 2004. "June 30 Goal Is Questioned by 2 Senators." *New York Times*, 5 April.

Birch, Anthony H. 1966. "Approaches to the Study of Federalism." *Political Studies* 14 (1) (February).

Brams, Steven J, Ann Dougherty, and Mathew Weidner. 1994. "Game Theory." In *International Multilateral Negotiations*, ed. I. W. Zartman. San Francisco: Jossey-Bass.

Chan, Sewell. 2004. "U.S. Plan Seeks to Build a Civilian-Run Iraqi Army". *Washington Post*, Sunday March 28, A1.

Dikshit, Ramesh Dutta. 1971. "Research Note: Military Interpretation of Federal Constitutions: A Critique." *Review of Politics* 33: 180–89.

———. 1975. *The Political Geography of Federalism.* New Delhi: Macmillan.

Fawcett, John and Henry Tanner. 2004. "The Internally Displaced People of Iraq. The Brookings Institution-SAIS Project on Internal Displacement." Occasional Paper. Brookings Institution, Washington D.C., October.

Fisher, Roger and William Ury. 1987 (1981). *Getting to Yes: Negotiating Agreement Without Giving In.* London: Arrow Books.

Gelb, Leslie H. 2003. "The Three-State Solution." *New York Times,* 25 November.

Governing Council of Iraq. 2004. Law of Administration for the State of Iraq for the Transitional Period. (Transitional Law) Baghdad Governing Council of Iraq and Coalition Provisional Authority. <http://www.cpa-iraq.org/government/TAL.html>.

Hall, Lavina, ed. 1993. *Negotiation: Strategies for Mutual Gain, the Basic Seminar of the Harvard Program on Negotiation.* Newbury Park, Calif.: Sage.

Holbrooke, Richard. 1998. *To End a War.* New York: Random House.

Horowitz, Donald L. 1990a. "Ethnic Conflict Management for Policymakers." In *Conflict and Peacemaking in Multiethnic Societies,* ed. Joseph P. Montville. Lexington, Mass.: Heath. 115–30.

———. 1990b. "Making Moderation Pay: The Comparative Politics of Ethnic Conflict Management." In *Conflict and Peacemaking in Multiethnic Societies,* ed. Joseph P. Montville. Lexington, Mass., Heath. 451–75.

———. 2000. "Constitutional Design: An Oxymoron?" In *Designing Democratic Institutions,* ed. Ian Shapiro and Stephen Macedo. New York: New York University Press. 264–84.

Karkouti, Mustapha. 2002. "Exclusive: Post-Saddam Roadmap Envisions Federal State." *Gulf News,* 5 December.

King, Preston. 1982. *Federalism and Federation.* London: Croom Helm.

———. 2001. *Federalism and Federation.* 2nd ed. London: Frank Cass.

Makiya, Kanan. 2003. "A Model for Post-Saddam Iraq." *Journal of Democracy* 14 (3): 5–12.

McKay, David. 1996. *Rush to Union: Understanding the European Federal Bargain.* Oxford: Clarendon Press.

Naab, Richard M. 2004. "Why Keeping the Peshmerga Makes Sense." *Washington Post,* 1 April.

O'Leary, Brendan. 2003. "Multi-national Federalism, Power-Sharing, Federacy and the Kurds of Iraq." Paper presented at conference on "Multi-Nationalism, Power-Sharing and the Kurds in a New Iraq," George Washington University, Washington D.C., 12 September, <http://www.krg.org/docs/federalism/federalism-iraqi-kurds-paper-sep03.pdf>.

O'Leary, Carole A. 2002. "The Kurds of Iraq: Recent History, Future Prospects." *MERIA: Middle East Review of International Affairs* 6 (4) (December): 17–29.

Raiffa, Howard. 1982. *The Art and Science of Negotiation. How to Resolve Conflicts and Get the Best out of Bargaining.* Cambridge, Mass.: Belknap Press of Harvard University Press.

Riker, William H. 1964. *Federalism: Origin, Operation, Significance.* Boston: Little, Brown.

————. 1975. "Federalism." In *Handbook of Political Science*, ed. Fred I. Greenstein and Nelson W. Polsby. Reading, Mass.: Addison-Wesley. 93–172.

————. 1996. "European Federalism: The Lessons of Past Experience." In *Federalizing Europe? The Costs, Benefits and Preconditions of Federal Political Systems*, ed. Joachim Jens Hesse and Vincent Wright. Oxford: Oxford University Press. 9–24.

Stansfield, Gareth R. V. 2003. *Iraqi Kurdistan: Political Development and Emergent Democracy*. London: Routledge.

Washington Post. 2004. "Disarming Iraq's Militias." Editorial, 14 March.

Zartman, I. William. 1996. "Dynamics and Constraints in Negotiations in Internal Conflicts." In *Elusive Peace: Negotiating an End to Civil Wars*, ed. I. William Zartman. Washington, D.C.: The Brookings Institution. 3–29.

Zartman, I. William and Jeffrey Z. Rubin, eds. 2000. *Power and Negotiation*. Ann Arbor: University of Michigan Press.

Chapter 5

Not to Be Forgotten: Children's Rights in the Permanent Constitution

Molly McNulty

"Programmes designed during reconstruction can lay foundations for child protection and strengthen social infrastructures, particularly in relation to health and education. Children are rarely mentioned in reconstruction plans or peace agreements, yet children must be at the centre of rebuilding."
—*Graça Machel*, Impact of Armed Conflict on Children *(1996)*

Politicians consider children under the rubric of "special populations"—if they consider them at all—even though women and children comprise up to four out of every five people who are displaced, injured, or killed in wars and ethno-political conflicts around the globe (Machel 2000, 5; UNICEF 2003, 1). Children comprise almost half the population in Kurdistan and Iraq, yet the needs of children have been marginalized in reconstruction programs. Analyses of capital infrastructure and plans for political renovation have not assessed the best interests of children separately from the interests of adults, yet their interests are not identical. The choices made and priorities set during constitutional negotiations, structural decisions, and the design of donor aid packages have the potential to save many children's lives. But when children's needs for educated mothers, clean water, food, medical care, education, housing, and safe neighborhoods are designated as "soft" needs, or slotted into the "long-term" or "phase 2" columns of strategic plans, children's health may be needlessly damaged. Indeed, lives have already have been lost. A half million children in Iraq died during the previous decade from preventable causes, the casualties of leadership decisions deferring or demoting their distinctive needs (Blacker, Jones, and Ali 2003, 217). Children cannot eat democracy, federation, autonomy, or the Shari'a. New roads cannot warm new babies. Children's needs cannot wait the resolution of adult debates. The bill of rights in the transitional administrative law contained no specific guarantee of children's rights (see Chapter 2 of the TAL, in Appendix 2). Hopefully, when the permanent constitution is made in a more open, democratic, and transparent manner, the rights of children will be properly considered and fully included, and the Kurdistan National Assembly will independently create a children's bill of rights which will be vigorously implemented in law and policy.

This chapter reviews the status of children and youth from birth through age eighteen in Iraq and Kurdistan, examining the special needs of children for survival, health, and development, with a particular focus on the needs created by armed conflict and its aftermath. It ranks priorities for the reconstruction of Kurdistan and Iraq from the viewpoint of children and describes how choices related to constitutional law, federal political systems, and governmental structures can facilitate or hinder children's growth. Taking the definition of children's needs in the United Nations Convention on the Rights of the Child as the standard, it draws on practical examples from other countries' constitutions and political practices to implement child-friendly laws. The critical constitutional and policy questions related to children are these: What affirmative duties do governments have to children? What laws and governmental structures assure the best outcomes for children? What structures permit effective monitoring of governments' commitments to children and assure accountability for policy choices and the expenditure of funds?

The Status of Children in Kurdistan and Iraq

The populations of Kurdistan and Iraq include a large proportion of children, even by comparison with many other Middle Eastern countries. About 550,000 Kurdistanis and 17 percent of Iraqis are children below the age of five. The UN estimated the total population of the Kurdistan Regional Government (KRG) at 3,757,058, or approximately 16 percent of the estimated total population of Iraq (23,315,140). Demographic projections suggest a "continued and truly astounding population growth into the next half century" (Cincotta, Engelman, and Anastasion 2003, 13, 40; Fuller 2003, 4). This suggests that the demands of a growing population will not have even begun to tail off, or have barely stabilized, for the next half century, placing continuing serious long term strain on the state infrastructure and society. Furthermore, countries with large "youth bulges" (over 40 percent of the population) experience a greater likelihood of civil conflict; the five largest are in Yemen, the Occupied Palestinian Territories, Djibouti, the Sudan—and Iraq. Hence, the future and stability of Kurdistan and Iraq will depend upon its ability to meet the needs of this burgeoning sector of its population.

The most recent assessment of the status of children and youth throughout Iraq (including Kurdistan) was conducted in 2001 by UNICEF and the Iraqi Ministry of Planning (UNICEF and Republic of Iraq Council of Ministers 2001). UNICEF assessed the children of Kurdistan separately in 2002 (UNICEF 2002).

Table 5.1 displays a range of indicators of child welfare in Kurdistan and Iraq. Although twenty years ago children in Iraq fared well compared to their counterparts throughout the Middle East, indicators of maternal and child well-being began to decline in the mid-1980s, especially in Kurdistan after the Anfal campaign and the civil war, and in the rest of Iraq after the 1991 Gulf War and the imposition of sanctions. When the Oil-for-Food Programme began to deliver aid to children in the mid-1990s, only Kurdistan successfully used these assets to reduce child malnutrition and mortality. The situation of children in central and southern Iraq did not improve.

The needs of children in state reconstruction can be prioritized in two ways: by child-targeted services and by population-wide services with a differential impact upon children. Child-specific services include medical care during childbirth, infancy, and early childhood, child protection, and education. The disproportionate effects on children of population-wide planning decisions are equally important, but often overlooked. For example, safe drinking water is important to both adults and children, but fluoridation of water, a policy choice within water planning, is vital to children's future oral health (though of less import to adults). Timing is also paramount. Emergencies and development should not be separated, because "particularly for children, emergency aid—investment that secures their physical and emotional survival—will also be the basis for their long-term development" (Machel 1996, para. 243).

Children's very survival is a matter of urgency in Iraq and, to a lesser degree, in Kurdistan (UN Population Fund 2003; UNICEF 2003). Although reliable data on the death rate among children during the war is scarce, proxy measures of preventable mortality, such as rates of maternal mortality, infant mortality, and mortality among children under five, are extremely high (Blacker, Jones, and Ali 2003). The status of children in need of special protection is particularly dire; these include disabled children, street and working children, internally displaced children, children in orphanages, mine victims,

TABLE 5.1. INDICATORS OF CHILDREN'S HEALTH, SURVIVAL, AND EDUCATION IN
KURDISTAN AND IRAQ

Indicators	Kurdistan[1]		Iraq—central and south[2]	
	N or rate	Percent	N or rate	Percent
Demographics				
Population[3]	3,757,058	13.9	23,315,140	86.1
Children ages 0–5, % of total population	550,000	15.4	3,555,000	33.8
Children under age 1[4]	64,709	1.7	671,291	2.9
Mother and child mortality[1],[5]				
Maternal mortality rate (per 100,000 women)	120.0		204.0	
Infant mortality rate (per 1,000 live births)	58.7		108.0	
Children under age 5 mortality rate	71.8		131.0	
Disease risks[1],[2]				
Access to safe drinking water (%)		Urban 96.0		Urban 97.5
		Rural 83.0		Rural 51.5
Access to sanitation (%)		Urban 98.2		Urban 99.0
		Rural 82.6		Rural 78.0
Malnutrition[1],[6]				
Stunting (chronic malnutrition)		14.5		22.1
Underweight		13.4		15.9
Wasting (acute malnutrition)		4.1		6.0
Education[2]				
Adult literacy		74.0		73.5
Primary school attendance, ages 7–12	Boys 67.7			76.3
	Girls 76.4			

Sources: (1) UNICEF (2002); (2)UNICEF and Republic of Iraq Council of Ministers (2001); (3) Humanitarian Coordinator for Iraq and Health Coordination Group (2003); (4) WHO (2003); (5) Ali and Shah (2000); (6) Nutrition Research Institute, Ministry of Health, and UNICEF 2003.

children in conflict with the law, and traumatized children (Salem-Pickartz 2001a). The statistics of mortality and morbidity given in Table 5.1 indicate that the government of Iraq failed to fulfill its obligations to children and hence must increase future spending on preventive nutrition and medical programs to improve maternal and child health, survival, and development (Salem-Pickartz 2001b).

Federations and the Protection of Children's Rights

Discourse about federal political systems revolves around power–sharing, which is entirely appropriate for states like Iraq whose recent histories are marred by state-sponsored political, ethnic, and religious violence. But the power-sharing discourse usually neglects the aspect of political power that is most salient for children, affirmative governmental duties. Federal political systems tend to protect regional autonomy against power from the central government, sometimes construing rights in a negative way, as freedom from coercion. Affirmative governmental duties, however, are necessary if the rights of children are to be realized, whether at the federal or regional level. Human rights for children and affirmative government duties to secure the well-being of children have been clearly laid out in the United Nations Convention on the Rights of the Child (UNCRC), key sections of which relate specifically to children affected by ethnic and political conflict such as those of Kurdistan and Iraq, summarized in Table 5.2. Countries that have implemented the Convention during the past decade provide examples of constitutional law protecting children's rights and defining the corresponding governmental and family duties. Other important lessons may be drawn from these countries' experiences about implementation and evaluation.

The UNCRC is an international treaty that defines children's rights, government and family duties, and indicators for evaluating implementation, and makes special provisions for children affected by armed conflict (United Nations General Assembly 1989; United Nations General Assembly 2000). The UNCRC rests upon four principles: the right of the child to life and survival; the right to nondiscrimination; the duty of governments to act in the best interests of the child; and the child's right to participate in political debate. The UNCRC defines child-specific rights to development, health care, education, and gender equality and includes special rights for children in "difficult circumstances," including ethnic minority and indigenous children, refugee, orphaned, and homeless children, the disabled, and those affected by war. The UNCRC is more widely ratified than any other international treaty. Signatory states agree to provide implementation reports every five years.

The Convention on the Rights of the Child achieved global acclamation of children's rights as human rights. An important but lesser-known dimension of the Convention is its wonderful toolbox. The Convention has practical uses for countries undertaking reconstruction after armed conflicts. It provides a legal and policy framework for the establishment of social goals and measurable indicators of progress and implementation. It suggests rules and

TABLE 5.2. THE UNITED NATIONS CONVENTION ON THE RIGHTS OF THE
CHILD—SELECTED RIGHTS AND DUTIES OF SPECIAL IMPORTANCE TO COUNTRIES
EMERGING FROM ETHNOPOLITICAL CONFLICT

Child rights	CRC	Government duties
Definition of a child • Every human being below the age of 18 is a child.	Art 1	• Write consistent definitions of childhood in all applicable laws.
Non-discrimination • Irrespective of the child's or his or her parent's or legal guardian's race, color, sex, language, religion, political or other opinion, national, ethnic, or social origin, property, disability, birth, or other status • Support to all children living at risk, especially those living on the streets	Art 2	• State parties shall respect and ensure rights of convention without discrimination of any kind • Appropriate measures to ensure the child protected against all forms of discrimination or punishment
Best interests of the child • Primary consideration in all actions concerning children	Art 3	• State parties shall ensure protection and care for well-being • Ensure that the institutions, services and facilities responsible for care and protection shall conform with standards set by authorities
Implementation of rights in the convention • All rights implemented to the maximum extent of available resources. • Implies adequate budgetary analysis	Art 4	• State parties shall undertake all appropriate measures to maximum extent of their available resources
Parental guidance and the child's evolving capacities • The family is defined as the fundamental group of society and the natural environment for the growth and well-being of all its members and particularly children	Art 5	• State parties shall respect the responsibilities of parents or other persons legally responsible for child

TABLE 5.2. (CONTINUED)

Child rights	CRC	Government duties
Child's right to life and maximum survival and development • Requires measures of care and protections for children affected by armed conflict • Protection from trafficking • Protection from recruitment into armed forces	Art 6	• State parties recognize that every child has right to life • State parties shall ensure maximum extent possible the survival and development of the child
Birth registration, name, nationality, and right to know and be cared for by parents • Every person has a right to a given name and to the surname of his parents or that of one of them	Art 7	• Shall be registered immediately after birth and shall have the right to a name, acquire a nationality and to know and be cared for by parents • State parties ensure the implementation of rights
Separation from parents • Arises from armed conflict or when they have become refugees	Art 9	• State parties shall ensure that a child not be separated from parents against their will unless in best interest of child • State parties shall respect the right of the child who is separated from one or both parents to maintain personal relations • If separation results from action initiated by state party, child should be provided with information of absent member(s) of family
Respect for the views of the child • Participation of children at all levels of policymaking • Planning and provision of health services relevant to children	Art 12	• State parties shall assure to the child the right to express views in all matters affecting the child • Provided with opportunity to be heard in any judicial and administrative proceedings affecting the child

TABLE 5.2. (CONTINUED)

Child rights	CRC	Government duties
Child's right to protection from all forms of violence • Protection from witnessing or experiencing domestic violence • Protection from paramilitary or police punishments	Art 19	• State parties shall take all appropriate measures to protect the child from all forms of physical or mental violence, abuse, maltreatment while in the care of person who has the care of the child • Procedures for establishment of social programs to provide necessary support for child and those who have care for the child
Refugee children • Outside their country of nationality because of a fear of being persecuted • To obtain information for reunification with his or her family • Protection for children deprived of family, including safe camps and least restrictive orphanages • Includes children re-settled due to ethnic cleansing or forced migration.	Art 22	• State parties shall ensure refugee children protection and humanitarian assistance • State parties shall protect and assist a child to trace the parents in order to obtain information necessary for reunification with his or her family and if no parents or members of family can be found, the child shall receive same protection as other children deprived of family environment
Rights of disabled children • Armed conflict is a cause of injury and disability • Injury compounded by reduction or breakdown of health and other services • Increased need for special education services • Mental health therapy is a heightened need • Right to least restrictive housing and education.	Art 23	• State parties recognize that a mentally or physically disabled child should enjoy a full and decent life and right to special care, effective access to and receives education, training, health care services, rehabilitation services, preparation for employment and recreation opportunities • Shall promote the exchange of information in preventive health care and treatment in order to improve skills and to widen experience

TABLE 5.2. (CONTINUED)

Child rights	CRC	Government duties
Child's right to health and health services • Right to access services of equal quality regardless of ethnicity • Increased need for safe motherhood initiatives. • Protection from genocidal policies denying medical care • Protection from landmines and environmental threats • HIV/AIDS a heightened risk in conflict	Art 24	• State parties shall strive to ensure that no child is deprived of his or her right to access to such health care services • Shall take measures to diminish infant and child mortality, health care to all children, combat disease and malnutrition, ensure pre-natal and post-natal care for mothers, access to education in child health and nutrition, advantages of breast-feeding, hygiene, and environmental sanitation and the prevention of accidents
Child's right to education • Girls and rural children particularly neglected. • Education often disrupted in armed conflicts.	Art 28	• State parties recognize the right of the child to education • Make primary education compulsory and free • Encourage the development of different forms of secondary educations • Promote and encourage elimination of illiteracy
Children of minorities or of indigenous people • To enjoy his or her own culture, practice his or her own religion, use his or her own language	Art 30	• A child belonging to a minority or who is indigenous shall not be denied the right to enjoy his or her own culture, to profess and practice his or her own religion, or to use his or her own language
Protection of children affected by armed conflict • Under 18-year-olds recruited in armed forces • Effects of landmines	Art 38	• State parties undertake to respect and ensure rules or international humanitarian law applicable to them in armed conflicts which are relevant to the child • Refrain from recruiting any person who has not attained the age of 18 years into the armed forces, and ensuring that persons who have not attained the age of 15 years do not take part in hostilities • Protect the civil population in armed conflicts and take measures to protect and care for children affected by armed conflict

TABLE 5.2. (CONTINUED)

Child rights	CRC	Government duties
Rehabilitation of child victims • Victims of torture, inhuman or degrading treatment or punishment • Armed conflict	Art 39	• State parties shall take all appropriate measures to promote physical and psychological recovery and social reintegration of a child victim

Sources: Machel (1996); UNGA (1989, 2000).

measures of equity in budgetary and funding decisions. Finally, implementation of the Convention suggests particular choices in the design of federal political systems, which have particular import for societies divided by national, ethnic, religious, or linguistic fault-lines.

Iraq

Iraq ratified the Convention on the Rights of the Child in 1994 and approved a National Plan of Action in 1995 (UNHRC 1996). To the extent that Iraqi law is still considered binding on all former governorates, Kurdistan can be deemed to be a party to the Convention and responsible for all the governmental duties contained therein. Iraq filed its first implementation report with the United Nations Committee on the Rights of the Child in 1996. Authored during the government of Saddam Hussein, this report described the legislative framework relating to all the articles of the Convention. Iraq did not file its five-year implementation report, which was due in 2001. It did, however, participate in a UNICEF-led global assessment of indicators of children's well-being. This assessment's primary limitation was that no information was given about changes to the legal framework of children's rights. Fortunately, that same year a more thorough evaluation of implementation of the UNCRC in Kurdistan was conducted for UNICEF by the consultants Andrew de Carpentier and Samir Debabneh (UNICEF 2002). This report summarized the legislative and institutional framework for children within the KRG, while recognizing that this framework did not apply to the rest of Iraq. The UNICEF authors reported that, based on the classifications of children under the law, there is already a "detailed and sophisticated legislative framework covering the rights of the child in terms of personal status, education, labour, and criminal law" (UNICEF 2002, 17). Although an assessment of the degree of compliance of current laws in Iraq and Kurdistan with the Convention is beyond the scope of this chapter, it appears that there is a platform upon which to bring the legal and legislative framework into conformity with the Convention.

Constitutions and Children

Constitutional provisions for human rights and governmental duties that apply to citizens of all ages are insufficient to protect children. Their "physical, emotional and economic dependence on adults . . . may deserve special measures of protection within the constitution; and because the future prosperity of the State depends on them, it is also in the State's interest to accord them special constitutional rights" (Hodgkin and Newell 2002, 66). The UNCRC requires signatory states to "harmonize" their domestic law, including constitutions, legislation, and regulations, with all the provisions of the Convention. As a result, signing the Convention has prompted many countries to amend their constitutions, or to draft new constitutions with children as a component of human rights or populations in need of special protections.

The UNCRC has been in force for over a decade in most countries, and we are learning valuable lessons about legal provisions and their implementation. The countries discussed in this chapter fall into two categories: first, two post-colonial federations that have experienced major conflicts arising from ethnic, political, or international violence (India and South Africa); and second, two long-standing pluri-national federations (Canada and Switzerland). The first category is significant because countries that are rebuilding after ethnopolitical violence usually write new constitutions, and hence have an opportunity to redefine human rights that take children into account. The second category is important because countries recovering from such conflicts try to prevent future violence by creating equitable power-sharing structures, modeled on successful examples elsewhere that guarantee previously aggrieved groups a voice in the government. These four federations illustrate a variety of options for drafting constitutional rights, structuring governmental duty-sharing, and creating specific responsibilities for implementation.

India

The Indian constitution contains six broad categories of fundamental rights that are justiciable—that is, liable to legal remedy: equality, freedom of speech and expression; freedom from exploitation; freedom of religion, the conservation of culture; and constitutional remedies for the enforcement of all these fundamental rights. The constitution also includes certain "Directive Princi-

TABLE 5.3. LAWS APPLICABLE TO CHILDREN IN IRAQ AND KURDISTAN

Current Iraq civil law	Differences in Kurdistan law

Right to childhood
    Iraqi civil law defines a child as any person under the age of 18. The law for Juvenile Care (76) of 1983 further designates children as:
    • minors, if the child is older than 9 and younger than 18;
    • juveniles, if older than 9 and younger than 18. Juveniles are divided into two groups:
        • boys and girls—older than 9 and younger than 15
        • adolescents—older than 15 and younger than 18	

Right to nationality
    • Law of Birth and Death Registration (1971)—the licensed birth assistant who supervises a delivery fills in a birth certificate form for the new born. The birth assistant sends the form to the Civil Status Department, which issues a civil status card.
    • Civil Status Law—every Iraqi child has the right to a civil status card.[a]
    • Law of Nationality (1963)—gives a child the right to Iraqi nationality on the basis of the father's Iraq nationality.[b]
	However in Northern Iraq, this law was for some time implemented largely in urban areas only.

Right to health The parents are also responsible for the health of the child according to the Law of Public Health (1981).	

TABLE 5.3. (CONTINUED)

Current Iraq civil law	Differences in Kurdistan law

Parental Responsibilities
- Personal Status Law (1959) regulates the rights of the children in the family and the responsibility of the parents towards them. These include rights for lineage, nursing, guardianship, protection and spending on the child until she/he reaches maturity. The child's guardian, usually the father, is responsible for the child's upbringing and education.
- Primary school by-laws (1978), the parents should also be involved in their children's education through parent-teacher associations.

Inheritance
- The father can select someone to be a trustee for his child after his death to administer the minor's property. If he failed to do this or if the court considers the trustee incompetent, the court will select a trustee, giving preference to the mother (the Law of the Care to the Minors, article 34).
- Inheritance is based on the Shariʿa and assumes that the male is usually responsible for the expenses of the family. A child is entitled to half the share of her brother of property inherited from the father.

Education
- The National Pact of 1971 gives all Iraqi citizens the right to free education at all levels. In 1976, legislation made primary school education compulsory. Plans to make school attendance mandatory at the intermediate level could not be carried out.

TABLE 5.3. (CONTINUED)

Current Iraq civil law	Differences in Kurdistan law
Freedom of expression and religion	
• Article 97 of the Civil Code (1951) provides for children to express their views.	In Northern Iraq all religious groups and sects follow their religious practices freely. The Law of Political Parties in the Iraqi
• Iraq has expressed reservations on the issue of freedom of religion.	Region (1933) and the Law of Association Kurdistan Region (1993) allow for freedom of association.

Source: Based completely on UNICEF (2002), *The Situation of Children in Northern Iraq: An Assessment Based on the United Nations Convention on the Rights of the Child*, Br. Andrew de Carpentier and Mr. Samir Debabneh, "Consultancy Visit Report" for assessment, evaluation, and planning, March-April 2001, http://www.krg.org/986/unicef-children-sep-2002.pdf. The legal provisions are representative, and are *not* intended to provide a comprehensive legal overview of CRC compliance.
a. In the 1980s, when the Iraqi government encouraged population growth, the civil status card was an incentive that added substantially to the guardian's monthly salary. Since OFFP started in 1997, the monthly distribution of the food basket has been linked to the civil status card of each family member. This has encouraged birth registration, and according to UNICEF's Household Survey 2000, 98.9 percent of children under the age of five were registered.
b. However, children cannot choose between the nationality of mother and the father, if they have different nationalities, nor can they apply for nationality before the age of 18. Women do not have any say concerning the nationality of their children.

ples of State Policy" which, though not justiciable, are fundamental in the governance of the country, and it is the duty of the state to apply these principles while framing laws. The "Directive Principles" declare that the state shall strive to promote the welfare of the people by securing and protecting, as effectively as possible, a social order based on social, economic, and political justice. The principles also establish that the state shall provide opportunities and facilities for children to develop in a healthy manner, including free and compulsory education for all children up to the age of fourteen years. A distinctive feature of the Indian constitution is that the chapter on fundamental rights recognizes children as persons entitled to fundamental rights (UNCRC 2003b).

India reports that it created "special government mechanisms to promote, coordinate and monitor measures for children at central and district levels" (India 2003). The Department of Women and Child Development (DWCD) is the lead agency in the national government for all issues pertaining to children. India's federal government reports, "It is invariably consulted on all major initiatives relating to children, including amendments to existing legislation, or introduction of new legislation. This process enables the Government to reduce the possibility of any conflicts" (UNCRC 2003b, para. 123). Housed in the Ministry of Human Resource Development, this agency is responsible for matters concerning women and children at the central level. The Minister for Human Resource Development and the Minister of State for Human Resource Development head the department, while its personnel "comprise a mix of civil servants and technocrats." Each state government also has a Department of Women and Child Development with a similar organizational structure. The department "formulates plans, policies and programmes, enacts/amends legislation, and guides and coordinates the efforts of both governmental and nongovernmental agencies in the field of women and child development. The DWCD has the responsibility for a wide range of child development programmes and as being the nodal department for the implementation of the UNCRC and for coordinating the UNCRC reporting process, it has a strong children's agenda. It plays a complementary role to the other developmental programmes in sectors such as health, education and rural development" (UNCRC 2003b).

South Africa

South Africa's new constitution contains a specific article which guarantees children a number of rights and freedoms that are provided for under the UN Convention in the Rights of the Child (Hodgkin and Newell 2002, 67). Article 28 of the Bill of Rights reads:

(1) Every child has the right:
    (a) to a name and a nationality from birth;
    (b) to family care or parental care, or to appropriate alternative care when removed from the family environment;
    (c) to basic nutrition, shelter, basic health care services and social services;
    (d) to be protected from maltreatment, neglect, abuse or degradation;
    (e) to be protected from exploitative labour practices;
    (f) not to be required or permitted to perform work or provide services that
        (i) are inappropriate for a person of the child's age; or
        (ii) place at risk the child's well-being, education, physical or mental health or spiritual, moral or social development;
    (g) not to be detained except as a measure of last resort, in which case, in addition to the rights a child enjoys under sections 12 and 35 [relating to freedom and security of the person and rights of arrested, detained and accused persons], the child may be detained only for the shortest appropriate period of time, and the right to be:
        (i) kept separately from detained persons over the age of 18 years; and
        (ii) treated in a manner, and kept in conditions, that take account of the child's age; and
    (h) to have a legal practitioner assigned to the child by the State, and at State

expense, in civil proceedings affecting the child, if substantial injustice would otherwise result; and

(i) not to be used directly in armed conflict, and to be protected in times of armed conflict.

(2) A child's best interests are of paramount importance in every matter concerning the child.

(3) In this section "child" means a person under the age of 18 years. (Hodgkin and Newell 2002: 67, citing South Africa IR, para. 1)

The examples of India and South Africa are especially relevant to the situation in Iraq and Kurdistan, because both these federations have become pluralistic, multicultural, and democratic states and have sought to redress historic and current maltreatment of children. Constitutional provisions in South Africa and India register concerns with the protection of children from exploitation as laborers and with their rights to health, education, and welfare. The differences between the structures that these two federations established to protect the rights of children reflect their distinct historical circumstances. While the Indian constitution establishes a special bureau to oversee matters affecting women and children, who are conceptualized as vulnerable groups whose interests are bound up together, the South African constitution embeds these matters in fundamental rights and recognizes that some children have lost their parents and become involved in armed conflicts.

Canada

The example of Canada is particularly relevant to Kurdistan and Iraq, because in this pluri-national, bilingual, and democratic federation Québec, with its distinctive ethno-linguistic identity, enjoys considerable autonomy and power-sharing in the federal government. The substantial degree of decentralization in Canada directly and indirectly affects its legal provisions for the protection and implementation of the rights of children. In contrast to India and South Africa, Canada does not establish any child-specific rights or child-specific governmental duties in its constitution. The Canadian Charter of Rights and Freedoms does contain an applicability provision which includes age: "Every individual is equal before and under the law and has the right to the equal protection and equal benefit of the law without discrimination and, in particular, without discrimination based on . . . age" (Constitution Acts, 1867 to 1982, Canadian Charter of Rights and Freedoms, Schedule B to the Canada Act 1982, UK 1982, enacted 17 April 1982, chap. 11, section 15, subsection 1).

As a federation with two major ethnolinguistic groups, Canada recognizes the rights of both francophone and anglophone minorities throughout the country. An article of the Charter of Rights and Freedoms on "Minority Language Educational Rights" gives parents the right to have their children schooled in their own first language, regardless whether it is English or French, at public expense—even if the language of choice is the minority language of the province (Canadian Charter of Rights and Freedoms, sec. 23). In contrast to India, the Canadian governmental structure appears to be highly decentralized, with few federation-wide policies, plans, or programs targeted specifically at children. Canada is a federal state comprised of ten provinces and three territories. The federal government has jurisdiction over criminal justice and child custody in divorce, while the provinces have jurisdiction over other family and social issues. Before Canada ratified the UNCRC, the only monitoring mechanism for implementation of international human rights instruments was a federal-provincial-territorial continuing Committee of Officials on Human Rights, which functioned as an "instrument of liaison and exchange."

After ratification, Canada created a Children's Bureau, housed in the central Department of Health, designed to "enable the Government of Canada to keep a close watch on children's issues" and to ensure "consistency and coordination for all federal programmes and policies for children." These structures were found wanting by the UN oversight committee, and by the time of Canada's second report on implementation of the UNCRC Canada had created new federal mechanisms to oversee children's issues. Foremost was the National Children's Agenda (NCA), a "federal-provincial-territorial and multi-sectoral initiative, to develop a shared vision and common goals to enhance the well-being of Canada's children" (para 11). The Prime Minister created the new position of Secretary of State for Children and Youth, who "works with Federal Ministers such as the Minister of Human Resources Development and the Minister of Health, on issues affecting the well-being of children and youth" (para. 14). The Social Union Framework Agreement, signed by all first ministers except Québec to coordinate the renewal of Canada's social programs with support from the Health, Education, Social Services, and Justice sectors, replaced the Children's Bureau by a Childhood and Youth Division as a federal center for expertise, leadership, and coordination for issues, activities, and programs concerning children and youth. Housed within Health Canada, it delivers programs, supports policy development, and undertakes strategic analysis of future trends. The Childhood and Youth Division also helps to provide policy development and coordination related to the Convention on the Rights of the Child. Canada's Minister of Foreign Affairs appointed a Special Advisor on Children's Rights "with a mandate to provide advice on children's issues, and liaise with nongovernmental organizations, the academic community, the private sector and the public" (para 30). The organization of the report reflects this federal structure; as each province and territory reports separately on implementation of the Convention.

The Canadian province whose experience and aspirations are closest to those of Kurdistan is Québec. In contrast to Canada as a whole, Québec has incorporated the UNCRC into both its constitution (Charter of Human Rights and Freedoms) and its legislation (e.g., the Youth Protection Act). However, unlike Canada, Québec limits enjoyment of these rights on the basis of age, which is a category of identity protected from discrimination under international law. Québec is the only Canadian province to lodge the permanent monitoring mechanism for the rights of the child and the responsibilities of government within its Commission on Human Rights, which has been renamed the Commission on Human Rights and the Rights of Youth. The commission also has a mandate to investigate "any situation where it has reason to believe that the rights of a child or of a group of children have been encroached upon by persons, establishments or bodies, unless the Court is already seized of it," to "conduct a program of public information and education relating to the protection of young persons' rights," to conduct assessments of the extent to which Québec law harmonizes with the charter, "to direct and encourage research and publications relating to fundamental rights and freedoms or to the rights of children; and to make recommendations, in particular to the Minister of Health and Social Services, the Minister of Education and the Minister of Justice concerning the rights of children."

The consequences of decentralization for the situation of children across Canada are difficult to assess, because Canada does not collect the data necessary for the computation of the index of children's well-being that was adopted by the World Summit for Children in 2002. Canada's favorable standing on the index may simply reflect its high level of economic prosperity and its broad distribution of wealth rather than any distinct policy or budgetary commitment to the needs of children. A Canadian parallel for Kurdistan is offered by Québec; the culturally and nationally most distinctive province that enjoys the greatest degree of autonomy has made the most progress toward implementing the rights and duties guaranteed by the UNCRC.

Canada's experience with highly decentralized authority represents an example of the dynamic tension between the global effort to improve the well-being of children through a centralized agenda and pluri-national states's desire to maintain social peace by deference to local cultural traditions and by power-sharing. Compliance with the UNCRC has increased federal governmental Canadian structures devoted to children's rights, despite the trend toward devolution and decentralization in the Canadian federation. Provinces are free to implement the UNCRC agenda more vigorously than the federal government chooses to do. Canada may be an apposite model for a future federation of Iraq, and Québec may be a model for Kurdistan.

Belgium

Belgium, which has a complex federal system and a pluralist population organized into German-speaking, Flemish-speaking, and French-speaking communities, now has substantial experience addressing the challenges that diverse societies and federalist structures pose to implementing the UNCRC. Questions raised in Belgium related to federalism have been: What proportion of the official budget is allocated to social programs for children, at both the national and community levels? What indicators are available, and what objectives have been set? Has the government established a mechanism at the national level to coordinate and evaluate measures for implementing the Convention? (United Nations Office of the High Commissioner for Human Rights 1995, paras. 5, 7).

Belgium, like Canada, was unable to report what proportion of the official budget is allocated to social programs for children at the federal level or for all of its ethno-linguistic communities. At the time of Belgium's first report to the United Nations, the German-speaking community was able to produce indicators related to implementation of the Convention "to the maximum extent of resources" by identifying the proportion of its budget spent on children and the proportion of the children's budget spent on education. The French- and Flemish-speaking communities were not able to provide this information; instead, they reported the total funds spent on various child and youth programs. The federal government of Belgium did not collect statistics on how many children were served by its primary social assistance programs (Belgium 1995a, 6–9).

In 1995, Belgium reported that a working committee had been established within the Ministry of Justice to examine the feasibility of a permanent monitoring structure for all the human rights instruments to which Belgium is party (Belgium 1995a, 14). A private-sector initiative had established a working committee to examine structural options for monitoring the Convention on the Rights of the Child (Belgium 1995a, 14–15). Belgium had not yet established such a structure when it submitted its first report, and apparently had no existing government agency upon which to build. Similar to Canada's protestations in its first report to the UN, Belgium claimed that since it had broad human rights protections in place for all persons, these protections applied to children as well, and thus no new special attention, rights, or mechanisms were required. In Belgium, as in Canada, one region performed better than the others at establishing regional monitoring structures with policy authority. The Flemish government established a Centre for the Promotion of Social Assistance for Children and Families (Belgium 1995a, 3–4).

Harmonizing the provisions of the UNCRC with domestic law has proven difficult in Belgium. In its first hearing before the UN, Belgium reported that, after several failed attempts "in the course of constitutional review procedures, to incorporate into law a general principle designed to bring the authority of treaties into line with that of the provisions of internal law," the judiciary intervened in 1971 and affirmed the primacy of provisions of international treaties with direct effects on internal law over provisions created by primary legislation passed by the Belgian parliament, even laws passed subsequent to ratification (UNCRC1995b, 20).

Five years later, when Belgium submitted its second report to the UN Committee on the Rights of the Child, the committee responded with even more pointed questions about the mechanisms for implementing the Convention at all levels of government. Issues related to federalism raised by the committee included how Belgium achieved "inter-sectoral co-ordination and co-operation on child rights at and between Federal, Community and Regional levels of government; receiving and addressing complaints of violations of child rights at the following levels: Federal, the German-speaking Community, and the Walloon and Brussels-Capital Regions; and the collection and analysis of disaggregated data, in order to design and evaluate policies and programmes affecting all persons under 18 years." The committee inquired if "any overlap or duplication exists in the areas of competence, inconsistencies in policies, or differences in priorities among the different governments, what is done to remedy this?" (UNHCHR 2002a, 3) The UNHCHR indicated its intention to discuss "coordination of child rights policies, including the use of child impact assessments at the Federal, Regional and Community levels of government" (UNCRC 2002a, 4).

In its concluding observations, the UN Committee on the Rights of the Child reiterated its "principal subjects of concern": the lack of coordination of rights, monitoring structures, and data collection at the national level; and the absence of an independent mechanism to monitor implementation of the Convention and to receive and address complaints in the German-speaking community and at the federal level (UNCRC 2002b, 3, 4). To improve coordination, Belgium had established a new Inter-Ministerial Conference for the Protection of Child Rights and had agreed upon on the creation of a federal commission for the rights of the child. However, the UN committee remained

concerned "at the absence of a global vision of children's rights and its translation into a national plan of action; that different laws governing different
administrative jurisdictions may lead to discrimination in the enjoyment of
children's rights across the State party; that the absence of a central mechanism
to coordinate the implementation of the Convention in Belgium makes it difficult to achieve a comprehensive and coherent child rights policy" (UNCRC
2002c, 3).

Specific recommendations to improve Belgium's implementation
included to "assign coordination of the implementation of the Convention to
a highly visible and easily identifiable permanent body with an adequate mandate and adequate resources; prepare and implement a comprehensive
national plan of action for the implementation of the Convention, paying special attention to children belonging to the most vulnerable groups (e.g., poor
households, asylum-seekers), through an open, consultative and participatory
process; and to continue and expand the use of child impact assessments in the
formulation of budgets and policies" (UNCRC 2002b, 3). Two of Belgium's
communities did establish permanent mechanisms; the Flemish-speaking
community created a Children's Rights Commissioner, and the French-speaking community created a Délégué général aux Droits des Enfants. The UN
committee recommended that Belgium "establish independent human rights
institutions in the German-speaking community and at the federal level, in
accordance with the Paris Principles (General Assembly resolution 48/134), to
monitor and evaluate progress in the implementation of the Convention. They
should be accessible to children and empowered to receive and investigate
complaints of violations of child rights in a child-sensitive manner and to
address them effectively." It was important to ensure that all the human rights
institutions had formal advisory functions with the respective legislative bodies
and that they established formal links with each other. Regarding data collection, the UN committee repeated its concern expressed in the first report
about "the absence of a nationwide mechanism to collect and analyze data on
the areas covered by the Convention" (UNCRC 2002b, para. 14). The committee recommended that Belgium establish "a nationwide system such that disaggregated data are collected on all persons under 18 years for all areas covered
by the Convention, including the most vulnerable groups (e.g., non-nationals,
children with disabilities, children of economically disadvantaged households,
children in conflict with the law, etc.), and that these data are used to assess
progress and design policies to implement the Convention" (UNCRC 2002b,
para. 15).

Putting the needs of children first was a new challenge for federations like
Belgium and Canada, because the degree of decentralization within their fed-

eral systems made it difficult to establish uniform regulation of rights of children across the country, to undertake child-oriented policy initiatives, and to assess whether the UNCRC's provisions were being implemented to the maximum possible extent. The UN Committee on the Rights of the Child has been especially concerned about the lack of uniform, country-wide monitoring mechanisms.

That concern is not merely a bureaucratic preoccupation. The committee has focused attention on the possibility that different levels and types of social service provision between regional or local governments might inadvertently create inequalities between children of different ethnic, linguistic, cultural, and/or religious groups. In Switzerland, for example, an NGO Alternative Report to the United Nations Committee on the Rights of the Child reported that both schooling and maternity benefits vary substantially between cantons, to the disadvantage of children in some localities. "This situation entails that the federal authorities, despite having ratified the international treaty, do not always have the competence to ensure its implementation. Therefore the competence of the federal authorities is often limited to issuing recommendations, supervision and co-ordination only" (Comité Suisse pour l'UNICEF 2002, 24). Since children's enjoyment of their human rights entail entitlements to social services such as education and health care, variations in funding for such benefits may result in discrimination or violations of human rights.

The principled federalist will respond that authentic federalism means precisely that different regions and localities may have divergent policy priorities and preferences. If, for example, the provisions for the delivery of social services to children differ from one ethnolinguistic community to another, that may be a valid expression of their cultural differences. Family relationships, kinship systems, and the conduct of childrearing in more or less private or public domains are among the most variable dimensions of societies. The principled human rights analyst whose primary concern is the welfare of children, rather than the federalist structuring of government or the conservation of cultural differences, would reply that, while diverse policy preferences are certainly valid, the standards for public services and monitoring mechanisms, which are created and defined by law, must apply uniform floors to all regions and localities.

Practically speaking, such uniform standards and methods of accountability would mean that Iraq would be forced to give Kurdistan its fair share of public resources for children, if the federation obtains a strong position over the collection of governmental revenues and foreign aid in the permanent constitution. Kurdistan has done well by children during its decade of de facto autonomy under the KRG, and in a new Iraqi federation a judicious combination of constitutional guarantees for the rights of children and the affirmative duties of government, power-sharing at the center, and autonomy in the delivery of necessary services would enable it to continue the comparatively strong record it has attained under difficult circumstances

Implementation

Article 4 of the Convention on the Rights of the Child obliges signatory states to adopt all appropriate legislative, administrative, and other measures required to implement the Convention. "With regard to economic, social and cultural rights, States Parties shall undertake such measures to the maximum extent of their available resources and, where needed, within the framework of international cooperation" (United Nations General Assembly 1989, 53). The primary tasks for implementing children's rights under law are: to assess domestic law, including a comprehensive review of constitutional and domestic legislation, judicial decisions, and remedies for violations of rights; to develop a comprehensive national strategy for children; to delineate the power and authority of government agencies for implementation, policy coordination, and monitoring; and to adopt indicators to measure progress in the economic, social, and cultural rights of children to the maximum extent of available resources (Hodgkin and Newell 2002).

Many countries have moved to decentralize or devolve government powers, especially when peace agreements and constitutions are written for divided territories. Evaluations of decentralized systems have shown that decentralization can improve the equitable allocation of resources if specific rules of allocation and need surveillance are in place (Bossert et al. 2000; Bossert et al. 2003). However, decentralization may also result in the fragmentation of planning and a decline in services for children. Concern about the worldwide trend toward decentralization of responsibility for human rights compliance has reached a high enough level that the United Nations Committee on the Rights of the Child issued a General Comment in October 2003 making these observations about the effects of federalization, decentralization, and "delegation" or devolution on children:

Where a State delegates powers to legislate to federal regional or territorial governments, it must also require these subsidiary governments to legislate within the framework of the Convention and to ensure effective implementation. The Committee has found it necessary to emphasize to many States that decentralization of power, through devolution and delegation of government, does not in any way reduce the direct responsibility of the State party's government to fulfill its obligations to all children throughout its jurisdiction, regardless of the state structure.

The Committee reiterates that in all circumstances, the State which ratified or acceded to the Convention remains responsible for ensuring the full implementation of the Convention throughout the jurisdiction. In any process of devolution, States Parties have to make sure that the devolved authorities do have the necessary financial, human and other resources effectively to discharge responsibilities for the implementation of the Convention. The governments of States Parties must retain powers to require full compliance with the Convention by devolved administrations or local authorities and must establish permanent monitoring mechanisms to ensure that the Convention is respected and applied for all children throughout its jurisdiction without discrimination. Further, there must be safeguards to ensure that decentralization or devolution does not lead to discrimination in the enjoyment of rights by children in different regions. (UNCRC 2003, paras. 1, 40, 41)

This counsel may be important to recall in the promised federalization of the rest of the former Iraq. But Kurdistan's better monitoring of and investment in child development suggest that in this case children have benefited from the region's autonomy from the central government of Saddam Hussein and will do well under a more established decentralized federation. A counterbalance to the dangers of decentralization has been established in many countries: a high-level government ministry is responsible for developing countrywide goals, strategies, and measurable indicators of progress. Each local or regional governmental unit may be made responsible for assuring that each of its sectors or departments establishes budgets, goals, and service priorities aligned with the federal or country-wide plan for children.

The comparison between children's rights and duty-sharing structures in the more decentralized federations of Canada and Belgium with those in the more centralized state structures of India and South Africa highlights the challenges that can result when the federal government retains international legal responsibility for assuring implementation of children's rights in all regions and localities, yet devolves or privatizes delivery of the services necessary for the achievement of those rights and data collection on outcomes. Even in highly decentralized federal political systems, the constitution must establish a floor of rights and duties below which no province or region may fall. The federal government must also establish a country-wide set of minimum services, which the federal and/or regional governments are responsible for delivering. Measuring the implementation of human rights requires the collection of a common set of indicators across all affected populations and geographic regions. Comparative monitoring of spending on basic social services across geographic regions, and comparative monitoring of indicators of children's well-being, are not possible unless the standards and measures are uniform across all jurisdictions.

Finally, the federation (as distinct from the federal government) should have a single agency, comprised of regional and governorate officials, interacting with civil society and children themselves, to monitor outcomes for children and to measure the performance of the regional and local governments, with a single information system, a minimum required data set, and uniform software and data collection methods across Iraq. This agency used to be the Child Welfare Commission, which was linked to the office of the Vice President. Data must be disaggregated enough to allow assessment of possible inequalities by age, ethnicity, place of residence, poverty level, family composition, and other markers of social and health inequality. This interregional agency will therefore have a significant training and education duty toward the regional and local government and private sectors. The oversight committee for the Convention on the Rights of the Child has consistently urged countries with decentralized or localized governance structures to improve implementation by the following strategies: a single central or federal governmental agency focused on children; a single central or federal governmental action plan to implement those goals with time-specific, measurable objectives; and country-wide, uniform data collection. These recommendations may not be welcome to those intent on a distinctly federalist structure of Kurdistan and Iraq, but each region ought to structure its new government so that all three components are in place, optimally in versions that allow the federal government to conduct cross-jurisdictional comparisons of children's well-being and to measure the adequacy of spending on basic social services.

During Kurdistan and Iraq's process of negotiating a permanent constitution, decision-makers should comply with the UNCRC requirement that priority be given to children's issues, particularly in light of the principle of "First Call for Children" included in the final document adopted by the World Conference on Human Rights (Hodgkin and Newell 2002). The Convention guidelines counsel that "in the formulation of policy options and proposals there should be an accompanying assessment of its impact on children so that decision makers can be better advised when formulating policy as to its effect on the rights of the child."

The UNCRC requirement that signatories undertake all measures conducive to the well-being of children "to the maximum extent of their available resources" implies budgetary analysis, and this provision applies to donor aid as well as to domestic revenue and spending. The UN oversight committee "reminds States Parties that resource allocation for basic social services has the greatest impact on the realization of child rights" (Hodgkin and Newell 2002, 60, citing the committee Report on the twenty-second session, September/October 1999, CRC/C/90, para. 291). This provision is of particular import for the current reconstruction and future of Iraq and Kurdistan. Neglect of domestic social needs is one of the hallmarks of war. Turning attention to children's needs is critical for the future health of a people.

Recommendations

Constitutions should include explicit rights for children, and correlative affirmative duties of the governments authorized by the constitutions to provide services to fulfill this right to the maximum extent possible, bearing in mind the resources of the society. Constitutional rights should include: (1) the definition of a child as a legal person entitled to protections under the law; (2) a child's right to life, survival, and development; (3) the rights of the family to choose education, religion, and language for their children; and (4) a right to non-discrimination on the basis of age, ethnicity, sex, or religion.

Laws and legal frameworks in Iraq should create a single federal organization responsible for coordinating federal and regional action plans, measuring the well-being of children, and monitoring the performance of government agencies and private contractors, across all social sectors and across all jurisdictions. These indicators should be collected in an open and transparent manner, be used for needs-based allocation and evidence-based policymaking, and be disaggregated by age, sex, ethnicity, and locality. A child welfare and development unit should be attached to the personal office of the Minister of Finance in the KRG and in the governor's council in the reconstructed governorates.

Budgets should take into account the best interests of the child and require this criterion to be used in assessing the comparative costs and benefits of policy and program options. Legislation and budgets should be subject to an assessment of their equalizing or discriminatory effects to assure that all children, regardless of where they live, enjoy the same basic social services, freedoms, and rights that allow them to flourish to their full potential. Fundamental political decisions about constitutional law, power-sharing arrangements in federal political systems, and government structures affect child survival, health, and development more than do such time-limited matters as annual budgets. Political leaders typically fail to assess the impact of these core decisions upon children and, therefore, upon the future course of their peoples. Political leaders have a moral, economic, and legal duty to address children's needs. The neglect of children's welfare creates particularly harsh consequences for the children who have suffered from war and conflict. Violent environments, forced migrations, interrupted schooling, and denial of preventive health care call not just for redress of standard government child neglect but also for compensatory investment in equality laws, ethnic inclusion from birth in all social structures, restoration of family rights, proactive gender initiatives, and better health and education. The future of a new Kurdistan and Iraq can be assured only if children are kept at the forefront of political decisions, if there is a federal and regional investment in children, and public accountability measures, mechanisms, and agencies are put in place. The future of Kurdistan and Iraq lies with its children.

Note

The author gratefully acknowledges the assistance of the World Health Organization Iraq; Katrina Gerber, Health and Society student at the University of Rochester School of Arts and Sciences, Rochester, New York, Brendon O'Leary, and Grey Osterud, editor, University of Pennsylvania Press.

References

Ali, Mohamed M. and Iqbal H. Shah. 2000. "Sanctions and Childhood Mortality in Iraq." *Lancet* 355, 9218 (27 May): 1851–57.
Blacker, John, Gareth Jones, and Mohamed M. Ali. 2003. "Annual Mortality Rates and Excess Deaths of Children Under Five in Iraq, 1991–98." *Population Studies* (Cambridge) 57 (2): 217–26.
Bossert, Thomas J., Osvald Larrañaga, and Meir F. Ruiz. 2000. "Decentralization of Health Systems in Latin America." *Review Panamanian Salud Publica* 9 (1–2): 84–92.
Bossert, Thomas J., Osvald Larrañaga, Ursula Giedion, José Jesus Arbelaez, and Diana M. Bowser. 2003. "Decentralization and Equity of Resource Allocation: Evidence from Colombia and Chile." *Bulletin of the World Health Organization* 81 (2): 95–100.
Cincotta, Richard P., Robert Engelman, and Daniele Anastasion. 2003. *The Security Demographic: Population and Civil Conflict After the Cold War*. Washington, D.C.: Population Action International.
Comité Suisse pour l'UNICEF. 2002. Swiss NGO Report: Comments on the Swiss Government Report to the Committee on the Rights of the Child. Convention on the Rights of the Child Session 30, 20 May-7 June 2002. London: Child Rights Information Network.
Fuller, Graham E. 2003. "The Youth Factor: The New Demographics of the Middle East and the Implications for U.S. Policy." U.S. Policy Towards the Islamic World Analysis Paper 3. Brookings Project on U.S. Policy /Towards the Islamic World. Washington, D.C.: The Brookings Institution.
Hodgkin, Rachel and Peter Newell. 2002. *Implementation Handbook for the Convention on the Rights of the Child*. New York: United Nations Children's Fund.

Machel, Graça. 1996. *The Impact of Armed Conflict on Children.* United Nations General Assembly, A/51/306.

———. 2000. *The Impact of Armed Conflict on Children: A Critical Review of Progress Made and Obstacles Encountered in Increasing Protection for War-Affected Children.* Winnipeg, Ont.: International Conference on War-Affected Children.

Salem-Pickartz, Josi. 2001a. *Situation Analysis of Women and Children in Northern Iraq: The Right to Special Care and Protection of Vulnerable Children.* Amman: Jerusalem Forum.

———. 2001b. *The Review of the Child Protection Programme (1990–2000).* Amman: Jerusalem Forum.

UNICEF. 2002. *The Situation of Children in Northern Iraq: An Assessment Based on the United Nations Convention on the Rights of the Child.*

———. 2003. *Iraq: The Big Picture.*

UNICEF, International Red Cross, SC-Alliance, and World Vision International. 2003. *Incorporating Child Protection in Humanitarian Response.*

UNICEF and Republic of Iraq Council of Ministers. 2001. *Multiple Indicator Cluster Survey for the Year 2000.*

United Nations General Assembly (UNGA). 1989. United Nations Convention on the Rights of the Child. General Assembly Resolution 44/25, 20 November.

United Nations General Assembly. 2000. Optional Protocol to the Convention on the Rights of the Child on the Involvement of Children in Armed Conflicts. General Assembly Resolution A/Res/54/263, 25 May.

United Nations High Commissioner for Human Rights, Committee on the Rights of the Child (UNCRC). 1995a. *List of Issues. Belgium. February 17 1995.* CRC/C.9/WP.4.

———. 1995b. *Core Document Forming Part of the Reports of States Parties: Belgium.* HRI/CORE/1/Add.1/Rev.1.

———. 1995c. *Reply to List of Issues: Belgium.* CRC/C/11/Add.4.

———. 1996. *State Party Report. Iraq.* CRC/C/41/Add.3.

———. 2002a. *List of Issues: Belgium.* CRC/C/Q/BELG/2.

———. 2002b. *Concluding Observations/Summary. Belgium.* CRC/C/15/Add.178.

———. 2003a. *General Comment No. 5 (2003): General Measures of Implementation of the Convention on the Rights of the Child (arts. 4, 42 and 44, para. 6).* CRC/GC/2003/5. 27 November.

———. 2003b. *State Party Report. India.* CRC/C/93/Add.5.

———. 2004. *State Party Report. Canada.* CRC/C/78/Add.3.

United Nations Population Fund. 2003. Press Release, "Maternal Deaths Nearly Triple in Iraq, Survey Shows." United Nations Population Fund, 3 November.

Humanitarian Coordinator for Iraq and Health Coordination Group. Selected Health Information on Iraq: March 2003. (from table 5.1)

Nutrition Research Institute, Ministry of Health and UNICEF. 2003. Nutritional Status Survey of Under-Five Children in Baghdad, Iraq. 29 April.

World Health Organization. 2003. Communicable Disease Profile: Iraq. 19 March.

PART THREE

Legacies of the Past

Chapter 6

Autonomy in Kurdistan in Historical Perspective

Ofra Bengio

Wars as Windows of Opportunity

The twists and turns in the fate of the Kurds of Iraq have been shaped by the major wars that have been fought in the region, as well as the intermittent guerrilla war that the Kurds themselves have conducted against the central government. Their fate has also been a reflection of their numbers: too large to be utterly crushed, not enough to dictate outcomes. The exact number of Kurds in Iraq today is not known, although it is thought that they comprise at least one-fifth of the population. According to the General Census of 1947, the Kurds numbered 900,000; the governorates of Erbil and Sulaimania were almost 100 percent Kurdish, Kirkuk more than 50 percent, and Mosul about 35 percent (Edmonds 1957, 438–40). The future of the Kurds of Iraq, as before, will be shaped by the military outcome of the new Gulf War and what uses the Kurds make of their numbers.

The First World War and the division of the Ottoman Empire ended with the formation of new Arab states, including Iraq. But it left the Kurds of the new state in an ambiguous situation for some seven years. In 1918 the British occupied Mosul *wilayet*, populated by a very clear majority of Kurds, and added it to the other parts of Mesopotamia (the rest of the future Iraq) that they had occupied earlier. During this period, the British fed Kurdish aspirations for autonomy and independence. The indecisive, ambiguous, and inconsistent policies of the British and the struggle between Turkey and Iraq over the inclusion of the Mosul *wilayet* in their respective states enabled the Kurds to enjoy de facto autonomy until the end of 1925, even though the promise of an independent Kurdistan had been withdrawn. By 1925, Britain, with vested interests in this oil-rich region, put all its weight behind the annexation of Mosul *wilayet* to Iraq. (They had also left Turkish territorial nationalists with grievances.)

The Second World War brought new challenges and new expectations to the Kurds of Iraq. Led now by the charismatic Mustafa Barzani, the Kurds took advantage of the unstable situation in the country in the aftermath of Rashid 'Ali al-Gaylani's revolt against the British in May 1941 to initiate an insurrection against the central government in Baghdad. But the pressure of the Iraqi army and the establishment in December 1945 of the Kurdish Republic of Mahabad in neighboring Iran under the auspices of the Soviets moved Barzani, together with 2,000 Kurds, to join the first true experiment of an independent Kurdish state. Sentenced to death in absentia in Iraq, Barzani was declared Field Marshal in the new republic (Longrigg 1968, 327). But the collapse of the Republic of Mahabad at the end of 1946 compelled Barzani and some 400 of his supporters to seek refuge in the Soviet Union. This forced exile lasted until the July 1958 coup of 'Abd al-Karim Qasim, who decided to call Barzani and his men back to Iraq with the aim of achieving reconciliation. The honeymoon period ended in September 1961, when the Kurds initiated a new round of insurrections, which continued until the fall of Qasim in February 1963 and from then on flared up intermittently until March 1970.

The decade of Kurdish insurrection brought about surprising results for the Kurds. The second Ba'th regime that came to power in 1968, at the initiation of its strongman, Saddam Hussein, recognized in March 1970, for the first time in Iraq's history, territorial autonomy for the Kurds (on this short-lived grant of autonomy, see Ghareeb 1981; Gunter 1992, 14–19; and for its legal content, Hannum 1996, ch. 9). This daring move shocked neighboring Syria, Turkey, and Iran, which feared spillover effects on their own Kurdish populations. But, what had seemed to be a major strategic reconstruction of relations between the Kurds and the Iraqi state turned out to be a merely tactical maneuver aimed at gaining time for the government to consolidate its power. The best proof for this was the failed attempt on the life of Mustafa Barzani on 29 September 1971, engineered by none other than Saddam Hussein himself: one source claimed that Saddam was directly involved in the attempt through Barzani's son, Ubaydallah (*Al-Nahar Arab Report*, 11 October 1981). This outbreak of hostilities developed into a full-fledged war in April 1974, four years after the autonomy agreement.

This war between the Kurds and Baghdad, which lasted for one year, became a turning point because it regionalized the issue of the status of the Kurds in Iraq. Iran was drawn into this previously internal conflict. But Iran's support for the Kurds of Iraq stopped abruptly when the two rivals, the Shah of Iran and the strongman of Iraq, reached an agreement in 1975. The Iraqi concession of delineating the border in the Shatt al-'Arab region according to

Iranian demands was reciprocated by the termination of Iranian aid to the Kurds. This pact resulted in the collapse of the Kurdish rebellion, Mustafa Barzani's second exile (from which he would never return), and the dispersal of many Kurds to Iran, other parts of Iraq, and many other countries. The brief experiment in autonomy ended in a national catastrophe for the Kurds that erased their previous achievements.

The recovery of the Kurdish movement from the 1975 collapse was very gradual, and it came to a halt with the eruption of the war between Iraq and Iran, which lasted for eight years from September 1980 until August 1988. The Kurds were drawn into the war, willy-nilly, as part of their conflict with the Iraqi central government and their ambiguous relations with Iran that drove (some of) them to side with Tehran against Baghdad. The price they eventually paid during this war was the worst catastrophe in their modern history. In the infamous genocidal Anfal campaign of the summer of 1988, the Iraqi government used chemical weapons in Halabja and other places, destroyed thousands of Kurdish villages, and, according to Human Rights Watch, killed at least 50,000 people (Middle East Watch 1993a, 1993b, 13).

The Kurds of Iraq had hardly recovered from the Iran-Iraq war when, three years later, the United States and its coalition allies defeated Iraq after Saddam Hussein's attempted conquest of Kuwait. The crushing defeat of the Iraqi army encouraged the Kurds (and the Shi'a) to rise in rebellion against the central government. Once again, however, the Kurdish population paid a heavy price. The non-intervention of the U.S.-led coalition and the swift reaction of the Iraqi army forced more than one million Kurds to flee to Turkey and Iran in the spring of 1991. Yet this event proved an opportunity and a boon in the long run. The U.S. and the UK felt obliged to declare a "no-fly" zone in northern Iraq and to create a "safe haven" for the Kurds. This shift eventually led to the withdrawal of the Iraqi army from Kurdish-dominated areas and to the formation of the Kurdistan Regional Government (KRG).

The war that the Americans, the British, and their allies initiated against Iraq in March 2003 will prove, for better or worse, another turning point for the Kurds. The questions that loom ahead are obvious: Will the United States for geopolitical reasons opt against the Kurds, as Britain had done before? Will the Kurds once again miss a historic opportunity to establish either autonomy or federation? Will Iraqi Kurdistan revert to its previous status? Assessment of what is likely to occur must focus on the three major developments of the last decade: the transformations in the Kurdish region itself, the shifting balance of power among the different states surrounding Iraqi Kurdistan, and the role of international players.

Autonomy in the Making

The most important development since 1992 as far as the Kurds are concerned is the autonomy they and the minorities within the jurisdiction of the KRG have enjoyed for over a decade. This phase of autonomy may usefully be compared with the political performance of the Kurds of Iraq in earlier periods, with that of other ethnic or religious groups in Iraq, and with that of the Kurds in other states.

For the Kurds of Iraq, this has been the longest period within a century in which they have experienced autonomous self-rule. The de facto autonomy of sorts that prevailed after World War I lasted for some seven years, and that of the Ba'th era for only four years. There is hardly room for a comparison between the present experience of autonomy and past instances. The early 1920s contributed very little to Kurdish identity and the creation of autonomous socioeconomic and political infrastructures. The autonomy of the 1970–1974 period, which enjoyed the blessing of the central government, was partial and too short to make any difference, and even during this interregnum the Kurdish autonomous government was in constant conflict with the Ba'th. No less important, the region's previous experiences of autonomy did not evolve under a protective great-power or international umbrella of the sort the region had enjoyed since 1991. To the contrary: in the 1920s, Britain used its own air force to subdue the Kurds and protected the central government against them (Longrigg 1968, 144, 146, 152, 194).

The most important achievement of the last decade has been the forging of a more cohesive Kurdish identity. This has been made possible by a combination of factors: the modernization of Kurdish society; vital support from the outside world; and the disappearance of the Baghdad government. This growing Kurdish regional identity has taken substantive and symbolic forms. The Kurdish language has been developed and employed in the public sphere, including schools, universities, the administration, and broadcasting and print media. There has been widespread development and display of national symbols, such as Kurdish flags (beside or instead of the Iraqi flags), a Kurdish hymn, and the erection of statues and portraits of Kurdish heroes, such as Mustafa Barzani and Mahmud Barznji. (The Kurds even experimented for a while with a new calendar, with the year 2001 parallel to the year 2700 of the Kurdish calendar.)

Another important boost for Kurdish identity and confidence in self-rule has come from the development of the local socioeconomic infrastructure. Under Baghdad's control, the region's infrastructure had been entirely dependent on the central government, and later much of it was destroyed in war.

The fact that the Kurds have managed to rebuild this infrastructure almost from scratch, albeit with outside support, speaks volumes about their aptitude for self-government. Last but not least, the Kurdish region created a political framework that has functioned independently of the Ba'th regime in the center. This framework has included the management of local government in different parts of Kurdistan by Kurdish officials not appointed by the Ba'thists; the open and free activities of Kurdish parties, something formerly the monopoly of the Ba'th party or pro-Ba'th Kurdish parties, and the institutionalization of a Kurdish parliament with more or less free elections, which took place in May 1992 (*Agence France Press*, 22 May 1992; *Le Monde*, 24–25 May 1992). Together these events and developments have constituted a Kurdish government and moved toward a de facto state. Notwithstanding its many mistakes and weaknesses, this government has, for the first time in decades, given the Kurds the sense that they are masters of their house. A new political language has emerged which refers to these institutions in the terminology of statehood: Kurds speak of the "Government of Kurdistan," the "Prime Minister," "cabinet ministers," and the like.

The experience of the Kurds contrasts sharply with the situation of the Shi'a of Iraq. Theoretically speaking, the Kurds and the Shi'a could have been in a similar position, for they had simultaneously started an Intifada against the Ba'th in 1991 and later both enjoyed the protection afforded by "no-fly" zones. Moreover, the position of the Shi'a as a numeral majority in Iraq should have given them an edge over the Kurds. In reality, however, the situation of the Shi'a became much worse than before the Intifada (Al-Milal wal-A'raq 1995, 47–52). In contrast with the Kurdish movement, the Shi'a have lacked organization, cohesiveness, integrated socioeconomic, religious, and political organizations, and real support from the outside world (even Iran has neglected them). In post-Saddam Iraq, the Shi'a, unlike the Kurds, have had to start from scratch.

The situation of the Kurds of Iraq also contrasted with that of the Kurds in other countries. Until the Kurdish Intifada, Baghdad used to boast of its magnanimous treatment of "its Kurds," claiming to have allowed them more autonomy than either Iran or Turkey did "their Kurds." It was not true then, but it became the case against the will of regime after 1991, when the Ba'th pulled out of the region. At present, in no other state do the Kurds enjoy autonomy of any sort, cultural or political. The precedent set by the Kurds of Iraq appears so threatening to the surrounding states that they have regularly vowed to fight it, lest the contagion spread to their own Kurds.

The unique situation of the Kurds of Iraq was due, above all, to the distinct situation created by the unfinished aftermath of the liberation of Kuwait.

Part of it may be attributed to the deliberate decision Saddam made to withdraw the Iraqi army from Kurdistan at the end of 1991. Saddam later rationalized this withdrawal: "we said let us withdraw the Army because it cannot perform its duty when things have reached such a low level" (*Al-Thawra*, 22 March 1991). But, in fact, his decision was based on two erroneous assumptions. First, he believed that the Kurds would not be able to survive without the services of the central government even for one day and would rush quickly back to the arms of the Baʿth. Second, he thought that the world would remain indifferent to the fate of the Kurds, as had been the case after the chemical attacks against them in 1988. Saddam fully expected that his regime would return to Kurdistan at the invitation of the Kurds themselves, no doubt after internal conflict among them. He was wrong. Even though there was internal fighting later, the Kurds were able to dispense with the services of the Baʿthist state. During the regime's last decade, the autonomy of Kurdistan came to haunt the central government, which feared that the same democratic aspirations might infect Baghdad itself, or at least the Shiʿa and Iraq's minority ethnic and religious communities.

Another factor working in favor of the Kurds was the enhanced international humanitarian awareness of their plight. The poignant flight of some one million Kurds after the Intifada dramatized the Kurdish cause and won it international attention and recognition. The immediate outcome was the installation of an effective "no-fly" zone in the north (in contrast to the ineffective one in the south)—an internationally enforced measure that made possible the emergence and survival of Kurdish autonomy. Since it already enjoyed autonomy, the Kurdistan Regional Government has raised the political stakes in post-Saddam negotiations, moving from an insistence on autonomy to demanding federation with the rest of Iraq. The Kurds had declared this to be their goal already in 1992, after long deliberations between the Kurdistan Democratic Party (KDP), led by Masoud Barzani, and the Patriotic Union of Kurdistan (PUK), led by Jalal Talabani. A resolution in early October 1992 by the Kurdistan National Assembly stated a unanimous commitment "to determine its fate and define its legal relationship with the central authority at this stage of history on the basis of a federation (*al-ittihad al-fidirali*) within a democratic parliamentary Iraq" ("Voice of the People of Kurdistan," 5 October 1992, *Daily Report*, 7 October). This formula was a compromise between Talabani's camp, who since 1988 had called for independence, and the more moderate and perhaps more realistic camp of Barzani, who had opted for autonomy. (This characterization of the two parties does not apply to their respective KRGs, however; in the KDP-controlled areas only the Kurdish flag flies, whereas in PUK-controlled areas both the Iraqi and Kurdish flags fly.)

On the whole, the Kurds of Iraq have been cautious in the past in not voicing the goal of independence so as not to over-antagonize the central government or their potential supporters in the surrounding states. But they have insisted on their inherent right to self-determination, and many decision-makers in Ankara, Damascus, and Tehran assume that the Kurds are acting to establish an independent Kurdish state.

Another interesting development was that that the Kurds of Iraq were allowed para-diplomatic representation in Turkey, Iran, France, Britain, and most importantly the United States—at a time when Baghdad itself had no ambassador or other representative in Washington. This was a far cry from the days when Washington concealed its contacts with the Kurds under a blanket of secrecy. (When the legendary Kurdish leader Mustafa Barzani came to Washington for treatment of his fatal cancer in 1979, he was treated under total anonymity; see Korn 1994.) There were three main reasons for the change: there was a compelling need to work with the KRG; to keep the pressure on Baghdad through the Kurds; and to prevent the possibility that any one out-side player would have too much influence at the expense of another. It is true that the Kurdish representatives abroad have lacked formal diplomatic status. Nevertheless, they have managed to advance the Kurdish cause in key capitals, have had some influence on decision-making, and may ultimately leave some enduring impact on the future status of the Kurds.

The Kurds' Achilles Heel

The picture, however, has had its darker side. Worst of all is the fact that the Kurdish national movement still lacks full-scale cohesiveness, and tribal and sectional interests at times overshadow national ones (van Bruinessen 2003). The prime example is the war between the KDP and the PUK, which raged for more than two years between May 1994 until October 1996 and required American mediation. The causes for the fighting were manifold, including his-torical enmity between the parties' leaders dating from the time when the KDP was headed by Mustafa Barzani, Masoud Barzani's father; local land disputes; rivalries over oil revenues, which were controlled by the KDP (through whose territories the transactions were made with Turkey); and dissatisfaction of both parties over the power-sharing formula in the parliament and cabinet established in 1992.

The fighting broke all records in its intensity and folly and nearly proved the merits of Saddam's gamble. The KDP called the Iraqi army to its help in August 1996—the same army that had been responsible for the Anfal campaign eight years earlier. The PUK called for the U.S. to help them, which did nothing to prevent the return of the Erbil governorate to the KDP. The fighting resulted in a high number of Kurdish casualties (an exaggerated claim of 15,000 PUK losses is cited by the *Daily Report*, 3 September 1996; a credible source, the *International Herald Tribune*, 4 September 1996, talked of 1,000–2,000 dead). The KRG region was divided into two rival entities: the KDP governed "Barzanistan" (with its yellow flag), while the PUK governed "Talabanistan" (with its green flag). Kurdistan had two executive jurisdictions, two premiers, two cabinets, and two armies (*peshmerga*). The unique window of opportunity for a unified autonomous region seemed to have been lost because of the Kurds themselves, not because of any external force.

Since 1997, the fighting has stopped, and the trend is toward reconciliation and even cooperation. Notably, both parties participated in the opening of the national assembly in October 2002. One might even argue that the rivalry between the two major Kurdish groups—the KDP and the PUK—has enabled the development of a more democratic and pluralistic system than in Baghdad, which has been dominated by one party for more than three decades. However, the achievement of peace between the two groups required the mediation of the United States, Britain, Turkey, Iran, and some Arab countries, giving all these countries additional leverage over the Kurds. Their unity in the future constitutional negotiations over the future of Iraq will be a prerequisite of their success.

The withdrawal of the Iraqi central government from Kurdistan, the establishment of the vulnerable KRG, and the more open and liberal atmosphere that has prevailed in the Kurdish autonomous region have allowed the entry of new political forces that may be a harbinger of helpful pluralism, but may also hamper Kurdish unity. These elements include the Turkish Kurdistan Workers Party (PKK); various radical Islamist groups, Turkomen groups and parties; and other smaller groups—all vying for influence. Clashes between the KDP and the PKK erupted in 1992, shortly after the establishment of the KRG, and went on intermittently for the greater part of the 1990s. The KDP established working relations with Ankara, which needed the KDP for Turkey's fight with the PKK, which attempted to establish new bases inside Iraq. The PUK, initially a conditional tacit ally of the PKK, moved against it at the end of the 1990s, mainly with a view to improving its relations with Turkey. Kurdish Islamist groups in Iraq, for their part, began clashing with the PUK as early as 1993. Similarly, tensions and latent struggles for power exist between the Kurds and the Turkomen in Iraq. The Turkomen are supported or even instigated by Turkey, which has made them a lever for containing the ambition of the Kurds of Iraq. Turkey has inflated the number of Turkomen in Iraq, estimating this population at two-and-a-half million, or about 10 percent of Iraq's population. In reality, they number no more than 500,000. In the Iraqi census of 1932 they comprised 2 percent of the population, a figure similar to that given by later authorities (Baer 1960, 105; Batatu 1978, 40; Dann 1969, 2). This mushrooming of rival groups and interests may be problematic for self-rule in Kurdistan: it will be essential for the KRG to be seen to manage the Turkomen reasonably.

Geopolitical constraints are another stumbling block. There is nothing new about this phenomenon; what is new is the redistribution of the relative weights of the regional players. From the 1960s to the 1990s, Iran was the key external regional actor. But, since the early 1990s, Turkey has replaced Iran. Turkey's attitude toward the Kurds of Iraq is thoroughly ambivalent. It has held the key to the survival and even the flourishing of Kurdish autonomy, but it is now formally fiercely opposed to the Kurds' plans for federation. In many ways Ankara has become as important a player as Baghdad itself, and its interests and goals in the region are in constant flux. Looming over Kurdish plans for federation (or even continued autonomy) is Turkey's obsessive fears about its own territorial integrity—a fear that may lead to Turkish military involvement in Iraq in an attempt to control Kurdistan. This time, however, Turkey has a potential veto over its entrance into the European Union standing over its performance with respect to the Kurds of Turkey.

The Kurds' other point of weakness is that they are not considered a strategic asset by the United States or Britain. True, the Kurds played an important role in weakening the Ba'th regime and an even more important one in ousting Saddam from power. However, this role might be a transient one, and the fact that the United States has refrained from publicly supporting the planned federation is ample evidence of the limits of Kurdistan as an asset in American eyes. It is perhaps to redress this weakness that the Kurds are now raising the stakes by demanding the inclusion of oil-rich Kirkuk, which they claim as one of their historic and sacred cities. But, even the basic demographic facts are disputed (according to one source, in 1949 the Kurds formed only 25 percent of the city's population; see Edmonds 1957, 435). Kirkuk was subjected to coercive "Arabization" by the Ba'th regime and excluded from the Kurdistan region. Kurdistan's claim to Kirkuk is a strategic one. After all, oil has been the main incentive for U.S. support for other small states in the Gulf region. The Kurds' hope is driven both by national affinity and geopolitical realism: if they manage to control an important oil-producing region, they will gain the strategic importance they have always lacked.

Whither Kurdistan?

Overall, the balance sheet of Kurdish autonomy in Iraq has been a positive one. The autonomy of the KRG region has survived longer and been more meaningful than any other Kurdish autonomous experiment in recent history. Indeed, it has become a possible model for Iraq as a whole—and Iraq, in the minds of some, is destined to become a model for the Arab world. But the Kurds' situation now is more paradoxical than ever. First paradox: only if the Kurds are united can they face internal and external challenges, but it is exactly the possibility of such unity that frightens the surrounding states and invites their intervention. Second paradox: to mobilize the Kurdish population, the leadership has to set clear-cut goals, but once such a goal is declared—as was the case with the federation—it immediately unites the Kurds' enemies against them. Third paradox: The Kurds need the U.S. to guarantee their autonomy, but this dependence on a superpower might turn them back into a disposable card in the game of great and regional powers. The latest war between the American and British coalition and Iraq provided another window of opportunity for the Kurds of Iraq, but its aftermath might result in disillusionment. The role that the Kurds have played in this war was unique in many respects. For the first time in the modern history of Iraq, Kurds fought side by side with a non-Muslim superpower. The Kurds' contribution was not secret, but made in broad daylight. Nor was it trifling support: sometimes the Kurds played the main role in the fighting while the Americans only provided air cover or intelligence support. In this war the Kurds forsook their habitual mode of fighting in their mountainous strongholds and moved to fight in the plain and to liberate the two major cities of Mosul and Kirkuk. Their role was crucial for the American war effort, because without their help the Americans could not have opened the northern front simultaneously with the southern one (given Turkey's last-minute decision not to allow the passage of American troops through its territory). Because the war had started before the U.S. could move troops to the north, the Kurdish *peshmerga*, who had the necessary intelligence about and experience in fighting against the Iraqi army, carried out the burden of the fighting on the ground on the northern front. The PUK and, to a certain extent, the KDP have proved their usefulness to the Americans by fighting their common enemy, the Islamist radical Kurdish group Ansar al-Islam, which was believed to have ties with al-Qaida. The Kurdish role was underlined because other Iraqi opposition groups, such as the Iraqi National Congress (INC), or the Supreme Assembly of the Islamic Revolution in Iraq (SAIRI), which the U.S. and Britain had contacted before the war, were not asked or allowed to participate in the actual fighting.

What are the repercussions of the Kurds' stance during the war for their future? On the positive side, they have proved to the Americans that they are skilled and loyal fighters, a factor magnified in importance by Turkey's passive or neutral role. Although the American stance toward the Kurds of Iraq has always been dictated by their consideration for Turkish sensitivities on this issue, it seems less likely that this time they will grant a prize to Turkey by altogether forsaking their new-old Kurdish allies. The Kurds' traditional role as a balance to the central government is likely to be reinforced, at least during the transitional period. Kurdish members have played key roles on the Iraqi Governing Council under the Coalition Provisional Authority. The Kurds' military achievements and capacity on the ground may also translate into assets when reshaping the Iraqi state. The fact that they have enjoyed self-rule for a decade has relieved the Americans of the burden of setting up an administration in that region. Most important of all, their case for demanding the formation of a federal or confederal state has been strengthened significantly.

But this fluid situation is also fraught with dangers. One possible negative result is that the estrangement between the Arab population and the Kurds might grow stronger, precisely because the Kurds are regarded, especially by Sunni Arabs, as having betrayed the state by collaborating with the enemy. This difference may cause collision rather than reconciliation between the parties. In early April 2003, the *peshmergas'* entrance into Kirkuk and Mosul was accompanied by severe looting and street fighting between Arabs and Kurds (reminiscent of the inter-communal fighting in the cities under 'Abd al-Karim Qassim; see Dann 1969, 172–77, 223–24). Another negative result might be that the surrounding states with Kurdish minorities—Turkey, Syria, and Iran— join forces to frustrate the Kurdish enterprise. Turkey, which for a decade was a lifeline for the KRG, might decide to stop this policy and blockade its borders; there are already signs of reduced cooperation on the borders. In such circumstances, will the U.S. forfeit its strategic alliance with Turkey for the sake of its more recent tactical alliance with the Kurds? Will it fight another war to guarantee federal status for the Kurds of Iraq?

In 1924, when the fate of the former Ottoman *wilayet* of Mosul had not yet been decided, King Faisal I, the monarch installed by the British in Baghdad, said this about the province, which was populated by a Kurdish majority: "I consider it impossible . . . both strategically and economically for a government in Baghdad to live if Mosul is detached . . . Mosul is to Iraq as is the head to the rest of the body" (Edmonds 1957, 398, citing League of Nations, "Questions of the Frontier Between Turkey and Iraq," Commission of Inquiry Report, 16 July 1925, 7). In the final analysis, it was Britain that decided among the three alternatives of granting autonomy to Kurdistan, ceding the region to

Turkey, or incorporating it into Iraq. Britain, with its vested interests in this oil-rich region, annexed it to Iraq. Seventy-five years later, Saddam Hussein reverted to the same image of Mosul as the head for Iraq in his ghostwritten novel, *al-Qal'a al-Hasina* (*The Fortified Fortress*) (Saddam 2001). In the novel, Mosul and Kurdistan are the center of the plot, as is the Kurdish heroine Shatrin. The illustration on the front page is that of a woman's head fused with a mountain, the Al-Aqsa Mosque in Jerusalem, and missiles. Whether Saddam was aware specifically of Faisal's simile or not, he was certainly aware of the region's importance and the great similarities between the two periods. In both eras, the vacuum that existed in the region after a war allowed the Kurds to carve out a certain autonomy for themselves. In both cases, Iraq and Turkey were the main forces vying for influence in the area, and in both, an outside power became the main arbiter of the fate of the Kurds. At the end of Saddam's novel, the "ideological" love between the Kurdish woman, Shatrin, and the Ba'thist hero, Sabah, reaches a testing point. Shatrin, who is about to marry Sabah, suggests that the fortress they are about to inhabit be divided into three parts for the sake of promoting "privacy," "democracy," and "independence." One part will be reserved for Sabah's mother, another for Sabah's brother and his wife, and the last for the prospective newlyweds. The idea shocks everybody, but only Sabah's mother Salha is courageous enough to come out against it outright, saying that the fortress should remain united. He who thinks otherwise, she says, "should stand at the doors of the foreigners . . . who will throw him a bone or throw him into the sea" (Saddam 2001, 702–12).

As in the novel, the Kurds of Iraq are now at a crossroads. Once again they stand to be betrothed, by the wishes of others, to the Iraqi state. What sort of fortress will they inhabit? Much of the answer will depend upon regional and international players, especially the United States and Turkey. But it will depend even more upon the Kurds. If they manage to overcome their own problems and act in a cohesive, wise, and prudent manner, they should be able to prevent the return to the catastrophic status of the Ba'th years. The years of autonomous rule are a fait accompli, difficult for the world to disregard.

References

Al-Milal wal-A'raq. 1995. *1995 Report*. Cairo: Ibn Khaldun Center.
Baer, Gabriel. 1960. *Population and Society in the Arab East*. London: Routledge and Kegan Paul.

Batatu, Hanna. 1978. *The Old Social Classes and the Revolutionary Movements of Iraq: A Study of Iraq's Old Landed and Commercial Classes and of Its Communists, Ba'thists, and Free Officers.* Princeton, N.J.: Princeton University Press.

Dann, Uriel. 1969. *Iraq Under Qassam.* Jerusalem: Israel Universities Press.

Edmonds, Cecil J. 1957. *Kurds, Turks and Arabs.* Oxford: Oxford University Press.

Ghareeb, Edmund. 1981. *The Kurdish Question in Iraq.* Syracuse, N.Y.: Syracuse University Press.

Gunter, Michael M. 1992. *The Kurds of Iraq.* New York, St. Martin's Press.

Hannum, Hurst. 1996. *Autonomy, Sovereignty, and Self-Determination: The Accommodation of Conflicting Rights.* Rev. ed. Philadelphia: University of Pennsylvania Press.

Korn, David. 1994. "The Last Years of Mustafa Barzani." *Middle East Quarterly* 1 (2) (June): 13–27.

Longrigg, Stephen H. 1968. *Iraq, 1900 to 1950.* Beirut: Libraire du Liban.

Middle East Watch. 1993a. *The Anfal Campaign in Iraqi Kurdistan: The Destruction of Koreme.* New York: Human Rights Watch.

———. 1993b. *Genocide in Iraq: The Anfal Campaign Against the Kurds.* New York: Human Rights Watch.

Saddam (Anonymous). 2001. *Al-Qual'a al-Hasina.* Baghdad: Dar al-kutub wal-watha'iq.

van Bruinessen, Martin. 2003. "Kurds, States and Tribes." In *Tribes and Power: Nationalism and Ethnicity in the Middle East,* ed. Faleh A. Abdul-Jabar and Hosham Dawod. London: Saqi. Chap. 6.

Chapter 7
Awaiting Liberation: Kurdish Perspectives on a Post-Saddam Iraq

Sophia Wanche

The Kurds of Iraq were cautiously optimistic about the future even before the invasion and occupation of Iraq and the removal from power of Saddam Hussein and his Ba'th party. In August and September 2002, when I conducted field research in Kurdistan (as well as in Turkey and Iran), the Kurds believed that an American attack and a change of regime in Baghdad were only a matter of time. Despite the risks that war entails, the Kurds felt confident of their prospects in post-Saddam Iraq. After all, they had enjoyed a decade of relative autonomy within the country, and their international standing had risen in the post-Soviet world. Although the Kurds had long been treated as a pawn by both the great powers and neighboring states, they were convinced that they would be a major player in the postwar restructuring of Iraq.

The Kurds' positive attitude toward regime change in Baghdad is underscored by three major considerations which reflect their historical experience. First, the removal of Saddam Hussein and his associates reduced Kurds' sense of vulnerability. Their pervasive insecurity was based on their persistent and eminently reasonable fear of reprisals from Saddam because of their refusal to accommodate themselves to Ba'thist rule. Second, regime change brought an end to Saddam's policy of intermittent genocide and persistent ethnic cleansing, especially the coercive Arabization of strategic areas. The many internally displaced people may now return to their homes. Third, restructuring the country's political system offers an opportunity to improve the region's economy. The UN Oil-for-Food Program had only limited humanitarian goals; the large-scale, international effort to rebuild the country may offer support for sustained development.

The realization of these potential advantages depends, first and finally, on the successful political reconstruction of Iraq. Before supporting the policy of regime change, the Kurds sought and apparently obtained international security guarantees, although relations with neighboring states remain tense. Political developments in Kurdistan might take many different directions in the post-Saddam period. This chapter considers four plausible scenarios: (1) independence, an aspiration held broadly by the Kurdish people, but which the leadership consistently disavows; (2) a federal system, which most Kurdish leaders advocate; (3) autonomy, a less preferred but possibly acceptable settlement; and (4) a return to the situation that existed before 1991, when Kurds were subordinated within an authoritarian Iraqi state, which is the outcome the Kurds fear most deeply. This chapter assesses these four plausible alternatives from the point of view of the Kurds of Iraq, rather than from an outside expert's viewpoint, and it places these possibilities in longer-term perspective, drawing on ideas the Kurds expressed between 1991 and 2002.

Perhaps the most crucial yet fraught issue, which none of the four scenarios that follow fully resolves, is the status of Kirkuk. The city and surrounding region have been a source of conflict between the Kurds and Iraqi central governments for many years. The area's rich oil resources, combined with the determined resolve of the various ethnic groups that now make up its inhabitants to exercise their perceived rights to the city, make its future governance a very explosive subject. Formerly the city was predominantly Kurdish. Ba'thist Arabization campaigns targeted this area because of its high concentration of natural resources. Throughout the 1990s, Baghdad conducted ethnic cleansing in Kirkuk under a program called "nationality correction," which aimed at changing the ethnicity and language of all the inhabitants to Arab and Arabic respectively. If non-Arabs refused to change their nationality, they were deported, their land and belongings were confiscated, and Arabs from the south were brought in to take their places and provided with strong material incentives to entrench themselves in the city. The massive, forced relocation of people that resulted from this policy is one of the most destructive legacies of Saddam Hussein's regime. The Kurds, who were most seriously affected by this practice, along with the new authorities in the rest of Iraq, are left with the politically difficult task of reversing this social engineering in a way that safeguards the conflicting rights of all those who were involuntarily subject to this policy. But make no mistake: Kirkuk is as vital for Kurds' national identity as Jerusalem is for Jews and Palestinians. Arabs, Kurds, and Turkomen may exercise power jointly over this "Iraqi Jerusalem," with the region's rich resources allocated equitably to all. This option may be feasible only with the involvement and supervision of the United Nations, although Kurdistan Regional Government leaders have proposed that Kirkuk be a power-sharing city and region within Kurdistan. Final status negotiations should not take place until stability has been achieved in the country. To allow Kirkuk to fall under the unilateral and exclusive control of any one of Iraq's ethnic groups, even if its claim can be justified historically, would reduce the chances for a peaceful transition to a democratic, pluralistic Iraq.

Independence

An independent Kurdish state is what the Kurdish people desire in their hearts. There is general public agreement on the boundaries of Greater Kurdistan as envisioned by nationalists (see Natali 2001, 256–58). There is, however, no powerful present sentiment to push for a Greater Kurdistan. Instead, the Kurds of Iraq seek the Kurdish majority areas of northern Iraq and to include Kirkuk within their region as its capital. Failing that, the current administrative center of the existing autonomous region, Erbil, would have to serve as the capital if the Kurds of Iraq were to pursue independence. Without Kirkuk and its oil, the Kurds might find it difficult to ensure the economic and geopolitical viability of their state. But Kurdish leaders' reluctance to pursue the dream of an independent Greater Kurdistan is based primarily on their realistic assessment of the situation in the region as a whole.

The major threat to the existence of an independent Kurdistan is the certain hostility of neighboring states. Turkey and Iran both harbored deep fears that the autonomous region might transform into a sovereign entity in the wake of a military operation against Iraq and the removal of Saddam Hussein from power. No state voiced such concerns more forcefully than Turkey. Ankara was acutely aware that the sovereignty of Iraq was already compromised by the decade of de facto independence enjoyed by Kurdistan in Iraq, and its officials feared that the proclamation of an independent Kurdish state could be a simple formality if chaos were to follow the collapse of the regime in Baghdad. The Kurds might exploit the absence of a strong central authority to assume control over Kirkuk and proceed with the declaration of independence. The Turks' nightmare scenario continued with some Western states recognizing a breakaway Kurdish state (as some European Union member-states did when smaller states, such as Slovenia, broke out of the former Yugoslav federation). Such a development would create serious complications for Turkey, which is a candidate for membership in the EU. Some Turkish leaders would regard the establishment of a Kurdish state as a declaration of war, and most would want to intervene militarily to prevent its consolidation. Skeptics observe, however, that Ankara would need a green light from Washington and that such an intervention would terminate Turkey's ambitions to join the European Union.

Governments of neighboring states oppose the perceived long-term ambitions of the Kurds of Iraq because they fear a Greater Kurdistan would include the Kurdish minorities within their own states. An independent Kurdistan is thus viewed as a threat to their own nation's sovereignty and territorial integrity. One rather gloomy Turkish scenario envisaged the autonomous region as the embryo of a pan-Kurdish movement that would target the Kurdish southeast of Turkey, with its vital water resources. However, the Kurds of Iraq exhibited no willingness or capacity to encourage secessionist sentiments among the Kurds of Turkey, and creating such bonds does not appear to be on the agenda. The campaign waged in the 1980s and 1990s by the Kurdistan Workers Party (Partiya Karkeren Kurd, or PKK) actually damaged cross-border ties among Kurds, both at the level of the Kurdish parties and among the people.

In the early 1990s, leaders in the Kurdistan Regional Governments—both the KRG in Erbil led by the Kurdistan Democratic Party (KDP) and the KRG in Sulaimania led by the Patriotic Union of Kurdistan (PUK)—feared that proclaiming an independent state would prompt Iran and Turkey to close their borders. Cross-border commerce was a lifeline for the KRG, which was then subject to the double embargo of UN sanctions on Iraq and Baghdad's internal embargo on the north. Trade with Turkey and Iran remains of crucial importance for the Kurds of Iraq, and if they attempted to achieve independent statehood they would face not only political but also severe economic isolation.

Only compelling international support and pressure could sustain a new state in the Middle East, and such pressure would have to be rooted in the strong strategic interests of the one remaining superpower and its allies. Since the Kurdish *peshmerga* fought alongside the Americans, the Kurds have some credit in the bank. But Israel is the only country in the region that might benefit from the establishment of a Kurdish state. Tel Aviv might view an independent Kurdistan as a potential bulwark against perceived threats from Iran, especially if an anti-ballistic missile system could be positioned there. However, Israel has generally prioritized its alliance with Turkey. Regional conditions are highly unlikely to favor a new Kurdish state in the foreseeable future. Moreover, the Kurds are entirely unwilling to subordinate themselves to the self-interest of other states. Their long experience of geopolitical betrayal by global powers makes the Kurdish leadership hesitant to entrust any outside forces to impose a solution on reluctant neighbors.

An independent Kurdistan is most likely to come into being as a result of either the failure of negotiations for the reconstitution of Iraq or the subsequent breakdown of a new constitutional order. If independence were to materialize, the state's legal sovereignty would probably exceed its actual power. A Kurdish government's ability to exert full sovereignty over its people and territory cannot be taken for granted. Just as the nation-states of Eastern Europe were sovereign only in name, incapable of forming their own policies independently of the Soviet Union in matters that the Soviets considered critical to their interests, so too a Kurdish state might find itself dependent on powerful neighbors for its continued existence. The Kurdish leadership in Iraq is well aware that it would be dangerous and unwise to proclaim an independent Kurdistan, because such a move would reduce the chances for a peaceful postwar transition in Iraq and endanger stability in the entire region. The overwhelming majority of political parties in autonomous Kurdistan dismissed such a step, and both the PUK and the KDP have repeatedly denied any suggestions that their aim is to establish an independent Kurdistan. Nonetheless, the longing for an independent state persists among Kurds, and many Kurds insist on independence as a distant possibility or long-term goal. The Kurds of Iraq may prove more nationalist and less prudent than their current leaders.

Federation

The leaders of the KDP and the PUK and most of the Kurds of Iraq realize that independence is not immediately feasible. They have no illusions that sympathetic attitudes toward an independent Kurdistan might surface within the international community or in neighboring states. So, for both strategic and tactical reasons, the Kurds propose that Iraq be governed by a federal system in which they have a strong voice. In mid-2002, they envisioned a binational federation of Kurds and Arabs based on agreement between two equal parties. Rather than advocating a simple continuation of regional autonomy, they sought power-sharing at the center, with representation in a democratically elected executive and parliament. There would be two federal assemblies, one representing the citizens of the federation as a whole and one representing each of the two federal regions. This arrangement would give power and security to the Kurds that an easily revocable autonomy law does not provide. The KDP, with the support of the PUK, put forward a federation proposal and draft constitution that they say would provide a coherent, sustainable sociopolitical framework for Kurdish-Arab coexistence. The key points include the incorporation of the province of Kirkuk into Kurdistan, Kurdish exercise of rights over oil wealth and national defense, and courts that are independent of Baghdad. This draft constitution also stipulated that the KRG parliament would have the power to negotiate international treaties and conduct its own monetary polices.

It may prove impossible for the Kurds to obtain the necessary regional and international support for the inclusion of Kirkuk and surrounding areas into the Kurdish regional government. Whoever assumes power in Baghdad is unlikely to cede the core of Iraq's productive resources to the Kurds. The Kurds will have to offer to share the wealth in order to calm their local and regional neighbors. Turkey adamantly refuses to accept Kurdish control of Kirkuk and its oil resources, even under a federal Iraqi system, because Ankara fears this would fuel the Kurds' political ambitions and make a Kurdish state economically viable.

The Kurds of Iraq have officially advocated federalism for Iraq since October 1992, when they announced the formation of a Kurdistan Regional Government, which was then recognized by the Iraqi opposition. Throughout the 1990s the Kurds held the same line: they respect the territorial integrity of Iraq and envisage their future within the framework of an Iraqi state. Given its population of Sunni Kurds, Sunni Arabs, and Shiʿa Arabs, a federal state of Iraq would encompass cross-cutting cleavages, which might give the system stability. The religious differences between Sunni and Shiʿa would, in this view, prevent an enduring Arab majoritarianism.

A federal arrangement would grant the Kurds political institutions they could see as their own, legitimizing any settlement. An arrangement that reduces the power of the federal government over Kurdish areas would give the Kurds and others autonomous political space without having to demand elusive sovereignty. If Iraq were to develop into a well-functioning federation between Kurds and Arabs, the Kurds of Iraq would have far less to fear from geopolitical power games. The Kurds seem to realize that their future prosperity will largely depend upon having a significant stake in a future federal government.

Autonomy

If opposition to a bi-national federation or any other form of federation proves too strong, the Kurds would fall back to their entrenched autonomy within the framework of a democratic Iraqi state. They seek, above all, to prevent a return to the previous unacceptable status, given the repression they previously suffered under strong central governments. If the international community does not support federation, the Kurds will have to enter into direct negotiations with the future central government. Regional autonomy may be as far as the Arabs are willing to go. Autonomy may be the only arrangement that does not run the risk of being overturned by the central government or a neighboring state at the first opportunity. Turkey's opposition to any structure in which the Kurds would constitute a federal unit carries a certain political weight, suggesting that in the absence of international support autonomy may be a more feasible and realistic goal to pursue than federalism.

The long history of autonomy negotiations between the Kurds and Baghdad has never yielded a stable settlement. Although Iraq has employed the most brutal methods to gain control over its Kurdish population, it is, ironically, also the only state where the Kurds have periodically enjoyed self-rule. Whenever a negotiated settlement of military conflicts between the north and the central government has been proposed, the Kurds have called for a revival and full implementation of the 1970 autonomy agreement, which provides the most substantial degree of autonomy for the Kurds to which the Iraqis have ever agreed even in principle. Its key articles include the recognition of Kurdish alongside Arabic as the official language in areas with a Kurdish majority and the full participation of Kurds in the central government, including access to key posts in the cabinet and the army. Moreover, the agreement provides for the return of displaced people, Arabs and Kurds alike, to their former places of habitation, which is even more relevant now than in 1970.

Establishing the borders of the Kurdish region is of paramount importance if this or any other autonomy agreement were to be implemented. The text of the 1970 agreement makes frequent references to the application of the new measures to areas with a Kurdish majority. But the agreement did not provide a definite clarification of the Kurdish majority areas the autonomous region would incorporate, which was a major cause of its failure. If this thirty-year-old settlement were to be dusted off, efforts must be made at the outset of negotiations to agree on the precise geographical areas that are to be included in a Kurdish autonomous region (see Figure 7.1). The changes imposed in the intervening decade by Saddam Hussein's Arabization programs must be reversed rather than respected in order to avoid further conflict.

International support for Kurdish autonomy may be more readily forthcoming than for a bi-national federation. For instance, Great Britain expressed interest in setting up autonomous or semi-autonomous Kurdish regions loosely attached to the central Iraqi administration as early as the 1920s, and in the EU recently reiterated its support of Kurdish autonomy.

A Return to the Situation That Prevailed Before 1991

The Kurds may end up with a return to the situation that prevailed before 1991 if their efforts to negotiate an Iraqi federation or a regional autonomy agree-

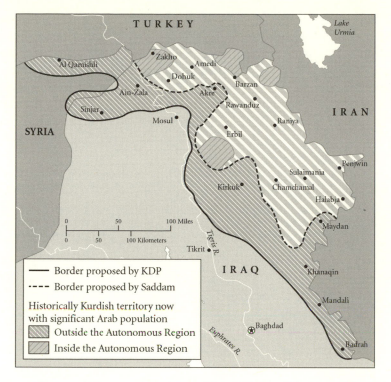

Figure 7.1. The 1974 Autonomy Law. Adapted from McDowall (2000, 334) by permission of I.B. Tauris.

ment are defeated by more powerful forces. This outcome could result if an initial positive development in the country derails and the regime in Baghdad refuses to accommodate Kurdish demands and overturns any agreement between the federal or central government and the Kurds. If such a government remains pro-American, Washington is likely to do little to advance Kurdish interests. In this scenario, the Kurds would be forced back into rebellion, which would lead to a new round of repression.

The Kurds dread this nightmare scenario and made a concerted effort to obtain guarantees from Washington that they would not be left to fend for themselves once U.S. interests in Iraq were secured. The Kurds made considerable progress in many areas during their decade-long experience with self-rule. But this development was possible only because of American and British enforcement of the northern "no-fly" zone and the UN involvement in Iraq. If international involvement were drastically reduced or brought to an end before a stable settlement was achieved, the Kurds would find it very difficult to continue their everyday affairs undisturbed.

The events of 1991 which facilitated the de facto autonomy of the Kurdish region disrupted the pattern that had been imposed on the region more than half a century earlier, when a variety of new Middle Eastern states appeared on the map. Although regional powers have not attempted to reconstitute the pre-1991 geopolitical order, their policies have been formulated so as to contain the situation. They anticipated an end to the abnormal state of affairs in northern Iraq and hoped that the Kurds of Iraq would be brought back under the firm control of Baghdad. The Turkish military in particular favors a post-Saddam Iraq ruled by a strong center which is able to control the borders and provide the security Ankara demands.

American bureaucrats, despite their official, publicly proclaimed vision of a democratic, pluralist state emerging after Saddam, have sometimes argued for the replacement of Saddam with another military ruler in the interests of ensuring stability within and beyond Iraq. The U.S. military occupation is intended to continue until stability is achieved. Officials have hesitated to employ the Afghan model in Iraq, setting up a provisional government run by Iraqis themselves with the inclusion of Kurds, because they fear the country might descend into civil war. During a transitional period, the Kurds may well be returned to the status they had before the 1991 uprising, with no clear prospect for either federalism or autonomy. For the Kurds, this would mean a dramatic reversal of their achievements of the past decade and an uncertain accommodation with the occupying power.

Note

The research on which this chapter is based was conducted for the International Crisis Group, a conflict-prevention and conflict-resolution organization. The chapter is a revised version of my presentation at the conference "Iraqi Kurdistan, 10 Years On," held in Odense, Denmark, in December 2002. Since the invasion and occupation of Iraq occurred well after my field research, I have refrained from commentary on the current situation. However, because the Kurds of Iraq expected military intervention, they were prepared for the future that has now arrived.

References

McDowall, David. 2000. *A Modern History of the Kurds*. London: I.B. Tauris.
Natali, Denise. 2001. "Manufacturing Identity and Managing Kurds in Iraq." In *Right-Sizing the State: The Politics of Moving Borders*, ed. Brendan O'Leary, Ian S. Lustick, and Thomas M. Callaghy. Oxford: Oxford University Press, 253–88.

Chapter 8

Governing Kurdistan: The Strengths of Division

Gareth Stansfield

At first glance, it would seem that the Kurds of Iraq have made substantial progress toward consolidating their current level of autonomy within the future Iraqi state. The Transitional Administrative Law (TAL) signed on 8 March 2004 enshrines federalism as the basis for the system of government (Article 4) and recognizes the Kurdistan Regional Government (KRG) as an official regional government within a unified Iraq (Article 53(a)).[1] However, the TAL presents two notable problems for the future: one of the whole of Iraq, and one for the Kurds in particular. The first problem is that the TAL discusses federalism as based on geography, history, and "the separation of powers" (what the TAL means by this latter point is unclear), rather than on ethnicity or sectarian affiliation (Art. 4). But the TAL then goes on to recognize the authority of the KRG, which many inhabitants of Kurdistan rightly or wrongly associate with a distinctly Kurdish national agenda. The celebratory demonstrations that occurred in Kirkuk after the signing of the TAL were wholeheartedly Kurdish, and many demonstrators believed that its provisions for autonomy might lead to independence from the Iraqi state. Ibrahim Hassan, a Kirkuk merchant, spoke for many when he said the TAL "means democracy at last for the Kurds and a new future in a federal state. This is what we have always wanted. This is the first step towards our independence, I hope."[2]

The hopes that Hassan articulated may be seriously misplaced, not only because of the variety of federal structures available to those drafting the permanent Iraqi constitution but also because of the ambiguous status of the KRG. This is, in effect, a second notable problem for the future: what *is* the Kurdistan Regional Government, which the TAL so benevolently recognizes as an official regional government? To start with, the verb should be plural, rather than singular. For, despite the TAL's generously euphemistic language, the KRG is not unified except in its common parliament, the Kurdistan National

Assembly. It is composed of two separate entities. While the Kurdistan Democratic Party (KDP) and the Patriotic Union of Kurdistan (PUK), which dominate the activities of the KRGs in Erbil and Sulaimania respectively, have continued to promise to unite their executives, evidence to suggest that this is happening in quite limited. Even if the executives of Kurdistan were unified, it is not clear how wise such a move would be and what benefits would result. The political life of Kurdistan has been characterized by divisiveness for many decades. Can unity now emerge between two parties which have proved as ready to fight each other as to work together? If Kurdistan emerges from the ashes of Iraq as one part of a bi-national federation, or as one component of a federal entity, internal Kurdish politics will be of great importance, and it is far from clear how political life in Kurdistan would develop in such circumstances.

The Recent Political History of Kurds in Iraq

To the outside observer, it would seem that the Kurdish representatives on the Iraqi Governing Council (IGC) display considerable unity of purpose. At the moment, perhaps, they do, but the political history of the major Kurdish parties and their leaders is one of mistrust, rivalry, and betrayal. Only on rare occasions has conflict been replaced by begrudging cooperation, nearly always with the involvement of external powers (such as the U.S. involvement in the Washington Agreement of 1998). Even a brief survey of the troubled internal political history of the Kurds warns us to be cautious at this time of heightened hopes and aspirations in Kurdistan.

The principal political agents within Kurdistan (listed by date of formation) are the Kurdistan Democratic Party (KDP), led by Masoud Barzani, and the Patriotic Union of Kurdistan, led by Jalal Talabani. Other influential political groupings in the region include prominent tribes (the Surchi, Zebari, and Baradosti, for example), Islamist parties (the Kurdistan Islamic Union (KIU) led by Salahadin Bahaddin and the Islamic United Movement of Kurdistan (IUMK) led by Ali Abdul Aziz), and a range of socialist and communist-oriented formations. But it is fair to say that the political development of Kurdistan has been dominated by the interaction of the PUK and KDP (Gunter 1999; Stansfield 2003a), and the future of Kurdistan will to a great extent be governed by their continued interaction.

The KDP was formed in 1946 as an uneasy alliance between groupings of leftist intelligentsia under the guidance of Ibrahim Ahmed and a tribally based *peshmerga* under the leadership of Mustafa Barzani. The relationship between the two leaders was poor from the outset, which is not surprising given the differences in their political bases and initial ideological perspectives. By 1964 the KDP had effectively split into two wings, one led by Barzani and the other led by Ahmed and his young protégé, Jalal Talabani (McDowall 1996, 315–20). The central government proved adept at playing one group off against the other, and in 1966 Talabani's wing fought alongside the Iraqi government against Barzani.[3] In 1970, Barzani and the Ba'thists agreed on the autonomy proposals known as the March Agreement (McDowall 1996, 327). The honeymoon between the Kurds and the regime in Baghdad did not last long. By 1972, tensions were again running high, principally over the status of oil-rich and predominantly Kurdish Kirkuk. When the Autonomy Law of 1974 failed to satisfy Kurdish demands regarding Kirkuk, the Kurds revolted. But this Kurdish revolution collapsed in 1975 when Saddam concluded the Algiers Agreement with the Shah of Iran, which curtailed Iranian aid to the Kurds. The Kurdish movement in Iraq divided again. After fleeing Iraq in the aftermath of the collapse of the Kurdish revolution, the KDP returned to Kurdistan under the leadership of Idris and then Masoud Barzani (sons of Mustafa Barzani), while Jalal Talabani formed the PUK from various moderate to extreme left-wing groups (Gunter 1999, 26; Stansfield 2003a, 83).

By that time, ideological differences between the two political parties were increasingly irrelevant to the divisions between them. The KDP was commonly more associated with conservative tribalism and the PUK with radical Marist-Leninism and Maoism, but the reality was more complex. Over time, the two parties became more similar in their composition and ideological orientation. The KDP included a new range of leftist cadres, while the PUK relied on the goodwill of tribes opposed to the Barzanis. Competition among Kurdish parties in Iraq cannot fully be accounted for by sociologically based or principled ideological differences. Sadly for the Kurds, the political parties themselves were responsible for fracturing Kurdish unity, as the leaders of each party became motivated primarily by antipathy toward their opponents.

Competition between the two parties culminated in ruthless fighting between the PUK and KDP at Hakkari in 1978.[4] The Iraqi central government again divided the parties during the 1980s. The KDP and PUK put aside their differences only in the face of the genocidal Anfal campaign, which aimed systematically to rid Kurdistan of any form of opposition to Saddam's regime. Serious and lasting damage had been done; years of competition produced deep-rooted mistrust and antipathy between the two leaderships. Both Masoud Barzani and Jalal Talabani coveted the position of supreme leader of the Kurds of Iraq. Talabani challenged Barzani's belief in the sanctity of his tribe and his presumption that leadership was his birthright. Barzani never forgave the affront to his father's memory and questioned the revolutionary legitimacy advanced by Talabani and his supporters. In his eyes, the left-wing position of the PUK had limited popular appeal. Still, over the years, especially since 1991, the KDP and PUK came to resemble each other. The KDP expanded, new leaders appeared after mergers with other parties, and a new social-democratic platform became the norm, even though the KDP leaders remained (perhaps unfairly) associated with a distinctly tribal approach to politics. Similarly, the PUK moved toward the center of the political spectrum, leaving behind its Marxist-Leninist and Maoist positions and becoming socialist rather than communist, although many of its leaders found it difficult to drop their hard-line Marxist rhetoric.

After 1991, attempting to describe how the two parties differed in their social bases and political program was a futile exercise; only their mutual antipathy remained. However, perhaps because the two parties became so similar, with personal differences creating an actor-based political system, it proved an impossible task to reconcile the leaderships of the two parties and ignore forty years of bloodstained competition. Kurdistan has been divided territorially since 1996 with a KDP-dominated executive in Erbil and a PUK-controlled executive in Sulaimania. Their reunification is still being addressed in negotiations as this chapter goes to press. While the two parties seem to agree on the terms of reunifying Kurdistan, the process of actually bringing the two administrations together has been tortuously slow, perhaps betraying a lack of political will to implement such a policy.

The withdrawal of the military forces and administrative agencies of the Iraqi government from Kurdistan provided the Kurdish parties with a unique opportunity to administer their own region (Marr 2004, 253–59). The establishment of the KRGs was the most important single event in the history of the Kurdish national movement in Iraq. There had been other periods in Iraq's history when the Kurds had managed to secure some autonomy from central authority. Indeed, the central government agreed to devolve power to the Kurds at moments of weakness (for example, in 1970, when the Ba'ath Party was in the process of consolidating its power in Baghdad), only to reassert its authority at later times (such as in 1975) (Natali 2001, 253; Anderson and Stansfield 2004, 155–83).

The Development of Kurdistan's Self-Governance

Analyses addressing the development of Kurdistan during the 1990s have understandably tended to focus on internal conflicts rather than on more subtle and substantive indicators of its performance (see, for example, Perthes 1998). Many accounts presume that the KDP and the PUK were unable to refrain from internecine fighting and from allowing Baghdad and the neighboring powers to become involved in their internal affairs.[5] These problems certainly did exist. Even though a great deal of the fighting was the result of partially successful policies of destabilization pursued by the central government and neighboring states, they reflect the multiple fault lines which exist in Kurdish political identity, between rural and urban areas and between tribal association and socialist sentiment—all focused onto the personalities leading the two dominant parties of the KDP and PUK. The divisions are overlapping and often mixed. These multiple fault lines are illustrated by the fact that the territorial division between KDP-dominated and PUK-dominated areas does not map neatly onto rural vs. urban areas or regions marked by tribal versus class divisions. The division has some rough correspondence with the division of dominant dialects, but that is not reflected in the parties' leadership or rank and file. Some observers suggest that enrollment in the *peshmerga* is more salient in identification with the KDP or PUK. Voting records of the three major cities do not indicate a cleavage based on differences between traditional and modernized society, or on tribal configurations. However, Dohuk remains very morally conservative, despite the recent development of the city and the influx of investment it has enjoyed. Sulaimania remains a paragon of liberalism, and Erbil is increasingly influenced by an Islamist tendency. The electoral results display considerable overlap, as demonstrated in the results of 1992; Dohuk voted overwhelmingly for the KDP, Sulaimania opted for the PUK, and Erbil divided almost equally between the two parties.

The question of how two political parties which are evenly matched in terms of military strength[6] and popular support could coexist in one small region requires attention as Kurdistan once again pushes toward a unified administration. During the early 1990s, when each party was seeking control over all of Kurdistan, unity, or even peace, could not be achieved. However, after the separation of the two parties into distinct executives in 1996, a degree of stability emerged in the region which has proven resilient in the face of destabilizing pressures. Inadvertently, the Kurdish parties stumbled into a political arrangement of elite accommodation which allowed them to manage their deep-rooted political grievances while gaining the experience, knowledge, and skills necessary to turn Kurdistan around. No longer a region of instability and insecurity, it enjoys an increasingly stable political environment and enhanced economic prosperity. Kurdistan since 1997 offers proof that Kurds can embrace democratic principles and norms. Of course, serious problems remained, and it would be a mistake to exaggerate the levels of development which occurred in Kurdistan (Niblock 2002, 163; Leezenberg 2003, 151). But, the Kurds' point of comparison—an Iraq severely damaged by the consequences of Saddam's adventurism since 1979—set a very low standard. For all their problems of divided government and internal mistrust, Kurdish successes were, and continue to be, significant and worthy of praise.

Kurdistan's self-governance throughout the 1990s, particularly in the period since the creation of the administrative divide in 1996 and the last round of factional fighting between the KDP and PUK in 1997, should be scrutinized to identify lessons that can be applied in the future.

Elections and Power-Sharing

Elections took place according to Law No. 1 of the Iraqi Kurdistan Front (IKF), an umbrella of the main political parties of Kurdistan, on 19 May 1992, under the observation of human rights organizations, parliamentary delegations from other states, and foreign journalists. The election was one of the most democratic to be held in the Middle East. Independent observers noted that "the turnout was an unambiguous sign of the population's awareness of the importance of democratic principles, and of protest against Saddam's regime'" (Hoff et al. 1992, 11).

The election results presented the participating parties with a quandary. The official division of seats in the Kurdistan National Assembly (KNA) would have given the KDP 51 and the PUK 49, with 5 reserved for the Christian list. However, the PUK did not accept its marginal defeat and, rather than taking on the role of the opposition party, as the deputy-leader Nawshirwan Mustafa Amin advised, Talabani disputed the outcome and moved a sizeable number of *peshmerga* into Erbil in a threatening move against the KDP. After negotiations between the two parties, a system was devised which had the dual intention to provide an administration for the region and satisfy the KDP and PUK in the short term until a new election took place. According to the plan adopted, the KDP and PUK each held 50 seats in the legislative KNA and divided all executive positions equally. Real power was, however, unofficially vested in the political bureaus (the highest decision-making offices) of the KDP and PUK.

The aim of what became known as the 50:50 system was to achieve an even division of power between the KDP and PUK in all government offices throughout the territory. If a minister was from the KDP, then his deputy would be from the PUK, but with equal powers. The decision-making process of the administration remained dominated by the KDP and PUK, preserving the influence of the parties' elites. Mohammad Tawfiq of the PUK Political Bureau noted that:

With the first and second cabinets, there was an unwritten understanding between the political bureaus of the KDP and PUK that all the decisions of the KRG must have [their] prior approval. So, there was a consensus of taking a decision. Both political bureaus discussed the main issues and then issued a message to the government. Sometimes it would be the government who would propose a policy, but it would still require the political bureaus to issue a decision.[7]

At the ministerial level, the deputy enjoyed the same power and influence as the minister; each needed the support of the other to plan policies and implement programs, and each possessed a veto. This arrangement existed throughout the governmental structures, from the cabinet to the town councils, and also included schools, health facilities, and internal security positions. Sitting on top of the whole structure were the political bureaus of the KDP and PUK led by the towering figures of Barzani and Talabani. Neither was prime minister or president, but the authority of both undermined the positions of the officials of the KRG and KNA, leading Denise Natali to note that "these [KRG and KNA] officials actually served as functionaries for their political party leaders" (Natali 1999, 11–12).[8]

This power-sharing system covered the activities of two consecutive cabinets. The first, under the premiership of the PUK's venerable Dr Fuad Massoum, had the unenviable task of governing Kurdistan during the most volatile period of the early 1990s. During the second, under the more partisan Kosrat Rasoul (again of the PUK), the weaknesses inherent in the power-sharing arrangement deepened the level of mistrust which already existed between the KDP and PUK. When localized land disputes broke out between supporters of the two parties, this dispute escalated into a Kurdish civil war in 1994 (Gunter 1999, 67–109). Rather than bringing the Kurds together, the power-sharing arrangement acted as a catalyst to heighten competition between the two parties as they struggled to coexist within a unified government to the point where even the slightest spark could ignite the fire of factional conflict. This precedent may bode ill for the future of a unified Kurdistan government.

The Divided Political System

When the fighting ended in 1994, the PUK controlled the majority of the region from Erbil, while KDP control was temporarily limited to Dohuk and the northern regions of Erbil governorate. Internal tensions had been magnified by the involvement of external forces. The PUK enlisted the support of Iranian military forces in the summer of 1996. Barzani responded by making a tactical alliance with Saddam himself, who was only too willing to get involved. On 31 August, the KDP forced the PUK out of Erbil with Iraqi assistance; eventually they routed their rivals from the whole of Kurdistan. However, with Iranian backing, the PUK regrouped and pushed the KDP back to the outskirts of Erbil governorate. The KDP maintained control over virtually all of the governorate (including the city of Erbil itself), while the PUK gained the town of Koysinjaq, located between Erbil and Sulaimania. As the situation became more and more dangerous, particularly because of its international dimension, the U.S., the UK, and Turkey brokered a ceasefire between the two parties, establishing a dividing line between them which remains in place today (Gunter 1999, 85–89; Stansfield 2003a, 96–100). Two lessons from this traumatic period are quite clear. First, both sides resorted to whatever means were available in order to displace the other. Second, external powers were necessary for the establishment and maintenance of peace between the parties.

Since late August 1996, Kurdistan has been divided into two distinct regions. The KDP consolidated its hold on Erbil and established the third cabinet of the KRG under the premiership of Dr. Roj Nuri Shaways, with Nechirvan Barzani as his deputy. The PUK secured its stronghold of Sulaimania and established its own third cabinet, again under the premiership of Kosrat Rasoul. Kurdistan was divided geographically and politically between a KDP-dominated north-to-east axis of Erbil-Dohuk and a PUK-dominated south-to-west axis of Sulaimania-Chamchamal (Kirkuk) (see Figure 8.1). Within each area, the ruling political party dominated the administration and, indeed, political life in general, resulting in further polarization. However, the war also created problems of legitimacy for both parties. Both their diasporic members and their local supporters were dismayed at the repercussions of factionalism and the inability of the KDP and PUK to bring peace and stability to Kurdistan.

Division and Stability

Awkward and cumbersome as the divided government appeared to be, this balanced division of power sustained a fragile peace through difficult times. When the sociopolitical tensions generated by holding the KDP and PUK together in a tight power-sharing system were removed, both sides could address the domestic affairs of the region in a more efficient manner without worrying about the activities of their counterparts. They focused on being gov-

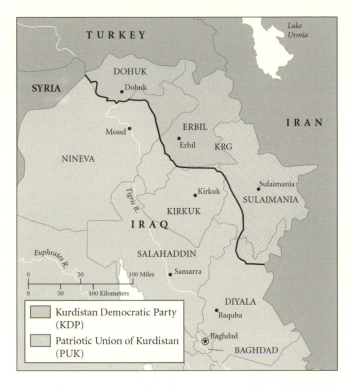

Figure 8.1. The de facto division of Kurdistan in Iraq since 1997. Adapted from KRG map.

ernments rather than parties. Fadhil Merani, the minister of interior of the third cabinet responsible for security within Erbil and Dohuk governorates, told me that, since 1996, the KDP and PUK have controlled the security of their respective regions in a more satisfactory manner than when they were joined together. He attributed this change to the organs of security now receiving instruction from one source, rather than from two:

After the separation of 1996, security was much improved, even in Sulaimania, because of the recognition of one executive power in both places. Each party and administration had less need to worry about the internal party situation within their respective areas; each was also trying to show that they were legal, powerful, and had an operating security and justice system.[9]

This division of Kurdistan and the obvious antipathy which exists between the leaderships of the KDP and PUK is a consequence of a peculiar political competition which exists between the political elites of the KDP and PUK. Government in each of the administrative regions is heavily controlled by the dominant political party.

Since the return of peace in 1997, conditions within the autonomous region have improved markedly. The UN-brokered Oil-for-Food Programme (OFFP) under the provisions of Security Council Resolution 986 allocated 13 percent of Iraqi oil export revenue to the three encapsulated northern governorates—the first time that Kurdistan had been allocated Iraqi oil revenue in proportion to its estimated population. Living standards in Kurdistan improved considerably (Niblock 2002, 163–69). This economic improvement was matched by a normalization of political relations between the two political parties following the U.S.-brokered Washington Agreement of September 1998, which called for increased cooperation between the KDP and PUK with the goal of holding multi-party elections to unify the two administrations. The two governments of Kurdistan became increasingly institutionalized within the region, and joint committees of their representatives engaged increasingly with the UN regarding humanitarian issues and with the U.S. regarding regime change, demonstrating that they could cooperate in the national interests of Kurdistan. New, more technocratic cabinets were established as the two political bureaus became less intent on dominating the civilian administrations. The KRG in Erbil is now headed by Nechirvan Barzani (Masoud's nephew), while the KRG of Sulaimania is led by Dr Barham Salih. Of course, Masoud Barzani and Jalal Talabani are still powerful presences, but when compared to the rest of Iraq under Saddam and, indeed, under the new ministries of the Iraqi Governing Council, the situation remains a relative improvement.[10]

The executive governmental structures have matured considerably under the divided political system. Despite needing twice as many staff as would be necessary if there were only one KRG, one of the silver linings of this situation is that twice as many bureaucrats have been exposed to the experience of governance, UN interaction, and NGO assistance. The Kurds had very limited numbers of bureaucrats with appropriate experience in 1991, but they now have a substantial body of trained administrators. The capability of Kurds to govern their own country has obviously been enhanced by these actions. Yet a deeper, even more important dynamic has emerged. The continued absence of the Iraqi government from the affairs of Kurdistan for over a decade, combined with the increased efficiency, legitimacy, and institutionalization of the indigenous KRGs, have given the Kurds a positive focus of national pride which, arguably, they have never had in their history. Until recently, Kurdish identity was built more on tragedy and grievance than on positive, autonomous achievements.

By 2001, the KRGs had presided over the lives of the Kurds of Iraq for a decade. People aged ten in 1991 are, in 2004, twenty-three-year-old adults with little recollection of life under Saddam's regime. Kurdish rather than Arabic is now the standard language. Indeed, at this time English is perhaps a more popular second language than Arabic for Kurds. The economy operates independently of Baghdad. "Government" is now synonymous with "Kurdistan," or one of its two executives, rather than with "Baghdad." To all intents and purposes, the people of Kurdistan (or, at least the Kurdish majority there), long distinct in their ethnic identity, have developed a vibrant Kurdish nationalism. Few are willing to be labeled "Iraqi" any longer (Anderson and Stansfield 2004, 177).

Kurdistan in the Future

The relationship between Kurdistan and the rest of Iraq could develop along several different lines, but Kurdistan's return to a position of marginalization seems improbable. The most likely possibility is for Kurdistan to remain an autonomous entity, or a federal unit constituted by a regional government (or two). Indeed, the Kurds would not willingly accept anything less. Because it extends the current situation, this scenario is one of the most likely, even if many Iraqi observers cannot yet bring themselves to admit it. So, what are the available options for organizing Kurdistan internally?

If there is one clear lesson to be learned from Kurdistan in the 1990s, it would be that the KDP and PUK have difficulty coexisting peacefully when asked to work closely together. There are instances of cooperative action, including their current involvement in the Iraqi Governing Council. But mistrust continues to be palpable, and competition underlies the entire relationship. While partisan competition is legitimate in politics and can become normalized, even routinized in a parliamentary system, this antagonism is so intense as to raise questions about whether these differences can be accommodated in the future. Furthermore, the stabilization of the political situation in Kurdistan from 1997 onward follows the division of territory between the parties that occurred in 1996. Questions about internal structures of governance in Kurdistan should therefore address the relative benefits of a unified administration and territory and an administration that continues to be divided.

The historical baggage of nearly half a century of continuous rivalry and episodic fighting weighs heavily on both the KDP and the PUK. How this legacy of violence and antagonism can be managed and eventually resolved should be actively, and realistically, considered. If the autonomous region of Kurdistan does indeed become a functioning federal unit in a reconstructed

Iraqi state, with the KRG held responsible for serving a population numbering as many as 5 million (accounting for returnees from the diaspora), it is essential that the leadership of the two parties confront the ghosts of the past and adopt mechanisms which allow the political system to normalize without empowering those forces which have the potential to undermine or even destroy the structures already established. Indeed, it is really these two parties which have to be managed, since they have acted as the main agents of conflict in Kurdistan over the past decade when they have been held together in the same political system. There is no longer any particular violent animosity within Kurdish society itself. It is simply wrong to assume that natural antipathy exists between different dialect groups (Soranis and Bahdinis), or that the inhabitants of different cities are predisposed toward violence against the others (although citizens of Sulaimania and Erbil joke about one another's intelligence). Political tensions resulting from the competition for resources and prestige between the KDP and PUK extend out into Kurdish society through a combination of political inertia and patronage, and it is this competition that is more than capable of tearing Kurdistan apart. The future stability of Kurdistan therefore depends upon accommodating both parties within a political structure which does not encourage them to compete.

To embark on a competitive multi-party democracy in a unified Kurdistan without considering the events of the 1990s would be unwise and potentially disastrous.[11] When the Kurds attempted this in 1992, it proved impossible for them to sustain a unified government with a nonviolent opposition. The attempts of the two parties to work together in a joint administration have consistently failed, ending in several rounds of civil war. If unity could be maintained, the KRG would undoubtedly carry more political weight with the U.S. and the international community, as the current arrangement is viewed as demonstrating that Kurds are unable to work together. Indeed, across the Middle East, it is a common refrain that an independent Kurdistan could never emerge because Kurdish political leaders cannot work together. However, the one result worse than a divided administrative system would be civil war over control of Kurdistan.

The lessons of Kurdish history must be acknowledged and used as a basis for designing a sustainable political arrangement for the future. The current system of divided authority has given Kurdistan the first period of extended peace it has enjoyed in years. It would be tragic to sacrifice this for a public relations exercise, or through a misguided belief in the political maturity of both parties. A more sustainable solution would therefore be one that recognizes the stability that has characterized divided Kurdistan. Perhaps Kurdistan itself could be "federal" and composed of two entities (one perhaps "Soran," the other "Bahdinan," under the leadership of the PUK and KDP respectively). Unity could be provided by a Kurdistan National Assembly (KNA) which has representatives of both parties (and others so far not represented, including Turkomen and Islamists) and ensures a thorough mix of representation by erecting a low threshold for election to parliament.[12]

In each of the two regions, it is clear that the KDP and PUK would continue to be the most significant political actors. There is no way of avoiding the problem of who would be the figurehead of Kurdistan, but the presidency could be a purely ceremonial position. Dual or collective premierships are common solutions to such difficulties. A shared presidency between Barzani and Talabani, both acting as watchdogs to defend Kurdistan against the political machinations of Baghdad and representing Kurdistan to the international community (as Québec's representatives behave toward Ottawa), might be mutually agreeable. Another possibility would be for one of the leaders to be Kurdistan's representative to the new Iraqi federal government and the other to serve as the Kurdish leader within Kurdistan itself.

Idealistic approaches to such sensitive matters are not necessarily impractical or unmanageable. This proposal for sharing power by dividing administrative authority would require both parties to staff the executive offices of the two KRGs of Erbil and Sulaimania. Joint committees would be established between corresponding ministries to coordinate the implementation of policies (as the two administrations already do in practice). This arrangement would control the interaction of the two parties, allowing them to grow into the political system rather than forcing them into competition. By progressively bringing together various uncontroversial public service ministries (as has already been agreed in principle and acted upon to a limited degree), the political system of Kurdistan would have the opportunity to develop in a sustainable manner, and the most serious potential cause of conflict—mistrust between the KDP and the PUK—would be managed.

Financial Considerations

How would an autonomous Kurdistan be financed? Arab opponents of increased autonomy for Kurdistan declare that the oilfields of Kirkuk are the national possessions of Iraq, and the revenue from them should be used to benefit all the peoples of Iraq rather than any one particular component of the population. This argument presupposes that the Kurds will demand exclusive ownership and control of the means of production and exclusive rights over the use of revenue. But, the leadership of the KDP and PUK seem willing to negotiate with their Arab counterparts on both issues.

The concerns of Arab Iraqis regarding the status of Kirkuk are understandable from their perspective and will influence future negotiations. For decades, the city and its oil have been a prize for both Kurdish nationalists and the central Arab government. Both sides have seen possession of Kirkuk as a nonnegotiable requirement. Unfortunately for the Kurds, successive central governments proved to be more capable of maintaining their hegemony over the disputed city and its environs. Under Saddam's leadership, the central government sought to eradicate the problem once and for all by undertaking the systematic removal of the non-Arab population and replacing them with Arabs. This infamous policy of "Arabization" affected many thousands of people and made Kirkuk a focal point for potentially devastating ethnopolitical instability—especially now that some Kurds who had been forced to live in squatter settlements in the Kurdish autonomous region have chosen to return to their homes in Kirkuk.[13] It is quite understandable that the Arab inhabitants of their homes (who number approximately 200,000 persons) do not take kindly to being forced out; some families brought by Saddam's "Arabization" campaign were themselves coerced to move north and have resided in Kirkuk for as many as three generations. Furthermore, the large Turkomen population in the city also strongly opposes the notion of making Kirkuk the capital of Kurdistan. Indeed, the Turkomen would respond that Kirkuk should become the capital of Turkmenali (literally, the "land of the Turkomen"), a region which would encompass Mosul, Erbil, and Kirkuk.

Kirkuk is a serious problem for which the Coalition Provisional Authority and the Iraqi Governing Council would be wisely advised to find a workable solution. However, this local problem of territorial ownership should not be confused with the greater issues of the Kirkuk oilfield. While ethnic conflict in the city could turn violent, it has little potential to act as a catalyst for civil war between Iraq's communities. Conflict over the largest oilfield is quite another matter. The Kurdish leadership has been sensibly cautious on this issue. Their caution may stem from a realization of the seriousness of the potential problem, but it also undoubtedly arises from an enlightened understanding that Iraq's oil can be shared.

This understanding developed under the UN Oil-for-Food Program (OFFP). The OFFP was created in 1996 as a humanitarian counterweight to the sanctions imposed against Iraq by UN Security Council Resolution 687 in 1991. The sanctions contained Saddam, but proved devastating for the rest of Iraq. Recognizing that the vast majority of Iraqis, who did not belong to the Ba'thist *nomenklatura*, were on the verge of suffering a humanitarian disaster of catastrophic proportions, the UN designed the OFFP to allow Iraq to sell an agreed amount of oil in order to purchase essential commodities. The implementation of the OFFP has its share of difficulties, and many observers feared that the UN was effectively creating a culture of dependency in Iraq. The economy of Kurdistan adapted to the flow of revenue by becoming almost wholly consumer-based; for example, local agriculture suffered from the immense amount of imports brought to the region by UN agencies.[14]

Even though the Kurds often disagreed with the UN Office of the Iraq Program (OIP) over expenditures, Kurdistan enjoyed the benefits of a "proportional" allocation of oil revenue. At 13 percent, the allocation remained less than fully proportional, but the benefits were immediately apparent. Between 1997 and 21 March 2003 (when the OFFP was terminated), the total oil sale proceeds for Iraq amounted to an estimated U.S.$ 64.2 billion, with approximately U.S.$ 8.4 billion allocated for Kurdistan. Humanitarian conditions remained serious in Kurdistan, but compared to the rest of Iraq, socioeconomic conditions visibly and measurably improved. Schools benefited from higher salaries for teachers and investment in buildings. Medicines were no longer rationed, and there was a significant decline in acute and chronic malnutrition (UNICEF 2002, 32). The improvements in water and sanitation provision are perhaps indicative of other sectors, with 72 percent of the population enjoying access to safe drinking water in 1999, as compared to 63 percent in 1996 (Niblock 2002, 163–64).

Despite these impressive results, the OFFP had serious deficiencies. The UN system of implementing development projects was notoriously inefficient, and substantial "leakages" occurred in the byzantine procurement procedures. If recent reports are accurate, the UN must also account for a missing U.S.$ 5 billion from the program; accusations of mismanagement are increasingly being aired in the international media.[15] Moreover, Kurdistan benefited from only half the funds allocated to to it by the program.[16] Of the U.S.$ 8.5 billion, an estimated U.S.$ 4 billion was actually spent, and not all procurements had been delivered. With the cessation of the program on 21 November 2003, all program assets were handed over to the Coalition Provisional Authority. The CPA handed over responsibility to the Iraqi Governing Council, and then to the Kurdistan Regional Governments for implementation of the outstanding initiatives in Kurdistan. Concerns have arisen within the KRG as to exactly how the funds have been transferred from the UN to the CPA, the IGC, and then the KRG, as the KRG was left with smaller amounts than initially projected.

Nevertheless, the OFFP may encourage the Kurds to adopt a more magnanimous position regarding Kirkuk's oil resources in future negotiations.

Kurds' previous attempts to change the political arrangements of Iraq have always faltered upon the Arab and Kurdish positions regarding the ownership of Kirkuk's oil fields. In the past, the government of Iraq has been victorious because the Kurds were divided, marginalized, and ignored by the international community. But times have changed. The Kurds are not openly divided, play a significant role in the Iraqi Governing Council, and are recognized by the international community. The KDP and PUK have brought Kirkuk under the sphere of influence of Kurdistan's political system in the post-Saddam chaos. To deny the Kurds any form of control over Kirkuk would be unrealistic, but to ensure that they do not monopolize Kirkuk's resources at the expense of the rest of Iraq is a goal shared by both Arab Iraqis and the CPA.

A compromise position obviously needs to be found that would recognize the city of Kirkuk as part of a Kurdistan autonomous region, but distribute revenue from all of Iraq's oilfields (including those in the south, as well as the north, and any that are yet to be discovered to the west) proportionally according to population. A proposal along such lines would be difficult to argue against. A distributive mechanism could be established centrally (as in the OFFOP), but it would almost certainly be opposed by the Kurdish leadership, which seems to be determined to gain some regional control of revenue. Another mechanism could be that employed by Alberta in Canada, where the province owns the resources and is constitutionally obliged to ensure the distribution of revenue across the entire pluri-national state. This arrangement would obviously appeal to the Kurds, but it would require similar arrangements for the south, and Arab nationalists would almost certainly object, since they would see this arrangement as tantamount to creating an independent Kurdish state.

These problems are obviously serious, and negotiations regarding Kirkuk are bound to be fraught with difficulty. But, the point is that the political battle for Kirkuk's oil resources and revenues need not be fought as a zero-sum game, as has been the case in the past. The Kurds are now too powerful and well-organized to be crushed by the weakened forces of the federal government as it is currently envisaged, but they are not in a strong enough position to defy the rest of Iraq and the international community by seizing Kirkuk and its oil outright. According to this logic, a compromise has to be found. The Kurds, from their relative position of local power, could use the negotiating process as a means to gain good will from their Arab counterparts and the international community by finding a mechanism to share Kirkuk's oil wealth—unless, of course, Kurdish popular sentiment forces the Kurdistani political leadership to consider independence.

Without Kirkuk's oil, is Kurdistan economically viable? As an autonomous component of a federal Iraqi state, Kurdistan would receive some resources from the federal government. But, it is a useful exercise to consider a scenario whereby the future KRGs have to find other sources of funding, in addition to revenue from oil. Before the OFFP, Kurdistan existed under a double embargo: an externally imposed one from the UN, and an internally imposed one from Saddam's regime. Even in this heavily constrained environment, Kurdistan succeeded in trading with neighboring countries, benefiting from its geographic positioning between Saddam's Iraq (which needed to find a way to earn hard currency) and those willing to ignore the constraints of the sanctions, particularly in Turkey and Iran. Indeed, for business interests wanting to deal with the Iraqi regime, Kurdistan performed the role of a conveniently placed "gateway" state. It was under sanctions, but its sanction-busting indiscretions were often politely ignored by the West; after all, the Kurds were an ally against Saddam. The relatively weak state structures that emerged in Kurdistan and the heavy personal involvement of Kurdish politicians in business also made business activities in the region trouble-free, as long as key figures within Kurdistani society were given their share of access to commercial opportunities. The most significant trading route links Mosul with Turkey, via Dohuk and Zakho. This route, dominated by the KDP, was capable of generating as much as U.S.$ 1–2 million per day at its height, with Kurdish-owned companies dealing with conglomerates of Turkish businessmen and military figures in southwest Anatolia (Niblock 2002, 166; Stansfield 2003a, 51). The PUK managed to generate sizeable trade across its border with Iran, although not at the same level as the KDP's Turkish trade. Both parties taxed goods crossing the internal boundary between them. In effect, a free-market trading economy emerged in the 1990s which was already vibrant before the OFFP came into being. Of course, poverty was prevalent, along with great disparities of wealth, but Kurdistan's ability to earn externally derived revenue through trade and taxation was significant. Kurdistan could indeed be an oil state, but it could also be an economic "gateway" state, benefiting from its central position between Iraq, Iran, Turkey, and Syria.

Petrochemical reserves that could be developed in the future exist within areas indisputably within the sphere of administration of the KRG. Proven oilfields lie in Taq-Taq (near Koysinjaq) and Chamchamal, and others may well be found. While these reserves are likely to be modest, the per capita size of an indigenous Kurdistan oil industry would not be insignificant. Of course, any such development in what would be a land-locked entity could only be pursued with the agreement of neighboring states, which would be needed to export the oil. But, those routes and mechanisms have already been established through Turkey and Iran. If the opportunity is right, the politico-military–

business groupings of southwest Turkey in particular could be expected to forget their distrust of the emerging Kurdistan entity in Iraq; after all, they have a decade-long history of dealing with their Kurdish business partners.

The Future Beckons

The pitfalls of attempting to resolve the situation of the Kurds within the political reconstruction of Iraq are legion. The Kurds are determined to maintain their gains and to ensure that they are never again left at the mercy of a genocidal dictator. The Kurds seek a significant degree of self-government, substantial involvement in the affairs of Iraq, and an independent relationship with the international community (particularly the U.S.) as the ultimate protector of their freedoms. On paper, it sounds as though this policy would be an easy public relations "sell" for the U.S. administration. However, the political realities of the Middle East region threaten to thwart Kurdish aspirations. Turkey has serious misgivings about any form of Kurdish autonomy in the north of Iraq, because of the demonstration-effect of a successful Kurdistan entity among their own Kurds (Fuller 2003).

If this serious external problem were not enough to keep Kurdistan's parties and leaders occupied, there are two other spheres in which Barzani and Talabani must operate: the internal political sphere of Kurdistan, and the wider theatre of Iraqi politics. Within Kurdistan, the KDP and the PUK have not continued to enjoy the unquestioning support of all the populace. Indeed, an increasingly vocal opposition to both parties focuses upon the fact that the KDP and PUK have been underachievers in the game of securing Kurdish rights. Some observers suggest that the KDP and the PUK no longer enjoy a monopoly on the power they once held, and both leaders are now seen to be "out of step" with a more radical nationalist agenda that demands independence for Kurdistan, rather than autonomy within Iraq.[17] It is possible that the two parties may be outflanked as more extreme groups benefit from changing public opinion, which may believe they have sold their patrimony for pottage in Baghdad. Along with this nationalist challenge, a further political force exists that is common across the Middle East: the rise of political Islamism. This trend cannot be ignored, as parties such as the Kurdistan Islamic Union (KIU) have already made inroads into the support bases of both parties, much to the chagrin of Barzani and Talabani.

In the Iraqi political arena, Arab public opinion, Shi'a and Sunni alike, considers Iraq to be an Arab state, as do all other Arab Middle East states. The positioning of Kurdistan in the sensitive northern border regions, along with the incessant Kurdish claim to the important oil-rich city of Kirkuk, suggest that any Arab-dominated Iraqi government would fall into disagreement with the Kurds over the federalization of power at a very early moment in the history of the new Iraq. Indeed, the disagreement is already apparent within the Iraqi Governing Council as the Arab representatives now forward their own federal model for Iraq. The position of the Shiʿi Hizb projects a federal structure designed not according to ethnicity but historical administrative geography. The model was articulated in 2002 in a document by Adel Abdul Raheem, *Hawllah Mashruʾ Taghyeer al-Nidhaam as-Siyiassi fi al-Iraq*, or *On the Project to Change Iraq's Political System*. The position taken by the Shiʿa parties in the IGG and when the TAL was being signed in March 2004 should not have surprised anyone in Kurdistan. The warnings have been apparent for some time, and disagreement will almost certainly recur in the next round of constitution-drafting in 2005.

Even though Arab opposition to the creation of a Kurdistan region is well documented, the Kurdish leadership was apparently shocked by the positions taken by their Arab counterparts in the Iraqi Governing Council. Indeed, sources close to the IGC negotiations have indicated with incredulity that the ethnic distinctiveness of Kurds has been questioned; for example, the Kurdish language has reportedly been referred to as nothing more than a dialect of Arabic, or pronounced inferior to the language of the Koran. The Kurdish negotiators believed that such basic issues of identity had been resolved and accepted years before. But perhaps the Kurdish leaders have been naïve.

The problem the Kurds now face is that, no matter how extensive their lobbying before the removal of Saddam, they never received any guarantees from the U.S. as to what their position in a future Iraq would be. Agreements made with the Iraqi opposition in the 1990s now seem to have been made on the Arab side with no intention of actually implementing them after the fall of Saddam. Even from their own partners within the opposition movement, very few parties showed explicit support for Kurdistan's autonomy; most paid lip service to the Kurdish position in order to secure their much-needed support. The Iraqi National Accord (INA) led by Dr. Iyad Allawi, for example, as a party with strong Arab nationalist interests, found it difficult to accept the levels of autonomy proposed by the KDP and PUK. Even the position of the Iraqi National Congress (INC) of Dr. Ahmad Chalabi has proved to be changeable, as virtually no non-Kurdish members of the Iraqi Governing Council were willing overtly to support the Kurdish line for the internal nationally oriented division of Iraq.

But, at least for now, Baghdad and the Arab Iraqis are incapable of forcing their plans onto Kurdistan, and the Kurds know it. The future contains both great promise and considerable danger for Kurdistan. Several times in the past, when faced with a resurgent Kurdistan in Iraq, the government in Baghdad and neighboring powers have proven remarkably skilful at exploiting the unresolved competition which exists between the KDP and the PUK, and it is logical to assume that they will make such attempts in the future. It is therefore of paramount importance that the KDP and PUK recognize that their propensity to fight each other must be controlled. The best way of doing this is for them to remain geographically divided. The 1990s show what happens when the two parties attempt to run before they can walk, and come together in a unified political system which required disputes to be resolved by civil negotiation rather than by military confrontation. Quite simply, they find it easy to fall into conflict, and there is not enough evidence to suggest that this has really changed. Only time can encourage the normalization of the political system in Kurdistan, and the continuation of the managed division of Kurdistan seems to be the only framework by which this can be successfully achieved.

Notes

This chapter draws on research undertaken in Kurdistan and Iraq in April 2004, funded by the Leverhulme Trust. It also benefits from earlier research published in my book, *Iraqi Kurdistan: Political Development and Emergent Democracy* (London, RoutledgeCurzon, 2003). Sections relating to the position of Kurdistan in post-Saddam Iraq have benefited from work with Liam Anderson of Wright State University in Ohio, recently published as *The Future of Iraq: Dictatorship, Democracy, or Division?* (New York: Palgrave Macmillan, 2004).

1. An extremely informative and useful commentary by Nathan Brown, an expert on Arab constitutions at George Washington University, can be found at <http://www.geocities.com/nathanbrown1/interimiraqiconstitiution.html>

2. Ibrahim Hassan, quoted in Beaumont (2004).

3. The 1964–1966 split between Talabani and Barzani remains controversial to this day, not only among the parties involved but also among expert observers. This account emphasizes the power of Baghdad in splitting the Kurds rather than Ahmed's and Talabani's defection from the KDP. Remaining KDP leaders regarded this split as a defection and felt that Ahmed and Talabani had betrayed the Kurds' nationalist agenda by allying with Baghdad. However, Ahmed felt that this decision, while regrettable, had been forced upon him by his unresolved dispute with Barzani and that he made the right choice.

4. The confrontation at Hakkari remains a contentious event, with partisans from both sides, expert observers, and historians disagreeing about the motivation of the event and its details. Units of the PUK and KDP clashed in the Hakkari region of northern Kurdistan (southern Turkey) under confused circumstances. In the aftermath, the senior PUK figure Ali Askari was captured and executed. The killing of Ask-

ari is an historical event which continues to have ramifications in the relationship between the two parties today, because he was a popular figure in the PUK and in Kurdistan. Whether the event constitutes a "massacre" or not (the PUK would contend that it does, and the KDP that it does not) is not the point. Who did what to whom, or which party has the worse record, are secondary issues of historical argument compared to the more pertinent fact that partisan disagreements still matter. The "Hakkari massacre" retains a strong negative influence in the contemporary relationship between the KDP and the PUK. See detailed discussion of these disputed matters in Stansfield (2003a, 86–89 and the notes on 223).

Editors' Note: As Dr. Stansfield correctly suggests, this episode is indeed deeply controversial, and we entirely agree with him that partisan disagreement over what happened still resonates. In January 2004 in Kurdistan two of the editors interviewed the leader of the KDP unit at Hakkari (Sami Abdulrahman), and, separately, two other senior KDP and PUK figures involved in the military action. The PUK man who surrendered became the prisoner of the other KDP figure we interviewed (and we interviewed these two men together). The three men all observed that the event was not a "massacre," namely "the killing of a lot of people, especially people who cannot defend themselves" (*Longman Advanced American Dictionary*). A PUK detachment, under written instructions to destroy KDP bases, was ambushed by a KDP unit, which had got wind of their opponents' intentions. There were casualties on both sides, and the PUK losses were significantly higher than those of the KDP, but the estimated total losses according to the three participant interviewees were over eight times lower than the highest figure given to Dr. Stansfield by his interviewees. The PUK surrender was respected. The executions of Askari and (and his deputy) occurred after the engagement. Sami Abdulrahamn found the account of the Hakarri encounter in David McDowall's *A Modern History of the Kurds* (2000: 344–45) accurate, but declared that the executions were a collective KDP decision, and not simply the result of his orders, as McDowall's account might be read to imply. Sami Abdulrahman's recollection that the execution was a collective decision was confirmed by our KDP interviewee. He explained that "Ali Askari was executed on principle. Ordinary peshmerga had lost their lives through in-fighting, but not leaders who had been allowed to change sides several times. We wanted to stop that."

5. Internecine fighting often commenced with localized disputes and personal squabbles, which escalated into greater affairs. Conflicts involving individuals from opposing parties soon took on a partisan dimension. For example, the 1994 round of fighting started with a small land dispute in Qala Diza (Kurdistan Democratic Party 1994).

6. Some caution is advised in this point. The CPA and the parties agree that there are many more KDP *peshmerga* than PUK *peshmerga*, but the relative efficiencies of each outfit must be taken into account. The important point is that neither side has the ability to defeat the other without the support of an outside, non-Kurdish force, such as that from Baghdad or Tehran. So the matter depends, ultimately, on politics.

7. Mohammad Tawfiq, PUK Political Bureau member, interviewed by author, Kalarcholan, 7 August 1999.

8. There is some dissent on this point among scholars. While some observers note that the two political party leaders seldom interfered in day-to-day matters, leaving most administrative decisions to functionaries, others emphasize the fact that they could and occasionally did intervene, with incontrovertible effects on policy.

9. Fadhil Merani, Minister of Interior of the third cabinet, responsible for security within Erbil and Dohuk governorates, interview by author, Erbil, 26 August 1999.

10. The KRG did have some complaints against the Oil-for-Food Program. No provision was made for local purchasing, so the entire "food basket" allocated to every registered Iraqi was imported, and no items were purchased in Iraq or Kurdistan. After showing signs of recovery following the Anfal operations in the 1980s, the Kurdistan agricultural sector went into decline once the Oil-for-Food Program was implemented in 1997. See Stansfield (2003a, 54–57).

11. In a tribally organized and segmented society, competitive electoral politics is especially liable to become fractious. Given the history of internecine strife among Kurds, the parties should be aware of the risk of civil war if political conflict were to get out of hand.

12. This last point is particularly important, as the setting of the threshold at a high level (7 percent) in 1992 led to the KNA being dominated by the KDP and the PUK, as smaller parties did not succeed in exceeding the voting limit. The KDP and PUK received 48 percent and 45 percent of the vote respectively. The third-placed IMK only received 4 percent, with the KSP gaining less then 3 percent (Stansfield 2003a, 130).

13. As with many malodorous practices in Iraq, "Arabization" was not an invention of Saddam; he merely copied it from the period of British occupation earlier in the century. The first round of "Arabization" in Kirkuk commended in the 1930s as the British sought to ensure that the labor force for the increasingly prosperous and important oil sector was predominantly Sunni Arab, rather than majority Kurdish. See Human Rights Watch (2003, 2); Talabany (2001, 20–21).

14. See Rosett (2004).

15. See, for example, "Oil for Scandal," *Wall Street Journal*, 18 March 2004, A16.

16. These figures were assembled by the KRG (Erbil) from the UN Office of the Iraq Program (OIP) open sources available at <www.un.org/dept/oip>. The KRG (Erbil) website can be found at www.krg.org.

18. This problem was avoided in the negotiations for the TAL, which focused on the territorial boundaries and final status of Kirkuk; the ownership of the oil fields was treated as a separate issue to be resolved later.

19, The most obvious indicator of this rise of a separatist tendency within Kurdistan was the collection of 1.7 million signatures between 24 January and 15 February 2004 by a group calling itself the 'Referendum Movement'. The petitioners demand a referendum to take place in Kurdistan to decide whether the region should be part of a federal Iraq, or be independent. See Valentinas Mite, "Kurds Demands Vote on Independence," Radio Free Europe/Radio Liberty, 26 February 2004, accessed at www.kurdistanobserver.com.

References

Anderson, Liam and Gareth R.V. Stansfield, eds. 2004. *The Future of Iraq: Dictatorship, Democracy or Division?* New York: Palgrave Macmillan.

Beaumont, Peter. 2004. "Premature Rejoicing in Kirkuk." *Guardian*, 9 March.

Cole, Juan. 2003. "The United States and Shi'ite Religious Factions in Post-Ba'athist Iraq." *Middle East Journal* 57 (4): 543–66.

Danner, Mark. 2002. "The Struggle of Democracy and Empire." *New York Times*, 9 October, 27.

Falk, Richard. 1991. "The Cruelty of Geopolitics: The Fate of Nation and State in the Middle East." *Millennium* 20 (3): 383–93.

Fuller, Graham. 2003. "Kurds Pose a Moment of Truth for Turkey." *Los Angeles Times*, 21 April.

Galbraith, Peter. 2003. "Kurdistan and a Federal Iraq: How the Kurds Created Facts on the Ground." *Arab Reform Bulletin* 1 (5). Washington, D.C.: Carnegie Endowment for International Peace. <http://ceip.org/files/Publications/ARB-11-15.asp?-from = pubtype#Kurds>.

Graham-Brown, Sarah. 1999. *Sanctioning Saddam: The Politics of Intervention in Iraq.* London: I.B. Taurus.

Graham-Brown, Sarah and Zina Zackur. 1995. *The Middle East: The Kurds—A Regional Issue.* Geneva: UNHCR.

Gunter, Michael. 1993. *The Kurds of Iraq: Tragedy and Hope.* New York: St. Martin's Press.

———. 1999. *The Kurdish Predicament in Iraq: A Political Analysis.* New York: St. Martin's Press.

Hoff, Ruud, Michiel Leezenberg, and Pieter Miller. 1992. *Elections in Iraqi Kurdistan: An Experiment in Democracy.* Brussels: Pax Christi International.

Human Rights Watch. 1993. *Genocide in Iraq: The Anfal Campaign Against the Kurds.* New York: Human Rights Watch.

———. 2003. *Iraq: Forcible Expulsion of Ethnic Minorities.* Report vol. 15, no. 3(E), March. New York: Human Rights Watch.

Kirşci, Kemal and Gareth Winrow. 1997. *The Kurdish Question and Turkey: An Example of a Trans-State Ethnic Conflict.* London: Frank Cass.

Kurdistan Democratic Party. 1994. *What Happened in Iraqi Kurdistan, May 1994?* Salahaddin, Erbil: KDP Research Department.

Leezenberg, Michiel. 2003. "Economy and Society in Iraqi Kurdistan: Fragile Institutions and Enduring Trends." In *Iraq at the Crossroads: State and Society in the Shadow of Regime Change*, ed. Toby Dodge and Steven Simon. London: International Institute of Strategic Studies and Oxford University Press.

Marr, Phebe. 2004. *The Modern History of Iraq.* 2nd ed. Boulder, Colo.: Westview Press.

McDowall, David. 1996. *A Modern History of the Kurds.* London, I.B. Taurus.

Natali, Denise. 1999. *International Aid, Regional Politics and the Kurdish Issue in Iraq After the Gulf War.* Abu Dhabi: Emirates Center for Strategic Studies and Research.

———. 2001. "Manufacturing Identity and Managing Kurds in Iraq." In *Right-Sizing the State: The Politics of Moving Borders*, ed. Brendan O'Leary, Ian S. Lustick, and Thomas Callaghy. Oxford: Oxford University Press. 253–88.

Niblock, Tim. 2002. *"Pariah States" and Sanctions in the Middle East: Iraq, Libya, Sudan.* Boulder, Colo.: Lynne Rienner.

Perthes, Volker. 1998. *Iraq Under Sanctions: A Regime Defiant.* London: Royal Institute of International Affairs.

Project for the New American Century (PNAC). 2000. *Rebuilding America's Defenses: Strategy, Forces and Resources for a New Century.* Washington, D.C.: PNAC.

Raheem, Adel Abdul. 2002. *Hawllah Mashru' Taghyeer al-Nidhaam as-Siyiassi fi al-Iraq* (*On the Project to Change Iraq's Political System*). Damascus: Islamic Center of Political Studies.

Rosett, Claudia. 2004. "The Real World: A New Job for Kay: Let Him Investigate the UN Oil-for-Food Scam." *Wall Street Journal*, 25 February.

Stansfield, Gareth R. V. 2003a. *Iraqi Kurdistan: Political Development and Emergent Democracy*. London: RoutledgeCurzon.

———. 2003b. "The Iraqi Kurds: A New Start or Repeated History?" *RUSI Newsbrief* 23 (4): 40–41. London: Royal United Services Institute for Defence Studies.

———. 2003c. "The Kurdish Dilemma: The Golden Era Threatened." In *Iraq at the Crossroads: State and Society in the Shadow of Regime Change*, ed. Toby Dodge and Steven Simon. London: International Institute of Strategic Studies and Oxford University Press.

Talabany, Nouri. 2001. *Arabization of the Kirkuk Region*. Uppsala: Kurdistan Studies Press.

Tripp, Charles. 2000. *A History of Iraq*. Cambridge: Cambridge University Press.

UNICEF. 2002. *The Situation of Children in Northern Iraq*. United Nations Children's Fund.

Williams, Daniel and Karl Vick. 2003. "Kurds Redrawing Map by Memory, with Force." *Washington Post Foreign Service*, 17 April.

Chapter 9
Turkey's New Neighbor, Kurdistan

Michael Gunter

"In a state governed by the rule of law the opinion of the army on such an issue [Cyprus] should be politically irrelevant."

—Oostlander Report of the European Parliament (2004)

"Europe is turning away from power, or to put it a little differently, it is moving beyond power into a self-containing world of laws and rules and transitional negotiation and co-operation. It is entering a post-historical paradise of peace and relative prosperity, the realization of Immanuel Kant's 'perpetual peace.'"

—Robert Kagan (2003)

Turkey's prospects of joining what Kagan has called the "post-historical paradise" of the European Union (EU) will be decisively determined in two domains. The first is in its external relations. How Turkey manages the Cyprus question will be crucial, as will its response to the crisis created by the U.S.-led coalition's intervention in Iraq. Accession to the European Union is entirely dependent upon successfully and peaceably resolving territorial disputes with neighboring states. That requires Turkey to settle border and status disputes with Greece, Cyprus, and Iraq (some of the Turkish political and military classes still hanker after the former Ottoman "Mosul *wilayet*"). The second is in its domestic political constitution, in both form and substance. What matters here is whether Turkey can meet the EU standards of democratization, legality, liberalization, and respect for national and ethnic minorities. Like the new member-states from Eastern Europe, it must show it has unambiguously met the criteria for membership of the world's club of exemplary democracies. The full parliamentarization of its political system is a sine qua non. Elected officials and civilians must demonstrably exercise control over the military. This requirement amounts to an end to the military's self-defined mission as the domestic guardian of the Turkish nation. The European Commission and Parliament have both declared Turkey's secret state, the State National Security Council, unacceptable in a candidate country. Turkey's full liberalization is also necessary. Freedom of expression, association, and religion in political, media, legal, policing, and military institutions are warranted. Turkey's existing human rights standards are unacceptable.

The European Parliament, which has co-decision rights over the accession of new member-states, recently endorsed a report which requires "revolutionary change" in Turkey's constitution (Oostlander 2004, 13/33). The existing constitution and penal code still contain provisions which restrict freedom in order to combat terrorism and protect the unity of the state and which prohibit insulting or deriding state institutions. Torture must be eradicated in practice, the European Parliament declares; its recent legal eradication is commendable but insufficient until fully implemented. Turkey's judiciary must demonstrate independence from the executive. The protection of the legal personality of religious minorities who do not benefit from what is bitingly described as "the present minimalist interpretation" of the Treaty of Lausanne (1923) must also be addressed. If the accession path of the former communist countries is followed, then Turkey will also face evaluation by the office of the Organization for Security and Cooperation in Europe's High Commissioner on National and Ethnic Minorities (HCNM)[1] or its functional equivalent. Under its first high commissioner, Max van der Stoel, the HCNM quietly but effectively obligated numerous post-communist states to alter discriminatory provisions in their constitutions and laws, and their practices as well.

These are tall orders.[2] The European Parliament's report shows how far Turkey is from meeting these standards (Oostlander 2004). Turkey became a candidate member-state of the European Union in 1999. Most of its political class is bent on achieving membership, although they are not universally aware of how much will be required. Some remain under the illusion that these matters are negotiable or can be addressed after accession, or even that EU membership could be based on Turkey's membership in security alliances, such as NATO and the OSCE. These illusions will be punctured. The membership standards of the "Kantian paradise" provide leverage that will limit Turkey's freedom of maneuver on the construction of a federation in Iraq, and may oblige it to cease denying the reality of Kurdistan in Iraq. Turkey's candidacy for the European Union will certainly limit its discretion on interventions in Iraq in ways that are presently unimaginable to Syrian and Iranian governments. Few Turkish leaders foresaw this vista before 1991, the year of the collapse of the Soviet Union, the first Gulf War, and the emergence of an

Figure 9.1. What might have been: The Treaty of Sèvres. The treaty proposed a sovereign Kurdistan in what is now Turkey, with the right of Kurdish majority districts in the former Mosul *wilayet* (Kurdistan in Iraq) to opt-in to this new state.

autonomous Kurdistan in Iraq, all of which radically reshaped Turkey's internal and external agendas.

Official Turkish attitudes toward the Kurds in general, and the Kurds of Iraq in particular, are deeply rooted in the historic fear of territorial dismemberment. This fear was made palpable by the Treaty of Sèvres (1920) (Figure 9.1), which would have completed the European attrition of the borders of the Ottoman Empire—the dominant fact of the previous century—by carving out huge swaths of its historic core in Asia Minor. This humiliating vista was overturned by Mustafa Kemal Atatürk, who through force of arms and political ruthlessness entrenched the modern Turkish "rectangle" in the minds of his citizens, as both the natural expression of the Turkish nation and a sacred trust. His success was ratified in the Treaty of Lausanne. The new Turkish nation-state saw itself as having finally halted European and Russian encroachments that had provoked successive secessions from the erstwhile empire, especially through the manipulation of religious and linguistic minorities. Today in the Kemalist mindset this abiding fear of amputation is represented by the fear of Kurdish secession from Turkey, a fear confirmed by the fierce armed struggle of the Kurdistan Workers Party (PKK) in the 1980s and 1990s, which was concentrated in what Kurdish nationalists call northern Kurdistan and Turks describe as southeastern Turkey.

The imperative of avoiding dismemberment led to the project of a centralized, unitary, and indivisibly sovereign and assimilationist nation-state, modeled on French Jacobin thought. Ottoman traditions were decisively rejected. Until the first third of the nineteenth century, the Ottoman Empire had been decentralized and organized through heterogeneous forms of indirect rule (İnalcik 1973). The *millet* system of religious communities had offered the "peoples of the book" a certain degree of legal, educational, and ecclesiastical autonomy (Shaw and Shaw 1977; Karpat 1973).[3] To save itself from European and Russian encroachments, the Ottoman Empire began to centralize, rationalize, and impose more bureaucratic direct rule from the 1830s (Lewis 1968). This turn to direct rule eliminated the autonomy long enjoyed by the Kurdish emirates (McDowall 1996, 38–65; van Bruinessen 1992, 133ff) and eventually provoked conflict.

World War I brought the defeat and collapse of the Ottoman Empire. Mustafa Kemal (Atatürk) created the Republic of Turkey from its rump, and, as proof of the transformation, abolished the Caliphate. When Atatürk first fashioned the Turkish nation-state, however, it was not clear what constituted a Turk (Lewis 1968, 1–5). Indeed, in appealing for Islamic unity against the Christian (Greek and Armenian) invaders, İsmet İnonu, Atatürk's famous lieutenant and eventual successor, initially spoke of the new state as a "homeland for Kurds and Turks" (Vanly 1970, 54). Kurdish troops had played an indispensable role in the Kemalists' victory in 1922. The new parliament in Ankara included 75 self-identified Kurdish deputies. For a while Atatürk even toyed with the idea of cultural and linguistic Kurdish autonomy in the new state, as the minutes of the Amasya interview and the proceedings of the Erzurum and Sivas congresses in 1919 make clear (Olson 1991).

Kurdish autonomy proved to be the road not taken. The Sheikh Said rebellion in 1925 convinced the Turkish authorities that the Kurds were a mortal danger to the territorial integrity of the Turkish rectangle (Olson 1989). The Kurds were reclassified as "Mountain Turks," a term that signaled a plan for their eventual assimilation into the larger Turkish population (Yavuz 2001). In addition, until 1926, Turkey also continued to claim the lost *vilayet* of Mosul, called Kurdistan (Edmonds 1957, 398ff). If this claim had been implemented, Turkey would have had even more Kurds to digest, but its leaders had enough on their plate in managing their own Kurdish question.

In consequence, until the early 1980s, Turkey largely considered the Kurds of Iraq an internal problem for Iraq and thus not a matter of direct concern. It also made no serious effort to act as the external guardian of the Turkomen whom it lost in the collapse of the Ottoman Empire. But the Iran-Iraq war in the 1980s opened opportunities for Kurdish self-determination in both of these warring states and began to reinternationalize the Kurdish question (Gunter 1992, 37–48). At approximately the same time, the rise of the Kurdistan Workers Party (PKK) in Turkey and its development of bases in northern Iraq from which it could attack southeastern Turkey constituted a major challenge. Until the mid-1980s, the PKK received help from the Kurdistan Democratic Party (KDP). Gradually, however, the then-Marxist PKK began to fall out with the KDP over a number of issues, including their different attitudes toward Turkey.[4] Increasingly, Turkey and the KDP began to cooperate (Gunter 1997, 115–25). In 1988–1989, at the end of the Iran-Iraq war, Turkey was confronted by a major new challenge: 60,000 Kurdish refugees who fled from Saddam Hussein's wrath.

The results of the 1991 Gulf War made dispositions towards the Kurds of Iraq an even more urgent policy issue. A half-million Kurdish refugees fled to the Turkish border after their uprising against Saddam Hussein was not supported by the U.S. This human tragedy threatened to overwhelm Turkish administrative capacities and resources and created predictable security anxieties. But, surprisingly, "safe havens" within Iraq were proposed by British Prime Minister John Major and Turkish President Turgut Ozal to protect the refugees, stem further flight, and enable an orderly return of refugees and internally displaced persons in due course. Turkey also offered its bases for the U.S., UK, and France to use in enforcing the "no-fly" zone to protect these safe havens. Over time, this region developed into the jurisdiction of the Kurdistan Regional Government described elsewhere in this book by Gareth Stansfield, Ofra Bengio, Brendan O'Leary, and Khaled Salih.

On 8 March 1991, Turkey broke its longstanding policy against negotiating with any Kurdish groups when it received a representative of the KDP, Mohsin Dizai, and the leader of the Patriotic Union of Kurdistan (PUK), Jalal Talabani. Talabani declared that "a new page had been turned in relations between Turkey and the Kurds of Iraq" and added that he believed "we were able to convince them we do not pose a threat to Turkey. . . . Our goal is to establish a federation of Arab, Turkomans, and Kurds" (FBIS-NESA 1991). When he returned to Turkey in late 1991, Talabani concluded that "Turkey must be considered a country friendly to the Kurds" (FBIS 1991). By the time he met with the Turkish prime minister Suleiman Demirel in June 1992, the Turkish prime minister was referring to the PUK leader as "my dear brother Talabani," while the Kurdish leader declared that "the people in northern Iraq will never forget the help of the Turkish Government and people in their difficult days" (FBIS-WE 1992b). Hoshyar Zibari, a leading figure in the KDP (who served as foreign minister of the Iraqi Governing Council after the regime change in Baghdad in 2003), explained in 1992: "Turkey is our lifeline to the West and the whole world in our fight against Saddam Hussein. We are able to secure allied air protection and international aid through Turkey's cooperation. If Poised Hammer [the no-fly zone] is withdrawn, Saddam's units will again reign in this region and we will lose everything" (FBIS-WE 1992a).

At the end of the remarkable year of 1991, the Kurds of Iraq had two representatives in Ankara, one for the KDP and the other for the PUK. To explain his heretical actions, Turkish President Özal even declared: "It must be made clear that those in the Iraqi Kurdish area are relatives of Turkish citizens. So the borders are to some extent artificial, dividing people into two sections" (FBIS-WE 1991) This opened a brief golden moment in relations between Turkey and the Kurds of Iraq. Overcoming Turkey's traditional fear of the Kurds, Özal sought to win their support against the PKK and to dissuade them from trying to establish their own independent state.

This imaginative Turkish sponsorship and attempted cooption of the Kurds of Iraq was a short-lived experiment. His Kemalist critics complained that Özal's actions were threatening Turkey's territorial integrity. If the Turkish president could countenance federal solutions for the Kurds in northern Iraq, might he not also be contemplating one for the Kurds in Turkey? The question was never answered because on 17 April 1993 Özal died suddenly from a heart attack, and with him ended this brief spring of positive initiatives between Turkey and the Kurds. During the following years, key Turkish politicians and key military securocrats regarded the autonomous entity of Kurdistan evolving in northern Iraq as a threat because it set a deeply dangerous precedent for "their own" Kurds (Stansfield 2003; Gunter 1999). Ankara's new policy was aided by intra-Kurdish political divisions and fighting; it sought to play the KDP and PUK off against each other and repeatedly intervened across its borders in attempts to eliminate the PKK. By 1998 the very same Talabani who had welcomed Ozal's initiative had concluded that "the Turkish Government is against any type of Kurdish national identity. . . . They want to finish our experiment with democracy at all costs" (FBIS-NESA 1998).

Turkey's implacable opposition to Kurdish nationalism and its strong strategic alliance with the United States since the days of the Truman Doctrine promulgated in 1947 have been two of the principal explanations of the inability of the Kurds to create any independent state after the collapse of the Ottoman Empire. Although the U.S. regularly paid lip service to the idea of

Kurdish rights, when the chips were down, it backed its strategic NATO ally, Turkey, or its Iranian ally, in the time of the Shah, or its tacit ally, Saddam Hussein, when he was engaged in a war with Iran's ayatollahs. Only after 1991, when the United States once again perceived the Kurds of Iraq as a useful foil against Saddam, did it begin to take a more favorable stance toward them; at no stage did it support the PKK. This new tactical U.S. support for the Kurds of Iraq did not inhibit Turkey from unilaterally intervening in autonomous Kurdistan in hot pursuit of the PKK during the 1990s. But, arguably, the U.S. support for the Kurdistan Regional Government, coupled with disagreements between Turkey and the U.S. over sanctions and support for regime change in Baghdad, marked the first signs of a serious tear in the longstanding U.S.-Turkish alliance.

The U.S.-led war to remove Saddam Hussein from power in 2003 brought American-Turkish relations into a dramatic crisis and even partially reversed alliance partners. For the first time since the creation of Iraq, the Kurds of Iraq—at least for the moment—have the most powerful ally in the world. This ironic situation arguably resulted from the Turkish parliament's refusal to allow the U.S. to use its territory as a base for a northern front to attack Saddam's army in March 2003. Courtesy of this decision, which pleased many of Turkey's prospective EU allies, the Kurds of Iraq suddenly were thrust into the role of the sole local U.S. ally, a novel position they eagerly and successfully assumed. On the northern front of the war, joint Kurdish *peshmerga* liberated the oil-rich Kirkuk and Mosul governorates from the Ba'thists. These particular liberations would have been unthinkable encroachments upon Turkish diplomatic "red lines" had Turkish armies anchored the northern front.

The novel situation was brought home in July 2003 when U.S. troops apprehended 11 Turkish commandos in the Kurdish city of Sulaimania who were intent on destabilizing the Kurdistan Regional Government and were suspected of organizing an assassination plot. Previously, as the key regional U.S. strategic ally, Turkey had carte blanche to do practically anything it wanted in what it insists on calling "northern Iraq," especially if done in pursuit of the PKK. This is no longer true. The "Sulaimania incident" caused what one high-ranking Turkish general called the "worst crisis of confidence" in U.S.-Turkish relations since the creation of the NATO alliance (*Turkish Daily News* 2003; and see Kralev 2003). Under international law, the occupation authority is obliged to defend Iraq's borders, but the episode also illustrated that the U.S. was willing to protect Kurdistan from unwanted Turkish interference.

Vehement Kurdish opposition, supported by Iraq's Governing Council, was mobilized against the deployment of 10,000 Turkish troops in the fall of

2003. Even deployment in areas of Iraq south of Kurdistan was opposed by an unexpected Kurdish-Arab alliance, not least because the troops would have marched through the KRG area. The Turkish parliament took the decision to agree to assist the coalition authorities in October 2003 in an effort to revive its failing fortunes with the U.S. and to achieve some control over the future of Kurdistan. The united opposition within Iraq helped oblige Turkey to rescind its offer shortly after it was issued. The U.S. Congress continued its offer of an $8.5 billion loan and credits to Turkey on the condition that its army refrain from entering northern Iraq unilaterally. The Kurds of Iraq also demanded that Turkey remove some 1,700 of its troops that have been in northern Iraq since 1997, supposedly to contain the PKK. Osman Faruk Logoğlu, the Turkish ambassador to the United States, complained that the U.S. was giving "excessive favors" to the Kurds of Iraq and thus encouraging future civil war and Kurdish secession (Wright 2003).

As the Kurds of Iraq embarked on negotiations leading to the Transitional Administrative Law (TAL) and made plain their determination to achieve Kurdistan's official recognition as a national and federative entity, General İlker Basbug, Turkey's deputy chief of staff, declared "if there is a federal structure in Iraq on an ethnic basis, the future will be very difficult and bloody" (Williams 2004). Turkish Prime Minister Recep Tayyip Erdoğan accused the Kurds of Iraq of "playing with fire" by trying to annex the oil-rich Kirkuk area to their prospective federal state.[5] Official Turkish opposition to ethnic federalism in Iraq reflects the Kemalists' longstanding security fears that any federation in Iraq—especially in favor of the Kurds—will inevitably encourage the Kurds in Turkey to seek territorial autonomy and eventually separation. In the name of stability, Turkey officially remains an inveterate opponent of an ethnically based federal system in the new Iraq.

The most that official Turkish spokespersons and independent Turkish intellectuals (Yavuz 2000; Sonar 2004) seemed willing to approve was some type of geographic federalism, perhaps based on the boundaries of the 18 governorates established under Saddam's regime, an arrangement that would have diluted Kurdish ethnic concentration and partitioned historic Kurdistan. Turkey argued that geographic federalism would dampen ethnic animosities which might be aroused by ethnic federalism by encouraging multi-ethnic and multi-sectarian civic nationalism.

Many observers have noted the inconsistencies between Turkey's aversion to Kurdistan's independence or to ethnic federalism in Iraq and its demands for either an independent Republic of Northern Cyprus or an ethnically based federalism in Cyprus.[6] When I brought up this inconsistency at a scholarly conference held at the Eastern Mediterranean University in northern (Turkish) Cyprus in April 2003, I was sharply informed that there was no inconsistency. The Turkish position in Cyprus had been guaranteed by its constitution and the international treaty that had originally established a bi-national Cypriot state in 1960, they explained. My Turkish interlocutors neglected the fact that Kurdistan in Iraq had been officially recognized by the Baʿthist government in 1970, and they appeared not to notice one implication of their argument: if Kurdistan is recognized, as it is now, under the negotiated TAL, then the Kurds of Iraq may enjoy the same rights that Turks now presume to be possessed by the Turks of Northern Cyprus.

Turkey is inescapably Kurdistan's and Iraq's neighbor. Its tremendous military superiority over Kurdistan remains. It has the ability, which it exercises regularly, to choke commercial and personal traffic at the key border junctions which were previously the lifelines of the Kurdistan Regional Government, especially the Erbil executive. Its capacity to threaten Kurdistan remains formidable, especially because inertia might restore Turkey's strategic relationship with the U.S. The U.S. geo-strategic understanding of its interests in central Eurasia has led it consistently to want Turkey as a NATO partner to balance Iran and the Russian federation. Even if the Kurds of Iraq offered the U.S. ready bases as a substitute for Turkey, they do not have many bargaining chips.

What should be the disposition of the political leadership of the Kurds of Iraq against this background? They have a historic opportunity, with American support, to achieve what Turkey has always opposed: either national status within a federal Iraq or, if this proves impossible, an independent Kurdistan (for further thoughts on an independent Kurdistan, see Anderson and Stansfield 2004, as well as the discussions elsewhere in this volume). Prudence suggests that the Kurds of Iraq would be well advised to proceed with as much consent as possible from Turkey because, in the end, the U.S. and its allies will leave Iraq and Turkey will remain next door. The Kurds of Iraq initially should be rather modest and, from their new-found position of relative strength, work with Turkey, not against it (Bengio 2003; Yavuz and Gunter 2001). Kurdistan's leaders must try to persuade Turkey that greater stability and common prosperity will stem from a democratic federal Kurdistan unit, rather than a recentralized authoritarian Iraq that leaves the Kurds of Iraq disgruntled. To win Turkish approval, the Kurds of Iraq must be seen to be sincere in trying to make a democratic federal Iraq work. If such an Iraq proves impossible to achieve, as some suggest the historical record demonstrates (Dodge 2003; Menon 2004), the Kurds of Iraq might then be seen as having the right, in the name of a stability that would also benefit Turkey, to move toward independence. Whether Kurdistan seeks a federation, or moves toward independence after an implosion in the rest of Iraq, the new Kurdistan must continue to assure Turkey it will not foment armed rebellion among the Kurds in Turkey, either directly or indirectly. It must continue to be visibly fair to the Turkomen minority in Kurdistan, giving Turkey no excuse for an intervention, as Greek Cypriots did in 1974. Flexible power-sharing arrangements for Kirkuk, in which Kirkuk's Turkomen have their fair share, are also well-advised.

Kurdistan has another piece of leverage it has never had before, in addition to U.S. support for the Kurds of Iraq. It can become the gatekeeper for Turkey's membership in the Kantian paradise. Kurdistan's treatment by Turkey will be inspected by EU parliamentarians determined to ensure that Turkey is worthy of membership. This issue raises, in acute form, both the external and the internal criteria for membership with which this essay opened. The Kurds of Iraq, and the Kurds of Turkey, should encourage Turkey to meet EU accession standards. There is no better long-run way peacefully to settle the Kurdish question in Turkey. Turkish membership in the EU would reduce the incentive for the Kurds of Turkey to want to secede—or, at least, ensure that they sought secession only on a parliamentary basis. Turkey's membership, with good relations with Kurdistan, would mean better security arrangements at the EU's "external border." After Turkey has met the conditions for EU entry, the influence of the Turkish military on political decisions over Kurdistan will diminish. A fully liberal and democratic Turkish government ready for EU membership would be less likely to fear an independent Kurdistan in Iraq.

In the interim, Kurdistan in Iraq and Turkey have joint interests in commercial cross-border cooperation that will be of interest to the Eurpoean Parliament as it oversees Turkey's candidacy. Economic cooperation has been hampered for years because of the instability caused by Iraq's wars against Iran and the U.S., as well as the U.S.-led sanctions against Iraq that hurt Turkey. Improved economic relations between Turkey and the Kurds of Iraq would also help benefit the Kurds in Turkey, who so badly need sustained economic development.

On the other hand, if Turkey is kept out of the EU, at least some of its senior military would be more likely to continue to view the Kurdish issue through traditional national security perspectives, which are hostile both to an autonomous Kurdistan in a free and federal Iraq and toward an independent Kurdistan. Why Turkey failed to meet the membership criteria would be important in determining its future behavior. Failure because it did not meet the high EU standards of entry might embolden reformers to complete the rejection of Kemalist mentalities, but failure because of "Islamophobia" or racism within the European Union would harden the reflexes of the unreconstructed among Turkey's power elite. Cast adrift from the European Union and the United States, Turkey would be a danger to all its neighbors—and, as regards Kurdistan, more likely to seek succor from Syria and Iran and those Arabs in Iraq who would like to overturn the partial successes of Kurdish nationalists.

So far, I have suggested the prudent approach Kurdistan should adopt to forestall the worst dispositions of which the existing Turkish state is still capable. But that does not mean that Turkey's existing institutional and policy regimes should be treated as unavoidable facts of life. Turkey must come around to trusting more in its inherent strength, rather than revisiting its outdated fears. As Ilnur Çevik, a leading Turkish journalist, observed: "Instead of seeking confrontation and friction with the Iraqi Kurdish leaders, some people in Turkey could change their attitude dramatically and start seeking ways to forge closer ties with them and actually treat them as regional partners." Çevik elaborated to make the striking and potentially correct claim that "the Kurds of Iraq are our natural allies. They were part of the Ottoman Empire and we lived with them for centuries." Therefore, he reasoned that it was only natural that the Kurds of Iraq should be treated "as our relatives," just like the Turkomen of Iraq: "Some people who do not seem to appreciate this will have to change their attitude if they want to live in a realistic world" (Çevik 2003b). Turkey needs more such voices and appraisals. Masoud Barzani, president of the KDP, reciprocated when he told Çevik and Cengiz Çandar, another leading Turkish journalist, that "when the situation is good in Iraq and in the north of the country, this would be beneficial for Turkey. . . . We should walk together [Turkey and the Kurds], and take joint steps to help each other to solve problems" (Çevik 2003a). Turkey needs to realize that as the more powerful partner it could become the natural leader and protector of either a national Kurdistan in a federal Iraq or an independent Kurdistan which would serve as a buffer between Turkey and possible Islamist-driven instability to the south. Fears about a Kurdish *kukla devlet* (puppet state) that would be the first stepping stone on the road to partition Turkey are anachronistic. Self-negating prophecies of the kind the late Turgut Özul initiated are required, rather than the public recycling of ancient nightmares. Özul's experiments suggested that the arguments advanced here for Turkish-Kurdish cooperation are not utopian. The promise of entry, and of meeting the standards for entry, to the European Union create the possibilities of better Turkish and Kurdish futures.

Notes

1. The High Commissioner on National and Ethnic Minorities is an office of the Organization for Security and Cooperation in Europe, responsible for peacefully addressing national minority questions within the OSCE.

2. Other bitter pills are in the offing. The same report, while nodding toward "Turkish sensitivities," signaled the European Parliament's "great interest" in "the Armenian question," which may foreshadow that acknowledging the last century's genocide will constitute the final requirement for Turkey's entry into the European Union.

3. There are strikingly contrasting views of the nature of the *millet* system. Braude and Lewis, by and large, portray it as a version of tolerant multiculturalism, whereas Ye'or highlights the degree of hierarchical control over the despised *dhimmi* in Islamic polities in general, and within the Ottoman empire in particular (Braude and Lewis 1982; Ye'or 1985). For a survey of the literature, see Karpat 1988.

4. The KDP espoused more "traditional" cultural and social values, while the PKK was socialist.

5. This was reported in *Anonymous*, a Turkish news weekly that does not list authors for its articles.

6. Furthermore, Turkey's support for the independence of ethnic Turkic-speaking states in central Asia, in Azerbaijan, Kazakhstan, and Turkmenistan, suggested that the Turks have accepted breaking up other peoples' federations.

References

Anderson, Liam and Gareth R. V. Stansfield, eds. 2004. *The Future of Iraq: Dictatorship, Democracy, or Division?* New York: Palgrave Macmillan.

Anonymous. 2004. "Turkey's Growing Uneasiness over Iraqi Kurds." *Briefing*, 19 January, 7.

Bengio, Ofra. 2003. "Iraqi Kurds: Hour of Power?" *Middle East Quarterly* 10 (3) (Summer): 39–48.

Braude, Benjamin and Bernard Lewis, eds. 1982. *Christians and Jews in the Ottoman Empire: The Functioning of a Plural Society*. 2 vols. New York: Holmes and Meier.

Çevik, Ilnur. 2003a. "Barzani: Iraq Is Not an Exclusively Arab State." *Turkish Daily News*, 24 July.

———. 2003b. "Iraqi Kurds in Baghdad Administration." *Turkish Daily News*, 15 July.

Dodge, Toby. 2003. *Inventing Iraq: The Failure of Nation Building and a History Denied*. New York: Columbia University Press.

Edmonds, Cecil J. 1957. *Kurds, Turks and Arabs: Politics, Travel and Research in North-Eastern Iraq, 1919–1925*. London, Oxford University Press.

Foreign Broadcast Information Service—Western Europe (FBIS-WE). 1991a. "Talabani Calls on PKK to End Armed Action." Broadcast in Ankara Anatolia in Turkish, 1415 GMT, 18 October, 58.

———. 1991b. "Ozal on Syrian Aid to Terrorist Groups." Cited from Al-Hayah (London), 15 December, 5; 18 December, 42.

———. 1992a. "Iraqi Kurds Reportedly to Block Terrorist Attacks." Broadcast Ankara TRT Television Network 1600 GMT, 8, 9 April, 43.

———. 1992b. "Meets with Demirel." Broadcast Ankara TRT Television Network in Turkish, 1600 GMT, 8 June, 11 June 11, 42.

Foreign Broadcast Information Service—Near East and South Asia (FBIS-NESA). 1991.

"Kurdish Leader on Significance of Talks in Ankara." Citing broadcast Ankara Anatolia in English, 1515 GMT, 14, 15 March, 39.

———. 1998. "Our Democracy Is Unique." Cited from Bretioslav Turecek, Tyden (Prague), 28 April, 102, and 30 April, 1–2.

———. Gunter, Michael M. 1992. *The Kurds of Iraq: Tragedy and Hope*. New York: St. Martin's Press.

———. 1997. *The Kurds and the Future of Turkey*. New York: St. Martin's Press.

———. 1999. *The Kurdish Predicament in Iraq: A Political Analysis*. New York: St. Martin's Press.

İnalcik, Halil. 1973. *The Ottoman Empire: The Classical Age, 1300–1600*. London: Wiedenfeld and Nicolson.

Kagan, Robert. 2003. *Of Paradise and Power: America and Europe in the New World Order*. New York: Knopf.

Karpat, Kemal. 1973. *An Enquiry into the Social Foundations of Nationalism in the Ottoman State: From Social Estates to Classes, from Millets to Nations*. Princeton, N.J.: Princeton University Press.

———. 1988. "The Ottoman Ethnic and Confessional Legacy in the Middle East." In *Ethnicity, Pluralism and the State in the Middle East*, ed. Milton J. Esman and Itamar Rabinovich. Ithaca, N.Y.: Cornell University Press. 35–53.

Kralev, Nicholas. 2003. "U.S. Warns Turkey Against Operations in Northern Iraq." *Washington Post*, 8 July.

Lewis, Bernard. 1968. *The Emergence of Modern Turkey*. 2nd ed. Oxford: Oxford University Press.

McDowall, David. 1996. *A Modern History of the Kurds*. London: I.B. Tauris.

Menon, Rajan. 2004. "Iraqi Kurds May Want to Go Their Own Way." *Los Angeles Times*, 12 April.

Olson, Robert W. 1989. *The Emergence of Kurdish Nationalism and the Sheikh Said Rebellion, 1880–1925*. Austin: University of Texas Press.

———. 1991. "Kurds and Turks: Two Documents Concerning Kurdish Autonomy in 1922 and 1923." *Journal of South Asian and Middle Eastern Studies* 15 (Winter): 20–31.

Oostlander, Arie M. (Rapporteur). 2004. Report on the 2003 Regular Report of the Commission on Turkey's Progress Towards Accession. Brussels European Parliament Final A5-0204/2004 (RR29363EN.doc PE 329.63).

Shaw, Stanford and Ezel Shaw. 1977. *History of the Ottoman Empire and Modern Turkey*. Vol. 2, *Reform, Revolution and Republic: The Rise of Modern Turkey, 1805–1917*. Cambridge: Cambridge University Press.

Stansfield, Gareth R.V. 2003. *Iraqi Kurdistan: Political Development and Emergent Democracy*. London: Routledge.

Turkish Daily News. 2003. "Okzkok: Biggest Crisis of Trust with U.S." 7 July.

van Bruinessen, Martin. 1992. *Agha, Shaikh and State: The Social and Political Structure of Kurdistan*. London: Zed Books.

Vanly, Ismet Cheriff. 1970. *Le Kurdistan irakien: entité nationale*. Neuchâtel: Éditions de la Baconnière.

Williams, Daniel. 2004. "Iraqi Kurdish Leader Demands Guarantees: Minority Seeks Autonomous Region, Expulsion of Arabs Under New Government." *Washington Post*, 18 January.

Wright, Jonathan. 2003. "Turkey Accuses U.S. of 'Favoritism' in Iraq." Reuters, 4 November.

Yavuz, M. Hakan. 2001. "Five Stages of the Construction of Kurdish Nationalism in Turkey." *Nationalism and Ethnic Politics* 7 (Autumn): 1–24.

———. 2004. *"Provincial* not *Ethnic* Federalism in Iraq." *Middle East Policy* 11 (1) (Spring): 126–31.

Yavuz, M. Hakan and Michael M Gunter. 2001. "The Kurdish Nation." *Current History* 100 (January): 33–39.

Ye'or, Bat. 1985. *The Dhimmi: Jews and Christians under Islam.* Trans. David Maisel, Paul Fenton, and David Littman. Rutherford, N.J.: Fairleigh Dickinson University Press.

PART FOUR

Immediate Issues

Chapter 10

What Went Wrong

Peter W. Galbraith

In the year since the U.S. Marines pulled down Saddam Hussein's statue in Baghdad's Firdos Square, things have gone very badly for the United States in Iraq and for its ambition of creating a model democracy that might transform the Middle East. As of today the United States military appears committed to an open-ended stay in a country where, with the exception of the Kurdish north, patience with the foreign occupation is running out and violent opposition is spreading. Civil war and the breakup of Iraq are more likely outcomes than a successful transition to a pluralistic Western-style democracy.

Much of what went wrong was avoidable. Focused on winning the political battle to start a war, the Bush administration failed to anticipate the postwar chaos in Iraq. Administration strategy seems to have been based on a hope that Iraq's bureaucrats and police would simply transfer their loyalty to the new authorities, and the country's administration would continue to function. All experience in Iraq suggested that the collapse of civil authority was the most likely outcome, but there was no credible planning for this contingency. In fact, the U.S. effort to remake Iraq never recovered from its confused start when it failed to prevent the looting of Baghdad in the early days of the occupation.

Americans like to think that every problem has a solution, but that may no longer be true in Iraq. Before dealing at considerable length with what has gone wrong, I should also say what has gone right.

Iraq is free from Saddam Hussein and the Ba'th Party. Along with Cambodia's Pol Pot, Saddam Hussein's regime was one of the two most cruel and inhumane regimes in the second half of the twentieth century. Using the definition of genocide specified in the 1948 Genocide Convention, Iraq's Ba'th regime can be charged with planning and executing two genocides—one against the Kurdish population in the late 1980s and another against the Marsh Arabs in the 1990s. In the 1980s, the Iraqi armed forces and security services systematically destroyed more than four thousand Kurdish villages and several small cities, attacked over two hundred Kurdish villages and towns with chemical weapons in 1987 and 1988, and organized the deportation and execution of up to 182,000 Kurdish civilians.

In the 1990s the Saddam Hussein regime drained the marshes of southern Iraq, displacing 500,000 people, half of whom fled to Iran, and killing some 40,000. In addition to destroying the five-thousand-year-old Marsh Arab civilization, draining the marshes did vast ecological damage to one of the most important wetlands systems on the planet. Genocide is only part of Saddam Hussein's murderous legacy. Tens of thousands perished in purges from 1979 on, and as many as 300,000 Shiʿas were killed in the six months following the collapse of the March 1991 Shiʿa uprising. One mass grave near Hilla may contain as many as 30,000 bodies.

In a more lawful world, the United Nations, or a coalition of willing states, would have removed this regime from power long before 2003. However, at precisely the time that some of the most horrendous crimes were being committed, in the late 1980s, the Reagan and Bush administrations strongly opposed any action to punish Iraq for its genocidal campaign against the Kurds or to deter Iraq from using chemical weapons against the Kurdish civilians.

On 20 August, 1988, the Iran-Iraq War ended. Five days later, the Iraqi military initiated a series of chemical weapons attacks on at least forty-nine Kurdish villages in the Dohuk Governorate (or province) near the Syrian and Turkish borders. As a staff member of the Senate Foreign Relations Committee, I (along with Chris Van Hollen, now a Maryland Representative) interviewed hundreds of survivors in the high mountains on the Turkish border. Our report, which established conclusively that Iraq had used nerve and mustard agents on tens of thousands of civilians, coincided with the Senate's passage of the Prevention of Genocide Act of 1988, which imposed comprehensive economic sanctions on Iraq for crimes against the Kurds. The Reagan administration opposed the legislation, in a position orchestrated by national security adviser Colin Powell, calling such sanctions "premature."

Except for a relatively small number of Saddam Hussein's fellow Sunni Arabs who worked for his regime, the peoples of Iraq are much better off today than they were under Saddam Hussein. The problems that threaten to tear Iraq apart—Kurdish aspirations for independence, Shiʿa dreams of dominance, Sunni Arab nostalgia for lost power—are not of America's making (although the failure to act sooner against Saddam made them less solvable). Rather, they are inherent in an artificial state held together for eighty years primarily by brute force.

American liberation—and liberation it was—ended the brute force. Iraqis celebrated the dictatorship's overthrow, and in Baghdad last April ordinary citizens thrust flowers into my hands. Since then, however:

- Hostile action has killed twice as many American troops as died in the war itself, while thousands of Iraqis have also died.
- Terrorists have killed the head of the UN Mission, Sergio Vieira de Mello; Iraq's most prominent Shi'a politician, the Ayatollah Baqir al-Hakim; and the deputy prime minister of the Kurdistan Regional Government, Sami Abdul Rahman, along with hundreds of others.
- Looting has caused billions of dollars of damage, most of which will have to be repaired at the expense of the U.S. taxpayer.
- $150 billion has already been spent on Iraq, an amount equal to 25 percent of the non-defense discretionary federal budget. (By contrast, the first Gulf War earned a small profit for the U.S. government, owing to the contributions of other states.)
- Discontent with the U.S.-led occupation boiled over into an uprising in the Shi'a areas of Iraq on the first anniversary of liberation and a persistent insurgency in the Sunni Triangle degenerated into a full-scale battle in Fallujah. Many on the U.S.-installed Iraqi Governing Council strongly opposed the US military response, and the U.S.-created security institutions—the new Iraqi police and the paramilitary Iraqi Civil Defense Corps—refused to fight, or in some cases, joined the rebels.
- U.S. credibility abroad has been undermined by the failure to find weapons of mass destruction. Spain's elections, Tony Blair's sinking poll results, and the prospective defeat of Australia's Howard government underscore the political risk of too close an association with the United States.
- Relations with France and Germany have been badly hurt, in some cases by the gratuitous comments made by senior U.S. officials.
- The United States does not now have the military or diplomatic resources to deal with far more serious threats to U.S. national security.

President Bush rightly identified the peril posed by the nexus between weapons of mass destruction and rogue states. The greatest danger comes from rogue states that acquire and disseminate nuclear weapons technology. At the beginning of 2003 Iraq posed no such danger. As a result of the Iraq war the United States has neither the resources nor the international support to cope effectively with the very serious nuclear threats that come from North Korea, Iran, and, most dangerous of all, our newly designated "major non-NATO ally," Pakistan.

With fewer than one hundred days to the handover of power to a sovereign Iraq on 30 June, there is no clear plan—and no decision—about how Iraq will be run on 1 July 2004. Earlier this month, the Bush administration praised itself generously for the signing of an interim constitution for Iraq—a constitution with human rights provisions it described as unprecedented for the Middle East. Three weeks later, as I write, the interim constitution is already falling apart.

As is true of so much of the U.S. administration of postwar Iraq, the damage here is self-inflicted. While telling Iraqis it wanted to defer constitutional issues to an elected Iraqi body, the U.S.-led Coalition Provisional Authority could not resist trying to settle fundamental constitutional issues in the interim constitution. The U.S. government lawyers who wrote the interim constitution, known formally as the Transitional Administrative Law (TAL), made no effort to disguise their authorship. All deliberations on the law were done in secret and probably fewer than one hundred Iraqis saw a copy of the constitution before it was promulgated. To write a major law in any democracy—much less a constitution—without public discussion should be unthinkable. Now that Iraqis are discovering for the first time the contents of the constitution, it should come as no surprise that many object to provisions they never knew were being considered.

Iraq's Shiʿa leaders say that the National Assembly due to be elected in January 2005 should not be constrained by a document prepared by U.S. government lawyers, deliberated in secret, and signed by twenty-five Iraqis selected by Ambassador Bremer. In particular, the Shiʿa object to a provision in the interim constitution that allows three of Iraq's eighteen governorates (or provinces) to veto ratification of a permanent constitution. This, in effect, allows either the Kurds or the Sunni Arabs, each of whom make up between one-fifth and one-sixth of Iraq's population, to block a constitution they don't like. (It is a wise provision. Imposing a constitution on reluctant Kurds or Sunni Arabs will provoke a new cycle of resistance and conflict.) The Shiʿa position makes the Kurds, who are well armed, reluctant to surrender powers to a central government that may be Shiʿa-dominated.

At the moment the Sunni Arabs have few identifiable leaders. The Kurds, however, are well organized. They have an elected parliament and two regional governments, their own court system, and a 100,000 strong military force, known as the *peshmerga*. The *peshmerga*, whose members were principal American allies in the 2003 war, are better armed, better trained, and more disciplined than the minuscule Iraqi army the United States is now trying to reconstitute. Early in 2005, Iraq will likely see a clash between an elected Shiʿa-dominated central government trying to override the interim constitution in order to impose its will on the entire country, and a Kurdistan government insistent on preserving the de facto independent status Kurdistan has enjoyed for thirteen years. Complicating the political struggle is a bitter territorial dispute over the oil-rich province of Kirkuk involving Kurds, Sunni Arabs, Shiʿa Arabs, Sunni Turmen, and Shiʿa Turkomen.

It is a formula for civil war.

How did we arrive at this state of affairs?

I arrived in Baghdad on 13 April 2003, as part of an ABC news team. It was apparent to me that things were already going catastrophically wrong. When the United States entered Baghdad on 9 April 2003, it found a city largely undamaged by a carefully executed military campaign. However, in the two months following the U.S. takeover, unchecked looting effectively gutted every important public institution in the city with the notable exception of the Oil Ministry. The physical losses include:

- The National Library, which was looted and burned. Equivalent to our Library of Congress, it held every book published in Iraq, all newspapers from the last century, as well as rare manuscripts. The destruction of the library meant the loss of a historical record going back to Ottoman times.
- The Iraqi National Museum, which was also looted. More than 10,000 objects were stolen or destroyed. The Pentagon has deliberately, and repeatedly, tried to minimize the damage by excluding from its estimates objects stolen from storage as well as displayed treasures that were smashed but not stolen.
- Hospitals and other public health institutions, where looters stole medical equipment, medicines, and even patients' beds.
- Baghdad and Mosul Universities, which were stripped of computers, office furniture, and books. Academic research that took decades to carry out went up in smoke or was scattered.
- The National Theater, which was set ablaze by looters a full three weeks after U.S. forces entered Baghdad.
- On 16 April, looters attacked the Iraqi equivalent of the U.S. Centers for Disease Control, stealing live HIV and live black fever bacteria. The UN arms inspection agencies UNMOVIC and UNSCOM had long considered the building suspicious and had repeatedly conducted inspections there. The looting complicates efforts to understand and account for any Iraqi bioweapons research in the past. A Marine lieutenant watched the looting from next door. He told us, "I hope I am not responsible for Armageddon, but no one told me what was in that building."

- Although U.S. troops moved onto the grounds of Iraq's sprawling Tuwaitha nuclear complex, they did not secure the warehouse that contained yellowcake and other radiological materials. Looters took materials that terrorists could use for a radiological weapon, although much of that material was eventually recovered. The looted nuclear materials were in a known location, and already had been placed under seal by the International Atomic Energy Commission.
- Ten days after the U.S. took over Baghdad, I went through the unguarded Iraqi Foreign Ministry, going from the cooling unit on the roof to the archives in the basement, and rummaging through the office of the foreign minister. The only other people in the building were looters, who were busy opening safes and carrying out furniture. They were unarmed and helped me look for documents. Foreign Ministry files could have shed light on Iraqis' overseas intelligence activities, on attempts to procure WMD, and on any connections that may have existed with al-Qaida. However, we may never know about these things, since looters scattered and burned files during the ten days, or longer, that this building was left unguarded.

Even more surprising, the United States made no apparent effort to secure sites that had been connected with Iraqi weapons of mass destruction (WMD) programs or buildings alleged to hold important intelligence. As a result, the United States may well have lost valuable information that related to Iraqi WMD procurement, paramilitary resistance, foreign intelligence activities, and possible links to al-Qaida.

The looting demoralized Iraqi professionals, the very people the U.S. looks to in rebuilding the country. University professors, government technocrats, doctors, and researchers all had connections with the looted institutions. Some saw the work of a lifetime literally go up in smoke. The looting also exacerbated other problems: the lack of electricity and potable water, the lack of telephones, and the absence of police or other security.

Most important, the looting served to undermine Iraqi confidence in, and respect for, the U.S. occupation authorities. In the parts of Iraq taken over by rebels during the March 1991 uprising, there had been the same kind of looting of public institutions. In 2003, the United States could not have prevented all the looting but it could have prevented much of it. In particular, it could have secured the most important Iraqi government ministries, hospitals, laboratories, and intelligence sites. It could have protected the Iraq National Museum and several other of Iraq's most important cultural and historical sites.

In the spring of 2003, Thomas Warrick of the State Department's Future of Iraq Working Group prepared a list of places in Baghdad to be secured. The Iraq National Museum was number two on the list. At the top of the list were the paper records of the previous regime—the very documents I found scattered throughout the Foreign Ministry and in other locations. What happened next is a mystery. My State Department informants tell me the list was sent to Douglas Feith, an undersecretary in the Department of Defense, and never came out of his office. Feith's partisans insist that uniformed American military failed to take action. In either case, the lack of oversight was culpable.

During the war in Kosovo, the Clinton White House was criticized for insisting on presidential review of proposed targets. President Bush, notorious for his lack of curiosity, seems never to have asked even the most basic question: "What happens when we actually get to Baghdad?"

The failure to answer this question at the start set back U.S. efforts in Iraq in such a way that the U.S. has not recovered and may never do so.

The Bush administration decided that Iraq would be run by a U.S. civilian administrator—initially, retired general Jay Garner—and American advisers who would serve as the de facto ministers for each of the Iraqi government ministries. All this was based on the expectation that the war would decapitate the top leadership of the Saddam Hussein regime and the next day everyone else would show up for work.

Predictably, this did not happen. In 1991, all authority disappeared in the areas that fell into rebel hands. But even had things gone as the Bush administration hoped, it was not prepared to run Iraq. As the war began, the Bush administration was still recruiting the American officials who would serve as the de facto Iraqi ministers. The people so recruited had no time to prepare for the assignment, either in learning about Iraq or in mastering the substantive skills needed to run the ministry assigned to them. Many mistakes were made. For example, the U.S. official in charge of prisons decided to work with Ali al-Jabouri, the warden of Abu Ghraib prison, apparently unaware of the prison's fearsome reputation as the place where tens of thousands perished under Saddam Hussein. The coalition rehabilitated Abu Ghraib and today uses it as a prison. The symbolism may be lost on the U.S. administrators but it is not lost on Iraqis.

In late 2002 and early 2003, I attended meetings with senior U.S. government officials on Kirkuk, the multi-ethnic city just west of the line marking the border of the self-governing Kurdish region. When Kirkuk, which is claimed by the Kurds, was held by Saddam Hussein, horrific human rights abuses had taken place there. I had been to Kirkuk in the 1980s, and I was concerned that Kurds brutally expelled in the 1980s and 1990s would return to settle scores with Arabs who had been settled in their homes. The week the war began, I asked the U.S. official responsible for Kirkuk how he planned to deal with this problem. We will rely on the local police, he explained. I asked whether the local police were Kurds or Arabs. He did not know. It remains astonishing to me that U.S. plans for dealing with ethnic conflict in the most volatile city in all of Iraq rested on hopes about the behavior of a police force about which they did not have the most basic information.

The Kirkuk police were, in fact, Arabs, and had assisted in the ethnic cleansing of the city's Kurds. They were not around when Kurdish forces entered the city on 10 April 2003. Many other Arabs also fled, although this was largely ignored by the international press. The U.S. political strategies in Iraq have been no less incoherent. General Garner arrived announcing that he would quickly turn power over to a provisional Iraqi government. Within three weeks Ambassador Bremer and a new structure, the Coalition Provisional Authority (CPA), replaced him. U.S. officials indicated that Iraqi participation would be limited to an advisory council and that the United States expected to stay in Iraq for up to three years. The U.S. would write a democratic constitution for the country and then turn power over to an elected government. After a few weeks, Bremer changed course and announced he was sharing power with a representative Iraqi governing council. In November, as Bush's poll numbers plummeted, Bremer was summoned back to Washington to discuss a new strategy. The U.S., it was decided, would turn power over on 30 June 2004, to a sovereign Iraqi government that would be chosen in a complicated system of caucuses held in each of Iraq's governorates. By January this plan was put aside (it was widely described as "election by people selected by people selected by Bremer").

The latest strategy—based on the interim constitution and a takeover of sovereignty on 30 June by an as yet undetermined body—the fifth in a year by my count, is now falling apart in the face of Shi'a opposition and mounting violence.

The Bush administration's strategies in Iraq are failing for many reasons. First, they are being made up as the administration goes along, without benefit of planning, adequate knowledge of the country, or the experience of comparable situations. Second, the administration has been unwilling to sustain a commitment to a particular strategy. But third, the strategies are all based on an idea of an Iraq that does not exist.

The fundamental problem of Iraq is an absence of Iraqis.

In the north the Kurds prefer almost unanimously not to be part of Iraq, for reasons that are very understandable. Kurdistan's eighty-year association with Iraq has been one of repression and conflict, of which the Saddam Hussein regime was the most brutal phase. Since 1991, Kurdistan has been de facto independent and most Kurds of Iraq see this period as a golden era of democratic self-government and economic progress. In 1992 Kurdistan had the only democratic elections in the history of Iraq, when voters chose members of a newly created Kurdistan National Assembly. During the last twelve years the Kurdistan Regional Government built three thousand schools (as compared to one thousand in the region in 1991), opened two universities, and permitted a free press; there are now scores of Kurdish-language publications, radio stations, and television stations. For the older generation, Iraq is a bad memory, while a younger generation, which largely does not speak Arabic, has no sense of being Iraqi.

The people of Kurdistan almost unanimously prefer independence to being part of Iraq. In just one month, starting on 25 January 2004, Kurdish nongovernmental organizations collected 1,700,000 signatures on petitions demanding a vote on whether Kurdistan should remain part of Iraq. This is a staggering figure, representing as it does roughly two thirds of Kurdistan's adults.

In the south, Iraq's long-repressed Shiʿa express themselves primarily through their religious identity. In early March I traveled throughout southern Iraq. I saw no evidence of any support for secular parties. If free elections are held in Iraq, I think it likely that the Shiʿa religious parties—principally the Supreme Council for Islamic Revolution in Iraq (SCIRI) and the Daʿwa (the Call)—will have among them an absolute majority in the National Assembly.

The wild card is Moqtada al-Sadr, the leader of the Shiʿa uprising. If he is allowed to compete in elections, he will certainly take a share of the Shiʿa vote. If he is excluded (or imprisoned or killed), his supporters will likely influence the policies of the mainstream Shiʿa parties, or conceivably disrupt the elections. None of this is good for hopes of creating a stable, democratic Iraq.

The Shiʿa are not separatists, but many of them believe their majority status entitles them to run all of Iraq, and to impose their version of an Islamic state. They also consider connections with Shiʿa elsewhere as important as their nationalist feelings about Iraq. Iranian Shiʿa, such as the Ayatollah al-Sistani and, from the grave, Ayatollah Khomeini, have enormous political and spiritual influence in southern Iraq. Their portraits are ubiquitous. Mainstream Iraqi Arab Shiʿa, such as SCIRI's leader Abdul Azziz al-Hakim, often advocate a very pro-Iranian line.

Sunni Arabs have always been the principal Iraqi nationalists, and a part of the anti-U.S. uprising in the Sunni Triangle is a nationalist one. The Sunni

Arabs have long been accustomed to seeing the Iraqi state as a part of a larger Arab nation, and this was a central tenet of the Ba'th Party. As Sunni Arabs face the end of their historic domination of Iraq, they may seek to compensate for their minority status inside Iraq by further identifying themselves with the greater Arab nation. Connections with other Sunni populations may eventually become even more important among the Sunni Arabs than pan-Arabism. As elsewhere in Arab Iraq, the Sunni religious parties appear to be gaining ground in the country's Sunni center at the expense of the secular parties.

Radical Sunni Islamic groups, including those with recent links to al-Qaida, appear to have an ever more important part in the uprising in the Sunni Triangle (which explains the increasing use of suicide bombers, not a tactic that appeals to the more worldly Ba'thists). By attacking Shi'a religious leaders and celebrations (for example, the deadly bombings in March 2004 during the as-Shoura religious holiday in Baghdad and Karbala, and the car bomb assassination of SCIRI leader Baqir al-Hakim), Sunni extremists seek to provoke civil war between Iraq's two main religious groups.

The U.S. strategy is to hold Iraq together by establishing a strong central government. So far, all its successes have been on paper. The interim constitution gives the central government a monopoly on military force, control over natural resources, broad fiscal powers, and oversight over the judiciary.

Little of this will come to pass. The Kurdistan National Assembly has put forward a comprehensive proposal to define Kurdistan's relations with the rest of Iraq. In it the Kurdistan National Assembly retains lawmaking power for the region, preserves its fiscal autonomy, and would eventually own the region's natural resources. Kurdistan will retain the *peshmerga* (which would be converted into an Iraqi Kurdistan National Guard nominally under the overall authority of the Iraq central government) and other Iraqi armed forces could only enter Kurdistan with the consent of the Kurdistan National Assembly. Iraq would be fully bilingual (Arabic and Kurdish) and Kurdistan would remain secular.

This places the Kurds on a collision course with the Shi'a and the Sunni Arabs. The Shi'a religious parties insist that Islam must be the principal source of law throughout Iraq. Both Shi'a and Sunni Arabs object to downgrading Arabic to one of two official languages. Sunni Arab nationalists and Shi'a religious leaders object to Kurdistan retaining even a fraction of the autonomy it has today.

There are also acute conflicts between Shi'a Arabs and Sunni Arabs. These have to do with the differing interpretations of Islam held by the two groups' religious parties and conflicts between pro-Iranian Shi'a and Arab nationalist Sunnis.

Shi'a are now providing moral and material support for the Sunni insurgents in Fallujah. An anti-American alliance of radicals from both confessions will not necessarily lead to political unity, nor will it erase Sunni fears of Shi'a domination. That said, the confessional divide between Iraq's Arabs is far less than the ethnic gulf between Arabs and Kurds. Democracy requires tolerance and a willingness to compromise. Except tactically, none of these traits is apparent in a political culture (except for the north) which has been ruled by absolutists.

In my view, Iraq is not salvageable as a unitary state. From my experience in the Balkans, I feel strongly that it is impossible to preserve the unity of a democratic state where people in a geographically defined region almost unanimously do not want to be part of that state. I have never met a Kurd of Iraq who preferred membership in Iraq if independence were a realistic possibility.

But the problem of Iraq is that a breakup of the country is not a realistic possibility for the present. Turkey, Iran, and Syria, all of which have substantial Kurdish populations, fear the precedent that would be set if Iraqi Kurdistan became independent. Both Sunni and Shi'a Arabs oppose the separation of Kurdistan. The Sunni Arabs do not have the resources to support an independent state of their own. (Iraq's largest oil fields are in the Shi'a south or in the disputed territory of Kirkuk.)

Further, as was true in the Balkans, the unresolved territorial issues in Iraq would likely mean violent conflict. Kirkuk is perhaps the most explosive place. The Kurds claim it as part of historic Kurdistan. They demand that the process of Arabization of the region—which some say goes back to the 1950s—should be reversed. The Kurds who were driven out of Kirkuk by policies of successive Iraqi regimes should, they say, return home, while Arab settlers in the region are repatriated to other parts of Iraq. While many Iraqi Arabs concede that the Kurds suffered an injustice, they also say that the human cost of correcting it is too high. Moreover, backed by Turkey, ethnic Turkomen assert that Kirkuk is a Turkomen city and that they should enjoy the same status as the Kurds.

It will be difficult to resolve the status of Kirkuk within a single Iraq; it will be impossible if the country breaks up into two or three units. And while Kirkuk is the most contentious of the territories in dispute, it is only one of many.

The best hope for holding Iraq together—and thereby avoiding civil war—is to let each of its major constituent communities have, to the extent possible, the system each wants. This, too, suggests the only policy that can get American forces out of Iraq.

In the north this means accepting that Kurdistan will continue to govern its own affairs and retain responsibility for its own security. U.S. officials have portrayed a separate Kurdistan defense force as the first step leading to the breakup of Iraq. The Kurds, however, see such a force not as an attribute of a sovereign state but as insurance in case democracy fails in the rest of Iraq. No one in Kurdistan would trust an Iraqi national army (even one in which the Kurds were well represented) since the Iraqi army has always been an agent of repression, and in the 1980s, of genocide. The Kurds also see clearly how ineffective are the new security institutions created by the Americans. In the face of uprisings in the Sunni Triangle and the south, the new Iraqi police and civil defense corps simply vanished.

Efforts to push the Kurds into a more unitary Iraq will fail because there is no force, aside from the U.S. military, that can coerce them. Trying to do so will certainly inflame popular demands for separation of the Kurdish region in advance of January's elections.

If Kurdistan feels secure, it is in fact more likely to see advantages to cooperation with other parts of Iraq. Iraq's vast resources and the benefits that would accrue to Kurdistan from revenue sharing provide significant incentives for Kurdistan to remain part of Iraq, provided doing so does not open the way to new repression. (Until now, most Iraqi Kurds have seen Iraq's oil wealth as a curse that gave Saddam the financial resources to destroy Kurdistan.) In the south, Iraq's Shiʿa want an Islamic state. They are sufficiently confident of public support that they are pushing for early elections. The United States should let them have their elections, and be prepared to accept an Islamic state—but only in the south. In most of the south, Shiʿa religious leaders already exercise actual power, having established a degree of security, taken over education, and helped to provide municipal services. In the preparation of Iraq's interim constitution, Shiʿa leaders asked for (and obtained) the right to form one or two Shiʿa regions with powers comparable to those of Kurdistan. They also strongly support the idea that petroleum should be owned by the respective regions, which is hardly surprising since Iraq's largest oil reserves are in the south.

There is, of course, a logical inconsistency between Shiʿa demands to control a southern region and the desire to impose Islamic rule on all of Iraq. Meeting the first demand affects only the south; accepting the second is an invitation to civil war and must be resisted.

Federalism—or even confederation—would make Kurdistan and the south governable because there are responsible parties there who can take over government functions. It is much more difficult to devise a strategy for the Sunni Triangle—until recently the location of most violent resistance to the American occupation—because there is no Sunni Arab leadership with discernible political support. While it is difficult to assess popular support for the insurrection within the Sunni Triangle, it is crystal clear that few Sunni Arabs in places like Fallujah are willing to risk their lives in opposing the insurgents.

We can hope that if the Sunni Arabs feel more secure about their place in Iraq with respect to the Shi'a and the Kurds, they will be relatively more moderate. Autonomy for the Sunni Arab parts of Iraq is a way to provide such security. There is, however, no way to know if it will work.

Since 1992, the Iraqi opposition has supported federalism as the system of government for a post-Saddam Iraq. Iraq's interim constitution reflects this consensus by defining Iraq as a federal state. There is, however, no agreement among the Iraqi parties on what federalism actually means, and the structures created by the interim constitution seem unlikely to move from paper to reality.

In November 2003, Les Gelb, president emeritus of the Council on Foreign Relations, created a stir by proposing, in a *New York Times* Op-Ed piece, a three-state solution for Iraq, modeled on the constitution of post-Tito Yugoslavia. The Yugoslav model would give each of Iraq's constituent peoples their own republic.[1] These republics would be self-governing, financially self-sustaining, and with their own territorial military and police forces. The central government would have a weak presidency rotating among the republics, with responsibilities limited to foreign affairs, monetary policy, and some coordination of defense policy. While resources would be owned by the republics, some sharing of oil revenues would be essential, since an impoverished Sunni region is in no one's interest.

This model would solve many of the contradictions of modern Iraq. The Shi'as could have their Islamic republic, while the Kurds could continue their secular traditions. Alcohol would continue to be a staple of Kurdish picnics while it would be strictly banned in Basra.

The three-state solution would permit the United States to disengage from security duties in most of Iraq. There are today fewer than three hundred Coalition troops in Kurdistan, which would, under the proposal being made here, continue to be responsible for its own security. By contrast, introducing an Iraqi army and security institutions into Kurdistan, as the Bush administration says it still wants to do, would require many more Coalition troops—because the Iraqi forces are not up to the job and because coalition troops will be needed to reassure a nervous Kurdish population. If the United States wanted to stay militarily in Iraq, Kurdistan is the place; Kurdish leaders have said they would like to see permanent U.S. bases in Kurdistan.

A self-governing Shiʿa republic could also run its own affairs and provide for its own security. It is not likely to endorse Western values, but if the coalition quickly disengages from the south, this may mean the south would be less overtly anti-American. Staying in the south will play directly into the hands of Moqtada al-Sadr or his successors. Moderate Shiʿa leaders, including the Ayatollah al-Sistani, counseled patience in response to al-Sadr's uprising, and helped negotiate the withdrawal of al-Sadr's supporters from some police stations and government buildings. The scope of the uprising, however, underscores the coalition's perilous position in the south. The failure of the Iraqi police and the Iraqi Civil Defense Corps to respond highlights the impotence of these American-created security institutions. The sooner power in the south is handed over to people who can exercise it, the better. Delay will only benefit anti-American radicals like al-Sadr.

As for the Sunni Triangle, one hope is for elections to produce a set of leaders who can restore order and end the insurrection. Presumably this is an outcome the Sunni rebels do not want to see happen; they will use violence to prevent a meaningful election in large parts of the Sunni Triangle. In these circumstances, the United States may face the choice of turning power over to weak leaders and living with the resulting chaos, or continuing to try to pacify the Sunni Triangle, which may generate ever more support for the insurrection. There may be no good options for the United States in the Sunni Triangle. Nevertheless the three-state approach could limit U.S. military engagement to a finite area.

Baghdad is a city of five million and home to large numbers of all three of Iraq's major constituent peoples. With skilled diplomacy, the United States or the United Nations might be able to arrange for a more liberal regime in Baghdad than would exist in the south. Kurdish and Shiʿa armed forces and police could provide security in their own sections of the capital, as well as work together in Sunni areas (with whatever local cooperation is possible) and in mixed areas. Such an arrangement in Iraq's capital is far from ideal, but it is better than an open-ended U.S. commitment to being the police force of last resort in Iraq's capital.

Because of what happened to Yugoslavia in the 1990s, many react with horror to the idea of applying its model to Iraq. Yet Yugoslavia's breakup was not inevitable. In the 1980s, Slovenia asked for greater control over its own affairs and Milosevic refused. Had Milosevic accepted a looser federation, there is every reason to think that Yugoslavia—and not just Slovenia—would be joining the European Union in May 2004.

Still, a loose federation will have many drawbacks, especially for those who dreamed of a democratic Iraq that would transform the Middle East. The country would remain whole more in name than in reality. Western-style human rights are likely to take hold only in the Kurdish north (and even there not completely). Women's rights could be set back in the south, and perhaps also in Baghdad.

In administering elections and allowing a federation to emerge, the U.S. would badly need the help of the UN and other international organizations and, if it can get it, of the principal European nations as well. The alternative is an indefinite U.S. occupation of Iraq in which we have fewer and fewer allies. It is an occupation that the U.S. cannot afford. It also prevents the U.S. from addressing more serious threats to its national security.

The American involvement in Iraq will be a defining event for the U.S. role in the world for the coming decades. Will it be seen as validating the Bush administration's doctrines of preventive war and largely unilateral action?

In my view, Iraq demonstrates all too clearly the folly of the preventive war doctrine and of unilateralism. Of course the United States must reserve the right to act alone when the country is under attack or in imminent danger of attack. But these are also precisely the circumstances when the United States does not need to act alone. After 11 September both NATO and the UN Security Council gave unqualified support for U.S. action, including military action, to deal with the threat of international terrorists based in Afghanistan. After the Taliban was defeated, other countries contributed troops—and accepted casualties—in order to help stabilize the country; and they have also contributed billions to Afghanistan's reconstruction. Because the U.S. so quickly diverted its attention to Iraq, many acute problems remain in Afghanistan, including warlordism and the deprivation of basic rights. International support for helping Afghanistan remains strong, however, and the effort can be revitalized with a new administration.

In Iraq the United States chose to act without the authorization of the Security Council, without the support of NATO, and with only a handful of allies. Aside from the British and the Kurdish *peshmerga*, no other ally made any significant contribution to the war effort. The United States is paying practically all the expenses of the Iraq occupation. Even those who supported the unilateral intervention in Iraq seem by now to realize that it cannot be sustained. The Bush administration, having scorned the United Nations, is now desperate to have it back.

It turns out that there are some things that only the United Nations can do—such as run an election that Iraqis will see as credible or give a stamp of legitimacy to a political transition. But the most urgent reason to want United Nations participation is to share the burden. Internationalization is a key element of John Kerry's program for Iraq. Unfortunately, it is a far from easy policy to achieve. While a less confrontational U.S. administration would certainly be able to win greater international support and contributions, it will be a challenge to persuade the major European countries to have either the United Nations or NATO take over the major responsibilities in Iraq.

The reason is cost. Taking all expenses into account, one year of involvement in Iraq costs between $50 billion and $100 billion. Under the mandatory assessment scale for the United Nations this would cost France and Germany some $5 billion to $10 billion each, and they would face pressure to put their own troops in harm's way. NATO assessments are similarly costly. While our allies may wish a Kerry administration well, they may not be willing to commit resources on this scale to help the United States get out of Iraq. As a European diplomat told me before last year's war, "It will be china shop rules in Iraq: you break it, you pay for it."

I believe U.S. policy is most successful when it follows international law and works within the United Nations, according to the provisions of the Charter. This is not just a matter of upholding the ideals of the UN; it is also practical. As our war in Iraq demonstrates, we cannot afford any other course.

Note

This chapter is a version of the first John Kenneth Galbraith lecture, which appeared in the *New York Review of Books,* 29 June 2004. It is reprinted by permission.

   1. I describe here my application of the Yugoslav model to Iraq, not Les Gelb's. We differ in our understanding of the Yugoslav model and of the subsequent history of that country. The differences, however, are not material to the arguments advanced here.

Chapter 11

State-Building After Saddam: Lessons Lost

Karin von Hippel

"To balance a large state or society, whether monarchical or republican, on general laws, is a work of so great difficulty that no human genius, however comprehensive, is able, by the mere dint of reason and reflection, to effect it. The judgments of many must unite in the work; EXPERIENCE must guide their labor; TIME must bring it to perfection, and the FEELING of inconveniences must correct the mistakes which they inevitably fall into in their first trials and experiments."
—David Hume, "The Rise of Arts and Sciences"

Just after midnight on 20 December 1989, almost one year into his presidency, President George Herbert Walker Bush ordered the invasion of Panama, a decision that would have far-reaching implications not just for Panamanians but also for the U.S. government as it assumed its lone superpower role. Indeed, the mistakes made before this operation, during the invasion itself, and in the post-conflict period taught U.S. and UN policy-makers valuable lessons about state-building in the 1990s. Many of these were subsequently applied in Haiti in 1994 (the intervention that restored Aristide to power, not the most recent one that overthrew him), as well as in Bosnia, Kosovo, and East Timor. While those involved in the operations had not developed a "nation-building doctrine" in the strict military sense of the word, a pattern of "best practice" had evolved due to these experiences.

By May 2004, with Arab Iraq, although not Kurdistan, in critical condition since the occupation began, it appeared that most of the lessons about interventions learned in the 1990s had been ignored or overlooked by the next President Bush, who was sworn into office on a platform opposed to "nation-building."[1] Before he took office, his choice for national security adviser, Condoleezza Rice, had outlined what would initially become President Bush's security strategy. She wrote: 'The president must remember that the military is a special instrument. It is lethal, and it is meant to be. It is not a civilian police force. It is not a political referee. And it is most certainly not designed to build a civilian society" (Rice 2000). On 26 February 2003, the *Washington Post* dug up a criticism of Al Gore made by George Bush the day before the presidential elections, which echoes Rice's doctrine: "Let me tell you what else I'm worried about: I'm worried about an opponent who uses nation building and the military in the same sentence." The tragedy of 11 September reversed President Bush's foreign policy, more closely aligning it to the activism of his father and of President Clinton. Not only did President Bush junior subsequently endorse military-assisted state-building in Afghanistan and Iraq, but he even sent troops into Liberia on a humanitarian mission in August 2003, a country not exactly of vital interest or strategic importance to the U.S. government, even given its special historical relationship as a state created by former American slaves.

Despite its eventual embrace of President Clinton's policy, the Bush administration has not incorporated the lessons learned in interventions in the 1990s with similar vigor. The consequences of that failure have been especially serious in Iraq. The American intervention there, unlike that in Afghanistan, was intended from the start to be an all-out state-building and democratization exercise. Indeed, if one considered the state of affairs in Iraq in May 2004, exactly a year after the official end of hostilities was declared, the situation looked dire: coalition soldiers were being cherry-picked on a daily basis, critical infrastructure regularly damaged by insurgents, and large car bombs had caused hundreds of deaths at the UN compound, the Jordanian Embassy, a mosque in Najaf, and several hotels and buildings housing international aid workers (one rocket attack narrowly missed Assistant Defense Secretary Paul Wolfowitz). For the U.S. alone, the costs have been enormous. By May 2004, more than one American soldier had died every day in Iraq since the official end of hostilities; the U.S. Central Command reported that nearly 500 had been killed since 1 May 2003, the day marking the official end of hostilities. The U.S. Treasury was doling out $1 billion a week just on military costs. In September 2003, President Bush requested and obtained from Congress an additional $87 billion for Iraq and Afghanistan. In an already ailing U.S. economy, the financial burden of the war ballooned the federal deficit. And that was the situation before the April 2004 uprising.

This chapter analyzes post-conflict reconstruction in Iraq, focusing primarily on the first six months. It examines what major lessons learned since the end of the Cold War were ignored and which were applied. The initial period after an intervention is crucial in determining the future course of a state emerging from violent conflict. Mistakes made during this time have lasting effects, and the intervening power can often spend years undoing the damage done. The intervening power must also get things right during this initial period because its own domestic support will still be high, and if a genocidal dictator is removed, the victim population will be initially supportive as well. At home, Americans stand tall at home as they watch their troops land in overwhelming numbers, win battles, feed the starving, and stop the killing. After a few months people become less willing to pay the enormous costs necessary to establish a stable democracy, particularly if American troops are being killed, while the Abu Ghraib prison scandal in May 2004 certainly did not make the war more popular in America. And, as unfolding events in Iraq have so dramatically demonstrated, if the initial policies adopted are unsuccessful or poorly conceived, the entire situation may deteriorate suddenly, with disastrous consequences for the occupied and the intervening power.

What lessons from the past fifteen years of interventions and state-building have been generally recognized as central for enhancing post-conflict reconstruction during this critical initial period? The cases referred to here are those in which the U.S. government played a major role in the military intervention, as well as in the post-conflict period. The cases of Panama, Somalia, Haiti, Bosnia, East Timor,[2] and Kosovo are instructive for understanding what has—and has not—happened in Iraq. From these experiences, numerous academic and policy studies have chronicled the lessons learned (see, for example, Caplan 2002; Center for Strategic and International Studies and the Association of the U.S. Army 2003; Dahrendorf 2003; Brahimi Report 2000; von Hippel 2000). Just before the war in Iraq began, a number of studies by prominent policy-makers and scholars pointed to these lessons and how they should be applied to Iraq (see, for example, Barton and Crocker 2003; Carnegie Endowment for International Peace and Foreign Policy 2003; Dobbins et al. 2003; Durch 2003; Pickering, Schlesinger, and Schwartz 2003).

This chapter emphasizes security-related matters because of the focus on the first six months, when security concerns are paramount, although other political and economic measures are necessary to kick-start successful reconstruction. A review of previous cases points to six lessons that have been unlearned, and only two that have been realized in this initial phase in Iraq. This critical review does not necessarily signify that Iraq will not develop into a stable democracy. Nor does it imply that the intervention would have avoided all serious obstacles from the beginning had planning and initial responses been better. What it does argue is that by ignoring previous lessons, the U.S.-led Coalition severely constrained progress and lost critical support, especially from the Arab population of Iraq. The negative impact because of the lives lost—of international civil servants and coalition soldiers as well as

Iraqi civilians—and the financial resources wasted or misspent could poten-tially have been minimized had planning and execution been more strategic and inclusive.

Lessons Unlearned

Hobbes's Lesson: Power Vacuums Lead to Looting and Criminality

Before implementing democratic reforms, security and the rule of law must be established, a point unanimously agreed by policy studies. Some experts even recommended the imposition of martial law in the crucial first few weeks of the occupation to prevent a dangerous power vacuum. (Indeed, some Iraqis themselves proposed this option, and army units were available, but they were not used.) Other experts suggested the deployment of international police officers alongside the military in the immediate post-combat phase to ensure that a civilian policing component was built-in from the start.[3] In the short term, the establishment of security is central to prevent widespread looting and criminal elements from establishing a foothold. Lessons learned in Pan-ama and Kosovo should have been instructive.

In Panama, the massive looting and collapse of civilian agencies through-out the country, especially in Panama City, came as a complete surprise to U.S. troops (Fishel 1992, 13, 26). The looting lasted throughout the first week, and government offices as well as shops were ransacked. Those who knew they would have no job to go back to because of their close affiliation with the Noriega regime carried away much of the booty. The looting gave the impres-sion that U.S. troops were not managing the situation they had created by the intervention. The estimate for overall damage reached $1 billion, a substantial sum in a country with fewer than three million inhabitants. Following the intervention in Panama, contingency planning for such pillaging was incorpo-rated into military strategy. In subsequent operations, looting was not as severe a problem. The massive looting that occurred in Iraq should thus have been anticipated. And, as soldiers on the ground noted, there were too few troops in theatre to stop the looting (see Judah 2003, 42). It also appears that the planners made the mistaken assumption that Iraqi police would remain in their posts and prevent such disorder from occurring.

Given the serious attention the U.S. military gave to this lesson learned after Panama, it is not clear why this was not a critical component in the plan-ning for Iraq. Whatever plans that might have been drawn up to deal with this contingency were not considered crucial by some in the Pentagon and therefore not utilized. As one senior U.S. soldier told me, "in Iraq, we didn't follow our own doctrine." Wesley Clark argued that "the military plan took unnecessary risks, because it skimped on the forces made available to the commanders" (Clark 2003). This policy, the Rumsfeld doctrine, combined with Turkey's refusal to allow U.S. troops to enter Iraq from Turkey, prevented an initial full deployment and ensured there were not enough troops inside Iraq to stop the looting. Clark added: "The ensuing disorder vitiated some of the boost in U.S. credibility that was won on the battlefield, and it opened the way for deeper and more organized resistance during the following weeks."

In Kosovo, the initial deployment of international police and other international security representatives was too slow, mostly for bureaucratic reasons and not because the Security Council did not approve of the intervention. A dangerous power vacuum was created, and, as with all power vacuums, was filled by the worst elements on the scene. The UN mission in Kosovo (UNMIK) was forced to spend far too much time during its first year trying to remove criminal gangs from political power in most of the municipalities as well as from businesses usurped when Serbs left the province in large numbers. The KFOR forces were reluctant to assume policing duties, though on all too many occasions they did. Kosovo today still suffers from criminality: the few lucrative businesses, such as large hotels, remain in the hands of gangs; illegal construction mars most cities; and smuggling and illegal trafficking of goods and people continue to blight most parts of the Balkans (see, for example, Yannis 2001, 37–38). In Iraq, the speed with which some of the national treasures were looted, particularly in Baghdad (but not in Kurdistan or the southern Shi'a areas), and likely transported out of the country suggests well-organized criminal gangs attuned to the political vacuum that would be caused by the entry of U.S. troops. Moreover, there are legitimate fears that if Iraq had any weapons of mass destruction, some of these materials might have been looted.

Juvenal's Lesson: *Sed quis custodet ipsos custodies?* Or, Who Guards the Guardians?

In a comprehensive security-sector reform package in any post-conflict situation which includes police, military, judicial, and penal reforms as well as civilian oversight of the military, predictable problems with the local military and police will certainly arise. In previous operations, the new governments or interim administrations have chosen to abolish the armed forces entirely and maintain only the police, as in Costa Rica, Haiti, or Panama. An alternative strategy has been to retrain the military for civil emergencies and related domestic concerns. The creation of a new police force has normally been necessary in order to ensure public safety and gain the confidence of the local population. The goal has been to achieve a comprehensive change in mindset of the local police and of the public, because previously the police in these countries often terrified civilians through extortion and torture, instead of providing protection. In Panama, the U.S. military considered it of utmost importance to have a working Panamanian presence on the streets so that American troops would not be seen as an occupying force.

In most of these previous cases, newly trained forces have inevitably included some members of the old force, given the lack of experienced personnel and the belief that it would take longer to train an entire corps of new officers than to retrain some of the old. Such a policy has not been without controversy, although the method initially applied in Haiti—phasing out the old force in increments, while recruiting and training new troops—appeared to garner more popular support. The model used in Bosnia displayed the advances in promoting accountability by international police trainers (Human Rights Watch 1998, United Nations 1999). In Kosovo, UNMIK initiated a similarly transparent multi-ethnic program that included comprehensive background checks.[4]

In Iraq, police training has been problematic. There was no planning, so the process has proceeded too slowly to keep up with the exigencies on the ground. Recruiting new officers has been difficult, given the opposition to what some perceive as collaboration with the occupation and the occurrence of terrorist reprisals against those applying to serve. Further, it is not clear whether the international police, once they are deployed to mentor the newly trained Iraqi force, will put up with the dangerous security situation on the street for very long.

On the military side, too, things have not been smooth. Many have argued that it may not have made sense to have disbanded the entire military, as CPA Administrator Bremer did in late May 2003, if only to keep thousands of trained, armed, and potentially disgruntled men busy. In Kosovo, one of the motivations for maintaining the Kosovo Protection Corps, created from the former guerrilla group, the Kosovo Liberation Army, was to keep these men under watch to prevent them from causing trouble. In Iraq, a large number of men had been employed in some form of security service, and while perhaps the top layers of the military and police, along with some of the paramilitary units, may have been tainted, many Arab Iraqis regarded the vast majority as professionals rather than hard-line Ba'thists.[5]

Democracy's Lesson: The Military Is Not Supposed to Govern

In the past half-century, one of the most important shifts in these operations concerns the role of the U.S. military in political reconstruction. A conspicuous change has been the gradual reduction of U.S. military control over state-building activities, with the Allied occupations of Germany and Japan representing the peak moment of military involvement in governance. Indeed, both of these operations were directed entirely by the military, with civilian agencies playing a subordinate role.

Panama was the last operation before Iraq in which the military overtly directed political reconstruction, although the American military had extensive experience and relations with Panamanians. Somalia was the last in which the military made important behind-the-scenes decisions, preparing state-building resolutions for the UN Security Council. By the time of the Haiti, Bosnia, Kosovo, and East Timor operations, the military's role was primarily confined to maintaining security and supporting democratization.

A cardinal rule of democracy is ensuring that the military is subject to civilian control. It is extremely important, for symbolic reasons, not to allow these roles to be reversed, particularly by the occupying power, and particularly when the entire interventionist exercise is intended to build a democratic and accountable state. In Iraq, the U.S. Department of Defense (DOD) did not transfer power to the State Department after the transition to the post-combat phase (although whether such a transfer would have prevented the multiple uprisings is impossible to predict). And even though Ambassador Bremer is a former State Department employee, he still reports to the DOD, which remains the lead department for political reconstruction in Iraq.

The Management Lesson: Joint Civilian and Military Planning Is a Good Thing

Improvements in relations between civilian and military agencies have been another striking development since Panama, where joint planning was ruled out by the need to maintain secrecy about the timing—and, indeed, the occurrence—of the invasion. This lack of cooperation delayed the democratization process. In Somalia, there was a conspicuous lack of cooperation on all sides, and regular turf wars took place between UN Headquarters in New York and UN operations in Mogadishu, between civilian and military operators in Mogadishu, and even between the U.S. and other militaries. While preparing for Somalia, in fact, there was no joint planning between the US military and the heads of relief organizations, even though the military was originally deployed to provide protection for those organizations. In such a climate, it was hardly surprising that it became extremely difficult to carry out the mandate.

By the time of the Haiti, Bosnia, Kosovo, and East Timor operations, both military and civilian bodies were closely involved in the planning and implementation of political reconstruction. Indeed, the 1994 Haiti operation experienced the fewest difficulties in implementation because military, humanitarian, and development agencies were melded in a tight partnership at the insistence of the Special Representative of the UN Secretary-General (SRSG), Lakhdar Brahimi, who was appointed by the UN Secretary General in 2004 as UN envoy for Iraq. In Haiti, the development agenda was integral from the beginning, civilian and military actors trained together before deployment, and a civilian directed the entire operation. Within the U.S. government, all civilian and military agencies that would be involved met regularly to plan the mission. This coordination could not guarantee that Haiti would develop a stable democracy; and indeed the major intervening power lost interest after a few years. But the point stands: a well-coordinated initial phase provides the best possible environment for democratic reforms to take root.

In Iraq, although a number of American and British agencies and think-tanks held planning exercises, the Pentagon did not participate to a significant degree, and Pentagon officials did not take any of the major recommendations on board. In fact, while the military tends to develop and fine-tune military plans for invasions of this kind over years, planning for the post-combat phase only occurred during the final few months before the war, just eight weeks before the invasion (Rieff 2003). Moreover, General Garner's Office of Humanitarian and Reconstruction Assistance in the Pentagon was poorly funded and under-staffed. Rieff noted, "Garner and his planners had to start more or less from scratch. . . . ORHA lacked critical personnel once it arrived in Baghdad" (Rieff 2003). General Wesley Clark added, "When planning finally began that autumn, it was based on the assumption that a U.S. invasion would be welcomed as a liberation by most Iraqis" (Clark 2003, 000). This was not the case apart from Kurdistan, where *peshmerga* actively fought with the U.S. and UK forces and American troops remain welcome. In Arab Iraq, the situation has been much different. In any case, as Louis Henkin remarked after Panama, "People have welcomed conquering armies since the beginning of time, especially when the conquering army is still there" (Henkin 1990, 251–52).

The NGO Lesson: Soldiers and Civilians Must Work Together

Beyond matters related to planning, the working relationship between civilian agencies and the military has deteriorated since Somalia and Bosnia in the early 1990s, when UN peacekeeping troops provided security for delivery of assistance. UN agencies in general were happy with the role the military played in Bosnia in particular, as UNPROFOR troops worked under the direction of the UN and did not act independently. In Kosovo, the military had to establish refugee camps because civilian agencies did not have the capacity. Here the UN considered that the military no longer worked under UN guidance but proceeded at its own discretion. Civilian agencies also worried about appearing too closely linked to belligerents.

In Afghanistan and Iraq, the military and civilian agencies have departed even further from the ideal mutually supportive roles. The coalition forces assumed a direct humanitarian role, delivering aid and supporting civic restoration projects, while also acting as belligerents. A few humanitarian organizations were involved in planning before the war in Iraq. Others prepared contingency plans for an eventual deployment. Yet, as the author established in interviews in early 2003 with numerous representatives of humanitarian agencies in Geneva, Brussels, Washington, D.C., and New York, the involvement of NGOs and UN agencies was deeply controversial within these groups themselves because many of these organizations' leaderships had opposed the war beforehand and did not want to become linked, at least in Sunni Arab Iraqis' eyes, with the aggressors. Because two of the major humanitarian donors in Iraq are belligerents, the issue became even more complicated for some agencies in terms of fund-raising for their operations.

Questions of neutrality and impartiality are of great concern to humanitarian and development agencies, and many organizations published guidelines for how they would coexist with the military in Iraq as well as in future operations (OCHA 2003). A further difficulty that arose in Iraq followed from the occupying powers' obligation under the Geneva Convention to ensure the security and well-being of civilians. Humanitarian agencies were reluctant to support the military in this role, preferring to do the work themselves. In the 1990s, the military and civilian agencies went through a long and difficult but necessary process of adjustment to adapt to one another's very different cultures and developed a modus vivendi and a modus operandi. Today, the gap between civilian and military agencies has reemerged.

The Lesson of Multilateralism: Fortune Punishes the Loner

The world's response to the decision of President Bush and Prime Minister Blair to lead a "coalition of the willing" and invade Iraq in the absence of a

UN Security Council resolution authorizing intervention was strikingly similar to what happened after the unilateral U.S. invasion of Panama. At the UN and the Organization of American States (OAS), the "U.S. aggression" in Panama was denounced on grounds justified at the time under international law. The UN General Assembly voted 75 to 20 on 29 December 1989 to condemn the invasion and demanded a U.S. withdrawal, while at the OAS, the count was 20 to 1 (the lone vote came from the U.S.) against the intervention. It must be pointed out, however, that while OAS members publicly opposed America's violation of Panamanian sovereignty, many privately approved of the invasion because they were glad to be rid of Noriega (von Hippel 2000, 46–47).

The U.S. administration appealed to the self-defense provisions in Article 51 of the UN Charter and Article 21 of the OAS Charter, arguing that all peaceful means had been tried to come to terms with the government of Panama. Thomas Pickering, U.S. ambassador to the UN at the time, argued that "the survival of democratic nations is at stake" (Scheffer 1991, 122). The executive was plainly stretching and reaching: beyond the patent absurdity of the self-defense rationale, which completely distorted the principles of necessity, proportionality, and immediacy that regulate its application, the still-intact Reagan Doctrine did not endorse military intervention in situations where the Soviet Union was not supplying arms. Furthermore, the U.S. Senate had earlier asserted that intervention in Panama would only be permissible in the event of a breach in the canal's neutrality, not as a result of domestic political events (Scheffer 1991, 113). Subsequent interventions during the Clinton presidency were multinational, international, and multilateral, and all but Kosovo were approved by the UN Security Council. Despite the obvious problems inherent in making decisions by committee, U.S. policy-makers considered the legitimacy conferred by international support and participation paramount.

The damage done to the U.S. government by essentially going it alone in Iraq (with the support of a handful of countries) will have reverberations far beyond the Americans' inability to obtain significant support from a larger coalition in the post-combat phase. Potential contributors of soldiers, civilian personnel, and financing have been wary of entering a situation that would not give them, or, at least the UN, commensurate decision-making authority. Leaving humanitarian concerns aside, they wondered why they should be responsible for cleaning up a mess caused by the U.S. government against their advice. They also wondered why they should entrust their soldiers to a coalition that was not winning hearts and minds, in an environment that was manifestly insecure. Even the unanimous passage of Security Council Resolution 1511 (October 2003) has not secured the troop and financial contributions hoped for by the United States. Preemptive unilateral interventions lack legitimacy if they are not perceived to be in response to an evident, imminent threat; they set a dangerous precedent in an already unstable international order; are extremely costly, and in this case, arguably undermine rather than assist the war against terror.

The manifestly American and British occupation, rather than UN supervision, of Iraq has served to humiliate even moderate Muslims in the wider world, enrage Islamic extremists, open the floodgates for *mujahidin* fighters, and contribute to anti-Americanism in many parts of the world (von Hippel 2003). While there was no established connection between Saddam Hussein and al-Qaida before the war, as all too many analysts predicted, the invasion and occupation of Iraq created one (Benjamin 2002). In general it has been extremely difficult distinguishing between Arab Iraqi nationalists opposed to foreign military occupation, hard-line Ba'athists resisting the planned transition to democracy, Sunni Arabs who resent losing the power they have wielded over other groups, members of al-Qaida who see this as an opportunity to attack America, and incoming *mujahadin* freelancers not directly associated with al-Qaida who nevertheless have heeded Osama bin Laden's call to fight the "infidel." No matter how rich and technically proficient the U.S. government is, a unilateralist foreign policy in a globalized world can only be unpopular, impractical, and counterproductive.

Lack of planning and coordination between civilian and military actors impairs an interventionist operation once it is underway. And a poor initial phase undermines the local support required to tolerate a foreign occupation, which is considered humiliating even in the best of circumstances. The late Sergio de Mello rightly pointed out just before he was assassinated: "This must be one of the most humiliating periods in history [for Arab Iraqis]. Who would like to see their country occupied? I would not like to see foreign tanks in Copacabana'" (*Economist*, 23–29 August, 73). Of course, those groups who did not see Saddam's Iraq as "their country," just as he did not see Kurds as "his own people," welcomed the removal of the regime. If the UN had been in charge of political reconstruction and the military had been a multinational force under the stewardship of NATO, the occupation might have been viewed as more legitimate. "Provisional authority" would have come to mean just that for Iraqis and others around the world who mistrust the motivation of the U.S. government.

Many other peace-support operations have shown that once the occupying power is no longer seen to be in control and providing security, the population will set up independent militias and attack that foreign power. This lesson was readily available to American policy-makers before the intervention in Iraq. The more anarchic the situation becomes, the more the population will tolerate another authoritarian ruler, if only for the sake of security, or the situation could lead to full-scale civil war. Neither are desired outcomes.

In Iraq, American officials have frequently remarked that they "underestimated" the challenges they were to face in the "post-combat" period and did not "anticipate" the sustained attacks against them. As is evident from the experiences in the 1990s, had they been willing to listen to and learn from their predecessors and even colleagues in the State Department, that should not have been the case. However, two crucial lessons may have been absorbed.

Lessons Learned

Overcoming the Body Bag Problem

The interventions in the 1990s taught extremists that the U.S. military and government were overly preoccupied with the protection of their own forces and had adopted what Thomas Weiss has called "a zero-casualty foreign policy" (Weiss 1996 91). Bin Ladin learned about Americans' aversion to body bags from Somalia. Not only did this disposition send the wrong message to terrorists, but it prevented American troops from providing the necessary leadership in peace-support missions and impeded relations with allies. Force protection policies have interfered with the realization of the mission in all the interventionist operations except Panama. Even there, ironically, one of the justifications for the invasion was the "threat to American lives," yet only one American citizen had been killed before the invasion, while 23 U.S. troops were killed during Operation Just Cause. By the time of the Somalia expedition, U.S. soldiers were no longer allowed to die, at least not on a humanitarian mission.

Fear of body bags has been mainly an American preoccupation, although in Bosnia, anxiety about Serb reprisals against British, Dutch, and French peacekeepers put a stop to NATO bombing sorties for some time, and this fear impeded the active apprehension of indicted war criminals, particularly Karadzic and Mladic, by NATO troops. Indeed, the British, French, and Dutch all lost more soldiers than the Americans did in Bosnia, while the Pakistanis suffered grave losses in Somalia without withdrawing. The safety of U.S. soldiers, like that of Iraqi civilians, would be enhanced by clearer and more robust rules of engagement. Moreover, if strong signals are consistently sent out to errant leaders that the mistreatment of foreign soldiers (and humanitarian workers) will be met with serious reprisals, both will operate in a more secure environment.

This policy of weighing military operations against the audit of the body count has changed since 11 September. The U.S. public has tolerated the deaths of American and Coalition troops in Afghanistan and Iraq in significant numbers, although many times fewer of them have died than their intended targets or civilians. The military now operates in a manner more appropriate to its training and mission. How patient the American public will be as deaths continue to mount from Arab Iraqi and some foreign resistance is another question. Certainly the lengthy deployment, the stressful demands on overburdened troops, and the insecure environment in Iraq have caused numerous complaints by U.S. soldiers.

Staying the Course

Past experiences, especially the hasty exits from Afghanistan and Somalia in the late 1980s and early 1990s, should have taught American policy-makers the dangers of short-term interventions. The lesson of Taliban-dominated Afghanistan is that the international community, and the United States in particular, ignores unpleasant parts of the world at its peril. Foreign policy myopia had its roots in a false lesson from Vietnam. In the early and mid-1990s, American policy-makers frequently referred to the fear of "mission creep," which negatively affected planning for all interventions. But once the Dayton peace process began to be realized on the ground in Bosnia, the policy-making vernacular evolved from "exit strategies" to "end states." In April 1999, Dave Scanlon, Stabilization Force (SFOR) spokesperson, told me that "SFOR is now working toward an 'end state,' not an 'end date.' Deadlines no longer apply to the mission here. . . . What is left is to ensure a stable and secure environment so that . . . a lasting peace [can be] established." A public commitment to a lengthy intervention was henceforth considered critical to allow confidence-building measures sufficient time to work. Coupled with this knowledge was the improved understanding by policy-makers in the U.S. government and the UN that support for transitional elections in any country, such as in Haiti during 1990, needs to be combined with meaningful, post-election programs that can cope with "inexperienced, weak, democratically elected governments coexisting with powerful anti-democratic structures of power" (Carothers 1995, 118). The common assumption among many policy-makers in the United States had been that the bulk of the foreign presence could leave once elections were held.

The oft-repeated public commitment by the U.S. administration to a democratic future for Iraq, which by definition requires a prolongation of the international presence, foreshadows a continuation of this trend, although there may be "electoralist" voices raised in favor of a fast exit. In April 2004, Rumsfeld noted, "The United States will stay the course, we will stay until the task is complete. As President Bush has said, 'We did not charge hundreds of miles into the heart of Iraq and pay a bitter cost of casualties to liberate 25 million people, only to retreat before a band of thugs and assassins'" (RFE/RL Iraq Report 2004). Earlier, on 27 August 2003, Bush cited the postwar Allied occupations of Germany and Japan, noting how long it had taken to turn those countries into stable democracies. Indeed, even after the Allies left, the U.S. government continued to support German political and economic reforms for years until Germany became a stable, democratic state. The American success in democratizing Germany has been described as follows: "Its accomplishment requires clarity of goals, complete cooperation among the occupying powers, and withal persistence in the face of inner doubts, resistance to external criticism, and acceptance of the glacial pace inherent to the process" (Merritt 1995, xiii). It remains to be seen whether political pressures and mounting American casualties will cause Bush to respond with the necessary persistence, despite the domestic political situation and international criticism. Ensuring the implementation of the constitutional arrangements overseen by the CPA will require especial vigor (along the line followed by the U.S. and the UN in the Balkans).

Conclusion

Digesting the fact that interventionists require willingness to sustain significant losses and commitment has been an important facet of the Bush administration. But these two lessons learned are outnumbered by the six they failed to learn. Numerous experts have argued that they had warned the U.S. government beforehand about what would happen if it was not prepared. Pundits who claim "I told you so" should display more humility, since it could be argued that it only goes to show the irrelevance of the pundit. Yet the studies cited here were well publicized among senior policy-makers and researchers from both sides of the party political divide and both sides of the Atlantic, and even within the Bush administration itself in the case of the State Department. The powers that be in the Bush administration simply refused to listen. After Panama, Richard Shultz explained, "At the most general level, the first [lesson] is the need to recognize post-conflict situations as important and complex missions for the Department of Defense. This was clearly not discerned in Panama. The U.S. did not have, at the time of Operation Just Cause, a policy for the period following the use of force" (Shultz 1993, 67). In too many ways, little has changed.

Notes

Epigraph: David Hume, "The Rise of Arts and Sciences," *Essays*, 1: 128, as cited by Alexander Hamilton, 1788, in Hamilton et al., *The Federalist Papers*, ed. Isaac Kramnick (New York: Penguin, 1987), 486.

1. The term "nation-building" is a misnomer that Americans often use to signify what is correctly known as "state-building," because they tend to confuse the term "state" with the 50 states that comprise the United States. "Nation-building" inaccurately depicts what the U.S. government is generally attempting to do in these types of organized interventions, because it rarely strives to create a nation—people who share the same collective identity. For example, when the U.S. government and the UN attempted to rebuild Somalia, they did not try to reunite all Somalis living in Djibouti, Kenya, and Ethiopia with Somalis in the former Somali Republic, which would have indeed created a Somali nation; rather, they focused on rebuilding the former Somali Republic.

2. The United States did not play such an overt role in East Timor, but it did play a role behind the scenes. East Timor is included as it is another example of an interim administration and a serious state-building effort led by the United Nations.

3. Several participants proposed this strategy at a conference on Public Security and the Rule of Law from a European Perspective, held in London by the Centre for Defence Studies, King's College London, and sponsored by the United Kingdom Department for International Development, on 6 March 2001.

4. Based on the author's own experience working for the UN mission throughout 2000.

5. This impression is based on discussions held at King's College London's Centre for Defence Studies before the war with a number of Iraqi exiles.

References

Benjamin, Daniel. 2002. "Combating Terrorism." Testimony of Daniel Benjamin, Senior Fellow, Center for Strategic and International Studies, Subcommittee on National Security, Veterans Affairs and International Relations, House Committee on Government Reform. Washington, D.C., House of Representatives, 16 April.

Barton, Federick D. and Bathsheena N. Crocker. 2003. "Post-War Iraq: Are We Ready?" Center for Strategic and International Studies, Washington D.C., 25 March.

Brahimi Report. 2000. *Comprehensive Review of the Whole Question of Peacekeeping Operations in All Their Aspects*. Report of the Panel on United Nations Peace Operations, Lakhdar Brahimi, chair. New York: United Nations, 21 August.

Caplan, Richard. 2002. *A New Trusteeship? The International Administration of War-Torn Territories*. Adelphi Paper 341. Oxford: Oxford University Press.

Carnegie Endowment for International Peace and Foreign Policy. 2003. *From Victory to Success: Afterwar Policy in Iraq*. New York: Carnegie, 24 July.

Carothers, Thomas. 1995. "Lessons for Policymakers." In *Haitian Frustrations: Dilemmas for U.S. Policy: A Report for the CSIS Americas Program*, ed. Georges A. Fauriol. Washington, D.C.: Center for Strategic and International Studies.

Center for Strategic and International Studies and the Association of the U.S. Army. 2003. Play to Win: The Commission on Post-Conflict Reconstruction. Washington, D.C., January.

Clark, General Wesley K. 2003. "Iraq: What Went Wrong." *New York Review of Books*, 23 October, 50–56.

Dahrendorf, Nici, ed. 2003. *A Review of Peace Operations: A Case for Change. Sierra Leone, Kosovo, East Timor, Afghanistan*. London: King's College.

Dobbins, James et al. 2003. *America's Role in Nation-Building: From Germany to Iraq*. Santa Monica, Calif.: Rand.

Durch, William J. 2003. "The UN System and Post-Conflict Iraq." Henry L. Stimson Center, 18 April.

Fishel, John T. 1992. *The Fog of Peace: Planning and Executing the Restoration of Panama*. Carlisle, Pa.: Strategic Studies Institute, U.S. Army War College, 15 April.

Henkin, Louis. 1990. *American Society of International Law: Proceedings of the 84th Annual Meeting, Washington, D.C.* Washington, D.C.: the Society.

Human Rights Watch. 1998. *Bosnia-Herzegovina Beyond Restraint: Politics and the Policing Agenda of the UN International Police Task Force*. New York: Human Rights Watch.

Judah, Tim. 2003. "The Fall of Baghdad." *New York Review of Books*, 15 May, 50–58.

Merritt, Richard L. 1995. *Democracy Imposed: U.S. Occupation Policy and the German Public, 1945–1949*. New Haven, Conn.: Yale University Press.

Office for the Coordination for Humanitarian Affairs (OCHA). 2003. *Guidelines on the Use of Military and Civil Defense Assets to Support United Nations Humanitarian Activities in Complex Emergencies*. New York, United Nations. March.

Pickering, Thomas R, James R. Schlesinger, and Eric P. Schwartz. 2003. *Iraq: The Day After, Report of an Independent Task Force Sponsored by the Council on Foreign Relations*. New York, Council on Foreign Relations.

Rice, Condoleeza. 2000. "Campaign 2000: Promoting the National Interest." *Foreign Affairs* (January/February). Website edition.

Rieff, David. 2003. "Blueprint for a Mess." *New York Times Magazine*, 2 November.

RFE/RL Iraq Report. 2004. Vol.7, 13, www.rferl.org/reports, 8 April.

Scheffer, David J. 1991. "Use of Force After the Cold War: Panama, Iraq, and the New World Order." In *Right vs. Might: International Law and the Use of Force*, ed. Louis Henkin. New York: Council on Foreign Relations.

Shultz, Richard H., Jr. 1993. *In the Aftermath of War: U.S. Support for Reconstruction and Nation-Building in Panama Following Just Cause*. Maxwell Air Force Base, Ala.: Air University Press.

United Nations. 1999. Report of the Secretary General on the Interim Administration Mission in Kosovo S/1999/987. New York, United Nations. 16 September.

Von Hippel, Karin. 2000. *Democracy by Force: U.S. Military Intervention in the Post-Cold World*. Cambridge: Cambridge University Press.

————. 2003. *American Occupational Hazards.* Available from <www.opendemocracy.net>, accessed 10 April.

Weiss, Thomas G. 1996. "Collective Spinelessness: UN Actions in the Former Yugoslavia." In *The World and Yugoslavia's Wars*, ed. Richard H. Ullman. New York: Council on Foreign Relations.

Yannis, Alexandros. 2001. "Kosovo under International Administration." *Survival* 43 (2) (Summer): 31–48.

Chapter 12
Kurdistan in a Federal Iraq

Peter W. Galbraith

The Birth of the Kurdistan Regional Government

The Kurdistan region of Iraq has functioned as a de facto independent state since 1991. Making the most of the first durable Kurdish state in modern history, the Kurds of northern Iraq have no intention of giving up the freedom and self-government they have enjoyed for over a decade. When the process of making a permanent constitution for Iraq begins, Kurdistan will be able to shape its terms.

Ironically, it was an American decision aimed at preventing any Kurdish state that gave the Kurds the opportunity they now enjoy. On 15 February 1991, President George H. W. Bush, then in the midst of the air campaign phase of the first Gulf War, called on the Iraqi military and people to overthrow Saddam Hussein. Bush delivered this message twice, first at the Raytheon plant in Andover, Massachusetts, where Patriot missiles were being made, and then in a second statement at the White House. When, just three weeks later, the Shi'a and Kurds of Iraq tried to do exactly what he had asked, the U.S. government was caught by surprise. Faced with an uprising that had reached the southern approaches to Baghdad and put Kurdish rebels in control throughout Kurdistan, the Bush administration confronted a policy dilemma. Bush's National Security Council feared that, if the Shi'a succeeded in throwing off the Ba'thist regime in the south, they would establish a pro-Iranian theocracy. If the Kurds succeeded in the north, the Americans feared, Iraq might break up. In the end, Bush decided to ignore the ever more desperate pleas of Shi'a and Kurdish rebels as Saddam Hussein's army regrouped and his tanks and helicopters moved, first south and then north, to suppress the rebellion.

The Shi'a paid a horrendous price for America's betrayal. Saddam's Republican Guards and security services massacred upward of 300,000 Shi'a in the six months following the uprising's collapse. Having experienced Saddam's vengeance in the late 1970s and 1980s, the Kurds were not going to wait around to see what he would do. As Iraqi forces advanced into Kurdistan over the weekend of 30–31 March 1991, cities and towns emptied; hundreds of thousands of people (myself among them) drove or walked to the Turkish and Iranian borders. Turkey's president, Turgut Ozal, refused to let the Kurds into Turkey, but he allowed the media access to the refugees as they huddled in freezing conditions on steep mountain slopes. Televised pictures of people dying in a sea of human agony outraged international public opinion, especially in Western Europe and the United States. After two weeks of equivocation, the Bush administration was forced to reintervene in Iraq, and a safe haven was declared.

The Iraqi army and police were ordered out of a triangular area in Dohuk governorate demarcated by Zakho, Dohuk, and Amadiya. This area promptly came under the political control of the Iraqi Kurdistan Front, and shortly thereafter hooked up with the swath of Kurdish territory in the east that Saddam had been unable to capture in his counteroffensive. In September 1991, Saddam decided to switch tactics. He tried to starve the Kurds into submission. He withdrew his administration, along with the Iraqi military, from Erbil and Sulaimania. The unintended effect was to give the Kurds control over the territory, population, and infrastructure for a state.

In May 1992, Kurdistan's authorities held the only genuinely democratic elections in the history of Iraq. Residents of the new enclave queued for up to eight hours to elect the Kurdistan National Assembly and a president. Unfortunately, these elections ended in a near dead-heat between the Kurdistan Democratic Party (KDP), led by Masoud Barzani, and the Patriotic Union of Kurdistan (PUK), led by Jalal Talabani. The two main parties decided not to have a presidential run-off election between Barzani and Talabani, but to share power in a Council of Ministers appointed by a parliament with 51 KDP members, 49 PUK members, and 5 members elected on the Christian minority lists. In the mid-1990s, these power-sharing arrangements broke down, in part over disputes about the sharing of revenue from smuggling. A nasty intra-Kurdish civil war ensued, which was ended in September 1998 thanks to American mediation.

Since then, the Kurdistan region has been divided into two administrations, one in Erbil and one in Sulaimania, with both claiming to be the Kurdistan Regional Government. In spite of all these difficulties, the two Kurdistan administrations started to function like the governments of a sovereign state. At the turn of the twenty-first century, both had dynamic young prime ministers, Nechirvan Barzani and Barham Salih, who focused on social services and institution-building. They were aided by United Nations Resolution 986, which earmarked 13 percent of Iraq's oil revenues for projects in the Kurdistan

Region. With the revenue from the Oil-for-Food Programme, Kurdistan began to thrive, despite its unrecognized status and the constant threat of the Iraqi Army across the "green line" that divided Kurdistan from the rest of Iraq.

Kurdistan and Federalism

In 1992, the then-unified Kurdistan Regional Government hosted the Iraqi opposition at a congress in Salahaddin. For the first time in the history of modern Iraq, the Kurds had an advantage over their Arab counterparts, controlling as they did territory, military forces, and financial resources. Talabani and Barzani made good use of their relative power vis-à-vis both secular Arabs and the Iranian-based Shi'a parties in the deliberations over the future of Iraq. The Salahaddin Congress created an umbrella organization, the Iraqi National Congress (INC), under the leadership of a secular Shi'a businessman, Ahmad Chalabi. As the quid pro quo for supporting this Arab-led project, Barzani and Talabani secured the INC's explicit endorsement of federalism as the governing system of a future Iraq. Chalabi himself went further, saying that he supported Kurdish self-determination, including Kurdistan's right to secede from Iraq. Exactly what federalism meant in the Iraq context was, however, never spelled out. Understandably, the Arab opposition focused mostly on removing Saddam Hussein, while the Kurds became preoccupied with developing internal structures protecting Kurdistan, and the escalating conflict between the KDP and the PUK.

September 11, 2001, changed the political calculus for Kurdistan's two major political parties. Having developed close ties with the neoconservatives dominant in the new Bush administration, they could see that the U.S. would go to war against Iraq. This led to renewed thinking about Kurdistan's role in a post-Saddam Iraq. The KDP reissued its 1992 draft constitution for the Kurdistan Region, as well as its proposed constitution for a federal Iraq, and secured the endorsement of the PUK. Jalal Talabani and Barham Salih, the PUK prime minister, traveled extensively abroad to promote the concept of federalism. In December 2002, as the Bush administration made the final preparations for the war, the Iraqi opposition met in London and reaffirmed the commitment to federalism. Once again, however, no details were decided.

In March 2003, President Bush gave federalism a large, if perhaps unintended, boost when he told a press conference that he favored an Iraq that was "a federation of Shi'a, Sunnis, and Kurds."[1] The statement caught senior officials in both the State Department and the Department of Defense off guard, as they had previously studiously avoided any endorsement of federalism out of deference to Turkish sensibilities.

In February 2003, the Turkish Parliament turned down an agreement the government had negotiated with the Bush Administration to allow the U.S. 4th Infantry Division to transit Turkey in exchange for U.S.$ 21 billion in aid and permission for the Turkish Army to send troops into northern Iraq. Subsequent Turkish equivocation further alienated a Bush administration already fuming at "disloyal" allies, such as France and Germany. While Turkey equivocated, the 4th Infantry Division sailed in circles in the eastern Mediterranean before being sent through the Red Sea to Kuwait, arriving too late to participate in the invasion. These proved to be extraordinarily fortuitous developments for Iraqi Kurdistan. The Pentagon improvised a new plan for a northern front, relying principally on the approximately 100,000-strong *peshmerga* and a few U.S. Special Forces. The Kurds had become America's most numerous ally in Operation Iraqi Freedom. Never had Kurdistan's stock been so high internationally, or within Iraq.

Negotiating the Interim Constitution

Kurdistan's major two parties and the Kurdistan National Assembly entered the process of negotiating the reconstruction of the Iraqi state with unprecedented advantages. At the end of the war, they had Iraq's only functioning government and its only remaining military force. As U.S. forces looked the other way, the *peshmerga* seized the artillery and other heavy weapons of the northern Iraqi armies. Their historic foes were no longer so threatening: Iraq was defeated, Syria and Iran were intimidated, and Turkey was on Bush's list of "unreliable" allies. Kurdistan's leaders had a clear idea of what they wanted out of the making of the Transitional Administrative Law, the first step in the new constitutional process. They wanted to retain the self-government they now enjoy, to enlarge Kurdistan to include those parts of Iraq with a Kurdish majority and areas which were historically Kurdish before Saddam's "Arabization" programs, and to play a prominent role in the federal government in Baghdad. They entered the constitutional negotiations well positioned to achieve all these goals.

On 13 February 2004, the speaker of the Kurdistan National Assembly, Dr. Roj Shaways, submitted a chapter, "Special Provisions for the Kurdistan Region" (see Appendix 1 to this volume), to be incorporated into Iraq's Transitional Administrative Law (TAL), then under discussion within the Coalition Provisional Authority (CPA) and Iraqi Governing Council (IGC). While Kurdistan did not did not succeed in getting the entirety of this proposal adopted in the TAL, the Kurdistan Chapter remains the basis for Kurdistan's proposals for the permanent constitution of Iraq. Some of its most important goals were achieved. Since Kurdistan existed as a de facto independent state, it did not need to sacrifice any of its powers to the federal government in the TAL. Failure to settle a matter meant that the status quo would continue. The Kurdistan delegation aimed to get as much as possible of what it sought in the TAL, but, where this proved impossible, to preserve its position for the negotiation of the permanent constitution.

The Kurdistan Chapter sought to consolidate Kurdistan's institutions and powers. It limited the role of the federal government, while establishing unequivocally the primacy of Kurdistan law in all matters outside those few which it saw as appropriately within the exclusive competence of the federal government. The proposal included detailed articles on military matters and natural resources that reflected Kurdistan's intense focus on security (a legacy of the Kurds' repressive eighty-year association with Iraq) and the importance of interests tied to petroleum. An article on fiscal matters sought to guarantee Kurdistan financial independence from the federal government, and a provision on ratification of the permanent constitution was designed to ensure that the status quo in Kurdistan could not be undone without the consent of the people of Kurdistan.

How did these provisions fare in the making of the Transitional Administrative Law? The Kurdistan Chapter sought to preserve the governmental institutions of the Kurdistan region, namely the Kurdistan National Assembly, the Council of Ministers, and the Kurdistan judiciary, and to have their sovereignty recognized over most matters within the territory that was administered by the Kurdistan Regional Government on 19 March 2003, the day the war against Saddam began. By limiting the mandate of the Kurdistan Regional Government to the three overwhelmingly Kurdish governorates (as well as small amounts of territory in adjacent governorates north and east of the "green line"), Kurdistan's leaders followed a pragmatic strategy of securing recognition of Kurdistan's existence before opening negotiations over Kurdistan's boundaries.

The Kurdistan Chapter proposed the establishment of Kurdistan law as the supreme law of the Kurdistan region on all matters, except the narrow set of issues delegated exclusively to the federal government. The federal government's powers would be limited to foreign policy, defense policy (but not implementation), monetary policy, and customs. The Kurdistan Government would exercise all other powers, including levying and collecting taxes; public spending; controlling the regional police; establishing and maintaining an independent judiciary; writing Kurdistan's criminal, civil, and commercial law; environmental protection; regulation of public land; running an educational system that includes three universities; and the definition and protection of human rights in the region.

In the TAL, Kurdistan conceded somewhat greater powers to the federal government, but it won recognition of the supremacy of Kurdistan law in all other matters. Article 55 of the TAL (see Appendix 2) gives the Kurdistan National Assembly the power to amend the application of all federal laws in Kurdistan except for those parts of federal law that touch on matters within the exclusive competence of the federal government. The list of exclusive federal competences in the TAL includes (in addition to those initially conceded in the Kurdistan proposal) management of natural resources (only for the transitional period), national fiscal policy (with Kurdistan retaining its own ability to tax and spend), and telecommunications policy.

In its proposal, the Kurdistan National Assembly emphasized the military security of Kurdistan. It envisaged an Iraqi Kurdistan National Guard that would be recruited primarily from the elite among the *peshmerga* units. The Kurdistan National Assembly would have exclusive authority to create and regulate the guard and to appoint its officers and commander. But, Kurdistan conceded a federal monopoly on military force by placing its proposed Iraqi Kurdistan National Guard under the overall command of the Iraqi civilian authorities, provided Iraq would remain a constitutional democracy and that any deployment of the Iraqi Kurdistan National Guard outside Kurdistan would require approval by a vote of the Kurdistan National Assembly. The Kurdistan Chapter also required the Kurdistan National Assembly to approve any deployment of the Iraqi armed forces into the Kurdistan Region and gave the Assembly the power to limit such presence to specific locations, specific numbers of troops, and a specific duration. Not surprisingly, the TAL left these military issues unresolved. The Coalition Provisional Authority negotiators saw Kurdistan's proposals as inconsistent with the unity of Iraq and America's ambitions to create a modern, democratic Iraqi military. Kurdistan's leaders felt the CPA had little appreciation for their history within Iraq, or for the role of the *peshmerga* as the lawfully constituted army of the KRG. For the Kurds, the Iraqi army has been the enemy, responsible for carrying out attacks on civilians ever since the founding of the modern Iraqi state. The Iraqi armed forces destroyed over 4,000 villages in Kurdistan during the 1970s and 1980s, used chemical weapons against the Kurds in 1987 and 1988, and participated in the deportation and execution of more than 100,000 civilians. The people of Kurdistan understandably do not believe that six months of U.S.-led "nation-building" provides any assurance of safety, especially as Shi'a leaders have publicly announced their intention to roll back constitutional protections for the Kurds. Kurdistan's negotiators saw the existence of an Iraqi Kurdistan National Guard (whose ultimate loyalty is to the Kurdistan National Assembly that would formally recruit it) and the proposed restrictions on the presence of the Iraqi army as insurance in the event that democracy failed to take hold in the rest of Iraq. The Americans, along with Iraq's neighbors, feared that the Kurdistan proposal was a first step to independence.

The Kurdistan Chapter proposed to make the Kurdistan Region the owner of all natural resources on, and under, the territory of Kurdistan, including all non-private land, water, minerals, and petroleum. Article 3 treated each resource somewhat differently for specific reasons. Much of the land in Kurdistan has no registered owner, or its title is uncertain. The Kurdistan Region wants to decide how this land is used and to prevent the federal government from using it to house Arab settlers or to create military bases, to cite two previous abuses that concern the Kurds. Water is a vital resource in the parched Middle East, arguably more important and contentious than oil over the long term. Kurdistan has lots of water—in lakes, in rivers originating in Kurdistan, and in rivers flowing through Kurdistan. Kurdistan wants to own the water to insure adequate supplies for local use and to continue to control the two hydroelectric facilities in Darbandikhan and Dukan, which supply much of Kurdistan's electricity. Of course, the Kurdistan National Assembly recognized that it has an obligation to downstream Iraqis, and therefore its proposal envisioned cooperative management of river water.

Petroleum is the key resource currently subject to controversy. With Kirkuk, Kurdistan would own 40 percent of Iraq's current petroleum production; without it, Kurdistan has no petroleum reservoirs in commercial production. Kurdistan does have fields with significant potential oil and gas resources in Taq-Taq, Chamchamal, and Zakho. With the status of Kirkuk unresolved, Kurdistan proposed to treat reservoirs currently in commercial production differently than new reservoirs. The federal government would manage currently producing oil fields, distributing the revenues to the regions on a per capita basis. Kurdistan would own and develop new reservoirs, although the proposal contemplates revenue-sharing should Kurdistan's share of petroleum be disproportionately large or small. Kurdistan sees ownership and management of oil as providing considerable economic benefit in terms of jobs and expertise, even if the revenues were pooled. Lurking behind the demand for ownership is the belief that Kurdistan's possession of petroleum reservoirs provides the only guarantee that Kurdistan will end up with its fair share of Iraq's wealth.

In the TAL, Kurdistan agreed to federal government management of the natural resources in consultation with the region, along with language that obscured the issue of ownership. The Bush administration had promised Turkey that Iraq's oil would be owned by the federal government, and the Kurdish leaders saw no reason to cross their American allies on an issue that would have no real effects during the transitional period (where the only relevant resource to be managed is oil from currently producing reservoirs).

The Kurdistan Chapter included provisions to insure the financial autonomy of Kurdistan, including exclusive tax powers within the region. In the TAL Kurdistan settled for a block grant to the Kurdistan Regional Government that is a percentage of Iraq's total revenue which is not less than Kurdistan's share of Iraq's population. The thorny issue of how federal taxes might be collected in a region where the federal ministries have no real presence was left unresolved.

Last, Kurdistan wanted to be sure that the permanent constitution could only go into effect in the Kurdistan Region with its consent, and therefore its leaders proposed a ratification clause saying just this. Initially, Administrator Bremer strongly opposed this approach, in effect agreeing with the Shi'a that a majority vote should be sufficient to ratify the permanent constitution. However, as the representatives of religious parties in the Iraqi Governing Council tried to roll back protections for women and sought to impose Islamic law even during the transitional period, Bremer became more sympathetic to Kurdistan's fears about the "tyranny of the majority." Kurdistan's leaders sent Bremer Article VII of the U.S. Constitution (which set a supermajority of nine of the thirteen states, with the constitution only coming into effect among those states so ratifying), and he relented. In any event, a constitution that is not acceptable to the Kurds, or for that matter to Sunni Arabs, is not likely to provide stability or unity for Iraq.

To accommodate its American ally, the Kurdistan delegation made concessions in the Transitional Administrative Law that were neither necessary, given the strength of Kurdistan's hand in the negotiating process, nor required to reach an accord on transitional arrangements. In particular, the delegation made significant (albeit temporary) concessions on the issue of natural resources and failed to regularize the status of their self-defense forces. A significant section of the Kurdish public has criticized these decisions, and many wonder whether the Americans will repay (or even appreciate) the sacrifices the Kurdish leaders made to please their ally. Yet, in spite of these concessions, Kurdistan will enter the negotiations on the permanent constitution with a strong hand. It still possesses the powers it wants, and concessions made in the TAL can easily be recalled—especially as Shi'a Arabs talk about repealing key features of the interim constitution.

The Territory of Kurdistan and Kirkuk

Enlarging the territory of the self-governing Kurdistan region poses a different negotiating challenge. Kurdistan is not in possession of the additional territory it seeks, and it can only expand the area it controls with the cooperation of Arab Iraq. The borders of the Kurdistan region as it existed on 19 March 2003 were determined by Saddam Hussein, who carefully excluded areas producing petroleum, as well as Kurdish-inhabited areas close to strategic Iraqi positions. For Kurdistan, enlargement would encompass territory with an overwhelming majority of Kurdish residents adjacent to the Kurdistan region and the city and region of Kirkuk. Kurdish-majority areas include—from southeast to northwest—Khaneqin, Akre the Yezidi town of Sheikhan, and Makhmur. Attaching these areas to Kurdistan may not be too controversial with other Iraqis. Their populations are almost entirely Kurdish, and they have been administered as if part of the Kurdistan Regional Government territory since liberation. The Mosul governorate made some effort to exercise authority in Makhmur, which was detached from Dohuk by Saddam in 2001, but the local population rebuffed the Mosul authorities, who then gave up.

On the other hand, Kirkuk's status will be difficult to settle. The Kurds claim Kirkuk as part of their historic national patrimony. Mustafa Barzani, the legendary founder of the Kurdistan Democratic Party and father of current leader, Masoud Barzani, described Kirkuk as the heart of Kurdistan. The 1974 autonomy agreement between Barzani and Saddam fell apart over whether Kirkuk would be included in the autonomous Kurdish area. In the 1980s, Jalal Talabani upped the rhetorical ante by calling Kirkuk "the Jerusalem of Kurdistan." In fact, there are no sacred sites particular to the Kurds in Kirkuk. But, Kirkuk sits atop Iraq's largest producing petroleum reservoir. The Kurds insist their claim to Kirkuk has nothing to do with this oil, but as the *New York Times* columnist William Safire has noted, in a paraphrase of Senator Dale Bumpers' eloquent defense of President Clinton in the impeachment trial, "when they say it's not about the oil, it usually is."

Unfortunately for the Kurds, three other communities claim Kirkuk. Two of them, the Arabs and the Turkomen, have powerful allies. Kirkuk's fourth national community, comprised of Chaldean and Assyrian Christians, has no outside protectors and merely wishes to continue to live in the governorate and practice its beliefs undisturbed. The Turkomen, by contrast, assert they are a majority within the city and have always been. Turkey has taken up their cause, although the suspicion lingers that Turkey is less motivated by concern for its ethnic kin than to deprive the Kurds of the economic resources that would facilitate the development of a viable independent state. Beginning during the late monarchy, Arabs began moving into Kirkuk in large numbers. Some of this migration was undoubtedly a response to economic opportunities in the rapidly growing oil industry. However, successive Iraqi regimes took increasingly forceful measures to bring Arabs to Kirkuk. In the 1970s, the Ba'th regime began also to expel Kirkuk's Kurdish—and, in some cases, Turkomen—population. In the 1980s and 1990s, this "Arabization" program became increasingly brutal. Several hundred thousand Kurds were expelled from Kirkuk and spent up to twelve years in tents just on the other side of the "green line" from their former homes. Saddam's regime turned Kurdish property over to Arabs, often from the Shi'a south, and provided significant financial subsidies to Arab newcomers in Kirkuk. Successive Iraqi regimes also altered the borders of Kirkuk governorate, transferring Kurdish districts to the adjacent Sulaimania and Erbil governorates and attaching Arab districts from Tikrit. "Arabization" and gerrymandering altered the demographic character of the province.

While Kurdistan's leaders insist on the validity of their historic claim to Kirkuk, they are willing to have Kirkuk's people determine its status in a referendum. But, they insist that, before such a referendum takes place, the effects of the "Arabization" programs must be reversed. They want to insure that Kurdish displaced persons return and recover their property. Arab newcomers should, they say, be offered financial incentives and other inducements to return to their places of origin. The Kurdish leaders are willing to have some Arab newcomers stay, but not to retain Kurdish-owned property. They insist that no one who came under the "Arabization" programs may vote in a referendum on its status. They also want Kirkuk to revert to its historic boundaries.

While both Iraqi Arabs on the Governing Council and the Coalition Provisional Authority concede that an injustice was done to Kirkuk's Kurds, there is no agreement on how to rectify the wrong. Specifically, there is no consensus on who came to Kirkuk under the "Arabization" program, or when "Arabization" began. No specific historical borders for Kirkuk have been accepted. While most agree to turning back the clock, it is unclear whether it should be turned back to 1991 (the time of the Kurdish uprising), 1981 (the start of an intense wave of repression), 1974 (after the collapse of the autonomy agreement), 1968 (the establishment of the Ba'th regime), 1958 (the end of the monarchy), or even earlier. Uncertainty about Kirkuk's status and the existence of powerful protectors for the Turkomen and Arabs makes Kirkuk potentially the most volatile place in Iraq. In 1974, the failure to resolve Kirkuk led to war, with devastating consequences for the Kurds and their dreams for self-government. Given the powerful forces with a vested interest in Kirkuk, gaining control of the province may prove a poisoned chalice for Kurdistan, providing a rationale for both Turkish and Arab intervention in Kurdistan's internal affairs.

While the Kurds are well positioned to secure recognition of the Kurdistan state and formalization of its powers within an Iraq federation, they have much less bargaining power on territorial issues, in particular the incorporation of Kirkuk into Kurdistan. The process to determine Kirkuk's status will have to be negotiated with Iraq's Arab majority. Among some of the secular parties in the Iraqi Governing Council, the Kurds have potential allies. However, the Shi'a religious parties, which seem likely to dominate after elections, are hostile to a Kurdistan region with substantial powers and are unlikely to be compromising on the issue of Kirkuk—especially because many of the Arabs who moved to Kirkuk are Shi'a. The Turkomen Shi'a are disposed to ally with them.

Power-Sharing in Baghdad

Kurdistan's leadership wants to play a substantial, if not disproportionate, role in the future Iraqi federal government. While there is an element of personal ambition in these aspirations, the Kurds see power-sharing as a way to protect a self-governing Kurdistan and as a way to ensure a benign Iraqi administration. Kurdistan's leaders recognize that their advantage over other Iraqis is temporary. Sooner or later, the rest of Iraq will develop a viable government. The United States is already trying to create a new Iraqi army, although with very limited success. In December 2003, a third of the first 700-man brigade resigned over pay issues. It was hardly an auspicious conclusion to a year-long effort (including planning) to develop a democratic military. While a well-armed Iraqi Kurdistan National Guard could make it very costly for Arab Iraq to take Kurdistan by force, it seems likely there will eventually be a reconstituted Iraqi army which could become a formidable adversary.

Furthermore, Kurdistan's well-being inevitably depends on relations with Baghdad. Even if Kurdistan wins the final arguments over ownership of petroleum, Kurdistan cannot export petroleum (the only way to generate revenues) in significant quantities without the consent of the Baghdad authorities. Kurdish farmers will want to sell their wheat into the Iraqi market and benefit from any subsidies. There are many practical issues where cooperation and coordination will be essential. Kurdistan's leaders hope that, by playing a major role in Baghdad, they can ensure a benign security environment and promote Kurdistan's economic interests.

During the first year after liberation, the Kurds exercised disproportionate influence in Iraq. The CPA administrator gave the Kurds 20 percent of the seats on the Governing Council, and the two major party leaders were among the nine rotating presidents. But, more importantly, Masoud Barzani and Jalal Talabani were the only members of the Iraqi Governing Council with demonstrable political support evidenced in free elections. This gave them a status above the rest of the members and allowed them on occasion to play the role of kingmakers. They were able to win support for some of their goals, including a clear statement on reversing the "Arabization" of Kirkuk. On the other hand, they have been less successful in protecting secularism in the face of Shi'a demands for Islamic rule. They were unable to stop Abdul Aziz al-Hakim, the leader of the Supreme Council of the Islamic Revolution in Iraq (SCIRI), from using his month-long presidency in December 2003 to win a majority to replace the civil code marriage provisions with Islamic law. The CPA administrator refused to sign the SCIRI proposal, and Kurdistan made it clear that even if it was ratified by the CPA its provisions would not apply in Kurdistan. The Iraqi Governing Council reconsidered and reversed this decision in a February 2004 vote.

Kurdistan's views on the future federal government remain ill defined. Its leaders seem to prefer a system in which the parliament is chosen under a party-list proportional representation electoral system. Their theory is that, in a multi-party parliament, they can both obtain positions and decide who else gets into power. For the transitional period, Kurdistan's parties support creating the three-person presidency that was incorporated into the Transitional Administrative Law. While the law does not say so explicitly, it was generally expected that the presidency (in fact, one president and two deputies who must operate by consensus on some issues) would include one Shi'a Arab, one Sunni Arab, and one Kurd. Kurdistan's views on other aspects of the organization of the federal government—the federal judiciary, a constitutional court, civilian control of the military—are much less well formed, partly because the Kurds see themselves as opting out of many of these institutions. Similarly, the Kurds have not been much engaged on the symbolic issues of the new state of Iraq, such as the emblem and flag, insisting only that it not be Saddam's Ba'thist flag and that they get to fly the Kurdistan flag.

The Kurds are deeply engaged on the issue of language and insist that Kurdish and Arabic be fully equal official languages of the federation. Kurds see the equality of their language as a proxy for the equality of Kurds and Arabs in the new Iraq. In insisting on bilingualism, the Kurds are explicitly trying to undo a Ba'thist ideology, which defined Iraq as part of the greater Arab nation and ultimately led to genocide against the Kurdish minority. The Kurds insist that they cannot be partners in a country that recognizes only one national group's language and disregards theirs. Here, they look to Canada, where bilingualism is the embodiment of the equality of the francophone population, which constitutes 20 percent of Canadians, with the anglophone majority. They also realize that bilingualism in Canada has given the French a role in the federal government considerably beyond their proportion of Canada's population; francophone Québécois have held the position of prime minister for much of the time since the mid-nineteenth century. Bilingualism in Canada has favored French speakers in other ways. Almost all educated Québécois speak English, but not all English-speaking Canadians speak French. Thus, in the competition for elite jobs in the federal bureaucracy, francophone Canadians have a distinct advantage. Since many educated Kurds speak Arabic, but few Iraqi Arabs speak Kurdish, a Canadian-style requirement of bilingualism for top jobs would very much favor the Kurds.

Curiously, the CPA resisted bilingualism. Paul Bremer, who had served as U.S. ambassador to the Netherlands, told Kurdish leaders that he considered bilingualism in Belgium a source of divisiveness in the country. Without any sense of irony, the CPA insisted that federalism should not be based on ethnicity, while also insisting that one group's language—Arabic—be the sole official language. In the end, however, the Kurds prevailed on language. Both Kurdish and Arabic are official languages in the new Iraq, will appear on new Iraqi banknotes, passports, and traffic signs, and will be used in laws, parliamentary debates, and government documents.

The TAL has been hailed, for good reason, as a remarkable document for the Middle East. It includes extensive protections for human rights, as well as radical innovations such as a nine-member U.S.-style supreme court. Unfortunately, the way the TAL was produced undermines its legitimacy. This may set the stage for renewed battles over the making of the permanent constitution, leading to conflict and perhaps ultimately to the break-up of Iraq. The CPA pretended that the TAL was an Iraqi product: "But I think the Iraqis, you could tell at the ceremony today, were justifiably proud of what they had done," declared an American official with no trace of irony.[2] In fact, the TAL was largely written by U.S. government lawyers and negotiated in secret by U.S. officials among a handful of Iraqis. Probably fewer than 100 Iraqis saw any version of the Transitional Administrative Law before it was adopted. The CPA insured there would be no public discussion, no hearings, and no public input. This approach, so alien to modern American democracy, has served to undermine the document's legitimacy as Iraqis discover what the Americans have in mind for their constitution.

In Kurdistan, NGOs and other members of civil society have criticized provisions that would sacrifice some of the autonomy Kurdistan now enjoys.

In the month leading up to the adoption of the Transitional Administrative Law, the Referendum Movement, a Kurdistan NGO seeking a vote on independence, collected 1,700,000 signatures in Kurdistan on a petition demanding a plebiscite. Overwhelming public sentiment for independence—1.7 million signatures may represent nearly three-fourths of Kurdistan's adults—makes it virtually impossible for the Kurdish leaders to accept much less than the current autonomy.

Shiʻa religious leaders seem intent on rolling back some of what Kurdistan gained in the Transitional Administrative Law. They argue that a document prepared in secret by Bremer and signed by 25 people he appointed does not have the authority to bind the National Assembly to be elected in January 2005. In particular, they state their intention to undo the TAL's ratification procedures that, by effectively giving Kurdistan a veto over the permanent constitution, insures a Kurdistan role in framing the federal government. The Shiʻa also object to Kurdistan's insistence on a continued role for its self-defense force. Kurdish leaders have warned that efforts to impose an Islamic state on their region would result in Iraq's dissolution. Eliminating Kurdistan's constitutional and military protections might well lead most Kurds to conclude that independence is less risky than staying in Iraq.

Over the long term, it is almost impossible for a democratic state to hold together if a people in a geographically compact area overwhelmingly prefer not to be part of that state. The people of Kurdistan equate Iraq with repression and genocide. Almost no one in Kurdistan would choose to be part of Iraq if there were an alternative. Therefore, if holding Iraq together by force is no longer an option, the people of Kurdistan must be induced to stay in Iraq voluntarily. In practical terms, this means accommodating their desires for self-government and security within a very loose federation while providing tangible benefits—in the form of shared petroleum revenues—for sticking with Iraq. Shiʻa demands for simple majority rule could seal Iraq's death warrant.

Notes

1. "President George Bush Discusses Iraq in National Press Conference," 6 March, East Room, The White House. <http://www.whitehouse.gov/news/releases/2003/03/20030306–8.html>

2. Washington File, U.S. Department of State, 8 March 2004.

Postscript: Vistas of Exits from Baghdad

Brendan O'Leary

"One must neither give reasons for things that don't exist, nor wrong reasons for things that do exist."
—Voltaire, On Hobbes, Grotius and Montesquieu

"Responsibility, n. A detachable burden easily shifted to the shoulders of God, Fate, Fortune, Luck or one's neighbor."
—Ambrose Bierce, The Devil's Dictionary

"One year later, the whole world knows that America does not have the financial or military means to control a country the size of Iraq."
—Emmanuel Todd, After Empire

This postscript is written in September 2004, as the death toll from political violence cumulates in Iraq. Civilians, foreigners, the security forces of the interim government and those interested in joining them, are the primary victims of political violence. Civilians are the prime victims of criminal assaults. As of 10 September, one estimate suggested that between 13,000 and 15,000 Iraqi civilians had died since 19 March 2003, of whom nearly 7,500 were killed in the major combat operations of the formal war before 1 May 2003 (Iraq Body Count 2004). As of September 22 over 1,300 people had been killed in mass casualty bombings executed by opponents of the Iraqi Governing Council and the Iraqi interim government since May 2003. As of 30 August more than 2,700 civilians had died in acts of war since May 2003; while the estimated death toll from criminality in the same interval ranges between 10,000 and more than 27,000 persons (Brookings Institution 2004). It should be emphasized that no completely reliable death tolls are available on the deaths of insurgents in Iraq, or on the deaths caused by the U.S.-led coalition. The graphic in Figure 1, adapted from the data in the Iraq Index of the Brookings Institution, sketches some of the estimated human horror and its monthly movements. As I write, it is widely expected that September will see another spike in violence, in both the death tolls and the numbers of attacks by the contending parties.

It bears emphasis that most of this violence has been occurring in Arab Iraq.[1] Moqtada al-Sadr's Mahdi army has sustained extremely high losses in intermittent battles with U.S.-led forces since the spring, but thus far the deaths of his paramilitaries, and the destruction they have caused, have enhanced rather than crushed the trainee cleric's political reputation as a champion of Shi'a and Arab interests. He now contends with Ayatollah Sistani for name-recognition among Shi'a Arabs, and is outbidding the leaders of the two principal Shi'a parties, the Supreme Council for the Islamic Revolution of Iraq (SCIRI) and the Da'wa ("Call"). Whether he will combine a ballot box and bombing strategy remains to be seen—current evaluations suggest he will stand in the elections scheduled for January 2005 on a platform with (Shi'a) Islamist and Iraqi nationalist colors. From what is universally but not entirely accurately known as "the Sunni Arab triangle" an intermittently holy—or unholy—coalition of Ba'thists and Islamists of every stripe, including allies and members of al-Qaida, launch extensive attacks on the forces of the U.S.-led coalition, as well as those of the interim government. The latter's new army and police units have been staggering to their feet only to come under fire or bomb-blasts—their opponents have made recruiting stations their most favored target. Inadequately trained, poorly paid, and afraid, many in the new police and army vote with their feet, while some defect to the insurgents. The American newspapers report as I write that the military command in charge of training Iraqi forces has fewer than half of its permanent headquarters personnel in place, and that the U.S. military war-dead toll since March 2003 has just passed the one thousand mark. In sum, no one doubts that there is now far more cumulative violent death among persons and organized damage to property in Arab Iraq than there had been when President Bush flew in to a celebration before a banner which declared "mission accomplished" in May 2003.

These facts and estimates of facts contrast sharply with the Bush administration's goals for Iraq, as specified in a White House New Year's Press briefing of January 1 2003, namely, "To disarm the country, dismantle the terrorist infrastructure, and liberate the Iraqi people." Saddam is disarmed, under arrest, and awaits trial. Yet Arab Iraq is now re-armed, but not under one integrated or widely legitimate government. Instead militias, insurgents, ex-Ba'thists and freelancing wahhabists contend for influence and local territorial control, and allow their cadres to run amok, constantly challenging the weak forces of the interim government. Kidnapping is a flourishing trade. New terrorist infrastructures have emerged: some are safe havens negotiated under

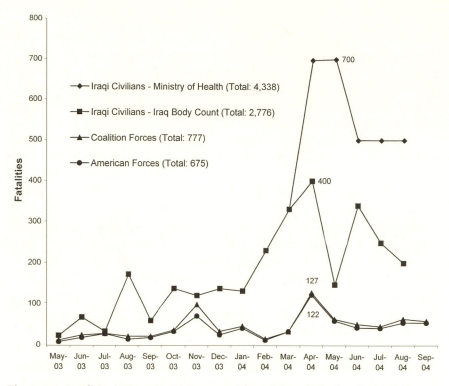

Figure 13.1. Fatalities in Iraq since May 2003. Adapted from "The Iraq Index," Brookings Institution (2004) <http://www.brookings.edu/fp/saban/iraq/index.pdf.> "Iraq Body Count" data on Iraqi civilian fatalities are the exclusive source until March 2004. There may be undercounts. Brookings began using this source as its lower limit of Iraqi civilian casualties in April 2004; it includes estimates of "civilians and police killed by fighting between insurgents and coalition forces, and as a result of mass casualty bombings." Arguably police should be counted as local security force casualties rather than as civilians. The "Iraq Index" acknowledges "estimates are most probably lower than the actual number as a result of the fact that many separate incidents go unreported or unnoticed." Data on American troop fatalities include only casualties suffered in hostile incidents; data on Coalition fatalities add those suffered by American troops in hostile incidents to those suffered by British and other coalition troops (including in nonhostile incidents).

U.S. auspices or connivance, formally in Falluja, informally in Ramadi, Baquba, and Samarra—the latter is scheduled for a recapture by the interim government as I write. The state terrorists who ran Saddam's Iraq are formally ousted from governmental corridors, but some remain contenders for power—fighting with and against many others determined to use terrorism against U.S. troops as well as those risibly known as their "fellow countrymen." Most Arabs in Iraq tell pollsters that they feel under occupation rather than liberated. The Christians of urban Arab Iraq are in flight. Of the major nationalities and confessions in Iraq only the Kurds feel liberated. External and insider observers can be heard counseling against holding Iraq-wide elections scheduled for the end of January 2005. These facts and the stories about them collectively speak for a U.S. policy disaster in Iraq. The failure to have them honestly recognized by the White House threatens to compound the disaster.[2]

Reflection on these facts gives rise to a grim satisfaction in some quarters. "We told you so" and "As you sow so shall you reap" are on the minds, if not always on the lips, of many European and North American opponents of the Bush administration's war to overthrow Saddam.[3] The media in the Arab and Muslim worlds showcase torture in Baghdad as the true verdict on America's commitment to human rights and democracy in the Middle East. The Coalition's support for the rights of women, and their rights to liberation—including sexual liberation, have been besmirched by the globally advertised spectacle of Private England engaged in the sexualized torture of naked Arab men in Saddam's dungeons. So far, accountability for the scandal of authorized torture—previously publicly counseled by some lawyers as a prudent U.S. policy option against terrorism (Dershowitz 2002)—remains confined to a few "rotten apples." But digesting the multiplying official secret and public reports on these grim matters it is impossible not to see the conduct of low-ranking military police or contractors as exactly what one would predict given the incentives, experience and rhetoric which shaped their tasks. It is equally impossible not to attribute responsibility all the way up the Pentagon's hierarchies (Taguba 2004; Jones and Fay 2004; Schlesinger et al. 2004). The Schlesinger Report is correct that "detainee abuse[s] in Iraq and Afghanistan . . . indicate a review of military ethics education programs is needed" (Schlesinger et al. 2004 124), but that is not where any review of ethics (or strategy) should stop. "Cordon and capture," the U.S.-led Coalition's large-scale use of detention without trial; the official acknowledgment in the Schlesinger Report that five detainees have been tortured to death by U.S. personnel—and that twenty-three further cases are under investigation; and the decision to incarcerate detainees with convicted criminals are all morally inexcusable, *and* they are politically and militarily counter-productive. They have wholly estranged the affected Arab population from which the Coalition's forces must necessarily seek intelligence. Whether these facts, and the policy disaster of which they speak, will decide the political fate of George W. Bush in November's imminent presidential elections is not yet known. Outside the ranks of those who will vote for Bush, and perhaps within them, what is known to the U.S. military as GWOT (the Global War on Terror) is becoming known as GERCC

(Global Exercise in Remarkably Crazy Crusading). Outside the U.S., the verdict of public opinion polls is clear. Sympathy for America as the victim of 9/11 has dissipated; and if the rest of the world had the relevant franchise it would dispatch President Bush from office, and many would want to prosecute him as a war criminal.[4] Within the U.S., opinion is far more polarized, and the incumbent has strong supporters of his intervention in Iraq. But if Bush were to lose in the Electoral College it would be assumed that it was because of the mess in Iraq; by contrast, if he were to win, by whatever margin, it would be considered an endorsement of his overall response to 9/11, including his decision to attack Saddam. Whoever wins, be it President Bush or Senator Kerry, will have to manage multiple policy follies on his Iraq in-desk.

The manuscripts of the chapters of my fellow contributors to *The Future of Kurdistan in Iraq*, as well as my own, went to press in late April 2004, shortly after the making of the Transitional Administrative Law in March, more or less coterminously with al-Sadr's April insurrection and the prolonged stand-off in Falluja, and before the exit of the Coalition Provisional Authority from Iraq and the concurrent formal restoration of Iraq's sovereignty on June 28. Together with my friends Peter Galbraith and Khaled Salih I worked in and for the Kurdistan National Assembly until the summer, in constitutional advisory work, particularly in advising on electoral arrangements for the Iraqi National Assembly—a matter in which Kurdistan's parties were justly successful in persuading the United Nations of the merits of party-list proportional representation using the whole of Iraq as one constituency.[5] The atmosphere in which we worked in Kurdistan was astonishingly different from that which we individually encountered in our occasional forays into Arab Iraq. We were working in and for a different nation. Returning to the U.S. has provided additional perspective on what has happened in Arab Iraq, and the likely prospects for Kurdistan, now that exit from Baghdad—or at least exit from the costs of Baghdad—has become the tacit preoccupation of senior Republicans and Democrats, and within the UK's Labour party, rhetoric to the contrary notwithstanding. This postscript will combine personal reflections with bringing readers up to date on key developments since our manuscript went to press.

When I returned from Kurdistan in June 2004, friends and acquaintances in Europe and North America interrogated me. Three questions were always posed. First, "Was the U.S.-led coalition right to invade and occupy Iraq?" Second, "How could the occupation of Iraq have been better organized?" (Not even devotees of *Fox News* think it was very well organized.) And third, "Can Iraq work now that the Coalition Provisional Authority has gone and is replaced by a formally sovereign Iraqi government?" More rarely was I asked about Kurdistan per se, rather than about Iraq as a totality, a matter to which

I shall return. My attempts to respond to these three questions prompt memories of a passage from a poem by W. H. Auden: "To ask the hard questions is simple, but the answers are hard, and hard to remember."[6] Here are my answers.

Answer 1. An appalling regime was removed, but for the wrong reasons.

As the editors emphasize in our Preface, Saddam's regime was genocidal, both before and after 1991. Member-states of the United Nations which are signatories to the UN Convention on the Prevention and Punishment of the Crime of Genocide (1948) are obliged to "prevent and punish" this crime, but this was not the key basis for the intervention by the Coalition. The Ba'thists ran a regime of mass destruction.[7] They were politicidal; opponents of the regime were killed, systematically tortured, as well as jailed. Saddam was a present danger to the majority of his subject peoples and their neighbors. He had twice initiated failed wars of conquest. His regime was unlikely to collapse, through either sanctions or reform. Ba'thists had taken KGB counsel on preventing coups. But these facts were not the principal justifications given for the enforced regime change.

The official case was threefold. The first premise was that Saddam had not complied with the UN treaty imposed after the Gulf War. This claim had merit, but its potency was de-fanged by subsequent UN resolutions. It is, mildly put, controversial whether prior UN resolutions gave the U.S. and its allies the authority to enforce through renewed war the resolutions that Saddam had sought to avoid. The legal case was at best casuistic, and as I write, the Secretary General of the UN has just publicly declared that the U.S. action was illegal, a judgment which is the consensus of the world outside Washington and Whitehall. The second premise was that Iraq possessed weapons of mass destruction that were imminent threats to international security. The WMD premise was thought true (even by many who opposed the war), although the intelligence on which it rested was challenged, most effectively by France at the UN. We all now know that the WMD theory was false. The third premise, asserted, implied, and insinuated, was that meaningful—or potential—linkage existed between Saddam's WMD regime and al-Qaida. This linkage theory involved deliberately inflated and misleading extrapolations. The bipartisan 9/11 Commission Report treats the issue soberly. It recalls that before 2002 Usama bin Ladin sponsored anti-Saddam Islamists in Kurdistan (those who formed Ansar al-Islam), and suggests that al-Qaida had more substantive links to Iran (National Commission on Terrorist Attacks on the United States 2004: 61, 468 n. 53, and chapters 2, 7 passim). That the attack on

Saddam was a diversion from the war on al-Qaida is a conclusion with which significant portions of mainstream America now concur.

Enforcing resolutions that the UN was unwilling to enforce, WMDs, and the linkage claim provided the public rationale for war-planners in Washington. After the invasion of Iraq, coalition leaders had an embarrassing difficulty, as we emphasize in our Preface. It is now crystal clear that the UN weapons-inspectors had done their job. Between 1991 and 1997–98 they decommissioned Saddam's WMD program and also contained its redevelopment (Blix 2004).[8] Most of the key intelligence services of the U.S. and the UK have now been officially declared wrong in their assessments of Saddam's WMD capabilities in 2002–3. The coalition's political leaders have therefore appeared either as awkward liars or, just as embarrassing, as the dupes of their intelligence agencies—themselves duped by their informants (the chief suspects being Ahmad Chalabi and his supporters), overly susceptible to pleasing their political masters, or just incompetent. The invasion itself has generated linkage, but through a self-fulfilling prophecy or "blowback" (Johnson 2001): al-Qaida and its allies and overthrown Ba'thists now collaborate in the Sunni triangle.

Kenneth Pollack, the author of the best book in favor of the U.S.-led intervention (Pollack 2002), has argued that the sanctions imposed on Saddam for noncompliance with U.N. resolutions were eroding, and that Saddam wanted to rearm (Pollack 2004).[9] But "smart sanctions"—smarter than the general sanctions that led to the deaths of children and mass-smuggling—had recently been approved by the UN. They had only been given a short time to work. Pollack is right that Saddam would have liked nuclear, chemical, and biological weapons, but the retrospectively astonishing question is: "Why did Saddam hide the fact that he was bereft of WMDs?" Why permit an invasion to begin on what he could have shown to be a false claim? And why at the end did he not do a better job of persuading the external world that he did not have WMDs? In the end the wolf was briefly innocent for once, but was assumed guilty by all. Perhaps Saddam thought the belief that he had WMDs acted as a deterrent. Perhaps he was misled by his intelligence agencies, who may have messed up their assessments of U.S. intentions as badly as their Western counterparts failed in their tasks. Perhaps his personal security and that of his (past) weapons program were so interlocked that he dared not "come clean." It is a subject for the historians.

The uneasy answer, therefore, to the question "Was the U.S.-led coalition right to invade and occupy Iraq?" is that an awful regime was overthrown that could have been overthrown lawfully, because it was genocidal, but was in fact overthrown in unlawful violation of orthodox international law, on premises that have been shown to have been false and misleading. The outcome has not only damaged the standing of the U.S., but also made the reconstruction of Iraq far more difficult. The U.S. needs to lead the UN in interventions against genocide and gross human-rights violations, but by making such a bad case for invading Iraq it has lost much of the legitimacy it so desperately needed. Legitimacy in international relations is like hard currency: it is tradable for desirable goods and services, and the Bush administration has deflated its state's assets. And it is not at all obvious that its actions have deterred other regimes intent on developing WMDs, as developments in Korea and Iran advertise on our news bulletins.

Answer 2. The occupation, handicapped by the unilateral and ill-considered basis for regime-change, was mismanaged because it was badly planned by the wrong people, poorly improvised, and driven by inappropriate political assumptions.

Only stranded platoons of neoconservatives now claim that the occupation went well after May 2003. It is true that the official military war was won quickly, efficiently, and effectively, that is, with minimal collateral damage to civilians and property, and with generally disciplined compliance with the laws of war. In the aftermath I saw multiple sites that appeared to be the results of very precise hits of military and regime targets. The U.S. war plans and their implementation targeted Saddam, Ba'thist leaders, and Saddam's apparatuses: the military and his intelligence and security services. The war saw no use of WMDs; there was no intervention by Turkey or Iran; Kurdistan's leaders and peshmerga ensured there was no significant ethnic conflict in the Kirkuk region; the oil-fields of Iraq were left intact—most damage to them has occurred through Ba'thist mismanagement and through subsequent insurgent actions. The military dimensions of the invasion and overthrow were therefore close to unqualified successes for their planners. The same could not be said of the occupation, which has been a strategic failure compounded by multiple tactically inept decisions. Since the occupation started the U.S. has had an expeditionary force with a policing mission it cannot fulfill: too small to be an army that quells dissent by sheer weight of numbers; too much of an army to be an effective police service. Wars are won both in formal battles and in their repercussions. In this case the war has yet to establish a peace; an unequal formal war has been replaced by multiple guerrilla and terrorist assaults on the victors in Arab Iraq.

Indeed, occupation policy appeared almost designed to provoke resistance and fragmentation in Arab Iraq, and to disorient Kurdistan. What went wrong? Peter Galbraith's and Karin von Hippel's chapters remain compelling and compatible answers to this question. Insufficient troops (including those with policing capabilities) were deployed in Arab Iraq to win the peace, despite prewar advice from many quarters, including from generals and the State Department-sponsored project on "The Future of Iraq." (The latter initiative, competently organized by area expert David H. Phillips, was trash-canned by the Pentagon as too "academic.") While the friends of Kurdistan, including most of the contributors to this volume, would be critical of many of the suppositions in the Future of Iraq project, it had the merit of being a plan based on considered evidence by careful, informed, and intelligent people. There is no compelling evidence that the Pentagon had a better plan, or even an alternative plan some would say. Defense Secretary Rumsfeld's doctrines on how to fight modern war proved quite effective, but not as recipes for peace. The Pentagon's forte is not state-building, and its senior officials behaved arrogantly, learning little from U.S. interventions in the 1990s.[10] At best they largely prepared for contingencies that did not happen—the impact of WMDs and large-scale refugee movements. It was presumed that Saddam's elite supporters would collapse, but that many institutions, especially the police, would remain intact. The complete loss of policing control and the spree of looting— abetted by Saddam's release of criminals—created a Hobbesian problem of disorder that was widely foreseen and could have been preempted. After some enjoyed brief elation during the looting, the poor planning of the occupation opened the door to a different kind of terrifying life for the inhabitants of Baghdad and the denizens of other Arab Iraqi cities. Instead of a criminal in charge of the state, ordinary criminals had a free run. The rapid dissolution of the Ba'th party and the Iraqi Army, coupled with a failure to take steps to render their leadership structures ineffective or to collect weapons, created significant numbers, among the elite and the rank and file, able and motivated to resist the U.S.-led occupation—and engage in crime. Insufficient troops and police meant that neither internal security nor effective sealing of the borders were achieved—thus aiding spoiling activities across the Syrian, Iranian, and Saudi borders, and inviting an influx of wahhabists. This picture remains true.

The Pentagon's planners appear to have bet all their political investments on outsider Ahmed Chalabi, seemingly in ignorance of his capacity to inspire distrust and to fall out with his own allies, while the CPA failed to build a properly wide and unified base of political support for a new order among Kurds and Shi'a Arabs—the two largest constituencies that had the most to gain from regime-change, that had been the most sustained victims of genocide and expulsion, and that together comprised over four out of five of Iraq's potential citizens. Poor politics and diplomacy were married to poor economics. For all the rash comparisons with Germany and Japan the Pentagon gave no prior deep thought to a Marshall Plan for Iraq. Risibly, the invasion's planners had assumed that the occupation of oil-rich Iraq would quickly become self-financing. Subsequent financial realities led to panicked budgetary requests to Congress, and to delays in organizing vital local expenditures, already confounded by maladministration within the CPA. The economic and political impact of this incompetence was not minor: well-directed expenditures could have consolidated support for regime change within Arab Iraq.

If there ever was ever a coherent post-invasion plan, its executors changed it quickly. Ambassador L. Paul Bremer replaced General Jay Garner. The Office for International Humanitarian Assistance was replaced by the CPA. Bremer was a more authoritative and authoritarian figure, but his improvisations lacked panache. He refused an immediate restoration of sovereignty to Iraq—something which, had Kurdistan been properly protected, might have assisted a more effective political renewal in Arab Iraq. As it was, Bremer's initial plans enabled many Arabs within and outside Iraq to portray America's plans as straightforwardly imperialist, and ensured that those Arab Iraqis and Kurds who worked constructively with the occupation would easily be deemed collaborators. Bremer's planned time-span of occupation, however, rapidly ranged from indeterminate ("as long as it takes" he said), to two years, to one year, with the abolition of the CPA eventually scheduled for June 30, 2004. (Garner by comparison had expected his mission to be over in "three months," which may have been the proximate cause of his recall.) Bremer considered thinking of governing without Iraqis at all, before eventually settling on the formation of an Iraqi Governing Council that had the merit of being broadly descriptively representative but was arguably insufficiently inclusive of potentially significant Shi'a stakeholders. Bremer equivocated as consequentially in another key transitional domain. He was unsure whether to rule out elections for the long term, canvass indirect elections to an interim assembly, or to negotiate with the UN to organize elections before or after the planned departure of the CPA. He ended up apparently supporting all these options, at different times. All this uncertainty itself encouraged anxiety—among Kurds and peaceful Shia such as al-Sistani—and resistance, and bids for power from ambitious contenders such as al-Sadr. This U.S. uncertainty, incoherence and incompetence undermined the one major achievement of Bremer's tenure, the negotiation of the Transitional Administrative Law (O'Leary 2004), the merits—and faults—of which I treated in Chapter 2, and the dumping of which I shall examine in a moment. Although Bremer failed in the high politics of the occupation, he might have been forgiven by historians had he presided over the first decent executive in Iraq. But it was not so. The internal governance of the CPA itself was frequently dreadful. The pathologies of contractors and privatized security personnel are worth books in themselves.[11] The civil and political planning of the U.S. army was not much better: the rapid rotation of the best U.S. officers on the ground was utterly counterproductive, from both a military and a political perspective. To add insult to incompetence, the CPA robbed Kurdistan. The CPA appropriated outstanding UN oil-for-food funds authorized for Kurdistan. Subsequently Kurdistan was allocated considerably less than its (probably underestimated) proportional share of public expenditures—although because it had self-government it was able to boost its local economy.

The CPA, in sum, presided over a chaotic mess in Arab Iraq. While the CPA offered farce, the Pentagon offered tragedy: creating a climate in which torture was practiced by authorized U.S. personnel in Saddam's dungeons in Abu Ghraib—to the shame of decent Americans everywhere. In the end, the CPA's most successful achievement was to leave two days ahead of schedule. The Pentagon's most damaging achievement has been to undermine the painful post-Vietnam reconstruction of the U.S. army's reputation as a non-racist force: it has allowed U.S. troops to be managed in such a way that they are seen as arrogant, ignorant, violent, and incompetent.

Bremer's CPA and the Pentagon should not, of course, be the sole legitimate targets of responsibility for what went wrong. Accountability should extend much higher, to the top. It was hubris for President Bush to organize television shots under a banner declaring "Mission Accomplished" in May 2003, and it was folly one year later to oscillate between determined coercion and appeasement in the treatment of al-Sadr's Mahdi army in Kufa, Najaf, and Baghdad. It was bizarre to decide to be ruthless toward Ba'thists dug inside Faluja, a key base for the organization of suicide-bombings, and then to retreat under media heat, enabling at least one critical journalist to write (in exaggeration), "A year after Bush declared major combat in Iraq over, insurgents have their own capital in Falluja" (Cockburn 2004).[12] As several contributors observe in the main text of our book, the combined failure by the Bush administration to sustain security, to organize an effective, credible and representative interim government, quickly to set in place credible electoral arrangements, or to proselytize on behalf of the Transitional Administrative Law, were bound to jeopardize all its transitional, democratic and federalizing ambitions for Iraq.

Our contributors have not been cynical about these ambitions, although most have been deeply critical about their mal-implementation or non-implementation. No one here has suggested that the invasion was "all about oil," or that Bush, Jr. deposed Saddam to avenge Saddam's assassination attempt on his father, or to demonstrate that he was a tougher man than his father, or to have another successful war to hide economic difficulties at home, to name just some of the favored diagnoses of the roots of the invasion. Such explanations are not empirically convincing. Doubtless it is to the advantage of the U.S. and western capitalism to have in Iraq an alternative source of secure oil supplies to those that come from pumps in Saudi Arabia—the land of wahhabism, and the home of bin Laden and the majority of the 9/11 hijackers. But, had the Bush administration been as driven by ruthless political economy as its self-styled realist or Marxist critics suggest, then after the invasion it was not obvious why it should have settled on a centralized and unified Iraq. To support the formation of a large Kurdistan in control of Kirkuk, and a large Shi'a state in the South would have made greater sense if oil was all that was at stake. Support for Chalabi—and Allawi—and American actions cannot be reduced to petrol supplies or prices. The administration's commitment to a centralized and integrated Iraq—and its incompetence in advancing that objective—strongly suggest it was ideologically motivated to showcase Iraq as the first step in the democratization of the Middle East.[13] Ideology was not the sole factor: the U.S. had to contain fears of regional destabilization, and it has usually supported the territorial integrity of existing states. That ideological vision of democratizing the Middle East was of course astigmatic, indeed myopic, based as it was on fears about Shi'a Islam (as opposed to Sunni wahhabism) that have proven partly self-fulfilling, and on a complete failure to integrate its policies toward Iraq and Palestine in ways that would have enhanced the reception of its dream within the region—and the planet. And that vision, precisely because it was just a vision, rarely translated into effective policy-making to deliver the outcome.

None of our contributors hold a priori convictions about the impossibility of reconciling democracy and Islam. To the contrary, none of us hold that either Muslim Kurds or Muslim Arabs are incapable of democratization. What we all fear is that Kurdistan and Arab Iraq may be on a new collision course, and that Arab Iraq is on route to a protracted civil war in which multiple parties, authoritarian and democrat, Islamist and secular, struggle for ascendancy. Noah Feldman, among others, has provided an eloquent defense of the thesis that Islamic countries can become democratic—that is, democratic and respectful of Islamic values (Feldman 2003), and his views were at least heard within the Bush administration and the CPA. With Feldman we may hope that the argument that Islam and democracy are intrinsically incompatible will one day be regarded in the same way as the now-defunct theses that Catholicism, Confucianism, and Hinduism are intrinsically incompatible with democracy. While Feldman and others quite properly worry about the protection of non-Muslim minorities and women in likely emergent Islamic democracies, he and others are more neglectful of two comparative insights of vital importance for Kurdistan and Iraq, insights that are not sufficiently appreciated. The first insight, from the work of Alfred Stepan, is that Arab-majority countries, controlling for the major variables thought likely to promote democracy, are prima facie more likely to be undemocratic than non-Arab countries. That is, it is Arab Muslim countries, not Muslim countries per se, that are less likely to be democratic than one would predict from their levels of development—indeed non-Arab Muslim majority countries are more likely to be democratic than other countries given their levels of development (Stepan and Robertson 2003). This comparative evidence suggests that there may be an Arab rather than a Muslim problem with democracy—that may owe something to Arab political culture as well as past U.S. foreign policy support for Arab autocracies. It also suggests that Kurdistan may find democratization easier than Arab Iraq, a thought that a current sojourn in both locations tends to encourage. The second comparative insight is this: with the interesting exception of Lebanon, Arab-majority countries have no track-record of recognizing their regimes as pluri-national, and many Muslim-majority countries have or have had similar difficulties (e.g., Turkey, Iran, Pakistan). The most difficult task in Kurdistan and Iraq in the light of preliminary comparative evaluations will be the attainment, not of a democratized regime or sets of regimes, but rather of a liberal and pluri-national federation that is also democratic.

Our contributors' fears about how the Bush administration might manage regime-change have, regrettably, been borne out. In Chapter 2, I showed that the TAL foresaw executive structures (a prime minister and three-person presidential council) that had some prospects of combining power-sharing, proportionality, and legitimacy, but appeared to give too much power to the prime minister. The Kurds, however measured, constitute the second largest collectivity in Iraq: the second largest nationality after Arabs, and the second largest collectivity after Shiʿa Arabs. For these reasons, Kurds expected that one of their number would be either interim prime minister or interim president in the three-person presidential council. In May 2004 U.S. Ambassador Blackwill told them otherwise: the prime minister was to be a Shiʿa Arab, the president a Sunni Arab (Galbraith 2004). The message and the messenger were regarded as spectacular hypocrisy: the CPA had lectured Kurds on how Iraq was to be a non-ethnic federation, on how all were to be just Iraqis, but here they were instructing Kurds that only Arabs could hold the symbolic and substantive positions in the interim government. This episode led to an official complaint from Kurdistan's two largest parties, and a threat to withdraw completely from the Baghdad government. This was the first time that exit from Baghdad has been canvassed in this conjuncture by Kurds. It may be a portent of things to come. The U.S. sought to pacify Kurdistan by supporting the appointment of one Kurdish deputy president and by creating a deputy prime minister without portfolio—a role that had not been envisaged in the TAL. The episode was symptomatic of American insensitivities and part of a wider failure to organize an institutionally rooted interim government.

Westerners and Arabs who opposed the war against Saddam generally regard the new interim government as stooges, collaborators, or as the *New Left Review* has put it members of "Vichy on the Tigris."[14] A typical academic summation of this orthodoxy derides "a supposedly sovereign interim government," treats the transfer of sovereignty as "another election ploy" by the Bush administration, and accuses the Americans and the interim government of preparing "a show trial in Baghdad" of Saddam (Byers 2004). When Western academic specialists in international law are keener to look out for Saddam's human rights than constructively to support the new government of Iraq, we can at least be certain that the occupation's handover to an interim government has not succeeded with non-American public intellectuals. It has also failed to win support with European public opinion.

The occupation the UN eventually ratified did not go well because the administration never seemed to resolve whether it was intent simply on removing Saddam and organizing a quick exit before the U.S. elections of November 2004, or on the comprehensive democratic reconstruction of Iraq, which requires a careful and judicious long-haul intervention, part of a wider proclaimed program to facilitate the democratization of the Middle East. The resultant confusion compromised both goals: Iraq got a Rumwolf, half of Rumsfeld, and half of Wolfowitz, which we may define as half-baked military ideas in conjunction with half-baked constitutional ideas.

No greater evidence of confusion can be found in how President Bush's administration handled the Transitional Administrative Law. The short version of the story is this: The CPA, the U.S. and its UK allies failed to have the Transitional Administrative Law rendered valid during the restoration of sovereignty to Iraq in June 2004. In doing so, they have created a constitutional "black-hole." The United Nations—at the request of the Coalition led by two of its Security Council members, the U.S. and the UK—had recognized the occupation of Iraq in 2003. Under international law occupation authorities are denied such sovereign capacities as the right to make binding constitutions or laws or to cede territory because these actions amount to conquest or the denial of the right of self-determination. For the TAL (and all other CPA legislation) to remain valid after the termination of the CPA's occupation in June 2004 therefore required one of two courses of action: either for the United Nations to recognize the TAL, while restoring Iraq's sovereignty, or for the new interim government to recognize the TAL (and the CPA laws). The Bush administration chose neither to petition the United Nations (perhaps for fear of being rebuffed), nor to organize an interim government that would legislate the enactment of the TAL as its first task. Iraq therefore presently lacks a formal interim constitution, and in consequence lacks agreed ground rules for the negotiation and ratification of the permanent constitution. One of the side effects is to render currently redundant some of the best-prospect analyses in Chapters 2 and 4, and, of course, the text of Appendix 2 of our volume.

Why did the Bush administration fail to protect the TAL? Peter Galbraith has suggested two explanations, which are, regrettably, compatible. One focuses on legal incompetence: "It appears that Bremer never realized that his decrees would not legally outlast the occupation. It was a rookie's mistake caused . . . by the lack of expertise on the part of his staff . . . [who] apparently neglected to consult an international lawyer" (Galbraith 2004). The second explanation focuses on a *realpolitik* decision to defer to majoritarian and anti-federal opinions among Arab Iraqis, especially Shi'a Arabs led by Ayatollah al-Sistani, who, as we saw (in the chapters by O'Leary, Eklund, O'Leary and Williams, Stansfield, and Galbraith), has consistently strongly opposed the federal and ratification proposals that Kurdistan successfully sought to embed in the TAL.

The TAL is not, however, completely dead. It leads a virtual and shadowy afterlife. That is because the new prime minister of the interim government, Iyad Allawi, promised Kurdistan's leaders and others that he would apply the TAL during his office. He refused, however, to legislate the TAL, and therefore it is not law, and he is not bound by it. It follows that the Iraqi Assembly that is scheduled to be elected in January 2005 is not officially bound to make any permanent constitution by the terms of the TAL. Article 61 of the TAL, to which we paid so much attention in Chapters 2 and 4, is not legally operative. Of course, what is sauce for the goose is also sauce for the gander. If Allawi, Iraq's Arab leaders, and the U.S. are not bound to support the TAL, then neither are Kurdistan's leaders—who prop up Allawi's government with key ministers, officials and combat-hardened and capable peshmerga. Kurdistan is politically likely to apply those provisions of the TAL which it approves, and to ignore those which it never sought or are inconvenient. Kurdistan may sensibly ask both U.S. presidential candidates for assurances that the U.S. will stand by the fair demand, one that the U.S. accepted in the TAL, that the people of Kurdistan should have the right to endorse or reject any permanent constitution that is negotiated in an Iraq-wide assembly. In my view, Kurdistan's leaders should also consider holding a simultaneous referendum in January mandating their leaders to consult with their citizens, and with the Kurdistan

National Assembly, before ratifying any draft permanent constitution for Iraq. In that way Kurdistan would affirm its principled negotiating position—and, incidentally, restore the relevance of the best-prospects analysis in Chapters 2 and 4. Kurdistan's optimal strategy might be to announce that it will compete in the elections scheduled for January 2005—or those held at a later date—but that its members will not sit in Baghdad unless the Assembly agrees that the people of Kurdistan and the Kurdistan National Assembly have the separate right to ratify the permanent constitution. Exit from Baghdad—not the same as formal secession—should be considered as a principled tactic.

The failure of the Bush administration to support the TAL may one day be regarded as the third great betrayal of the Kurds by American presidents, one that will rank alongside those of President Ford in 1975 and President Bush, Sr. in 1991.[15] But for now Kurdistan's geostrategic position is much better than on the occasion of these first two betrayals—as several of our contributors have noted, notably Michael Gunter in his appraisal of Turkey. By comparison with 1975 and 1991 Kurdistan is much better institutionalized and better able to defend itself militarily and politically against any resurgent rebuilders of Arab Iraq. It may also be better able to persuade any American administration that it is not in its political interests to allow secular Kurdistan to be coercively reintegrated into Iraq according to the majoritarian diktats of Shi‘a Ayatollahs—or for that matter by minoritarian Wahhabist authoritarians. But Kurdistan is vulnerable to an American withdrawal, either by the incumbent President if he cuts his losses, or by his successor, if driven there by a full shift in U.S. public opinion that cannot be ruled out. And Kurdistan has been rendered vulnerable to Islamist as well as Arabist reaction. In beheading three Kurds in September 2004, the Army of Ansar al-Sunna, another nom de guerre for Ansar al-Islam, al Qaida's Kurdish ally, complained that Kurdistan's parties are in alliance with Crusaders and Jews. The deployment of peshmerga outside Kurdistan in support of the CPA and the interim government has deepened antagonisms between some Arabs and Kurds. Some of the European and American governments and publics that opposed the unilateral U.S. intervention may sympathize with Kurdistan, but sympathy may not be of much use in future battlefields. The lack of questions I receive about Kurdistan, as opposed to Iraq, in the U.S. and the UK and elsewhere in Europe, not only suggests to me the higher salience that accrues to violence in global public opinion and comment. It also registers the weakness of the international public opinion that Kurdistan can draw upon. Kurds are no longer Saddam's victims; they are in danger of being dismissed as Bush's puppets.

The constitutional black hole created by the abandonment of the TAL creates truly urgent incentives for Kurds that have to be positively managed to control now more palpable threats. It makes imperative sense for the KDP and the PUK to proceed as soon as possible to achieve a unified government throughout Kurdistan—a matter on which I dissent from the well-argued position of Gareth Stansfield in this volume. The decision in KRG (Sulaimania) not to replace Barham Salih, its most recent prime minister, who is now serving as the deputy prime minister of Iraq, is suggestive. It makes more likely the unification of the KRGs under Nechirvan Barzani, currently the prime minister of KRG (Erbil). Fulfilling this objective will mightily enhance Kurdistan's future negotiating power, and spell out clearly to Arab Iraq the Kurds' determination that Kurdistan be properly recognized for what it is—the settled will of Kurdistan's people. In my view, it would also be wise for Kurdistan to draft its own fresh domestic constitution as part of its own reconstruction. Such constitutional renewal should take an open, public and deliberative form, involving the National Assembly, and a special constitutional forum, but only after the full unification of the KRGs.

So my second uneasy answer is that the U.S.-led Coalition could have done everything better, especially in security, economic, and institutional planning. The plan of attack, bereft of a wider UN-authorized alliance, has left the U.S. paying practically the full costs of the war, with small change contributed by the UK, Poland, and Australia. The plan of attack lacked a plan for peace, order, and good government. Order needed to be established with overwhelming numbers (the Powell doctrine applied to post-conflicts). Interim constitutional renewal should have been more openly made rather than driven in secret by Ambassador Bremer. Effective regime-changes are neither cheap nor easy. The Coalition missed its opening political moments of opportunity, failed to build properly on the goodwill especially available among Kurds and Shi'a Arabs to create a robust governing coalition, and allowed crushed pockets of resistance to reform. Counterinsurgency policy was not coherently married to constitutional rebuilding and political reconstruction, and U.S. foreign policy in the rest of the Middle East remains an easy target for critics within and outside the Arab world.

Answer 3. All is not yet lost; it is just far, far more difficult than it need have been.

The interim government of Iraq is not in fact comprised of mere stooges. The new prime minister, Iyad Allawi, a Shi'a and a former Ba'thist, did work for MI6 and the CIA against Saddam, but he was not the Pentagon's or Ambassador Bremer's or President Bush's first choice—which was originally Ahmad Chalabi. The president, Ghazi al-Yawar, was chosen by a critical alliance of

Kurds and Shi'a Arabs on the Governing Council, against Bremer's express preference for Adnan Pachachi—who had been Bremer's key vehicle for Sunni Arab interests during the negotiation of the TAL. Allawi appears to be pursuing a three-pronged strategy. First, he has sought to win the confidence of the Kurds after they threatened to withdraw from the Baghdad government by saying that he would apply the TAL. Second, he has sought to offer amnesty to those who did not surrender after the war and continued to fight the coalition. The strategy is soft before tough love: those who reject amnesty and political inclusion will face the full deployment of local and coalition forces under martial law. It seems clear that he would like to organize, with U.S. oversight, a drive to clear all sites of organized resistance to the interim government in Arab Iraq before elections are held in January, or after. Third, he is trying to ensure that he projects a new, independent Iraqi government, with an Arab and Kurdish face, and with a strongly Shi'a face in Arab Iraq.

Allawi's difficulties are obvious, and have been highlighted in our contributors' essays. Kurds minimally want to avoid the recentralization of Iraq. Many Shi'a Arabs want a centralized majoritarian democracy—and some want it to be theocratic for good measure. They are mostly democrats, but mostly illiberal democrats. It is difficult for Allawi to compromise with Kurdistan without losing Shi'a Arab support. It is difficult for Kurdistan to support Allawi without antagonizing Allawi's Arab rivals who are jockeying for future positions. Many Sunni Arabs still hanker after a neo-Ba'thist restoration; others are Islamists. Sunni Arab and Shi'a Arab liberal democrats, brave secular and human rights activists, male and female, are out-gunned, out-shouted, and drowned out in the rage that passes for news on Al-Jazeera and its local imitators. Allawi is dependent, for now, on coalition forces, and on a borrowed regiment from Kurdistan, which is the sole reliable element of the army of the interim government that is "Iraqi." He has inherited a post-totalitarian rump state and some rapidly dumped modular American institutions and practices, as well as the ill will of Islamists, especially wahhabists. The history of Iraq does not inspire facile optimism in his future. Indeed, many are predicting that Iraq will become a failed state, especially in Arab Iraq—Kurdistan is not a failed entity. It is already an established trope that the Bush administration has repeated, albeit faster, many of the errors made by the British in their intervention in Mesopotamia and Kurdistan during and after World War 1 (Dodge 2003; Keay 2003).

Some of these analogies are overdrawn and too deterministic. I may be wrong, but I do not yet see a unified resistance to the new government. Rather, most signs point to loose sets of armed networks of convenience, and the tactics of the resistance-organizers, especially the use of suicide-bombers, are no longer overtly, or sneakily, locally regarded as heroic, but rather are seen as the actions of fanatics as willing to smash infrastructure projects that help Muslims as they are to attack Christian churches. Even the apparent effectiveness of the attacks on U.S. forces can be exaggerated. On an annualized per capita basis, U.S. military war dead are fewer than the casualties sustained by the British Army at the hands of the IRA in Northern Ireland in 1972.[16] But that said, no one should underestimate the intensity of the significance of the current violence, or the capacity of the multiple networks that have emerged to sustain decades of vigorous paramilitary campaigning. There are currently multiple open and undeclared bids for power in Arab Iraq. And if that power struggle cannot be institutionalized democratically, protracted violence must be expected—leading to the emergence of a new authoritarian coalition throughout Arab Iraq, or of a three-state solution through armed conflict, or of a collapsed set of mini-regimes run by local warlords—Somalia with oil.

It is a mistake, of course, to read the violence after the transfer of sovereignty as mere chaos, banditry, and criminal lawlessness. There is some of all of that, especially of criminal violence in Baghdad. But there is also a political logic. The source of most of the violence, which does not openly speak its cause for obvious reasons, is the Sunni Arab minority, which lost power when Saddam's Ba'thists were toppled. It is mostly from this community, and what we might call a Sunni Arab International, that well-organized violence has been orchestrated: suicide-bombs against Kurdistan's two largest parties, the Shi'a holy shrines at Karbala, Christian churches, and attacks against the coalition forces, the new police, and the Governing Council and its successor, the interim government. This is a multi-headed insurrection against loss of dominance, one that cannot endorse democracy because that will ratify the Sunni Arabs' loss of power. The violence of al-Sadr's Mahdi army is the exception that proves the rule. Unlike his Sunni Arab counterparts al-Sadr can contemplate success through both bombs and the ballot box. Most Shi'a Arabs see no need for violence because they will be the primary stakeholders, both in the interim government and after free elections (which they support). If post-occupation Iraq works, it will be the first predominantly Arab state in which Sunni Arabs have been deposed from dominance since colonial times, which helps explains why Sunni al-Qaida wahhabists are in tactical alliance with ex-Ba'thists, and in undeclared war against Shi'a Arabs, Kurds, and the smaller minorities.

The security situation bequeathed by the CPA is widely agreed to be "sub-optimal," although appraisals of why this is so vary widely. Some commentators stress the failure to establish a self-standing Iraqi army and police service with Iraq-wide scope—seemingly oblivious to the fact that Kurdistan's people would regard a military and police with such scope as a genocidal hazard to be avoided at all costs. The U.S. tried to treat Kurdistan's peshmerga as another militia, equivalent to the party militias in Arab Iraq. The KRGs were asked to reconstitute the peshmerga as Mountain Guards, to which they were agreeable—but advised the American sent to negotiate the matter that the Kurdish translation for the said service would be "peshmerga." Given the removal of the thin constitutional security of the TAL, and with signs that America's political class is looking for the exit, be it short- or long-term, Kurdistan will keep its lawfully constituted army for the immediate future, and insist on its bottom-line negotiating preferences spelled out in Peter Galbraith's second chapter, and Appendix 1.

No one, of course, ever knows the future with certainty: good judgments are all that is possible. We encouraged our contributors to consider possible futures—involving both empirical predictions and normative prescriptions. Looking into the next decade one can see two basic scenarios for the Kurdistan of Iraq emerging, each with multiple variations. The first, the most benign, would see a unified Kurdistan extract the permanent recognition of the extensive autonomy it seeks. Kurdistan would be either a "federacy" in a semi-sovereign association with an otherwise centralized Arab Iraq, or a member-unit of a democratic pluralist federation of Iraq which is pluri-national, decentralized and consensual—and based on three, four, or five regions. For that to happen, there must be more signs that significant Shi'a players will consider such a design—the fact that some want to aggregate some southern governorates may point in this direction. The elections will have to return both Kurdish and Arab parties willing to renew Iraq in this manner. But the benign scenario, and its variants, presently looks much less likely, given the CPA and the Pentagon's mismanagement of the occupation, and the current rhetoric of some potential Shi'a and Sunni Arab contenders for power. The difficulties attendant upon making variants of the benign scenario have been spelled out by most of our contributors. Its realization should not be excluded, but it will need very constructive diplomacy and campaigning to make it emerge. Kurdistan must therefore work for the best and prepare for the worst.

The second scenario, by contrast, will involve the official break-up of Iraq. The ways in which this grim scenario might unfold are manifold. The least likely, I think, is a deliberate preemptive decision by Kurdistan to secede and declare itself independent. The existence of disputed territories and the possibility of neither American nor Turkish recognition strongly tempers this disposition—as does the possibility of a Turkish invasion. But withdrawal from participation in a Baghdad government, and the management of an undeclared de facto independence, as a tactical or strategic move certainly cannot be excluded, although it will have attendant costs. The more likely version of the malign scenario will involve Kurdistan playing the role of the best-standing survivor as Arab Iraq implodes and becomes a collapsed rather than a failed state. In the optimal variant Kurdistan will become the surviving independent unit of Iraq around which the U.S. will attach its diminished credibility, and which Turkey will decide to tolerate—partly because of U.S. pressure, partly because of its European Union ambitions and partly because some Turks may realize the benefits of seeing another secular parliamentary democracy emerging in their neighborhood. In the chaos of all versions of the malign scenario, difficult decisions will have to be taken as regards Kirkuk and the disputed territories. Some variants of the malign scenario could be catastrophic for Kurdistan—involving large-scale ethnic and confessional expulsions in mixed and disputed areas, the destabilization of Kurdistan as Arab Iraq implodes, the U.S. exiting ignominiously in a further betrayal of its commitments, and the regional powers invading Iraq or picking factions to support war by proxy. Foreknowledge of these potential catastrophes has tempered Kurdistan's collective urge to be free. Its leaders have been most responsible in trying to rebuild Baghdad rather than seizing the moment to depart.

The break-up of Iraq is on the agenda—which is not to say that it will happen. Iraq has no analogous cultural unity to Japan or Germany, which were reassembled under American auspices in the late 1940s. Indeed, it has been the dominant motif of our contributors that Iraq is not—and cannot be regarded as a nation. If it is to work as a state, as opposed to a nation, it must be as a pluri-national federation—which is not the advice that echoed within the White House, or that came from the Future of Iraq project that the Pentagon jettisoned or from among the Arabist scholars of the Middle East. Iraq is deeply diverse: Kurds and Arabs comprise different nations; Sunni and Shi'a Muslims are often as divided as Protestants and Catholics in early modern Europe; and in the territories in which they are concentrated the big three communities encompass small pockets of other religious and linguistic minorities (e.g., Chaldeans, Assyrians, Armenians, Turkomen, and Yezidis). The CPA's slogan that all should be "just Iraqis" was facile, inappropriate, and widely rejected.

A federation, which may later earn the shared respect of its citizens, may yet be built, and to avoid catastrophe needs to be built. If Iraq is to be rebuilt it needs to be rebuilt as a democracy. It needs to be a secular state at the federal level (or a religiously pluralist and tolerant state at the federal level), even if some of its regions may opt for an established religion. It needs to be a federation that treats women as equals and not as chattels. These are very tall orders, and will be extraordinarily difficult to deliver both in the negotiation of the permanent constitution and on the ground as institutionalized facts. It may yet be that a modus vivendi can be reached in which divergent public approaches to religion, morality, and regional relations apply in a three- or five-region federation. But as of now this vista describes aspirations and perhaps dreams. Suffice it to emphasize here that the rebuilding of Iraq cannot be engineered, either by insiders or foreigners, around the illusion that it has been, is, or can be one nation. The recognition of Kurdistan and its just constitutional treatment by Arab Iraq will be the decisive test of whether there can be a federal democratic Iraq. Kurdistan has disproved the thesis that people of predominantly Muslim beliefs cannot become democratic, secular, or tolerant of other nationalities and other ethnic, religious, and linguistic communities, and it can continue to do so, and deepen its democratization. But that will be possible only if it is given sufficient freedom to demonstrate its potential—by the rest of Iraq, by Iraq's neighbors, and by the great powers. U.S. policy under President Bush or a President Kerry must absorb the full implications of this lesson if Iraq is not to be added to the list of "failed" and "collapsed" states. Whether Arab Iraq's major politicians and publics can concur on a generous constitutional rapprochement with Kurdistan in 2005, and on their own constitutional governance, is not something my co-authors or I can presume to know. But we agree that the alternatives are grim.

Notes

My thanks to Peter Galbraith, Lina Hartocollis, Sam Hughes, John McGarry, Jack H. Nagel, and Khaled Salih.

Epigraph citations: Voltaire (1994: 91); Bierce (1993); Todd (2004: 206).

1. "Arab Iraq" is my short-hand expression for Arab-dominated Iraq outside of Kurdistan. I use the term to avoid using the "rest of Iraq," which might imply Kurdistan is an official part of Iraq—a matter that remains to be negotiated in a permanent constitution. Of course, non-Arabs, including Kurds and Turkomen, live in Arab Iraq, but Arab Iraq is predominantly Arab, by both ethnicity and language.

2. Disarray is, I think, a far more accurate portrait of what has happened than the claim of some Arabs and some of the western left, including its leading Pakistani diasporan (Ali 2004), that a recolonization of Iraq was, or is, underway.

3. The *New Left Review*, the leading English-language periodical of the Left, in which I am proud to have been published in the past, has gone to the lengths of comparing Iraq's interim government to France's Vichy regime (Watkins 2004). The *NLR* Editorial later undercuts its own comparison when it states that "the puppet government in Baghdad today enjoys less autonomy than Pétain's regime in Vichy; in that respect it is closer to Quisling's in Oslo" (Watkins 2004, 13). But let us pause at Vichy, and ignore Norway. Are we to understand from the *NLR* that the U.S.-led Coalition is

a Nazi-led axis? That Saddam's Ba'thist Republic resembled the French Third Republic? That al-Sadr's Mahdi Army and Ba'thists and Wahhabists are analogous to the Free French and the French Resistance, with local equivalents of Jean-Paul Sartre, Albert Camus, and Samuel Beckett working for their cause? That "the resistance" in Arab Iraq is the defender of minorities whom the "puppet" regime of the occupiers plans to assist in extermination programs? I shall avoid further questions. The analogy is shameful, and stupefying. But the article is symptomatic of a wider trend among some of the European left—which I trust is temporary. Its careless extremism in historical allusion suggests that "anti-Americanism" has become primary in rhetoric, displacing focused attention on matters that should be central to the agenda of any self-respecting democratic left, namely, the status of national and ethnic minorities, the secular interests of religious and irreligious minorities, and the status of women. The *NLR* Editorial endorses a resistance, which is not, contrary to its claims, nationally unified. And, if it were ever to become unified, it would be under an Arabist program, with a racist agenda for Kurds and an Islamist one for non-Muslims and Muslims. The *NLR* condemns Kurds for choosing the wrong partners—as if they had any better strategic options for secular and democratic partners than the U.S.—and asserts that "the Kurdish leadership has installed a network of Israeli intelligence agents and hit squads" (14). It is the *NLR* that has endorsed the wrong partners—providing written support for some of the worst political dispositions in current Arab and Muslim cultures because they are supposedly anti-imperialist; and making unsubstantiated claims on what the Kurdish leadership has done. The *NLR* article concludes that "the Iraqi *maquis* deserve full support in fighting to drive [the U.S.-led forces] out." In times past the word "critical" might have been inserted before "support," but critical thinking currently gives way to uncritical anti-Americanism.

4. Liberal French intellectual Emmanuel Todd speaks for many, and shows little of the hysteria of the *New Left Review* editorial rebuked in the note above: "When they denounce the evil ones, these people are not talking about rogue states and terrorists, they are talking about themselves. They have after all turned the 9/11 tragedy into an opportunity for external aggression; they have lied to the world, obviously with a certain amount of relish. . . . We must therefore consider the possibility that they are in fact "evil" (Todd 2004, 209).

5. This was a matter on which I worked personally. Fortunately, the UN Electoral Assistance Division regarded Kurdistan's proposals as far more practical than the much less feasible ideas articulated by the CPA's advisors. The merits of a PR party-list system in Iraq as a whole are as follows:

(1) It is relatively easy to administer, and for first-time voters to understand, and has previously been used in Kurdistan, the sole part of Iraq to have had any large-scale free election.
(2) It enables all voters, including internally displaced persons, to vote wherever they are in Iraq—and makes less controversial the potential impact of additional voters in exile;
(3) It is appropriate for the election of a constitutional convention—which should be free to choose other electoral systems for the future governments of Iraq.
(4) It avoids the potential clash of electoral districts and jurisdictions created by the TAL's recognition of both Kurdistan and the governorates—the CPA's advisors

had unwisely proposed electoral districts that would have cut across Kurdistan's current boundaries (and would have been utterly inconsistent with Kurdistan's federal regional status in the TAL).

(5) It lessens the potential difficulties in polling in disputed territories such as Kirkuk.

(6) It makes it easy both to ensure the representation of small nationalities and to organize the party law so that a significant quota of women are elected from each party-list.

(7) It will help avoid artificially boosting new parties in Arab Iraq that might have done better in smaller constituency-based elections.

6. I paraphrase from W. H. Auden, *Selected Poems*, ed. Edward Mendelson (London: Faber and Faber, 1979), 17.

7. For a thorough review of the failures of President Reagan and President Bush, Sr. to respond to the genocide against Kurds in the 1980s, see the salutary account of Samantha Power (Power 2002, 171–246). She shows the extent to which U.S. support for Iraq in the Iran-Iraq War led the White House to deny or remain indifferent toward evidence of genocide against Kurds, both before and after the use of chemical weapons, and describes the efforts of Senator Claiborne Pell and his foreign policy aide Peter Galbraith to pass a "Prevention of Genocide Act."

8. See also a powerful and lucid article in *Foreign Affairs* (Lopez and Cortright 2004). The authors go too far in claiming that "smart sanctions" had destroyed Saddam's war machine (97), and are too uncritical of the UN "oil for food program" in Arab Iraq.

9. He made the same argument in his book (Pollack 2002), and was much more nuanced and detailed than the predictable neo-conservative pro-war book (Kaplan and Kristol 2003). Pollack, unlike neo-conservatives and Pentagon officials, was innocent of bad counsel on post-occupation planning: he argued for a much larger troop deployment to ensure security, and for a principled "reconstruction" rather than a "pragmatic" approach to "Rebuilding Iraq" (387–424). (A calmly worded review of differences among American conservatives on the war can be found in an English political science journal: see Durham 2004.)

10. According to Bob Woodward, Colin Powell thought it "logical" that the planning authority for post-Saddam Iraq should be Defense rather than State: "It didn't cross his mind that this was out of the ordinary. It was exactly what had happened after World War II in Germany" (Woodward 2004, 282). Powell may have been thinking of scale of population; but it would have been more "logical" to deploy Arab and Kurdish expertise from State—and expertise on the multinational and multiethnic Balkans and Bosnia. Woodward separately records General Franks's assumptions of what was required for an effective war on Saddam: Number 8 was that "The Department of State would promote creation of a broad-based, credible provisional government as had been done in Afghanistan. . . . State would have to engage the United Nations or other countries to do this. The military did not do nation building very well, Franks said" (2004, 62).

11. Peter Galbraith has recently documented scathing criticism of the CPA's recruitment of its staff—which may account for the organization's incompetence in advice on matters of constitutional and international law, organizing public expenditures, and in putting together effective health care programs (Galbraith 2004).

12. The notion of a "capital" implies Iraqi nationalist unity in the resistance, which is, mildly put, a premature judgment. Mostly Sunni Baʿthists and al-Sadr's Shiʿa militia—partially sponsored by Iranian sources, are not natural bedfellows.

13. One account of one source of ideology within the Bush administration, the Straussian cult, may be found in the writings of Anne Norton, my colleague at the University of Pennsylvania (Norton 2004). She demonstrates that the Straussians within the Bush administration are neither fully faithful to Leo Strauss's philosophy nor informed about non-Christian philosophical traditions, and makes the insightful suggestion that "We have licensed anti-Semitism at home, and funded it abroad, on the condition that it take the Arab rather than the Jew as its target" (215).

14. See note 3 above.

15. Some would argue that George W. Bush would be the fourth American president to betray the Kurds if President Wilson is included among those whose commitments have been dishonored.

16. Northern Ireland's population of approximately 1.5 million is approximately 16 times less than Iraq's estimated population of 24 million. The Northern Irish Catholic population of over 700,000 is about 1/27 of the population of Arab Iraq. To be as effective as republican paramilitaries were against UK troops in 1972—when they killed 108 soldiers, Arab Iraqi opponents of the U.S. army need to kill 1,708 troops in one year if Iraq as a whole is treated as the unit of analysis, or 1,916 troops in one year if Arab Iraq is the unit of analysis.

References

Ali, Tariq. 2004. *Bush in Babylon: The Recolonization of Iraq.* London: Verso.
Bierce, Ambrose. 1993. *The Devil's Dictionary, Unabridged.* Mineola, N.Y.: Dover.
Blix, Hans. 2004. *Disarming Iraq.* New York: Pantheon.
Byers, Michael. 2004. "Alleged War Criminals." *London Review of Books,* 22 July, 30–31.
Brookings Institution. 2004. Iraq Index: Tracking Variables of Reconstruction & Security in Post-Saddam Iraq. Iraq Index Washington D.C.: The Brookings Institution. <www.brookings.edu/iraqindex>
Cockburn, Patrick. 2004. "Diary." *London Review of Books,* July 22, 34–35.
Dershowitz, Alan M. 2002. *Why Terrorism Works: Understanding the Threat, Responding to the Challenge.* New Haven, Conn.: Yale University Press.
Dodge, Toby. 2003. *Inventing Iraq: The Failure of Nation Building and a History Denied.* New York: Columbia University Press.
Durham, Martin. 2004. "The American Right and The Iraq War." *Political Quarterly* 75 (3): 257–65.
Feldman, Noah. 2003. *After Jihad: America and the Struggle for Islamic Democracy.* New York: Farrar, Straus and Giroux.
Galbraith, Peter W. 2004. "Iraq: The Bungled Transition." *New York Review of Books,* September 13. www.nybooks.com
Iraq Body Count. 2004. Available from www.iraqbodycount.net. (cited September 14).
Johnson, Chalmers. 2001. *Blowback: The Costs and Consequences of American Empire.* New York: Owl Books.

Jones, LTG Anthony R. and MG George R Fay. 2004. *AR 15–6 Investigation of the Abu Ghraib Prison and 205th Military Intelligence Brigade. The Fay Report.* Washington D.C.

Kaplan, Lawrence F. and William Kristol. 2003. *The War over Iraq: Saddam's Tyranny and America's Mission.* San Francisco: Encounter Books.

Keay, John. 2003. *Sowing the Wind: Seeds of Conflict in the Middle East.* New York: W.W. Norton.

Lopez, George A. and David Cortright. 2004. "Containing Iraq: Sanctions Worked." *Foreign Affairs* 83 (4): 90–103.

National Commission on Terrorist Attacks on the United States. 2004. *The 9/11 Commission Report: Final Report of the National Commission on Terrorist Attacks upon the United States, Authorized Edition.* The 9/11 Commission Report New York: W.W. Norton: pp. 567.

Norton, Anne. 2004. *Leo Strauss and the Politics of American Empire.* New Haven, Conn.: Yale University Press.

O'Leary, Brendan. 2004a. The Transitional Administrative Law, March 17 2004. Reported in *Khebat*, 8 April, p. 4, at Aweza Club, Hewler, Kurdistan, organized by Khattzeem,

———. 2004b. "Two Cheers for the Transitional Law of Iraq." *Pennsylvania Gazette* (May-June). <www.upenn.edu/gazette/0504/0504gaz09.html>

Pollack, Kenneth M. 2002. *The Threatening Storm: The Case for Invading Iraq.* New York: Random House.

———. 2004. "Spies, Lies and Weapons: What Went Wrong." *Atlantic Monthly* (January/February).

Power, Samantha. 2002. "Iraq: Human Rights and Chemical Weapons Use Aside." In Power, *"A Problem from Hell": America and the Age of Genocide.* New York: Basic Books. 171–46.

Schlesinger, James R, Harold Brown, Tillie K. Fowler, and Charles A. Horner. 2004. *Final Report of the Independent Panel to Review DoD Detention Operations.* The Schlesinger Report. Washington, D.C.

Stepan, Alfred and Graeme B. Robertson. 2003. "An 'Arab' More Than 'Muslim' Democracy Gap." *Journal of Democracy* 14 (3)(July): 30–44.

Taguba, Antonio M. 2004. *Article 15–6 Investigation of The 800th Military Police Brigade (Secret/No Foreign Dissemination).* The Taguba Report. Washington D.C.: Department of Defense. http://news.findlaw.com/hdocs/docs/iraq/tagubarpt.html

Todd, Emmanuel. 2004. *After the Empire: The Breakdown of the American Order.* Trans. C. J. Delogu. London: Constable.

Voltaire. 1994. "First Conversation. On Hobbes, Grotius and Montesquieu. In The A B C, translated from the English by Mr Huet." In *Political Writings.* Cambridge: Cambridge University Press. 87–100.

Watkins, Susan. 2004. "Editorial: Vichy on the Tigris." *New Left Review* 28 (July-August): 5–17.

Woodward, Bob. 2004. *Plan of Attack.* New York: Simon and Schuster.

Appendix 1
Kurdistan's Constitutional Proposal

Editors' Note. The text below, also known as "The Kurdistan Chapter," was submitted on 13 February 2004, for proposed incorporation into the Transitional Administrative Law of Iraq then under discussion. It was submitted by the Speaker of the Kurdistan National Assembly, Dr. Shaways, with the endorsement of both KRG executives and Kurdistan's two largest political parties.

Article 1: Continuity of the Kurdistan Region

Section 1: *The Kurdistan Regional Government:*—The Kurdistan Region is a selfgoverning egion, with its own laws and government. The Government of the Kurdistan Region includes the Kurdistan National Assembly, the Council of Ministers, and the Kurdistan Judiciary.

Section 2: *Territory of the Kurdistan Region:*—For the purposes of this Transitional Law, the Kurdistan Region consists of those territories in the governorates of Ninevah, Dohuk, Erbil, Kirkuk, Sulaimaniya, and Diyala that were administered by the Kurdistan Regional Government on March 19, 2003 and is the territory within Iraq that is north and west of the former cease-fire line ("Green Line") as it existed on March 18, 2003.

Section 3: *Continuation of Law:*—Except as otherwise provided in this law, all laws in force in the Kurdistan Region as of the effective date of this Transitional Law shall continue in force. Except as related to matters within the exclusive competence of the Provisional Government of Iraq, the Kurdistan National Assembly shall enact all laws in force in the Kurdistan Region. On the territory of the Kurdistan Region, law enacted by the Kurdistan National Assembly shall be supreme.

Article 2: The Iraqi Kurdistan National Guard; Security of the Kurdistan Region

Section 1: *Establishment of Iraqi Kurdistan National Guard*:—The Kurdistan National Assembly shall raise, regulate, recruit, and officer an Iraqi Kurdistan National Guard, and shall appoint its Commanding Officer. The Iraqi Kurdistan National Guard shall be a component of the Armed Forces of Iraq and under the command of the lawful civilian authorities of Iraq provided:

(1) The Iraqi Kurdistan National Guard may be deployed outside the boundaries of the Kurdistan Region only at the request of the lawful civilian authorities of the Provisional Government of Iraq and only after the Kurdistan National Assembly has authorized such a deployment, provided further that the Kurdistan National Assembly may restrict the deployment of the Iraqi Kurdistan National Guard outside the boundaries of the Kurdistan Region to a specific location and for a specified period of time;
(2) No weapons shall be removed from the possession and control of the Iraqi Kurdistan National Guard without the consent of the Kurdistan National Assembly; and
(3) The Provisional Government of Iraq is democratic and operating pursuant to all provisions of this Transitional Law.

Section 2: *Transition to Iraqi Kurdistan National Guard*:—Within a reasonable period of time after enactment of this Transitional Law, the Kurdistan National Assembly shall authorize the formation of the Iraqi Kurdistan National Guard. Peshmerga units shall be demobilized and all armaments (except for personal weapons) shall be transferred to the Iraqi Kurdistan National Guard.

Section 3: *Recognition of Peshmerga Contribution to National Liberation*:—The Kurdistan National Assembly and the Provisional Government of Iraq shall honor, through the striking of a medal or other appropriate means, the contribution the Peshmerga made to the liberation of Iraq.

Section 4: *Composition of Iraqi Kurdistan National Guard*:—The Iraqi Kurdistan National Guard shall be representative of all the peoples of the Kurdistan Region, including Kurds, Turcomans, Assyrians, Chaldeans, and Arabs.

Section 5: *Non-deployment of other Iraqi Armed Forces to Kurdistan*:—Except for the Iraqi Kurdistan National Guard established by this Article, the Armed

Forces of Iraq shall not enter the territory of the Kurdistan Region without the consent of the Kurdistan National Assembly. The Kurdistan National Assembly may confine the presence of any Iraqi Armed Forces to specified places within the Kurdistan Region and may limit the numbers and duration of any presence by Iraqi Armed Forces on the territory of the Kurdistan Region.

Section 6: *Protection of International Borders*:—In accordance with policies determined by the Provisional Government of Iraq and decided in consultation with the Kurdistan Regional Government, the Iraqi Kurdistan National Guard shall be responsible for the protection of Iraq's international borders that are the also the borders of the Kurdistan Region.

Article 3: Natural Resources in the Kurdistan Region

Section 1: *Ownership of resources*:—The Natural Resources located on the territory of the Kurdistan Region, including water, petroleum and subsoil minerals, belong to the Kurdistan Region.

Section 2: *Public Land*:—All public land in the Kurdistan Region belongs to the Kurdistan Region.

Section 3: *Water*:—(a) All water in the Kurdistan Region belongs to the Kurdistan Region. The Kurdistan Regional Government shall regulate the generation and distribution of hydroelectric power within the Kurdistan region, the exploitation of fish and other aquatic resources, and the irrigation of cropland within the Kurdistan Region.

(b) Water flowing though the Kurdistan Region shall be managed in close coordination with the relevant ministries of the Provisional Government of Iraq so as to assure an equitable division of water between the Kurdistan Region and other parts of Iraq.

Section 3: *Minerals and Petroleum*:—(a) Petroleum and minerals on or under the surface of the land of the Kurdistan Region belong to the Kurdistan Region.

(b) Except for petroleum from reservoirs in commercial production on the effective date, the Kurdistan Regional Government shall regulate the exploitation and sale of petroleum and minerals in the Kurdistan Region, and shall receive the proceeds from their sale.

(c) The exploitation of petroleum in the Kurdistan Region shall be managed in close coordination with relevant ministries of the Provisional Government of Iraq.

(d) Petroleum from reservoirs in commercial production on the effective date may be managed by the Provisional Government of Iraq for the benefit of all the people of Iraq, provided the Kurdistan Regional Government receives from federal budget the funds specified in Article 4.

(e) For the purposes of this article, commercial production means an average daily production over any consecutive twelve-month period since January 1, 1998 of 20,000 barrels per day.

Article 4: Fiscal Arrangements

Section 1: *Taxation*:—The Kurdistan Regional Government and the Provisional Government of Iraq shall conclude an agreement regarding the applicability of federal tax laws in Kurdistan, which shall be binding when approved by the Kurdistan National Assembly and the Transitional Assembly of Iraq. Pending such an agreement, only taxes enacted by the Kurdistan National Assembly shall be valid in Kurdistan.

Section 2: *Administration of Taxes*:—The Kurdistan Regional Government shall be responsible for the administration of all taxation laws within the Kurdistan Region. It shall remit to the Treasury of the Provisional Government of Iraq all revenues (less the costs of administration and enforcement) from any applicable federal taxes.

Section 3: *Block Grants*:—For the purpose of governmental functions in the Kurdistan Region, the Kurdistan Regional Government annually shall receive, after permitted deductions, a sum of money that is a percentage of the total revenues of the Provisional Government of Iraq that is not less than the percentage the population of the Kurdistan Region is of the population of Iraq.

Section 4: *Permitted Deductions*:—For the purpose of this Article, "permitted deductions" means (1) Kurdistan's proportionate share (based on population) of Provisional Government expenditures for activities within the exclusive competence of the Provisional Government, (2) an amount not more than the revenues anticipated from federal taxes in Kurdistan where such taxes are applicable all parts of Iraq except Kurdistan and (3) any revenues from the sale of petroleum retained by the Kurdistan Regional Government where the Kurdistan Region would retain more revenues from the sale of petroleum than any other region or governorate in Iraq.

Article 5: Kurdistan Region Ratification of Successor Laws to the Transitional Law

The Permanent Constitution of Iraq, or any successor law to this Transitional Law, shall be valid in the Kurdistan Region only if approved by a majority of the people of the Kurdistan Region voting in a referendum.

Article 6: Effective Date in the Kurdistan Region

This Transitional law will come into effect in the Kurdistan Region when conforming changes are made in the Constitution and laws of the Kurdistan Region.

Law of Administration for the State of Iraq for the Transitional Period (Transitional Law 040308)

Editors' Note. This is the complete text from the CPA web-site as published on 8 March 2004 (www.cpa-iraq.org). All spelling errors and grammatical mistakes and infelicities are the responsibility of the Iraqi Governing Council and the CPA.

Preamble

The people of Iraq, striving to reclaim their freedom, which was usurped by the previous tyrannical regime, rejecting violence and coercion in all their forms, and particularly when used as instruments of governance, have determined that they shall hereafter remain a free people governed under the rule of law. These people, affirming today their respect for international law, especially having been amongst the founders of the United Nations, working to reclaim their legitimate place among nations, have endeavored at the same time to preserve the unity of their homeland in a spirit of fraternity and solidarity in order to draw the features of the future new Iraq, and to establish the mechanisms aiming, amongst other aims, to erase the effects of racist and sectarian policies and practices. This Law is now established to govern the affairs of Iraq during the transitional period until a duly elected government, operating under a permanent and legitimate constitution achieving full democracy, shall come into being.

Chapter One—Fundamental Principles

Article 1.

(A) This Law shall be called the "Law of Administration for the State of Iraq for the Transitional Period," and the phrase "this Law" wherever it appears in this legislation shall mean the "Law of Administration for the State of Iraq for the Transitional Period."

(B) Gender-specific language shall apply equally to male and female.

(C) The Preamble to this Law is an integral part of this Law.

Article 2.

(A) The term "transitional period" shall refer to the period beginning on 30 June 2004 and lasting until the formation of an elected Iraqi government pursuant to a permanent constitution as set forth in this Law, which in any case shall be no later than 31 December 2005, unless the provisions of Article 61 are applied.

(B) The transitional period shall consist of two phases.

   (1) The first phase shall begin with the formation of a fully sovereign Iraqi Interim Government that takes power on 30 June 2004. This government shall be constituted in accordance with a process of extensive deliberations and consultations with cross-sections of the Iraqi people conducted by the Governing Council and the Coalition Provisional Authority and possibly in consultation with the United Nations. This government shall exercise authority in accordance with this Law, including the fundamental principles and rights specified herein, and with an annex that shall be agreed upon and issued before the beginning of the transitional period and that shall be an integral part of this Law.

   (2) The second phase shall begin after the formation of the Iraqi Transitional Government, which will take place after elections for the National Assembly have been held as stipulated in this Law, provided that, if possible, these elections are not delayed beyond 31 December 2004, and, in any event, beyond 31 January 2005. This second phase shall end upon the formation of an Iraqi government pursuant to a permanent constitution.

Article 3.

(A) This Law is the Supreme Law of the land and shall be binding in all parts of Iraq without exception. No amendment to this Law may be made except by a three-fourths majority of the members of the National Assembly and the unanimous approval of the Presidency Council. Likewise, no amendment may be made that could abridge in any way the rights of the Iraqi people cited in Chapter Two; extend the transitional period beyond the timeframe cited in this Law; delay the holding of elections to a new assembly; reduce the powers of the regions or governorates; or affect Islam, or any other religions or sects and their rites.

(B) Any legal provision that conflicts with this Law is null and void.

(C) This Law shall cease to have effect upon the formation of an elected government pursuant to a permanent constitution.

Article 4.

The system of government in Iraq shall be republican, federal, democratic, and pluralistic, and powers shall be shared between the federal government and the regional governments, governorates, municipalities, and local administrations. The federal system shall be based upon geographic and historical realities and the separation of powers, and not upon origin, race, ethnicity, nationality, or confession.

Article 5.

The Iraqi Armed Forces shall be subject to the civilian control of the Iraqi Transitional Government, in accordance with the contents of Chapters Three and Five of this Law.

Article 6.

The Iraqi Transitional Government shall take effective steps to end the vestiges of the oppressive acts of the previous regime arising from forced displacement, deprivation of citizenship, expropriation of financial assets and property, and dismissal from government employment for political, racial, or sectarian reasons.

Article 7.

(A) Islam is the official religion of the State and is to be considered a source of legislation. No law that contradicts the universally agreed tenets of Islam, the principles of democracy, or the rights cited in Chapter Two of this Law may be enacted during the transitional period. This Law respects the Islamic identity of the majority of the Iraqi people and guarantees the full religious rights of all individuals to freedom of religious belief and practice.

(B) Iraq is a country of many nationalities, and the Arab people in Iraq are an inseparable part of the Arab nation.

Article 8.

The flag, anthem, and emblem of the State shall be fixed by law.

Article 9.

The Arabic language and the Kurdish language are the two official languages of Iraq. The right of Iraqis to educate their children in their mother tongue, such as Turcoman, Syriac, or Armenian, in government educational institutions in accordance with educational guidelines, or in any other language in private educational institutions, shall be guaranteed. The scope of the term "official language" and the means of applying the provisions of this Article shall be defined by law and shall include:

(1) Publication of the official gazette, in the two languages;

(2) Speech and expression in official settings, such as the National Assembly, the Council of Ministers, courts, and official conferences, in either of the two languages;

(3) Recognition and publication of official documents and correspondence in the two languages;

(4) Opening schools that teach in the two languages, in accordance with educational guidelines;

(5) Use of both languages in any other settings enjoined by the principle of equality (such as bank notes, passports, and stamps);

(6) Use of both languages in the federal institutions and agencies in the Kurdistan region.

Chapter Two—Fundamental Rights

Article 10.

As an expression of the free will and sovereignty of the Iraqi people, their representatives shall form the governmental structures of the State of Iraq. The Iraqi Transitional Government and the governments of the regions, governorates, municipalities, and local administrations shall respect the rights of the Iraqi people, including those rights cited in this Chapter.

Article 11.

(A) Anyone who carries Iraqi nationality shall be deemed an Iraqi citizen. His citizenship shall grant him all the rights and duties stipulated in this Law and shall be the basis of his relation to the homeland and the State.

(B) No Iraqi may have his Iraqi citizenship withdrawn or be exiled unless he is a naturalized citizen who, in his application for citizenship, as established in a court of law, made material falsifications on the basis of which citizenship was granted.

(C) Each Iraqi shall have the right to carry more than one citizenship. Any Iraqi whose citizenship was withdrawn because he acquired another citizenship shall be deemed an Iraqi.

(D) Any Iraqi whose Iraqi citizenship was withdrawn for political, religious, racial, or sectarian reasons has the right to reclaim his Iraqi citizenship.

(E) Decision Number 666 (1980) of the dissolved Revolutionary Command Council is annuled, and anyone whose citizenship was withdrawn on the basis of this decree shall be deemed an Iraqi.

(F) The National Assembly must issue laws pertaining to citizenship and naturalization consistent with the provisions of this Law

(G) The Courts shall examine all disputes airising from the application of the provisions relating to citizenship.

Article 12.

All Iraqis are equal in their rights without regard to gender, sect, opinion, belief, nationality, religion, or origin, and they are equal before the law. Discrimination against an Iraqi citizen on the basis of his gender, nationality, religion, or origin is prohibited. Everyone has the right to life, liberty, and the security of his person. No one may be deprived of his life or liberty, except in accordance with legal procedures. All are equal before the courts.

Article 13.

(A) Public and private freedoms shall be protected.

(B) The right of free expression shall be protected.

(C) The right of free peaceable assembly and the right to join associations freely, as well as the right to form and join unions and political parties freely, in accordance with the law, shall be guaranteed.

(D) Each Iraqi has the right of free movement in all parts of Iraq and the right to travel abroad and return freely.

(E) Each Iraqi has the right to demonstrate and strike peaceably in accordance with the law.
(F) Each Iraqi has the right to freedom of thought, conscience, and religious belief and practice. Coercion in such matters shall be prohibited.
(G) Slavery, the slave trade, forced labor, and involuntary servitude with or without pay, shall be forbidden.
(H) Each Iraqi has the right to privacy.

Article 14.

The individual has the right to security, education, health care, and social security. The Iraqi State and its governmental units, including the federal government, the regions, governorates, municipalities, and local administrations, within the limits of their resources and with due regard to other vital needs, shall strive to provide prosperity and employment opportunities to the people.

Article 15.

(A) No civil law shall have retroactive effect unless the law so stipulates. There shall be neither a crime, nor punishment, except by law in effect at the time the crime is committed.
(B) Police, investigators, or other governmental authorities may not violate the sanctity of private residences, whether these authorities belong to the federal or regional governments, governorates, municipalities, or local administrations, unless a judge or investigating magistrate has issued a search warrant in accordance with applicable law on the basis of information provided by a sworn individual who knew that bearing false witness would render him liable to punishment. Extreme exigent circumstances, as determined by a court of competent jurisdiction, may justify a warrantless search, but such exigencies shall be narrowly construed. In the event that a warrantless search is carried out in the absence of an extreme exigent circumstance, the evidence so seized, and any other evidence found derivatively from such search, shall be inadmissible in connection with a criminal charge, unless the court determines that the person who carried out the warrantless search believed reasonably and in good faith that the search was in accordance with the law.
(C) No one may be unlawfully arrested or detained, and no one may be detained by reason of political or religious beliefs.
(D) All persons shall be guaranteed the right to a fair and public hearing by an independent and impartial tribunal, regardless of whether the proceed-

ing is civil or criminal. Notice of the proceeding and its legal basis must be provided to the accused without delay.

(E) The accused is innocent until proven guilty pursuant to law, and he likewise has the right to engage independent and competent counsel, to remain silent in response to questions addressed to him with no compulsion to testify for any reason, to participate in preparing his defense, and to summon and examine witnesses or to ask the judge to do so. At the time a person is arrested, he must be notified of these rights.

(F) The right to a fair, speedy, and open trial shall be guaranteed.

(G) Every person deprived of his liberty by arrest or detention shall have the right of recourse to a court to determine the legality of his arrest or detention without delay and to order his release if this occurred in an illegal manner.

(H) After being found innocent of a charge, an accused may not be tried once again on the same charge.

(I) Civilians may not be tried before a military tribunal. Special or exceptional courts may not be established.

(J) Torture in all its forms, physical or mental, shall be prohibited under all circumstances, as shall be cruel, inhuman, or degrading treatment. No confession made under compulsion, torture, or threat thereof shall be relied upon or admitted into evidence for any reason in any proceeding, whether criminal or otherwise.

Article 16.

(A) Public property is sacrosanct, and its protection is the duty of every citizen.

(B) The right to private property shall be protected, and no one may be prevented from disposing of his property except within the limits of law. No one shall be deprived of his property except by eminent domain, in circumstances and in the manner set forth in law, and on condition that he is paid just and timely compensation.

(C) Each Iraqi citizen shall have the full and unfettered right to own real property in all parts of Iraq without restriction.

Article 17.

It shall not be permitted to possess, bear, buy, or sell arms except on licensure issued in accordance with the law.

Article 18.

There shall be no taxation or fee except by law.

Article 19.

No political refugee who has been granted asylum pursuant to applicable law may be surrendered or returned forcibly to the country from which he fled.

Article 20.

(A) Every Iraqi who fulfills the conditions stipulated in the electoral law has the right to stand for election and cast his ballot secretly in free, open, fair, competitive, and periodic elections.
(B) No Iraqi may be discriminated against for purposes of voting in elections on the basis of gender, religion, sect, race, belief, ethnic origin, language, wealth, or literacy.

Article 21.

Neither the Iraqi Transitional Government nor the governments and administrations of the regions, governorates, and municipalities, nor local administrations may interfere with the right of the Iraqi people to develop the institutions of civil society, whether in cooperation with international civil society organizations or otherwise.

Article 22.

If, in the course of his work, an official of any government office, whether in the federal government, the regional governments, the governorate and municipal administrations, or the local administrations, deprives an individual or a group of the rights guaranteed by this Law or any other Iraqi laws in force, this individual or group shall have the right to maintain a cause of action against that employee to seek compensation for the damages caused by such deprivation, to vindicate his rights, and to seek any other legal measure. If the court decides that the official had acted with a sufficient degree of good faith and in the belief that his actions were consistent with the law, then he is not required to pay compensation.

Article 23.

The enumeration of the foregoing rights must not be interpreted to mean that they are the only rights enjoyed by the Iraqi people. They enjoy all the rights that befit a free people possessed of their human dignity, including the rights stipulated in international treaties and agreements, other instruments of international law that Iraq has signed and to which it has acceded, and others that are deemed binding upon it, and in the law of nations. Non-Iraqis within Iraq shall enjoy all human rights not inconsistent with their status as non-citizens.

Chapter Three—The Iraqi Transitional Government

Article 24.

(A) The Iraqi Transitional Government, which is also referred to in this Law as the federal government, shall consist of the National Assembly; the Presidency Council; the Council of Ministers, including the Prime Minister; and the judicial authority.
(B) The three authorities, legislative, executive, and judicial, shall be separate and independent of one another.
(C) No official or employee of the Iraqi Transitional Government shall enjoy immunity for criminal acts committed while in office.

Article 25.

The Iraqi Transitional Government shall have exclusive competence in the following matters:

(A) Formulating foreign policy and diplomatic representation; negotiating, signing, and ratifying international treaties and agreements; formulating foreign economic and trade policy and sovereign debt policies;
(B) Formulating and executing national security policy, including creating and maintaining armed forces to secure, protect, and guarantee the security of the country's borders and to defend Iraq;
(C) Formulating fiscal policy, issuing currency, regulating customs, regulating commercial policy across regional and governorate boundaries in Iraq, drawing up the national budget of the State, formulating monetary policy, and establishing and administering a central bank;
(D) Regulating weights and measures and formulating a general policy on wages;

(E) Managing the natural resources of Iraq, which belongs to all the people of all the regions and governorates of Iraq, in consultation with the governments of the regions and the administrations of the governorates, and distributing the revenues resulting from their sale through the national budget in an equitable manner proportional to the distribution of population throughout the country, and with due regard for areas that were unjustly deprived of these revenues by the previous regime, for dealing with their situations in a positive way, for their needs, and for the degree of development of the different areas of the country;

(F) Regulating Iraqi citizenship, immigration, and asylum; and

(G) Regulating telecommunications policy.

Article 26.

(A) Except as otherwise provided in this Law, the laws in force in Iraq on 30 June 2004 shall remain in effect unless and until rescinded or amended by the Iraqi Transitional Government in accordance with this Law.

(B) Legislation issued by the federal legislative authority shall supersede any other legislation issued by any other legislative authority in the event that they contradict each other, except as provided in Article 54(B)

(C) The laws, regulations, orders, and directives issued by the Coalition Provisional Authority pursuant to its authority under international law shall remain in force until rescinded or amended by legislation duly enacted and having the force of law.

Article 27.

(A) The Iraqi Armed Forces shall consist of the active and reserve units, and elements thereof. The purpose of these forces is the defense of Iraq.

(B) Armed forces and militias not under the command structure of the Iraqi Transitional Government are prohibited, except as provided by federal law.

(C) The Iraqi Armed Forces and its personnel, including military personnel working in the Ministry of Defense or any offices or organizations subordinate to it, may not stand for election to political office, campaign for candidates, or participate in other activities forbidden by Ministry of Defense regulations. This ban encompasses the activities of the personnel mentioned above acting in their personal or official capacities. Nothing in this Article shall infringe upon the right of these personnel to vote in elections.

(D) The Iraqi Intelligence Service shall collect information, assess threats to national security, and advise the Iraqi government. This Service shall be under civilian control, shall be subject to legislative oversight, and shall operate pursuant to law and in accordance with recognized principles of human rights.

(E) The Iraqi Transitional Government shall respect and implement Iraq's international obligations regarding the non-proliferation, non-development, non-production, and non-use of nuclear, chemical, and biological weapons, and associated equipment, materiel, technologies, and delivery systems for use in the development, manufacture, production, and use of such weapons.

Article 28.

(A) Members of the National Assembly; the Presidency Council; the Council of Ministers, including the Prime Minister; and judges and justices of the courts may not be appointed to any other position in or out of government. Any member of the National Assembly who becomes a member of the Presidency Council or Council of Ministers shall be deemed to have resigned his membership in the National Assembly.

(B) In no event may a member of the armed forces be a member of the National Assembly, minister, Prime Minister, or member of the Presidency Council unless the individual has resigned his commission or rank, or retired from duty at least eighteen months prior to serving.

Article 29.

Upon the assumption of full authority by the Iraqi Interim Government in accordance with Article 2(B)(1), above, the Coalition Provisional Authority shall be dissolved and the work of the Governing Council shall come to an end.

Chapter Four—The Transitional Legislative Authority

Article 30.

(A) During the transitional period, the State of Iraq shall have a legislative authority known as the National Assembly. Its principal mission shall be to legislate and exercise oversight over the work of the executive authority.

(B) Laws shall be issued in the name of the people of Iraq. Laws, regulations, and directives related to them shall be published in the official gazette and shall take effect as of the date of their publication, unless they stipulate otherwise.

(C) The National Assembly shall be elected in accordance with an electoral law and a political parties law. The electoral law shall aim to achieve the goal of having women constitute no less than one-quarter of the members of the National Assembly and of having fair representation for all communities in Iraq, including the Turcomans, ChaldoAssyrians, and others.

(D) Elections for the National Assembly shall take place by 31 December 2004 if possible, and in any case no later than by 31 January 2005.

Article 31.

(A) The National Assembly shall consist of 275 members. It shall enact a law dealing with the replacement of its members in the event of resignation, removal, or death.

(B) A nominee to the National Assembly must fulfill the following conditions:

(1) He shall be an Iraqi no less than 30 years of age.

(2) He shall not have been a member of the dissolved Ba'ath Party with the rank of Division Member or higher, unless exempted pursuant to the applicable legal rules.

(3) If he was once a member of the dissolved Ba'ath Party with the rank of Full Member, he shall be required to sign a document renouncing the Ba'ath Party and disavowing all of his past links with it before becoming eligible to be a candidate, as well as to swear that he no longer has any dealings or connection with Ba'ath Party organizations. If it is established in court that he lied or fabricated on this score, he shall lose his seat in the National Assembly.

(4) He shall not have been a member of the former agencies of repression and shall not have contributed to or participated in the persecution of citizens.

(5) He shall not have enriched himself in an illegitimate manner at the expense of the homeland and public finance.

(6) He shall not have been convicted of a crime involving moral turpitude and shall have a good reputation.

(7) He shall have at least a secondary school diploma, or equivalent

(8) He shall not be a member of the armed forces at the time of his nomination.

Article 32.

(A) The National Assembly shall draw up its own internal procedures, and it shall sit in public session unless circumstances require otherwise, consistent with its internal procedures. The first session of the Assembly shall be chaired by its oldest member.

(B) The National Assembly shall elect, from its own members, a president and two deputy presidents of the National Assembly. The president of the National Assembly shall be the individual who receives the greatest number of votes for that office; the first deputy president the next highest; and the second deputy president the next. The president of the National Assembly may vote on an issue, but may not participate in the debates, unless he temporarily steps out of the chair immediately prior to addressing the issue.

(C) A bill shall not be voted upon by the National Assembly unless it has been read twice at a regular session of the Assembly, on condition that at least two days intervene between the two readings, and after the bill has been placed on the agenda of the session at least four days prior to the vote.

Article 33.

(A) Meetings of the National Assembly shall be public, and transcripts of its meetings shall be recorded and published. The vote of every member of the National Assembly shall be recorded and made public. Decisions in the National Assembly shall be taken by simple majority unless this Law stipulates otherwise.

(B) The National Assembly must examine bills proposed by the Council of Ministers, including budget bills.

(C) Only the Council of Ministers shall have the right to present a proposed national budget. The National Assembly has the right to reallocate proposed spending and to reduce the total amounts in the general budget. It also has the right to propose an increase in the overall amount of expenditures to the Council of Ministers if necessary.

(D) Members of the National Assembly shall have the right to propose bills, consistent with the internal procedures that drawn up by the Assembly.

(E) The Iraqi Armed Forces may not be dispatched outside Iraq even for the purpose of defending against foreign aggression except with the approval of the National Assembly and upon the request of the Presidency Council.

(F) Only the National Assembly shall have the power to ratify international treaties and agreements.

(G) The oversight function performed by the National Assembly and its committees shall include the right of interpellation of executive officials, including members of the Presidency Council, the Council of Ministers, including the Prime Minister, and any less senior official of the executive authority. This shall encompass the right to investigate, request information, and issue subpoenas for persons to appear before them.

Article 34.

Each member of the National Assembly shall enjoy immunity for statements made while the Assembly is in session, and the member may not be sued before the courts for such. A member may not be placed under arrest during a session of the National Assembly, unless the member is accused of a crime and the National Assembly agrees to lift his immunity or if he is caught *in flagrante delicto* in the commission of a felony.

Chapter Five—The Transitional Executive Authority

Article 35.

The executive authority during the transitional period shall consist of the Presidency Council, the Council of Ministers, and its presiding Prime Minister.

Article 36.

(A) The National Assembly shall elect a President of the State and two Deputies. They shall form the Presidency Council, the function of which will be to represent the sovereignty of Iraq and oversee the higher affairs of the country. The election of the Presidency Council shall take place on the basis of a single list and by a two-thirds majority of the members' votes. The National Assembly has the power to remove any member of the Presidency Council of the State for incompetence or lack of integrity by a three-fourths majority of its members' votes. In the event of a vacancy in the Presidency Council, the National Assembly shall, by a vote of two-thirds of its members, elect a replacement to fill the vacancy.
(B) It is a prerequisite for a member of the Presidency Council to fulfill the same conditions as the members of the National Assembly, with the following observations:
    (1) He must be at least forty years of age.
    (2) He must possess a good reputation, integrity, and rectitude.

(3) If he was a member of the dissolved Ba'ath Party, he must have left the dissolved Party at least ten years before its fall.

(4) He must not have participated in repressing the *intifada* of 1991 or the Anfal campaign and must not have committed a crime against the Iraqi people.

(5) The Presidency Council shall take its decisions unanimously, and its members may not deputize others as proxies.

Article 37.

The Presidency Council may veto any legislation passed by the National Assembly, on condition that this be done within fifteen days after the Presidency Council is notified by the president of the National Assembly of the passage of such legislation. In the event of a veto, the legislation shall be returned to the National Assembly, which has the right to pass the legislation again by a two-thirds majority not subject to veto within a period not to exceed thirty days.

Article 38.

(A) The Presidency Council shall name a Prime Minister unanimously, as well as the members of the Council of Ministers upon the recommendation of the Prime Minister. The Prime Minister and Council of Ministers shall then seek to obtain a vote of confidence by simple majority from the National Assembly prior to commencing their work as a government. The Presidency Council must agree on a candidate for the post of Prime Minister within two weeks. In the event that it fails to do so, the responsibility of naming the Prime Minister reverts to the National Assembly. In that event, the National Assembly must confirm the nomination by a two-thirds majority. If the Prime Minister is unable to nominate his Council of Ministers within one month, the Presidency Council shall name another Prime Minister.

(B) The qualifications for Prime Minister must be the same as for the members of the Presidency Council except that his age must not be less than 35 years upon his taking office.

Article 39.

(A) The Council of Ministers shall, with the approval of the Presidency Council, appoint representatives to negotiate the conclusion of international treaties and agreements. The Presidency Council shall recommend passage of a law by the National Assembly to ratify such treaties and agreements.

(B) The Presidency Council shall carry out the function of commander-in-chief of the Iraqi Armed Forces only for ceremonial and protocol purposes. It shall have no command authority. It shall have the right to be briefed, to inquire, and to advise. Operationally, national command authority on military matters shall flow from the Prime Minister to the Minister of Defense to the military chain of command of the Iraqi Armed Forces.

(C) The Presidency Council shall, as more fully set forth in Chapter Six, below, appoint, upon recommendation of the Higher Juridical Council, the Presiding Judge and members of the Federal Supreme Court.

(D) The Council of Ministers shall appoint the Director-General of the Iraqi National Intelligence Service, as well as officers of the Iraqi Armed Forces at the rank of general or above. Such appointments shall be subject to confirmation by the National Assembly by simple majority of those of its members present.

Article 40.

(A) The Prime Minister and the ministers shall be responsible before the National Assembly, and this Assembly shall have the right to withdraw its confidence either in the Prime Minister or in the ministers collectively or individually. In the event that confidence in the Prime Minister is withdrawn, the entire Council of Ministers shall be dissolved, and Article 40(B), below, shall become operative.

(B) In the event of a vote of no confidence with respect to the entire Council of Ministers, the Prime Minister and Council of Ministers shall remain in office to carry out their functions for a period not to exceed thirty days, until the formation of a new Council of Ministers, consistent with Article 38, above.

Article 41.

The Prime Minister shall have day-to-day responsibility for the management of the government, and he may dismiss ministers with the approval of an simple majority of the National Assembly. The Presidency Council may, upon the recommendation of the Commission on Public Integrity after the exercise of due process, dismiss the Prime Minister or the ministers.

Article 42.

The Council of Ministers shall draw up rules of procedure for its work and issue the regulations and directives necessary to enforce the laws. It also has the right to propose bills to the National Assembly. Each ministry has the right, within its competence, to nominate deputy ministers, ambassadors, and other employees of special grade. After the Council of Ministers approves these nominations, they shall be submitted to the Presidency Council for ratification. All decisions of the Council of Ministers shall be taken by simple majority of those of its members present.

Chapter Six—The Federal Judicial Authority

Article 43.

(A) The judiciary is independent, and it shall in no way be administered by the executive authority, including the Ministry of Justice. The judiciary shall enjoy exclusive competence to determine the innocence or guilt of the accused pursuant to law, without interference from the legislative or executive authorities.
(B) All judges sitting in their respective courts as of 1 July 2004 will continue in office thereafter, unless removed from office pursuant to this Law.
(C) The National Assembly shall establish an independent and adequate budget for the judiciary.
(D) Federal courts shall adjudicate matters that arise from the application of federal laws. The establishment of these courts shall be within the exclusive competence of the federal government. The establishment of these courts in the regions shall be in consultation with the presidents of the judicial councils in the regions, and priority in appointing or transferring judges to these courts shall be given to judges resident in the region.

Article 44.

(A) A court called the Federal Supreme Court shall be constituted by law in Iraq.
(B) The jurisdiction of the Federal Supreme Court shall be as follows:
  (1) Original and exclusive jurisdiction in legal proceedings between the Iraqi Transitional Government and the regional governments, governorate and municipal administrations, and local administrations.
  (2) Original and exclusive jurisdiction, on the basis of a complaint from

a claimant or a referral from another court, to review claims that a law, regulation, or directive issued by the federal or regional governments, the governorate or municipal administrations, or local administrations is inconsistent with this Law.

(3) Ordinary appellate jurisdiction of the Federal Supreme Court shall be defined by federal law.

(C) Should the Federal Supreme Court rule that a challenged law, regulation, directive, or measure is inconsistent with this Law, it shall be deemed null and void.

(D) The Federal Supreme Court shall create and publish regulations regarding the procedures required to bring claims and to permit attorneys to practice before it. It shall take its decisions by simple majority, except decisions with regard to the proceedings stipulated in Article 44(B)(1), which must be by a two-thirds majority. Decisions shall be binding. The Court shall have full powers to enforce its decisions, including the power to issue citations for contempt of court and the measures that flow from this.

(E) The Federal Supreme Court shall consist of nine members. The Higher Juridical Council shall, in consultation with the regional judicial councils, initially nominate no less than eighteen and up to twenty-seven individuals to fill the initial vacancies in the aforementioned Court. It will follow the same procedure thereafter, nominating three members for each subsequent vacancy that occurs by reason of death, resignation, or removal. The Presidency Council shall appoint the members of this Court and name one of them as its Presiding Judge. In the event an appointment is rejected, the Higher Juridical Council shall nominate a new group of three candidates.

Article 45.

A Higher Juridical Council shall be established and assume the role of the Council of Judges. The Higher Juridical Council shall supervise the federal judiciary and shall administer its budget. This Council shall be composed of the Presiding Judge of the Federal Supreme Court, the presiding judge and deputy presiding judges of the federal Court of Cassation, the presiding judges of the federal Courts of Appeal, and the presiding judge and two deputy presiding judges of each regional court of cassation. The Presiding Judge of the Federal Supreme Court shall preside over the Higher Juridical Council. In his absence, the presiding judge of the federal Court of Cassation shall preside over the Council.

Article 46.

(A) The federal judicial branch shall include existing courts outside the Kurdistan region, including courts of first instance; the Central Criminal Court of Iraq; Courts of Appeal; and the Court of Cassation, which shall be the court of last resort except as provided in Article 44 of this Law. Additional federal courts may be established by law. The appointment of judges for these courts shall be made by the Higher Juridical Council. This Law preserves the qualifications necessary for the appointment of judges, as defined by law.

(B) The decisions of regional and local courts, including the courts of the Kurdistan region, shall be final, but shall be subject to review by the federal judiciary if they conflict with this Law or any federal law. Procedures for such review shall be defined by law.

Article 47.

No judge or member of the Higher Juridical Council may be removed unless he is convicted of a crime involving moral turpitude or corruption or suffers permanent incapacity. Removal shall be on the recommendation of the Higher Juridical Council, by a decision of the Council of Ministers, and with the approval of the Presidency Council. Removal shall be executed immediately after issuance of this approval. A judge who has been accused of such a crime as cited above shall be suspended from his work in the judiciary until such time as the case arising from what is cited in this Article is adjudicated. No judge may have his salary reduced or suspended for any reason during his period of service.

Chapter Seven—The Special Tribunal And National Commissions

Article 48.

(A) The statute establishing the Iraqi Special Tribunal issued on 10 December 2003 is confirmed. That statute exclusively defines its jurisdiction and procedures, notwithstanding the provisions of this Law.

(B) No other court shall have jurisdiction to examine cases within the competence of the Iraqi Special Tribunal, except to the extent provided by its founding statute.

(C) The judges of the Iraqi Special Tribunal shall be appointed in accordance with the provisions of its founding statute.

Article 49.

(A) The establishment of national commissions such as the Commission on
    Public Integrity, the Iraqi Property Claims Commission, and the Higher
    National De-Ba'athification Commission is confirmed, as is the establish-
    ment of commissions formed after this Law has gone into effect. The
    members of these national commissions shall continue to serve after this
    Law has gone into effect, taking into account the contents of Article 51,
    below.
(B) The method of appointment to the national commissions shall be in
    accordance with law.

Article 50.

The Iraqi Transitional Government shall establish a National Commission for
Human Rights for the purpose of executing the commitments relative to the
rights set forth in this Law and to examine complaints pertaining to violations
of human rights. The Commission shall be established in accordance with the
Paris Principles issued by the United Nations on the responsibilities of
national institutions. This Commission shall include an Office of the Ombuds-
man to inquire into complaints. This office shall have the power to investigate,
on its own initiative or on the basis of a complaint submitted to it, any allega-
tion that the conduct of the governmental authorities is arbitrary or contrary
to law.

Article 51.

No member of the Iraqi Special Tribunal or of any commission established by
the federal government may be employed in any other capacity in or out of
government. This prohibition is valid without limitation, whether it be within
the executive, legislative, or judicial authority of the Iraqi Transitional Government. Members of the Special Tribunal may, however, suspend their employment in other agencies while they serve on the aforementioned Tribunal.

Chapter Eight—Regions, Governorates, And Municipalities

Article 52.

The design of the federal system in Iraq shall be established in such a way as
to prevent the concentration of power in the federal government that allowed

the continuation of decades of tyranny and oppression under the previous regime. This system shall encourage the exercise of local authority by local officials in every region and governorate, thereby creating a united Iraq in which every citizen actively participates in governmental affairs, secure in his rights and free of domination.

Article 53.

(A) The Kurdistan Regional Government is recognized as the official government of the territories that were administered by the that government on 19 March 2003 in the governorates of Dohuk, Arbil, Sulaimaniya, Kirkuk, Diyala and Neneveh. The term "Kurdistan Regional Government" shall refer to the Kurdistan National Assembly, the Kurdistan Council of Ministers, and the regional judicial authority in the Kurdistan region.

(B) The boundaries of the eighteen governorates shall remain without change during the transitional period.

(C) Any group of no more than three governorates outside the Kurdistan region, with the exception of Baghdad and Kirkuk, shall have the right to form regions from amongst themselves. The mechanisms for forming such regions may be proposed by the Iraqi Interim Government, and shall be presented and considered by the elected National Assembly for enactment into law. In addition to being approved by the National Assembly, any legislation proposing the formation of a particular region must be approved in a referendum of the people of the relevant governorates.

(D) This Law shall guarantee the administrative, cultural, and political rights of the Turcomans, ChaldoAssyrians, and all other citizens.

Article 54.

(A) The Kurdistan Regional Government shall continue to perform its current functions throughout the transitional period, except with regard to those issues which fall within the exclusive competence of the federal government as specified in this Law. Financing for these functions shall come from the federal government, consistent with current practice and in accordance with Article 25(E) of this Law. The Kurdistan Regional Government shall retain regional control over police forces and internal security, and it will have the right to impose taxes and fees within the Kurdistan region.

(B) With regard to the application of federal laws in the Kurdistan region, the Kurdistan National Assembly shall be permitted to amend the application of any such law within the Kurdistan region, but only to the extent that this relates to matters that are not within the provisions of Articles 25 and 43(D) of this Law and that fall within the exclusive competence of the federal government.

Article 55.

(A) Each governorate shall have the right to form a Governorate Council, name a Governor, and form municipal and local councils. No member of any regional government, governor, or member of any governorate, municipal, or local council may be dismissed by the federal government or any official thereof, except upon conviction of a crime by a court of competent jurisdiction as provided by law. No regional government may dismiss a Governor or member or members of any governorate, municipal, or local council. No Governor or member of any Governorate, municipal, or local council shall be subject to the control of the federal government except to the extent that the matter relates to the competences set forth in Article 25 and 43(D), above.

(B) Each Governor and member of each Governorate Council who holds office as of 1 July 2004, in accordance with the law on local government that shall be issued, shall remain in place until such time as free, direct, and full elections, conducted pursuant to law, are held, or, unless, prior to that time, he voluntarily gives up his position, is removed upon his conviction for a crime involving moral turpitude or related to corruption, or upon being stricken with permanent incapacity, or is dismissed in accordance with the law cited above. When a governor, mayor, or member of a council is dismissed, the relevant council may receive applications from any eligible resident of the governorate to fill the position. Eligibility requirements shall be the same as those set forth in Article 31 for membership in the National Assembly. The new candidate must receive a majority vote of the council to assume the vacant seat.

Article 56.

(A) The Governorate Councils shall assist the federal government in the coordination of federal ministry operations within the governorate, including the review of annual ministry plans and budgets with regard to activities in the governorate. Governorate Councils shall be funded from the general budget of the State, and these Councils shall also have the authority to increase their revenues independently by imposing taxes and fees; to organize the operations of the Governorate administration; to initiate and implement province-level projects alone or in partnership with international, and non-governmental organizations; and to conduct other activities insofar as is consistent with federal laws.

(B) The *Qada'* and *Nahiya* councils and other relevant councils shall assist in the performance of federal responsibilities and the delivery of public services by reviewing local ministry plans in the afore-mentioned places; ensuring that they respond properly to local needs and interests; identifying local budgetary requirements through the national budgeting procedures; and collecting and retaining local revenues, taxes, and fees; organizing the operations of the local administration; initiating and implementing local projects alone or in conjunction with international, and non-governmental organizations; and conducting other activities consistent with applicable law.

(C) Where practicable, the federal government shall take measures to devolve additional functions to local, governorate, and regional administrations, in a methodical way. Regional units and governorate administrations, including the Kurdistan Regional Government, shall be organized on the basis of the principle of de-centralization and the devolution of authorities to municipal and local governments.

Article 57.

(A) All authorities not exclusively reserved to the Iraqi Transitional Government may be exercised by the regional governments and governorates as soon as possible following the establishment of appropriate governmental institutions.

(B) Elections for governorate councils throughout Iraq and for the Kurdistan National Assembly shall be held at the same time as the elections for the National Assembly, no later than 31 January 2005.

Article 58.

(A) The Iraqi Transitional Government, and especially the Iraqi Property Claims Commission and other relevant bodies, shall act expeditiously to take measures to remedy the injustice caused by the previous regime's practices in altering the demographic character of certain regions, including Kirkuk, by deporting and expelling individuals from their places of residence, forcing migration in and out of the region, settling individuals alien to the region, depriving the inhabitants of work, and correcting nationality. To remedy this injustice, the Iraqi Transitional Government shall take the following steps:

(1) With regard to residents who were deported, expelled, or who emigrated; it shall, in accordance with the statute of the Iraqi Property Claims Commission and other measures within the law, within a reasonable period of time, restore the residents to their homes and property, or, where this is unfeasible, shall provide just compensation.

(2) With regard to the individuals newly introduced to specific regions and territories, it shall act in accordance with Article 10 of the Iraqi Property Claims Commission statute to ensure that such individuals may be resettled, may receive compensation from the state, may receive new land from the state near their residence in the governorate from which they came, or may receive compensation for the cost of moving to such areas.

(3) With regard to persons deprived of employment or other means of support in order to force migration out of their regions and territories, it shall promote new employment opportunities in the regions and territories.

(4) With regard to nationality correction, it shall repeal all relevant decrees and shall permit affected persons the right to determine their own national identity and ethnic affiliation free from coercion and duress.

(B) The previous regime also manipulated and changed administrative boundaries for political ends. The Presidency Council of the Iraqi Transitional Government shall make recommendations to the National Assembly on remedying these unjust changes in the permanent constitution. In the event the Presidency Council is unable to agree unanimously on a set of recommendations, it shall unanimously appoint a neutral arbitrator to examine the issue and make recommendations. In the event the Presidency Council is unable to agree on an arbitrator, it shall request the Secretary General of the United Nations to appoint a distinguished international person to be the arbitrator.

(C) The permanent resolution of disputed territories, including Kirkuk, shall be deferred until after these measures are completed, a fair and transparent census has been conducted and the permanent constitution has been ratified This resolution shall be consistent with the principle of justice, taking into account the will of the people of those territories.

Chapter Nine—The Transitional Period

Article 59.

(A) The permanent constitution shall contain guarantees to ensure that the Iraqi Armed Forces are never again used to terrorize or oppress the people of Iraq.

(B) Consistent with Iraq's status as a sovereign state, and with its desire to join other nations in helping to maintain peace and security and fight terrorism during the transitional period, the Iraqi Armed Forces will be a principal partner in the multi-national force operating in Iraq under unified command pursuant to the provisions of United Nations Security Council Resolution 1511 (2003) and any subsequent relevant resolutions. This arrangement shall last until the ratification of a permanent constitution and the election of a new government pursuant to that new constitution.

(C) Upon its assumption of authority, and consistent with Iraq's status as a sovereign state, the elected Iraqi Transitional Government shall have the authority to conclude binding international agreements regarding the activities of the multi-national force operating in Iraq under unified command pursuant to the terms of United Nations Security Council Resolution 1511 (2003), and any subsequent relevant United Nations Security Council resolutions. Nothing in this Law shall affect rights and obligations under these agreements, or under United Nations Security Council Resolution 1511 (2003), and any subsequent relevant United Nations Security Council resolutions, which will govern the multi-national force's activities pending the entry into force of these agreements.

Article 60.

The National Assembly shall write a draft of the permanent constitution of Iraq. This Assembly shall carry out this responsibility in part by encouraging debate on the constitution through regular general public meetings in all parts of Iraq and through the media, and receiving proposals from the citizens of Iraq as it writes the constitution.

Article 61.

(A) The National Assembly shall write the draft of the permanent constitution by no later than 15 August 2005.

(B) The draft permanent constitution shall be presented to the Iraqi people for approval in a general referendum to be held no later than 15 October 2005. In the period leading up to the referendum, the draft constitution shall be published and widely distributed to encourage a public debate about it among the people.

(C) The general referendum will be successful and the draft constitution ratified if a majority of the voters in Iraq approve and if two-thirds of the voters in three or more governorates do not reject it.

(D) If the permanent constitution is approved in the referendum, elections for a permanent government shall be held no later than 15 December 2005 and the new government shall assume office no later than 31 December 2005.

(E) If the referendum rejects the draft permanent constitution, the National Assembly shall be dissolved. Elections for a new National Assembly shall be held no later than 15 December 2005. The new National Assembly and new Iraqi Transitional Government shall then assume office no later than 31 December 2005, and shall continue to operate under this Law, except that the final deadlines for preparing a new draft may be changed to make it possible to draft a permanent constitution within a period not to exceed one year. The new National Assembly shall be entrusted with writing another draft permanent constitution.

(F) If necessary, the president of the National Assembly, with the agreement of a majority of the members' votes, may certify to the Presidency Council no later than 1 August 2005 that there is a need for additional time to complete the writing of the draft constitution. The Presidency Council shall then extend the deadline for writing the draft constitution for only six months. This deadline may not be extended again.

(G) If the National Assembly does not complete writing the draft permanent constitution by 15 August 2005 and does not request extension of the deadline in Article 61(D) above, the provisions of Article 61(E), above, shall be applied.

Article 62.

This law shall remain in effect until the permanent constitution is issued and the new Iraqi government is formed in accordance with it.

Contributors

Ofra Bengio, Ph.D. (Tel Aviv), is Senior Research Fellow at the Moshe Dayan Center for Middle Eastern and African Studies and Senior Lecturer at the Department of Middle Eastern and African History, Tel Aviv University. She has published numerous essays on Iraq, the Kurds, and minorities in the Middle East. Her publications include *Turkish-Israeli Relations: Changing Ties of Middle Eastern Outsiders, Saddam's Word: Political Discourse in Iraq, The Kurdish Revolt in Iraq* (in Hebrew), *Saddam Speaks on the Gulf Crisis: A Collection of Documents, Minorities and the State in the Arab World* (coeditor with Gabriel Ben-Dor), and *Wine and Love Poetry* (cotranslator and editor), a collection of poetry by Abu Nuwwas (in Hebrew).

Karna A. J. Eklund, J.D. (Washington College of Law), B.A (North Park), is a Master's candidate at the School of International Service, American University. She is currently codirector of the Iraq/Kurdish program for the Public International Law and Policy Group and a Senior Research Associate on issues of shari'a law and other Middle East issues.

Peter W. Galbraith, J.D. (Georgetown University Law Center), M.A. (Oxford), B.A. (Harvard), is a specialist in negotiation. He served as the first U.S. ambassador to the Republic of Croatia and was a mediator of the 1995 Erdut Agreement that ended the Croatia War. As a staff member for the Senate Foreign Relations Committee, he documented Iraq's Anfal campaign against the Kurds, including the use of chemical weapons in Dihok governorate in 1988. His work led the U.S. to pass the Prevention of Genocide Act of 1988 to impose comprehensive sanctions on Iraq. He has been a professor at the National Defense University and a senior official with the United Nations in East Timor. He is currently Senior Fellow at the Center for Arms Control and Non-Proliferation and senior partner in Galbraith and Morrow, a firm specializing in international law and negotiation. He is presently an advisor to the Kurdistan Regional Government and Kurdistan National Assembly.

Michael M. Gunter, Ph.D. (Kent State), M.I.A., B.A. (Columbia) is Professor of Political Science at Tennessee Technological University in Cookeville, Tennessee. He is the author of several scholarly books on the Kurdish question, the most recent being *Historical Dictionary of the Kurds*; *The Kurdish Predicament in Iraq: A Political Dilemma*; and *The Kurds and the Future of Turkey*. He has published numerous articles on the Kurds in leading periodicals, including *Middle East Journal*; *Middle East Quarterly*; and *Orient*. He is a former Senior Fulbright Lecturer in International Relations in Turkey.

John McGarry, Ph.D. (Western Ontario), M.Sc. (Western Ontario), B.A. (Trinity College Dublin), is Canada Research Chair in Nationalism and Democracy at Queen's University, Ontario. He has edited, coedited, and coauthored several books, including *The Northern Ireland Conflict: Consociational Engagements*; *Northern Ireland and the Divided World*; *Minority Nationalism and the Changing International Order*; *Explaining Northern Ireland: Broken Images*; and *The Politics of Ethnic Conflict Regulation*. He has published in journals such as *Ethnic and Racial Studies*; *Government and Opposition*; *Nationalism and Ethnic Politics*; *Nations and Nationalism*; *Political Studies*; *Political Quarterly*; *Parliamentary Affairs*; *Journal of Conflict Studies*; and *Journal of Commonwealth and Comparative Politics*. He is presently an external advisor to the Kurdistan Regional Government and the Kurdistan National Assembly.

Molly McNulty, J.D. (NYU), A.B. (Smith), is a lawyer and public policy analyst. Formerly Professor of Public Health Practice at the University of Rochester School of Medicine, she is presently a consultant for UNICEF in Iran who specializes in implementation of human rights for women and children. Her publications include "Assuring Adequate Health and Rehabilitative Care for the Child," in *Children's Rights in America: United Nations Convention on the Rights of the Child Compared with United States Law*, and "Adolescent Health Spending and Measures in State Title V Maternal and Child Health Programs" in *Journal of Public Health Management and Practice*. She has provided consultation to U.S. senators, the U.S. Department of Health and Human Services, the Departments of Health of New York State and Vermont, the American Public Health Association, and the National Governors Association.

Brendan O'Leary Ph.D. (London School of Economics), M.A. (University of Pennsylvania, hon), B.A. (Oxford), is Lauder Professor of Political Science and Director of the Solomon Asch Center for the Study of Ethnopolitical Conflict at the University of Pennsylvania. His books on Northern Ireland, six with John McGarry, include *The Future of Northern Ireland*, *The Politics of Antagonism*, *Explaining Northern Ireland*, and *The Northern Ireland Conflict: Consociational Engagements*. He has authored, coauthored, or coedited *Theories of the*

State; *The Asiatic Mode of Production*; *Prime Minister, Cabinet and Core Executive: The Politics of Ethnic Conflict–Regulation*; and *Right-Sizing the State*. He has carried out constitutional advisory work for governments and parties in Northern Ireland, Somalia, and South Africa, and presently advises the Kurdistan Regional Government and Kurdistan National Assembly.

Khaled Salih, Ph.D., M.Sc., B.A. (Gothenburg), B.Sc. (Sulaimania), is Senior Lecturer in Middle East Studies at the University of Southern Denmark at Odense. He is the author of *State-Making, Nation-Building and the Military: Iraq 1941–1958*; *The Kurdish Question* (in Swedish); *The Kurdish Question in Turkey* (in Swedish); *Iraq Between Fear and Freedom* (in Swedish); and *The EU's Turkish Dilemma and Turkey's Kurdish Problem* (in Danish). He is presently an advisor to the Kurdistan Regional Government and Kurdistan National Assembly.

Gareth Stansfield, Ph.D., M.A., B.A. (Durham), is a Lecturer in Middle East Politics at the Institute of Arab and Islamic Studies at the University of Exeter and is Associate Fellow on the Middle East Programme at the Royal Institute of International Affairs, Chatham House, London. He currently holds a Leverhulme Trust Special Research Fellowship to research the political development of Iraq. His books on Kurdistan and Iraq include *The Future of Iraq: Dictatorship, Democracy or Division?* (with Liam Anderson) and *Iraqi Kurdistan: Political Development and Emergent Democracy*. Stansfield worked in Kurdistan between 1997 and 2001 as a Department for International Development-funded advisor to the Kurdistan Regional Governments. He has lectured in the U.S., UK, New Zealand, Switzerland, Turkey, and the Middle East on Iraq and Kurdistan and has advised several governments on policy toward Iraq.

Karin von Hippel, Ph.D. (London School of Economics), is a Senior Research Fellow at the Centre for Defence Studies, Kings College, London. She recently directed a project on European counter-terrorist reforms, funded by the MacArthur Foundation, and edited the volume *Europe Confronts Terror*. In 2002, she advised the OECD on what development cooperation can do to get at the root causes of terrorism, and has been a member of Project Unicorn, a counter-terrorism police advisory panel in London. Her publications include "Terrorism as a Problem of International Cooperation," in Thomas Weiss and Jane Boulden, eds., *Terrorism and the UN: Before and After September 11*; "The Roots of Terrorism: Probing the Myths," in Lawrence Freedman, ed., *Superterrorism: Policy Responses*; and *Democracy by Force: U.S. Military Intervention in the Post-Cold War World*, which was short-listed for the Westminster Medal in

Military History. She has also worked for the United Nations and the European Commission for over three years in Somalia and Kosovo.

Sophia Wanche, Ph.D., M.A. (Durham), B.A. (Uppsala), is a research consultant as well as a humanitarian affairs officer with the Swedish International Development Agency/United Nations Office for the Coordination of Humanitarian Affairs. Previously working for the Swedish Embassy in Tehran, she has researched the political situation in Iraqi Kurdistan for the International Crisis Group, and worked for Athens University on a variety of research projects. Her latest publication, resulting from a consultancy project for the United Nations High Commissioner for Refugees, is titled *An Assessment of the Iraqi Community in Greece.*

Paul R. Williams, Ph.D. (Cambridge); J.D. (Stanford); B.A. (University of California, Davis), holds the Rebecca Grazier Professorship of Law and International Relations at American University. During 1991–1993 he served as an attorney-advisor in the U.S. Department of State's Office of the Legal Advisor for European Affairs. During his legal practice, he has assisted nearly a dozen states and regional entities in international peace negotiations and served as a delegation member in the Dayton, Rambouillet/Paris, Key West, Lake Ohrid/Skopje, and Belgrade/Podgorica negotiations. He has advised fifteen governments across Europe, Africa, and Asia on matters of public international law.

Name Index

Subject Index

Page numbers in italics refer to figures and tables in the text.